The Radical Right in Western Europe

D1594354

The Radical Right in Western Europe

A Comparative Analysis

Herbert Kitschelt

In collaboration with
Anthony J. McGann

Ann Arbor
THE UNIVERSITY OF MICHIGAN PRESS

First paperback edition 1997
Copyright © by the University of Michigan 1995
All rights reserved
Published in the United States of America by
The University of Michigan Press
Manufactured in the United States of America
Ⓐ Printed on acid-free paper

2000   4   3   2

A CIP catalog record for this book is available from the British Library.

Library of Congress Cataloging-in-Publication Data

Kitschelt, Herbert.
    The radical right in Western Europe : a comparative analysis /
Herbert Kitschelt ; in collaboration with Anthony J. McGann.
        p.   cm.
    Includes bibliographical references and index.
    ISBN 0-472-10663-5 (hc : alk. paper)
    1. Socialist parties—Europe, Western. 2. Right and left
(Political science) 3. Europe, Western—Politics and government.
    I. McGann, Anthony J. II. Title.
JN94.A979K569 1996
324.24′038′09049—dc20   95-41373
                                                            CIP

ISBN 0-472-08441-0 (pbk. : alk. paper)

Contents

Preface

This study is a sequel to *The Transformation of European Social Democracy* (Kitschelt 1994). It extends and tests the core theoretical argument developed in that book but applies it to a new research object. In a nutshell, the dynamics of party systems in the advanced capitalist democracies cannot be explained primarily in terms of changes in social structure and political economy. While these boundary conditions constitute the scenario within which parties operate, the competitive struggle among parties themselves, their internal organizational patterns of interest aggregation, and the long-term ideological traditions in which they are embedded shape their ability to craft electoral coalitions. While the earlier study explored this argument in detail for the left side of the European party spectrum in the 1970s and 1980s, this study attempts to explain similarities *and* differences in the career of so-called radical rightist parties in Western Europe.

The key hypotheses of this study can be summarized in a single paragraph. The social structure and economy of advanced capitalism have given salience to a competitive dimension of politics with two aspects: economically leftist (redistributive) and politically as well as culturally libertarian (participatory and individualist) positions at one extreme and economically rightist, free-marketeering as well as politically and culturally authoritarian positions at the other. The strategic problem of moderate conservative parties is a mirror image of the problems of social democracy analyzed in the earlier study: how can parties appeal to moderate voters and thus build electoral coalitions that predestine them to become governing parties without antagonizing more extremist right-authoritarian (or left-libertarian) voters that call for a political "product differentiation" on the right (or left) spectrum of the dominant axis of party competition?

We are arguing in this study that the success of the extreme Right is contingent upon the strategic choices of the moderate conservative parties as well as the ability of the extreme-rightist leaders to find the electorally "winning formula" to assemble a significant voter constituency. The conditions for the rise of extreme-rightist parties become favorable if moderately left and right parties converge toward the median voter. Under these conditions, the established parties fail to attend to a wide uncovered field of more radical right-authoritarian voters who will search for a new political alternative. Whether or not such a new political alternative becomes successful, however, depends on the strategic appeal of right-wing political entrepreneurs. Only if they choose economic free market appeals that are combined with authoritarian and ethnocentric and even racist messages will they attract a broad audience. Parties that feature only racist and authoritarian positions but fail to highlight and embrace their commitment to free markets appeal only to modest segments of the blue-collar and lower white-collar electorate, primarily younger voters who have not been encapsuled by the organized working-class movement. If they also include free market slogans, they additionally attract small independent businesspeople, such as shopkeepers, family farmers, and craftspeople. Even successful extreme-rightist parties will always be underrepresented among the more educated citizens, those who work as employees or professionals in various branches of the service sector.

Extreme-rightist parties may diverge in two ways from the winning formula of right authoritarianism. On the one hand, in countries characterized by partocratic connections of politics and economics through patronage and clientelism, they can thrive on a broader political populism and antistate affect that exists beyond the bounds of their core electorate. In this situation, new rightist parties are well advised to tone down authoritarian or racist messages and focus their attention on a "market-liberal," antistatist appeal. On the other hand, right-wing parties may fail to find the winning formula, appeal solely to authoritarian and ethnocentrist sentiments, and therefore fail to succeed electorally. This situation typically comes about where generations of older activists are rooted in the organizational and intellectual legacy of strong fascist or national socialist movements. They prevent the contemporary rightist movement entrepreneurs from learning the electorally winning formula.

This book is written against several rival hypotheses about the rise and performance of the European extreme Right. First, some analysts have claimed that such parties thrive on a vague antielitist affect against the "political class" in advanced capitalist democracies. But the followers of the extreme Right have too sharply defined ideological propensities that situate them in a particular field of the competitive space for this argument to be true. Second, others see the extreme Right as a single-issue response to the stress of immigration from non-European countries. We show, however, that racism and ethnocentrism may be catalysts to get extreme-rightist parties started, but such appeals are successful in the longer run only if they are embedded in a broader right-authoritarian agenda. Where ethnocentric mobilization of immigrants is not linked to the winning formula, as in the case of the German Republicans, the party is doomed to failure once the issue attention cycle for immigration policy declines. Third, an interpretation of the new extreme Right as a simple continuation of the fascist or national socialist Right is just as misleading. Where the proximity between the historical and contemporary extreme Right is great, the contemporary parties are rather unsuccessful. The old extreme Right has not put enough emphasis on a free market organization of the economy to build a successful electoral coalition today. Finally, a few analysts have proposed to interpret the extreme Right as the "right-libertarian" counterpart to the "left-libertarian" social movements and parties. As we will show in detail, few libertarian elements can be identified in the elite appeal or the mass support of the European extreme Right. Moreover, we will argue that right-wing parties assemble characteristic electoral coalitions that vary with the specific nature of their programmatic appeal.

An empirical test of our theory would thus undermine our argument if one or both of the following observations were demonstrated. First, electorally successful extreme-rightist parties are racist but libertarian and/or not committed to free market liberalism. Second, votes and elite appeals are entirely focused on race but take widely varying or middle-of-the-road positions on economics, political organization, and social issues.

After having sketched what this book is about, let us also say what it is not. The book does not offer a detailed chronological account of the rise of rightist parties. The monographic literature on extreme-rightist parties that offers all of this information abounds, yet there is a dearth of systematic theory-guided comparative analysis. As a consequence, this book will not provide new insights to the country specialist who has read everything there is to read about the history and contemporary articulation of the extreme Right in a particular nation. The book also delivers no detailed analysis of the "inner life" of extreme-rightist parties. In five of the seven countries that will be compared, the career of the extreme Right can be explained well at the systemic level without need to open the black box of internal party politics. In the other two cases, the German and the Italian extreme Right, a number of detailed analyses provide sufficient background data to characterize the internal dynamics of these parties to the extent required by the explanatory claims of our argument.

Let us close this preface on a personal note. Politically, we find the preoccupation with the extreme Right in Western Europe thoroughly distasteful. We also would wish that the analytical upshot of this study, namely, that the extreme Right is here to stay and not just a fleeting phenomenon of short-term pressures of immigration, were untrue. At the same time, we have been driven by theoretical, political, and professional motivations to complete this book. In theoretical terms, it makes a nice complement to the earlier comparative analysis of the European Left. It is satisfying to apply an already existing theoretical argument to a new empirical object rather than to develop a new theoretical argument for each empirical object one begins to study. In political terms, we see a great many misconceptions about the extreme Right both in the American as well as the European mass media. These misconceptions are unrelated to the authors' ideological convictions as they are found equally among more conservative and more liberal observers. Particularly for opponents and enemies of the contemporary extreme Right, it is important to have an accurate assessment of what this new political force represents in order to more effectively fight it.

In professional terms, this book derives from the opportunity given to Herbert Kitschelt to deliver an exploratory paper on this topic at a conference on the "New Right in European Politics" in November 1991 at the University of Minnesota. The book has grown out of that first effort to examine the contemporary Right more seriously. In the initial phase of the data analysis, Brian Loynd and William T. Bernhard's assistance was indispensable. Anthony McGann joined the project early on and has designed and performed much of the data analysis documented in the case study chapters. Through this contribution, he has earned junior coauthorship, even though the theoretical framework that drives the argument is derived from and the text of this study is written by the senior author. Torben Iversen read and offered several important critiques of earlier versions of the book. Ronald Inglehart directed our attention to the 1990 *World Values Study* survey, with its wide range of pertinent questions, and provided useful comments on an earlier draft of this book. At various stages, this research project benefited from presentations to faculty and graduate students, particularly at Duke University. Finally, we have to thank two anonymous reviewers for University of Michigan Press whose detailed and incisive critical reviews of the last but one version of this study are highly appreciated. Nevertheless, none of these contributors to the project should be held responsible for the shortcomings of the final product.

Abbreviations

A	Austria
AP (SP)	Popular Alliance (now PP) (Alianza Popular)
BHE (FRG)	Federation of Expellees and People Deprived of their Rights (Bund der Heimatvertriebenen und Entrechteten)
C (S)	Center Party (Centerpartiet [Sweden])
C (N)	Center Party (Senterpartiet [Norway])
CD (DK)	Center Democrats (Centrum Demokraterne)
CeP (NL)	Center Party (Centrums Partij)
CDU (FRG)	Christian Democratic Union (Christlich Demokratische Union)
CSU (FRG)	Christian Social Union (Bavaria) (Christlich Soziale Union)
DC (I)	Christian Democrats (Democrazia Cristiana)
DK	Denmark
DNA (N)	Norwegian Labor Party (Det Norske Arbeiderparti)
DP (I)	Demoproletarians (Democrazia Proletaria)
DRP (FRG)	German Empire Party (Deutsche Reichspartei)
DVU (FRG)	German People's Union (Deutsche Volks Union)
Ecolo (F)	Ecologists/Greens (Ecologists/Verts)
F	France
Fi	Finland
FN (F)	National Front (Front National)
FP (S)	People's Party (Folkpartiet)
FP (DK)	Progress Party (Fremskridtspartiet [Denmark])
FPD (FRG)	Free Democratic Party (Freie Demokratische Partei)
FPDL (Fi)	Finnish People's Democratic Union (Suomen Kansan Demokraattinen Liitto)
FPÖ (A)	Austrian Freedom Party (Freiheitliche Partei Österreichs)
FRG	Federal Republic of Germany
FRP (N)	Progress Party (Fremskrittspartiet [Norway])
G (FRG)	Greens (Grüne)

GA (A)	Green Alternative (Grüne Alternative)
Gr (DK)	Greens (Gronne)
GRE	Greece
H (N)	Conservatives (Hoyre)
I	Italy
KDS (S)	Christian Democrats (Kristdemokratiska Samhällspar-tiet)
KF (DK)	Conservative People's Party (Det Konservative Folkesparti)
KOK (Fi)	National Coalition (Kansallinin Kokoomus)
KrF (DK)	Christian People's Party (Kristelig Folkeparti [Denmark])
KRF (N)	Christian People's Party (Kristelig Folkeparti [Norway])
M (S)	Moderates (Moderata Samlingspartiet)
MP (S)	Environment Party/Greens (Miljöpartiet de Gröna)
MRG (F)	Left Radicals (Mouvement Radicale de Gauche)
MSI (I)	Italian Social Movement (Movimento Sociale Italiano)
N	Norway
NA (SW)	National Action (Nationale Aktion)
ND (S)	New Democracy (Ny Demokrati)
NL (I)	Northern League (Lega Nord)
NL	Netherlands
NPD (FRG)	National Democratic Party (Nationaldemokratische Partei)
ÖVP (A)	Austrian People's Party (Österreichische Volkspartei)
PASOK (GRE)	Pan-Hellenic Socialist Movement (Panellenio Sosialistiko Kinema)
PCF (F)	French Communist Party (Parti Communiste Français)
PCI (I)	Italian Communist Party (Partito Communista Italiano)
PDS (I)	Party of the Democratic Left (Partito della Sinistra Democratica)
PFN (F)	Party of New Forces (Parti des Forces Nouvelles)
PLI (I)	Italian Liberal Party (Partito Liberale Italiano)
PR (I)	Radical Party (Partito Radicale)
PRI (I)	Italian Republican Party (Partito Repubblicano Italiano)
PS (F)	Socialist Party (Parti Socialiste)
PSDI (I)	Italian Social Democratic Party (Partito Socialista Democratico Italiano)
PSI (I)	Italian Socialist Party (Partito Socialista Italiano)
PSOE (SP)	Spanish Socialist Workers' Party (Partido Socialista Obrero Espanol)
PSU (F)	Unified Socialist Party (Parti Socialiste Unifié)

PvdA (NL)	Labor Party (Partij van de Arbeid)
REP (FRG)	Republicans (Republikaner)
RPR (F)	Rally for the Republic (Rassemblement pour la République)
RV (DK)	Radical Liberal Party (Det radikale Venstre)
S	Sweden
SAP (S)	Swedish Social Democratic Party (Sveriges Socialdemokratiska Arbetarparti)
SAP (Sw)	Swiss Automobilists' Party (Schweizer Autofahrerpartei)
SD (DK)	Social Democratic Party (Socialdemokratiet)
SF (DK)	Socialist People's Party (Socialistisk Folkeparti [Denmark])
SF (N)	Socialist People's Party (Socialistik Folkeparti [Norway])
SP	Spain
SPD (FRG)	Social Democratic Party of Germany (Sozialdemokratische Partei Deutschlands)
SPÖ (A)	Austrian Socialist Party (since 1990: Austrian Social Democratic Party) (Sozialistische Partei Österreichs) (since 1990: Sozialdemokratische Partei Österreichs)
SRP (FRG)	Socialist Empire Party (Sozialistische Reichspartei)
SW	Switzerland
UDF/CDS (F)	Union for French Democracy/Center Democrats (Union pour la Démocratie Français/Centre Democratique)
UDF/PR (F)	UDF/Republican Party (UDF/Parti Républicain)
UDF/RAD (F)	UDF/Radical Party (UDF/Radicaux de Gauche)
V (Dk)	Liberal Party (Venstre [Denmark])
V (N)	Liberal Party (Venstre [Norway])
VB (B)	Flemish Block (Vlaams Blok)
Verdi (I)	Greens (Verdi)
VPK (S)	Left Party (Communists) (Vänsterpartiet Kommunistarna)
VS (Dk)	Left Socialist Party (Venstresocialisterne)
VU (B)	Flemish People's Party (Vlaams Volksunie)
VVD (NL)	Party for Freedom and Democracy (Volkspartij voor Vrijheid en Democratie)

1

The Contemporary Radical Right:
An Interpretative and Explanatory Framework

Western Europe has experienced an unprecedented rise of new extreme "right-ist" parties some of which took off in the 1970s but most of which came into their own in the 1980s and early 1990s. They run in elections under such labels as "National Front" in Britain, France, and Wallonia; "Progress Party" in Denmark and Norway; "Republicans" and "German People's Union" in Germany; "Center Party" in the Netherlands, or regional self-identifications as the "Flemish Block" in Flanders and the "Northern League" in Italy. In Austria, even an established party, the "Freedom Party," is often counted as a member of the extreme Right after its strategic reversal in the mid-1980s. Beyond the vague feeling, however, that all these parties are somehow "on the right," it is unclear from the existing comparative literature whether these parties really can be lumped together. Do they represent a similar political appeal and electoral coalition? What is the meaning of their "rightist" appeal? Why are they sometimes successful, but sometimes not?

At least four hypotheses have guided the debate on the rise of the extreme "Right." The first is that it represents a revival of fascist and national socialist ideology in the midst of an economic crisis with high unemployment. According to the second hypothesis, the contemporary extreme Right is a single-issue racist and xenophobic backlash against the multi-culturalization of Western European societies caused by the influx of immigrants from non-Occidental civilizations, particularly from the Islamic, African, and Far Eastern regions. A third hypothesis focuses on domestic institutional changes in advanced capitalist democracies and singles out the increasing control of individual lives by a coalescing "class" of political and corporate leaders as the trigger for a "right-libertarian" and "populist" backlash against big government and consociational or corporatist politico-economic elites.

In this book we will argue that none of these perspectives is correct. Instead, we will advance an alternative hypothesis. Societal change in contemporary capitalism has increased the salience of political partisan appeals to economically rightist positions favoring market allocation over political redistribution of economic resources. At the same time, these positions support authoritarian and paternalist modes of collective decision making in the state, the corporation, and the family. The structural change of society that has made possible the rise of the extreme Right is the transition to a postindustrial economy in which citizens' political preferences and salient demands differ from those that prevailed in the Keynesian Welfare State of the post–World War II era, peaking in the 1960s. In a structural perspective, the New Right constitutes the mirror image and opposite political pole of a New Left that began to mobilize in the 1960s (Andersen and Björklund 1990; Inglehart 1990, 11; Leggewie 1990, 10). On the one hand, the New Left stands for "leftist" income redistribution by way of encompassing social policies in the economic sphere and "libertarian" democratic participation and maximum individual autonomy in politics and the cultural sphere. The New Radical Right (NRR), on the other hand, advocates rightist free market economics and "authoritarian" hierarchical arrangements in politics, together with a limitation of diversity and individual autonomy in cultural expressions. In other words, postindustrial politics is characterized by a main ideological cleavage dividing left-libertarians from right-authoritarians.

Up to this point, however, our line of theoretical reasoning can account for the often confusing variety of rightist parties and movements as incompletely as its rivals. Therefore, we must identify additional arguments that can be logically related to the master hypothesis and can explain in a systematic way different appeals and electoral payoffs of new rightist parties. We must explore why economically rightist and politico-culturally "authoritarian" appeal is sometimes approximated in the actual strategy of the new parties but sometimes discarded in favor of other strategies. While common tendencies of the contemporary Right may be driven by the change of popular demands for political messages, the variance in the rightist parties' appeals across countries, and even within countries over time, requires a theory of political institutions and strategic choice within party systems and party organizations. This argument builds on three elements.

First, structural and sociological analysis of political preference changes does not develop a theory about the "supply side" of parties that serve right-authoritarian constituencies, but merely the "demand side" of electoral constituencies. In some cases, right-authoritarian voters may be represented by moderate-conservative parties that, in turn, will do everything to preempt the emergence of an independent NRR. In some instances, such efforts fail and right-authoritarians build their own vehicles of political articulation. In order to understand the phenomenon of the NRR in the arena of political mobilization, and particularly party competition, we therefore must analyze the strategies established political actors have chosen to address the demand for right-authoritarian politics and the political institutions that have constrained their choices. The sociological account of right-authoritarian politics remains incomplete without a reconstruction of the strategies of political entrepreneurs that seize on opportunities to build genuinely new right-authoritarian parties.

Second, the rise of the contemporary Right is not just conditioned by the choices of the established moderate conservatives but also by the capabilities and choices of the incipient rightist entrepreneurs and parties themselves. Politicians may face a favorable opportunity structure but fail to create strategies that enhance their power at the polls and in legislatures. Before resorting to ad hoc explanations that attribute such failures to a lack of information on the part of decision makers or a lack of interest in accumulating more power, it is worth checking how internal party structures of interest aggregation as well as the composition of the party activists constrain parties in their strategic choices. Sometimes variance in the appeal of the contemporary Right, therefore, may be due to the intraorganizational dynamics of incipient new parties. This is particularly likely where rightist parties fail to choose a strategic formula that takes advantage of the opportunities the party system offers them to gain electoral ground at the expense of established parties.

Third, empirical evidence shows that the contemporary extreme Right is not a "single-issue" phenomenon that can be solely understood as a response to economic crisis or the rapid influx of non-Occidental immigrants into hitherto homogeneous Western European societies. To the contrary, a sense of alarm about such developments, taken by itself, is typically a weak predictor of right-extremist support, as will be shown both by ecological- and individual-level analysis in later chapters. Nevertheless, economic crisis and surges of immigration can serve as *catalysts* that crystallize right-wing extremism on the level of party competition if political entrepreneurs can embed xenophobic slogans in a broader right-authoritarian message for which they find a receptive audience. Structure-induced dispositions of the electorate and opportunities for party competition interact with conjunctural issue attention cycles in the rise of new parties. Strategic political entrepreneurs skillfully bring together long-term and short-term opportunities to mobilize voter coalitions.[1] In light of such processes, it would be naive to expect the disappearance of the NRR, as soon as a particular issue—such as immigration—became less important on the political agenda.[2]

Although contemporary rightist parties make a variety of appeals and attract different electoral coalitions, none of the NRR's incarnations precisely correspond to the "old" extreme Right with fascist or national socialist labels. The old Right and the NRR not only have different structural origins but also different constituencies and substantive demands. Moreover, the NRR is strong in countries where the fascist and national socialist Right of the interwar period remained weak. Most importantly, where contemporary parties build on the legacy of the interwar extreme Right, they typically fail to attract significant electorates.

The metaphors "left" and "right," and even more so such labels as "fascism" and "national socialism," are embroiled not only in scholarly, theoretical controversies but also in a political war of words: opponents of the NRR like to label such parties as (neo)fascist; their adherents deny the accuracy of such characterizations. But the conceptual assimilation of the New to the Old Radical Right may be theoretically inadequate to explain the new phenomenon as well as politically dangerous—particularly for the foes of the NRR. Bad analysis rarely leads to effective political (counter)strategy.

The tasks for this opening chapter are thus quite clear. First, we outline a theory of the "demand" for rightist parties in contemporary advanced industrial democracies. Next, we develop theoretical propositions about the "supply" of rightist parties, the conditions under which their appeal is expected to vary, and the electoral payoffs such parties derive from different appeals. Based on this analysis, we then specify the evidence that would count as support or falsification of our own theory and three rival arguments that we will discuss in detail. The final section of this chapter will be devoted to a discussion of the contemporary extreme Right and the historical fascist Right. We will argue that the two Rights are very different in their ideological appeal and their electoral coalitions. Moreover, we will show, they were produced by different societal conditions.

The Demand for NRR Party Alternatives

Political systems involve (1) a delineation of who is a "player" or citizen, (2) a choice of collective decision modes among players, and (3) policies that determine the ground rules for allocating scarce resources among players. Different views of citizenship, decision modes, and resource allocation therefore provide the critical dimensions along which opinions and beliefs in democracies may vary. With respect to citizenship, the alternative is between a narrow, exclusive definition of citizenship rights (e.g., excluding women, immigrants, adherents of certain ethnocultural groups) and a broad, inclusive, and universalistic conception of citizenship. If we focus on ethnocultural relations, the polarity can also be described as a conflict between "cosmopolitan" and "particularist" conceptions of citizenship. With respect to collective decision modes, the alternative is between individual freedom of political and cultural expression, combined with participatory choice procedures of collectively binding policies, at one extreme of the continuum, and collective norm compliance, combined with hierarchical choice procedures, at the other. We may refer to this polarity as the division between "libertarian" and "authoritarian" political preferences. Finally, with respect to the allocation of scarce resources, the key division is between (1) at one extreme, proponents of spontaneous market allocation and proportional (if not flat) taxation of citizens' income, regardless of differences in wealth and, (2) at the other extreme, advocates of egalitarian resource redistribution calling for progressive income taxation on citizens who are better off or radical measures of direct expropriation of those who own the means of production. Here, a market-liberal view is pitted against a "populist" or "socialist" preference for redistribution.

Positions on the three dimensions may not vary independently from each other, but the precise way cosmopolitan versus particularist, libertarian versus authoritarian, and redistributive versus market-liberal views interact with each other may be historically contingent.[3] In this section, we argue that contemporary postindustrial democracies generate a limited but distinctive demand for a political combination of ethnocentric, authoritarian, and free market liberal appeals. This demand is not evenly distributed across the entire population but is more likely to surface among social groups characterized by distinctive experiences and deprivations of life chances.

Conventional approaches that ground the emergence of political demands in social structure have typically latched on to class divisions, defined in terms of economic property rights, and simple occupational categories, such as manual versus nonmanual labor, shop floor versus managerial tasks, and so on. In advanced capitalism, however, simple class conceptions and related occupational distinctions constitute crude tracers of the social and economic conditions that shape political preferences over conceptions of citizenship, democratic procedure, and resource allocation. We will therefore present a somewhat more sophisticated, though still oversimplifying, phenomenology of citizens' social experiences that enables us to reconstruct the process of political preference formation in advanced capitalism and to show why promarket, authoritarian, and particularist dispositions, on the one hand, and redistributive, libertarian, and cosmopolitan positions, on the other, form important clusters of public opinion. Since this theory of social preference formation in postindustrial capitalism has been outlined in more detail in another publication (Kitschelt 1994), we will summarize the argument in a few paragraphs. We will then offer an explanation of how this sociological theory of preference formation relates to socio-psychological accounts of the divide between authoritarians and libertarians that was first presented in Adorno et al.'s (1950) study of the authoritarian character.

If economic class, in the Marxian sense of property relations, cannot explain the constitution of political preferences by itself, two other avenues may allow us to construct a linkage between social structure and political consciousness. In economic terms, drawing on Max Weber and much recent rational choice theorizing, citizens' "market situations" may be presumed to shape their political consciousness, particularly when policy alternatives between economic redistribution and spontaneous market allocation are concerned. Market situation concerns actors' skills and capabilities, their social ties, and their location in a particular economic sector.

In advanced capitalism, in a period of increasing international competition and accelerating pressures for structural and occupational learning within industries and at a time when most actors realize that short-term insulation from structural innovation in response to market pressures can be had only at the expense of long-term industrial adaptation, most employees develop an interest in the market viability of their firms and industrial sectors. As a consequence, where comprehensive welfare states exist that absorb considerable resources in order to protect citizens from downward mobility, employees in internationally competitive sectors become reluctant to endorse further redistributive measures that would drain resources from investment and private consumption. This preference for investments to enhance market flexibility over further redistributive policies tends to be greatest among sectors and occupations that are most vulnerable to the competitive pressures of the international economy, such as manufacturing and financial services. In contrast, employees in the public-service sector (but also many private-sector nontradable services) as well as industries sheltered from foreign competition,[4] are more favorably disposed to redistributive social policies than are employees in the internationally exposed manufacturing industries or in financial and business services. Unlike internationally competitive sectors of the economy, domestic services can roll rising labor costs and social contributions into prices.

Economic left/right attitudes are not simply influenced by employment sector but also by individual market skills, which determine opportunities to move across sectors. At the individual level, actors who have the option and intention to work in sheltered nontradable domestic sectors because of their unique skills and qualifications tend to be more sympathetic to economic redistribution. The orientation on the economic left/right dimension is thus primarily a matter of occupational qualifications and employment sector rather than of economic class. Overall, both the proportion of jobs in competitive and internationally exposed sectors, but also in public, protected social service sectors, have increased at the expense of private, domestically sheltered manufacturing and services.[5] As a consequence, popular support for redistributive policies has declined among private sector workers and employees. This has brought about an increasing political polarization between private competitive and (quasi)public, sheltered sectors, both of which have grown in the last several decades at the expense of private domestic sectors.

People's market experience and occupational market power, however, are not the only conditions that shape their political consciousness. A second dimension that can be loosely derived from Habermas's distinction between strategic and communicative interaction sheds light on another aspect of the process of political preference formation. People's orientation toward definitions of citizenship (universalistic-cosmopolitan or particularistic-culturally parochial) and modes of collective decision making (egalitarian-democratic or hierarchical-authoritarian) are shaped by their *communicative experiences and capabilities.* These communicative experiences occur both in work organizations as well as in the private sphere of family, friends, and neighborhood. In our simplified model, we will focus only on experiences in work organizations.

Most importantly, individuals who work in symbol- and client-processing organizations where social relations are at the heart of the work process—such as in education, social work, health care, or cultural production—have a much stronger orientation toward a reciprocal, egalitarian design of democratic politics and cultural institutions than do individuals who work in strategic and instrumental economic settings where they manipulate objects, documents, and spreadsheets generated by other instrumental players. In this second type of task structure, which is heavily guided by rules and orders, actors will find authoritarian visions of collective decision making more natural. Due to a shortage of suitable surveys, the empirical evidence for this hypothesis is still fragmentary, but generally supportive.[6]

In addition to the phenomenology of the work situation, people's cognitive capabilities play a critical role in predisposing them to more libertarian or authoritarian conceptions of citizenship and collective decision making in advanced industrial society. Individuals with greater cognitive skills develop a sense of mastery of their social environment that leads them to raise claims to political participation, equality, and self-governance in all social institutions. Higher education thus reinforces libertarian politics. Conversely, individuals with few cognitive skills, who are capable of only crude schematizations of social reality, are more inclined to opt for authoritarian modes of collective decision making.

Instrumental or communicative orientations in politics and culture may also be indirectly related to gender. Women's socialization predisposes them toward more communicative and symbol-producing occupations and, in fact, the occupational profile of sectors with different communicative experiences is clearly characterized by a sex bias. Younger, educated, professionally employed women should therefore display the strongest predisposition toward libertarian politics.

The six indicators of market and organizational experiences thus yield a two-dimensional space of political orientations, with one set of experiences impinging primarily on economic preferences over rightist spontaneous or leftist redistributive allocation of resources and the other on political and cultural preferences over libertarian-cosmopolitan versus authoritarian-particularist views of collective decision making.[7] This scheme, however, does not illuminate why the combination of economically rightist and politically authoritarian beliefs—the configuration we have postulated to characterize the NRR—as well as its opposite, the combination of economically leftist and politically libertarian orientations, should be more common than the other combinations of left-authoritarian or right-libertarian views in the disposition of voters and especially the appeal of politicians who put together programmatic "packages" and advertise them under party labels.

The "elective affinity" between economic leftism and political libertarianism, on the one side, and between economic rightism and political authoritarianism, on the other, is not intrinsically rooted in postulates of political and economic theory. Rather, it is rooted in the historically contingent clustering of market and work experiences to which individuals are exposed in advanced postindustrial capitalism. The occupations and sectors that are protected from international competition also tend to offer work experiences that require high educational qualifications and afford reciprocity with clients and colleagues and thus foster libertarian orientations. Conversely, occupations and sectors exposed to international competition tend to provide work experiences that often rely on limited skills or, more importantly, structure interaction in instrumental and strategic ways. Most jobs in manufacturing, communication, and transportation industries, but also in financial and insurance services, are typical examples.

At the same time, bundles of job experiences that would favor authoritarian socialist orientations are becoming less frequent, for example, lower clerical tasks in the general public administration or in formerly state-owned enterprises, such as the railroads, utilities, and postal systems, or blue- and white-collar jobs in highly subsidized heavy industries—all areas that are now exposed to international competition. Conversely, only some tasks in marketing and advertising agencies, the news media, and in some business services provide experiences that encourage the combination of libertarian-capitalist orientations.

At the macrolevel, the specific clustering of occupational experiences in advanced capitalism has been brought about by well-known technical and institutional processes that have been too widely discussed to deserve more than a brief enumeration: namely, the introduction of knowledge-intensive flexible and specialized production systems, the expansion of the welfare state, the decline of transportation and communications costs, and the ensuing intensification of global market competition.

Of course, citizens' preferences over economic distribution and the cultural and political organization of collective decision-making processes are not entirely driven by occupational and educational experiences. A full theory of political preference formation would have to include a phenomenology of *consumption styles* in which residential patterns of living, family organization, age, and exposure to environmental pollution would have to play a critical role.[8] Nevertheless, occupational experiences provide good tracers of the potential coalitions and divisions in society in the postindustrial era. In contrast, class categories reflect political divisions only in a highly indirect, fractured fashion.

To single out just one group, the "working class" is increasingly divided into different segments by sectoral market and occupational experiences. The shrinking number of less skilled workers in declining but protected sectors has an inclination to opt for left-authoritarian politics. Their market situation removes them from competitive pressures and predisposes them toward a more "leftist" economic policy preference. At the same time, their occupational experiences (processing objects) and their limited education predispose them toward more authoritarian political appeals. Higher skilled workers in internationally competitive industries, in contrast, are more likely to support middle-of-the-road economic policies and moderate cultural and political views. A culturally parochial and politically authoritarian potential is particularly strong among the losers of the economic modernization process within the working class, primarily manual workers with few or obsolete skills. Given their economic predicament, they may not fully endorse procapitalist economic policies, but they are available to the NRR primarily because of the latter's authoritarian and racist appeals. Such political visions may be particularly attractive for young workers who have never established close organizational and cultural ties to socialist parties, labor unions, and ancillary organizations surrounding them. In fact, it has been suggested that the rigidity of labor markets in Western European welfare states makes it so difficult for young unskilled workers to get an economic and a political foothold in these systems that they turn toward market liberalism in order to smash the institutions exacerbating their weak position in labor markets.[9]

Tests of the theoretical argument that we will present face the following empirical obstacles. Surveys typically do not allow us to measure several of the critical variables that are hypothesized to impinge on political preference formation, particularly private- or public-sector employment, domestic or internationally competitive sector employment, and occupational experience in client-symbol- or object-documents-processing task structures. At the same time, existing occupational and class categories muddle linkages between market-organizational experience and political preferences. Nevertheless, given this predicament, empirical research is forced to resort to traditional job classifications that are readily available and may reflect occupational experiences only in a very indirect fashion. In the empirical analysis, we will distinguish four categories of respondents and analyze their political and party preferences:

1. *Blue-collar workers:* Given the sectoral division between competitive and domestic sectors, blue-collar workers, as a whole, should no longer be economically leftist in a pronounced way. At the same time, given that the bulk of blue-collar workers is involved in object- and document-processing, has comparatively little education, and is predominantly male, this occupational group may express above average dispositions toward particularist and culturally parochial conceptions of citizenship and authoritarian decision making.

2. *"Petit bourgeois" small independents such as craftspeople, shop-keepers, and farmers:* Through manufacturers and wholesalers, small independent businesspeople tend to be exposed at least indirectly to the pressures of international competition. They are therefore likely to voice intense aversion to redistributive welfare state policies. More-over, they are more involved in object- and document-processing than social and symbolic tasks. They have received below average educa-tion and tend to be predominantly male. Among this group, both a particularist-authoritarian as well as a market-oriented liberal political preference structure may be dominant.

3. *White-collar employees, professionals, students:* These groups tend to be more typically employed (or strive for such employment) in the public or in nonprofit sectors, have high education, and work in client-interactive task structures. Many younger women can be encountered in these organizational settings. Overall, particularism and authoritar-ianism should be substantially below average among all of these groups. At the same time, these groups are internally divided over economic questions of allocation, with public-sector employees tilting to the redistributive side and private-sector employees and profes-sionals supporting market allocation. Independent professionals, such as lawyers, accountants, and providers of other business services, are probably the group with the greatest disposition toward economically rightist and politically libertarian conceptions.

4. *Residual population without employment (pensioners, homemakers, the unemployed):* Given the age distribution of the residual popu-lation, they typically have below average education and are more likely to have held jobs in object- and document-processing organiza-tions, favoring distinctly authoritarian tendencies. With respect to eco-nomic left/right divisions, no clear tendency emerges in this group. Working-class individuals on fixed incomes (public pensions, unem-ployment payments, etc.) will express more leftism, but other mem-bers of this broad category may be more supportive of free market capitalism.

In general, we would hypothesize that the potential to vote for new right-wing authoritarian parties is higher than average among blue-collar workers, petit bourgeois, and lower salaried employees. It tends to be lower than average among higher white-collar employees, business professionals, and especially social service employees and professionals. The former groups have a higher potential for authoritarian and ethnocentric dispositions and, at least in the case of the petit bourgeois, for vigorously market-liberal views against the tax burdens imposed by the welfare state as well. The relationship between actual voting for extreme-rightist parties and these general dispositions, however, may involve some unexpected complications.

In European advanced capitalist and democratic welfare states, vigorous racist, ethnocentric campaigns, but also the call for substantial reductions in the welfare safety net and for a reassertion of free markets, are nonconformist, if not outright challenges to taboos. In the same vein, supporting a new and radical party is an act of nonconformism that challenges the status quo. In contrast, authoritarian dispositions are often closely linked to conformism and compliance with the status quo. In other words, how can racist and market-liberal supporters of radical rightist parties also be authoritarians if voting for extremist parties goes against the grain of authoritarian compliance with order and hierarchy? We will argue that while supporters of radical rightist parties are in general more authoritarian than the population at large, there may be a marginally declining propensity to vote for new radical rightist parties beyond a certain threshold of authoritarianism. Empirically, therefore, voters of radical rightist parties are not necessarily more authoritarian than the voters of conventional conservative parties. If we compare the electorates of moderate conservative and of radical rightist parties, one of three configurations is likely. First, extremist voters are indeed more market liberal, authoritarian, and racist than conservatives. Second, radical rightist voters are more market liberal and more racist than the comparison group supporting conservative parties, but not more authoritarian. Third, at the level of voter dispositions, there are hardly any differences between conservative and radical right voters. The reason then why a significant proportion of individuals in the general right-authoritarian pool votes for radical parties rather than mainline conservatives is entirely accounted for by the strategic behavior of the conventional conservatives who for one reason or another are not able to project a credible image and build a reputation for serving right-authoritarian preferences. This leads us into the consideration of party elites and their behavior in the competitive electoral game, the subject of the next section.

Before we get to the analysis of party strategy, however, we will step back and confront the sociological and economic explanation of political preferences with rival and possibly complementary sociopsychological theories that also identify the importance of a cosmopolitan/particularist (in-group versus out-group) and a libertarian/authoritarian dimension in political attitudes. Adorno et al. (1950) were among the first to recognize that ethnocentric attitudes are not an isolated "single issue" but part of a broad constellation of authoritarian attitudes and beliefs. It is a different matter, however, to explain the emergence of such beliefs. Sociopsychological accounts can be roughly divided into psychoanalytical theories and social learning theories (cf. Altemeyer 1988, 51–55). The psychoanalytical theories that informed the Adorno et al. investigation of the authoritarian character put greatest emphasis on the early parent-child interaction and are clearly inconsistent with our framework. They ignore later learning experiences or even the explicit political ideology of the parents, which may be transmitted to children. Fortunately, the psychoanalytical theory of libertarian/authoritarian preference formation has found little support in empirical research. Its major measurement instrument, the F-scale (F stands for fascism) is biased and must be modified (Altemeyer 1988, chap. 1). Moreover, recent tests of the linkage between a shortened version of the F-scale and political party preference has found no correlation once political authoritarianism has been controlled for (cf. Middentorp 1993).

The relationship between sociopsychological learning theories of authoritarianism and the sociological approach outlined above is more complicated. On the one hand, there are a number of elements in learning theories that are directly consistent with the sociological approach. For example, education is seen as a major contributor to greater libertarianism.[10] The role of education is also highlighted in Lipset's (1981, 101–14) provocative argument that the working class has authoritarian dispositions because it lacks cognitive sophistication, power to abstract from concrete experience, and imagination (108).[11] Moreover, there are some indirect tracers of job experience measured in experiments of learning that are consistent with the role attributed to occupational experiences in our sociological framework. For example, Altemeyer's (1988, 93) comparison of changes of authoritarianism in liberal arts and administrative science majors shows that the former move faster and further toward libertarian politics than the latter over the course of four years of college education. In general, learning theory puts great emphasis on social encounters and interactions, a perspective that is critical for our sociological account as well.

At the same time, there are a number of areas where the predictions of sociological and learning theory are not directly comparable or are potentially inconsistent. We have not found empirical studies that would directly test the impact of organizational experiences on political consciousness because sociopsychological learning theories typically do not examine occupational life as a source of preference formation and ideology. Most difficult for the sociological theory may be finding learning theories that argue that the family and peer groups have a definite impact on libertarian-authoritarian dispositions, that is, experiences made long before individuals enter the labor market. Our sociological account suggests that there is no memory that connects what people experienced in their youth to their occupational life or even a medium-range memory that connects the succession of jobs they held during their occupational life.

At this point, we will make a partial concession to learning theory that, however, does not undermine the empirical regularities our sociological account has hypothesized, although it modifies the underlying causal model of preference formation. People's political consciousness may in fact derive in part from their parents' and their peer group's outlook on life; moreover, the choice of occupational career paths, for example, between client-interactive or document-processing occupations, may be in part endogenous to dispositions acquired in the socialization process. At the same time, however, the dispositions and interpretations of society that parents transmit to their offspring are linked to their own market and occupational experiences. Moreover, given that constraints on social mobility keep most people in similar market and occupational situations as their parents, the transmission of parental ideas often tends to be reinforced by the market and organizational experiences made in adult life. In this vein, sociological and sociopsychological theories of preference formation offer not necessarily contradictory but often complementary and mutually reinforcing accounts.

Finally, sociopsychological theories implicitly rely on sociological theories without fully recognizing this fact. Altemeyer (1988, chap. 1) notes that sociopsychological scales of authoritarianism require updating from time to time because some issues no longer load on the critical dimensions to be measured. Overall, in a fixed 12-item scale of right-wing authoritarianism annually tested on cohorts of students, the interitem correlation fell from .25 in 1973 to .13 in 1984 and then recovered slightly to .17 in 1987 (28). The changing response patterns over time to items in the scale, such as gender relations, sexual morality, the communist threat, authority, and interethnic relations, reflect social transformations that cannot be reduced to personality changes. Sociopsychological studies cannot explain why the salience of certain attitudes increases and why dispositions become more intense and politically salient. These limitations again show that socio-psychological research is not directly competing with or cannot serve as a substitute for sociological approaches to the study of political preference formation. Both approaches are based on the mechanism of learning, but in different ways. A complete model of the causal determinants of authoritarianism would have to take into account parental style and beliefs, education, as well as work and other experiences in daily life.

Party Competition and the Supply of Radical Rightist Parties

Let us first recapitulate the sociological situation with which parties are confronted in advanced capitalist democracies. Due to the expansion of public-sector employment, particularly in personal services with highly sophisticated professionals, the proportion of the population with economically leftist and libertarian orientations has been increasing. At the same time, the broader exposure of private-sector workers and employees in manufacturing and business services to international competition has triggered a general shift of popular opinion to the economic right, toward limiting the general economic burden of the welfare state. This shift has occurred both in the working class as well as in a variety of non–working-class occupations.

Overall, due to educational and occupational change the proportion of individuals in social locations that favor authoritarianism has, in general, declined. In particular, the share of people whose position makes them likely to support both authoritarian and leftist political preferences has eroded. Why, then, have explicitly authoritarian and rightist parties found greater support in the 1980s and 1990s than in the decades immediately following World War II?

This puzzle can be solved only if we abandon the idea that parties are nothing but the reflection of mass-level sentiments. This, of course, is an insight widely shared by theorists of party formation.[12] Parties seek power in a variety of ways, and voter preferences enter their calculations to the extent that they advance such political objectives. Thus, the distribution of political preferences in a space where most citizens and voters are located close to an axis ranging from left-libertarian to right-authoritarian positions does not by itself determine the shape of the party system of advanced postindustrial democracies. A sociological theory of preference formation can identify the clienteles of authoritarian politics, particularly elements of the working class and lower white collar sector, and of both authoritarian and promarket politics, particularly small business. It is insufficient, however, for predicting the rise of right-authoritarian parties because their emergence depends on the strategic interaction of existing parties in the competitive system. Not in all circumstances where right-authoritarian popular preferences are intense will corresponding parties manage to garner a substantial share of the electorate.

The future of the radical Right cannot be read from structural trends in the transformation of "post-Fordist" production systems, welfare states, or intensified international competition nor from the corresponding microlevel changes in the market location, task structures, and qualifications of individual employees. These macrochanges provide the scenario within which politicians choose objectives and strategies that influence the fate of political parties. Whether a successful NRR party emerges depends on the opportunity structure of party competition. Only if voters are sufficiently disaffected with the existing moderately conservative and moderately leftist or social democratic parties will the reservoir of potential right-authoritarian voters rally around a new political force.

The disaffection with moderate conservatives is also more likely where electorally successful radical left-libertarian parties exist that appear to authoritarian constituencies to be a political provocation not adequately countered by the existing moderate conservatives. The success of new rightist parties, however, does not entirely depend on the behavior of their competitors. Even if a strategic opening for a new rightist party does exist, right-wing political entrepreneurs must be able to build organizations and to design the appropriate appeal that seizes the moment and exploits the strategic weakness of the existing parties. New parties must assume issue leadership to crystallize a

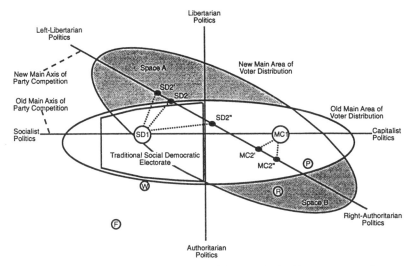

Fig. 1.1. The competitive space for political parties in Western Europe in the 1980s

potential electorate and mobilize it around a new cluster of political demands.[13]

The electoral opportunity structure for the emergence of NRR parties can best be understood against the background of the strategic dilemmas faced by conventional mass parties of the moderate Left and moderate Right. Previous work by one of this book's authors employed a scheme designed to shed light on the strategic difficulties encountered by the social democratic Left (Kitschelt 1994, chap. 1). A modified version of the scheme, reproduced here as figure 1.1, can be utilized to analyze strategic dilemmas on the Right as well as the opportunities for the emergence of extreme-rightist parties.

Figure 1.1 constructs an ideal-typical rendering of the voter distribution and ignores the effects of short-term issue cycles, variance in parties' issue leadership, and cross-national variations in the extent to which the main axis of competition rotates from a left/right to a purely economic left-libertarian versus right-authoritarian position. The curves that enclose the clear area constitute the main voter distribution in the previous cold war era of left/right competition when voters were primarily concerned with economic issues, such as the expansion of the Keynesian Welfare State. The curves that envelope the shaded area around the diagonal axis in figure 1.1 represent the main area of voter distribution from left-libertarian to right-authoritarian alternatives in advanced capitalist democracies. The overall share of authoritarians in the cold war era was certainly not smaller and was most likely greater than in postindustrial democracies. Yet they are now differently distributed. A relatively greater proportion of authoritarians is also located on the economically capitalist side of the political spectrum (shaded space B). At the same time, while support for the economic left has generally diminished, a strong new left-libertarian sector has emerged (shaded space A).

Consider now the strategic choices social democrats (SD) or moderate conservatives (MC) face relative to the evolving main space of voter distribution in advanced capitalist democracy.[14] If voters act rationally in a Euclidean space and support parties close to their own ideal position, most but not all parties will strategically locate their appeals within the ideological range covered by each time period's main area of voter distribution—provided the parties attempt to maximize their electoral support or legislative seats. Only parties representing small pressure groups on specific secondary issues may garner limited electoral support with positions outside these basic regions of the space in figure 1.1.[15]

In the first decades after World War II, when libertarian/authoritarian issues had only limited salience and voters were primarily divided along the socialist versus capitalist political axis, conventional leftist and rightist parties were positioned best at moderate positions on the socialist/capitalist axis, yet (almost) neutral on the libertarian/authoritarian axis (positions SD_1 and MC_1).[16] With the rotation and rightward shift of the main area of voter distribution and, consequently, also of the main axis of party competition, social democratic parties have been well advised to move toward (1) more libertarian and (2) more capitalist positions, for example location SD_2. Moderate conservatives may stay in place near MC_1 because more voters now share nonsocialist convictions about economic governance structures. Yet, at the same time, the structural transformation of postindustrial capitalism has created a new reservoir of voters for whom authoritarian positions become highly salient, particularly with the rise of a libertarian Left at the opposite end of the axis of political competition.

Space A represents the area where most libertarians are situated. Since they typically also subscribe to (moderate) social democratic economic positions, this competitive space is up for grabs between repositioned social democratic parties (located at SD_2, $SD_{2'}$, or $SD_{2''}$) and explicit left-libertarian parties in positions more extreme than $SD_{2''}$. Space B comprises a generally smaller but significant core space of those individuals who are economically on the moderate to extreme Right yet who are distanced from the center of the competitive space primarily by their support of authoritarian and racist positions. Electorally successful new rightist parties must situate themselves somewhere in this space. Their success depends, however, on the strategic appeal of MC and, to a lesser extent, SD parties, both of which are faced with strategic dilemmas.

Let us begin with the MC party. If the party stays near MC_1, it has the greatest chance to capture the "pivot" of the electoral space and stave off a leftist majority, that is, of social democratic and left-libertarian parties. At the same time, however, it creates a vast uncovered electoral space that may invite an NRR party to locate at strategic position R. As long as SD offers a fairly pronounced alternative to MC_1, for example, by staying at position SD_1 or by moving to $SD_{2'}$, MC_1 may still be attractive to voters sympathetic to the authoritarian Right by presenting itself as the "lesser evil": Only a moderate conservative government, uninhibited by a more right-wing competitor at R, can prevent a government even more unpalatable to the far Right than an MC government. This appeal of the moderate Right is particularly plausible and attractive as long as that party is confined to the opposition benches and a social democratic government is in office.

Yet as left parties move toward the median voter, for example, by assuming position $SD_{2''}$, the moderate conservative's appeal to the lesser evil loses plausibility for sympathizers of the authoritarian Right. Voters in the right-authoritarian opinion sector become cynical about politics, just as left-libertarians do who see social democratic parties move toward "centrist" positions. Cynical voters see no difference among the established parties and believe that party politicians form a closed "political class" that is only out to help itself to wealth and power at the expense of the "common man" in the streets. On the political right, this loss of trust in moderate conservatism is accelerated by longer episodes of mainstream conservative government that is likely to reveal the similarity of the policies pursued by moderately leftist and moderately rightist governments. Voters of the far Right will then perceive a "cartel" of established moderate SD and MC parties that have become virtually indistinguishable. *Convergence of SD and MC parties, together with an extended period of government participation by the moderate conservatives thus creates the electoral opening for the authoritarian Right that induces voters to abandon their loyalty to established conservative parties.* MC parties are then caught in a dilemma between "vote-maximizing" strategies that often may force them to appeal more clearly to their right-authoritarian supporters and to move their parties to MC_2, or even $MC_{2''}$, particularly in the presence of an NRR competitor, and "office-maximizing" strategies to capture the median voter and make the party pivotal for government coalitions and policy formation in the party system. Such office-maximizing strategies, however, may entail serious electoral losses benefiting new challenging NRR parties.

The same dilemma, of course, applies to social democrats as well, though with a twist. Given the disappearance of a fundamentalist socialist, or even Marxist, Left from the end of the 1970s onward, and especially after the fall of communism, social democrats have had to abandon position SD_1 to stay electorally viable, regardless of specific strategic considerations. Once they approach the new main axis of party competition, however, further strategic moves are likely to be *either* toward a more left-libertarian ($SD_{2'}$) *or* a more centrist appeal ($SD_{2''}$). Where they will locate themselves depends on (1) their electoral objectives and (2) their competitors' positions.

In a simple spatial model of multiparty competition among short-term vote maximizers, parties have an incentive to spread out across the ideological space rather than to gravitate toward the median voter (Cox 1990; Shepsle and Cohen 1990). If social democrats try to maximize votes in the short term, the most "profitable" location then depends on the "crowdedness" of the competitive space to the party's libertarian Left and its authoritarian Right. The more crowded a market segment is with serious competitors who can overcome entry costs into the game, the less attractive it is for parties to approach that segment. Rational parties locate themselves in the middle of their market, as far away from competitors as possible.[17] Social democrats may also pursue a different strategy than short-term vote maximizing, such as maximizing chances to hold government office by occupying the pivot of the competitive electoral space. Often a strategy of "pivoting" by moving to position $SD_{2''}$ will, on balance, cost the party votes but may increase its bargaining weight in coalition and policy formation.[18] In this vein, social democrats experience exactly the same dilemma as moderate conservatives.

In general, the constraints of the electoral arena compel vote- or office-seeking social democrats to move away from the left-authoritarian quadrant of figure 1.1. Such movements, however, have significant consequences for the parties' traditional working-class and lower white-collar clienteles and particularly those segments that are drawn to leftist positions because they are employed in a public sector or domestically protected or subsidized industry. The same groups are often attracted to authoritarian political positions because they have little education and work in object-processing occupations, for example, workers in heavy industries, but also lower blue- and white-collar employees in the post office, the railroads, or the security forces (police, military). Such occupational groups may be located near position W in figure 1.1. The further social democratic parties move from SD_1 to SD_2, the more alienated such traditional social democratic worker and lower white-collar constituencies will feel from their previously preferred party and the more such voters might be tempted to support, say, racist and xenophobic party R, which appeals to authoritarian resentments even though it diverges to some extent from these voters' commitment to the welfare state and redistributive economic policy. Alternatively, voters in position W may stay home and no longer vote in elections.

The success of NRR parties, however, is contingent not only on the choices of SD and MC and the general crowdedness of the party spectrum in different areas of the competitive space but also on the choices of the up-and-coming new rightist parties themselves. *Depending on where they locate themselves, they will draw different electoral coalitions and will have different "yield ratios" within the electorate.* In other words, contingent upon the new parties' strategic appeals, the composition of their following will be more working class or more non-working class, especially petite bourgeois and lower white collar. Positions *P, R, W,* and *F* in figure 1.1 are only ideal-typical examples of a continuum of positions over which new rightist parties may be distributed. If this theoretical conceptualization of their position is correct, however, each position should be associated with (1) different electoral constituencies and (2) different electoral payoffs. We will now describe the conditions under which each of these ideal-typical strategic positions of the contemporary Right may be chosen as well as the electoral coalitions and payoffs that are associated with them. This analysis will provide the hypotheses that will be initially explored in the comparative investigation of chapter 2 and then in more depth in the case study chapters that follow.

The "Master Case": Authoritarian and Capitalist Appeal of the NRR

The ideal-typical NRR position is associated with both authoritarian and capitalist appeals in the region of position *R* in figure 1.1. In our view, this position is the "master case" for the contemporary extreme Right because it promises a high electoral return given that it can appeal to a cross-class alliance: it attracts segments of the working class based on racist-xenophobic and authoritarian appeals. It rallies small business on additional promarket and antistate slogans, calling for the dismantling of public bureaucracies and the welfare state.[19] In this scenario, the main underrepresented social category will be white-collar professionals. As indicated above, the occupational categories are but indirect tracers of the true market and organizational experiences that characterize the electoral coalition around the NRR. If data were available to explore the proposition empirically, we would expect the lowest support for the NRR by far among university-trained professionals in public social service agencies (education, social welfare, etc.) and the highest support among craftspeople, shopkeepers, and blue-collar workers in industries that are losing ground in the international market competition.

The European NRR is commonly associated with two political issues that have become salient since the 1970s and 1980s in a variety of countries: the revolt against higher taxes, primarily direct income and property taxes, and the rejection of immigrants from non-Occidental cultures, nationalities, and ethnicities. Yet these two issues only highlight broader ideological orientations and dispositions toward political action that encompass a more complex universe of beliefs and aspirations on the three interrelated dimensions we have already introduced above: the scope of citizenship, the organization of collective decision-making procedures, and the principles of allocating scarce resources. In terms of citizenship, the NRR stands for an exclusionary, particularist definition of citizenship rights confined to a culturally homogeneous group of residents. In terms of collective decision-making procedures—whether in politics, enterprise, family, or church—the NRR stands for strong authoritarian-paternalist procedures and rejects participatory debate, pluralism based on the equal worth of citizens' voices, tolerance for disagreements in the decision process, and compromise between conflicting interests. In terms of economic and social policies, the NRR advocates the spontaneous allocation of resources through market institutions but rejects redistributive schemes of planned allocation regardless of whether they are guided by a central bureaucracy or democratic collective decision making. The state should be strong and authoritarian, but small. The NRR generally favors an ethic of hard work and investment that is reinforced by the individualization of choice in the marketplace over an ethic of consumption and hedonistic enjoyment that is promoted by collective and redistributive allocation modes. The conflict between authoritarian Right and libertarian Left thus extends over a wide range of policy issues among which the following presently enjoy particular salience:

1. *Gender conflict*—paternalism in the family versus gender equality and difference (policy issues: public child care, abortion rights, women's representation in politics);
2. *Multicultural conflict*—cultural homogeneity in an ethnically exclusionary society versus cultural pluralism in a cosmopolitan society (policy issues: immigration and political asylum, voting rights for residents with foreign nationality, the right to practice different religions and beliefs in public spaces, the role of national symbols, such as the flag, anthem, etc.);
3. *Environmental conflict*—industrial growth, a subordination of nature to material production, and the primacy of the Protestant work ethic versus protection and enjoyment of the environment, permitting only minimal intrusion by industry;
4. *Modes of political participation*—compliance with political authorities and participation only through voting versus a participation through sometimes disruptive forms of direct action in social movements (demonstrations, sit-ins, plant occupations).

The radical Right with an authoritarian bent is "new" because it combines promarket and authoritarian appeals. We will discuss the relationship between this "new" Right and the "old" interwar extreme Right in the final section of this chapter. We can now generate several hypotheses about the NRR:

Hypothesis 1. NRR parties are most likely to appear and to be electorally successful
   (a) in postindustrial societies with large welfare states and

(b) in circumstances where there has been a convergence between the main moderate left and right conventional parties.

Hypothesis 2. NRR parties will attract the following electoral coalition:
   (a) blue-collar workers will be somewhat overrepresented
   (b) small business will be most overrepresented
   (c) inactives in the labor market will be proportionally represented or somewhat overrepresented
   (d) white-collar employees, professionals, and students will be underrepresented.

Populist Antistatist Appeals

In figure 1.1, the populist antistatist strategy is symbolized by position *P,* but this is only one possibility among a range of positions that go from *P* up toward a procapitalist and actually more neutral, if not slightly libertarian, appeal. In other words, populist antistatist appeals are primarily directed against "big government" and the "political class" that dominates a country's politics through the conventional parties, but to a much lesser extent against the libertarian themes of multiculturalism, environmentalism, gender liberation, and direct political participation.

Populist antistatism thus should not be lumped together with the NRR. Political entrepreneurs might find populist antistatism electorally profitable where the established moderate left and right parties are firmly bound to a status quo in which a deregulation and liberalization of the economy also undercuts party power. This is typically the case in democracies with large public industries where governance of such industries has been run as a patronage racket shared by all the major parties. Under these circumstances, moderate conservative parties are totally unable to incorporate free market appeals in a credible way. Moreover, in such systems, the distance between moderate conservative and moderate leftist parties should be even smaller than in other countries where the convergence of the conventional Left and Right has triggered the possibility of NRR mobilization. The call for market liberalism on the populist Right is thus primarily a challenge to the incumbent political elites and their often corrupt and self-serving policies.[20]

Populist antistatist parties are also likely to attract a different and broader electorate than NRR parties, where conditions are favorable for this strategy. Faced with a patronage-driven, clientelist traditional party establishment, many educated white-collar professionals will also be cynical about the established parties and sense a desire to "teach them a lesson." If they are uninclined to vote for a left-libertarian party, no other alternative is more convenient than a populist antistatist party.[21] For the populist and antistatist strategy, we can thus derive the following hypotheses:

Hypothesis 3. Populist antistatist parties are most likely to appear and to be electorally successful:
(a) in postindustrial societies with large welfare states and
(b) in circumstances where there has been a convergence between the main moderate left and right conventional parties *and* this convergence is cemented by a clientelist/patronage-driven political economy;

Hypothesis 4. Populist antistatist parties will attract a true "cross-class" electoral alliance in which no single group will be clearly over- or underrepresented.

Racist Authoritarian and "Welfare Chauvinist" Appeals

This position is symbolized in figure 1.1 by the region in the vicinity of *W* (welfare chauvinism) and can stretch all the way to *F* (for fascism). Here, political entrepreneurs emphasize racist and authoritarian slogans but studiously stay away from an admiration of market-liberal capitalism. The main point is the mobilization of resentment on the authoritarian/libertarian axis. The attack on foreigners, the vilification of feminist and environmentalist movements (for example, in the fight against abortion rights or speed limits on freeways), and the stress on national symbols and historical reminiscences are critical for the racist-authoritarian strategy.

The racist-authoritarian strategy may explicitly move to the defense of income redistribution and of the "little people" in the street against the large corporations and trusts. At the same time, income redistribution and protection from the risks of labor markets can be woven into the racist-authoritarian message by appealing to "welfare chauvinism." The welfare state is presented as a system of social protection for those who belong to the ethnically defined community and who have contributed to it. Immigrants are depicted as freeloaders who do not contribute to the system but claim its benefits. Welfare chauvinism is particularly likely among social groups whose economic well-being is critically dependent on fiscally viable social policies that furnish satisfactory public pensions, medical benefits, and unemployment insurance. Quite clearly, citizens with lower incomes—blue-collar workers, lower clerks, pensioners—and few assets (stocks, bonds, real estate) are most sensitive to any threat to the continuing viability of social insurance systems. Since the generally below average level of education in these groups also renders them vulnerable to authoritarian appeals, such groups are most likely to express "welfare chauvinist" resentments.

A welfare chauvinist party strategy is not identical with a fascist authoritarianism that, at least in its rhetoric, directly attacks liberal capitalist market relations. At position *F,* we often encounter a combination of terrorist activities against foreigners and other targets of ethnic hatred with a resentment against capitalist market processes. As we will argue below, fascist parties, situated in historical settings with very different social structures and citizens' preferences than advanced capitalist democracies, under certain circumstances were able to become electorally successful with such appeals. In postindustrial capitalism, however, social fascist positions are likely to maneuver right-wing parties into a political desert. Strategy F appeals only to a minute constituency of people socially marginalized because of their youth, their lack of marketable skills, and other deficiencies that undermine their ability to compete in the marketplace. In contrast to the era in which fascist parties mobilized, in postindustrial democracies position F is typically propagated not by political parties aspiring to a mass following but by small sects for whom their internal communal life and their violent external pursuits, for example, against foreigners, are more important than winning votes.

Due to increasing affluence in advanced industrial capitalism, the potential target groups for welfare chauvinist appeals are also quite limited. Authoritarian, ethnocentric, and anticapitalist appeals are likely to fall onto much more fertile ground in less affluent postsocialist societies (cf. Kitschelt 1992; 1995). Why, then, would political entrepreneurs in advanced capitalism choose authoritarian welfare chauvinist appeals? How could a winning coalition be formed around such a strategy? In fact, short of a major economic catastrophe, it appears unlikely that the gradual structural transformation of Western economies will ever threaten or actually cut free a sufficiently large proportion of the workforce into unemployment to provoke the rise of significant authoritarian welfare-chauvinist parties. Parties with such appeals may do well for a while in depressed industrial areas or in regional protest elections but rarely on a national scale or for an extended period of time. There is no "structural location" in advanced capitalism in which they can entrench themselves.

This hypothesis implies that parties that follow the new rightist authoritarian and market-liberal "master strategy" should lose votes if they emphasize immigration, xenophobia, and race as their key issue but neglect market liberalism. In terms of figure 1.1, a movement from positions P or R toward W or F leads to a narrowing of the electoral coalition that can be rallied behind rightist parties.

At the systemic level of party competition, our theory has no explanation for the choice of welfare chauvinist strategies by the contemporary extreme Right that restrict electoral support coalitions. As a consequence, we must change the level of analysis and examine how *intraparty politics* may condition strategic choices such that the leadership will not pursue vote-maximizing power strategies. We are searching for internal impediments to a "rational" choice of party appeals at the systemic level of party competition. One obvious hypothesis has to do with the political experiences and inclinations of the extreme-rightist activists. Where these activists were socialized into a fascist tradition that patterns their political interpretations, it is unlikely that extreme-rightist parties can fully seize upon the opportunities offered by the contemporary electoral marketplace. In countries with a historical tradition of the extreme Right, particularly those where fascist movements founded fascist regimes, the perpetuation of an extreme-rightist discourse is organized such that a "winning coalition appeal" with a procapitalist and authoritarian strategy of the NRR is unacceptable to most hard-core followers of extreme-rightist parties.[22] Where the fascist tradition involves more social, if not socialist, elements, parties may locate between the strategic points W and F in figure 1.1. It is, however, possible that neofascist forces express more traditionalist authoritarian views that value property and hierarchical status outside the framework of a liberal market society. Also, here, neofascist parties will be unable to appeal to market liberalism and often also to racism as well. Yet they will not be welfare chauvinist and will have little ability to attract workers, but their authoritarian traditionalism will primarily rally small business and lower white-collar employees.

We are now ready to specify hypotheses for the authoritarian welfare-chauvinist strategy:

> *Hypothesis 5.* Authoritarian and welfare chauvinist parties will not be electorally successful in advanced capitalist democracies.
>
> *Hypothesis 6.* Such parties will draw on a clientele that overrepresents only blue-collar voters, yet none of the other main socioeconomic groups.
>
> *Hypothesis 7.* The systemically "irrational" authoritarian welfare chauvinist appeal will be chosen only by those parties of the extreme Right that are steeped in a legacy of strong fascist movements and political regimes with a national socialist bent.
>
> *Hypothesis 8.* More traditionalist neofascist groups also will be unable to increase their electoral appeal because they fail to highlight market competition and racism in their programs. They will draw primarily on small business and lower white-collar constituencies.

Theoretical Propositions about the Contemporary Extreme Right and Rival Hypotheses

To conclude this analysis, we can now specify the empirical findings that lend support to or falsify the theory we have laid out in this chapter (fig. 1.2). First, right-authoritarian or populist anti-statist electoral success presupposes an advanced industrial capitalism. Outside advanced capitalist democracies, the

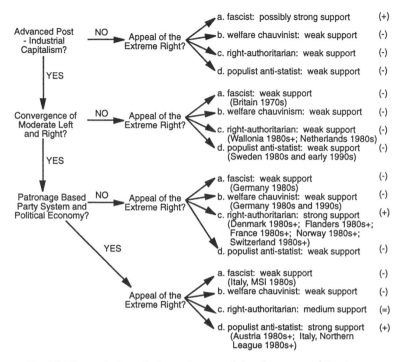

Fig. 1.2. Theoretical predictions of successful and unsuccessful extreme-rightist parties

party appeals and electoral coalitions that may attract a significant following inside contemporary Western democracies should find only weak support. Outside advanced Western societies, fascist parties may be quite attractive, provided they rise in an otherwise favorable political opportunity structure, which we will contrast with that promoting the contemporary Western extreme Right in the final section of this chapter.

Within today's Western democracies, a convergence of the main moderate left and right parties is the next precondition for the emergence of a powerful extreme Right. Where this condition is absent, no extremist party will be electorally important, no matter whether its appeal is fascist, NRR, or populist and antistatist. Among countries with a moderation of party competition, two further cases will be distinguished. Where this moderation is associated with a patronage-based political economy, populist antistatist parties with a broad cross-class basis will be electorally most attractive. Where there is a more clear-cut separation of politics from business, the "winning formula" of the extreme Right will be NRR, assembling an electoral coalition in which workers and small business are overrepresented. Populist antistatist appeals, but also welfare chauvinist appeals, are not particularly attractive in these circumstances.

We are now in a position to contrast our explanatory framework with several alternative views of the contemporary extreme Right that have been advanced in various scholarly and political debates. For each of these alternatives, we can specify a set of hypotheses that differs from the set of propositions we have introduced above.

The contemporary Right as "single-issue" politics. Interpretations of right-wing extremism in Western Europe as single-issue mobilization have focused on two separate issues that are hypothesized to stir political support— the fight against progressive income taxes in the 1970s and the opposition to the influx of immigrants and asylum seekers from non-Western European regions, particularly from the Middle East and from Africa. If the rightist parties in the 1980s mobilize around a single issue, their voters should be dispersed over the entire range of ideological alternatives on all other economic and sociopolitical issues but clearly stand out on a separate issue dimension dividing racist and parochial supporters of the New Right from the more cosmopolitan and universalist supporters of all the other parties. [23] In contrast, if NRR parties assume a distinctive configuration of positions on a broader cluster of issues that constitutes a dominant dimension of competition in a party system, spatial theories of multiparty competition may provide a superior account of their success. The extent to which racist and ethnocentric appeals explain voters' support for the extreme Right thus sheds light on the adequacy of rival theories of party competition.

Three "rival hypotheses" to those presented above can be derived from the "single-issue" theory of directional competition:

> *Rival Hypothesis 1.* Voters of extreme-rightist parties should stand out from the supporters of all other parties in only one respect, their support of containing and reversing the inflow of foreigners from different races and ethnicities. On all other issue dimensions, their position should vary randomly around the population mean.
> *Rival Hypothesis 2.* There is little social structuration of the extreme rightist parties of the electorate, whether measured in terms of market position, organizational affiliation, or age and education.
> *Rival Hypothesis 3.* In macrocomparison, those regions and countries that had to swallow the heaviest load of immigrants give rise to the strongest right-wing extremist parties.

The contemporary Right as a "right-libertarian" protest. In this view, the main momentum of the extreme Right is not right authoritarianism but right-libertarian politics, combining a commitment to free markets with an antiauthoritarian social individualism and a quest for antielitist, participatory politics, directed against the established party states. Contrary to our own argument, right-wing party followers should combine economic market liberalism with libertarian attitudes. Advocates of the hypothesis that the new Right revolves around libertarian market enthusiasts further claim that the extreme Right's commitment to racism is an exception within its otherwise libertarian bent, a single issue that has been grafted onto the much more crucial agenda of lowering taxes, reducing the welfare state, and dismantling state regulation in favor of market transaction.

The "right-libertarianism" hypotheses is to a large extent, but not entirely, inconsistent with our framework. Under the clearly specified circumstances of a highly party-penetrated patronage political economy, our propositions also envision that right-wing political entrepreneurs will tone down an authoritarian appeal in favor of populist antistatism. However, we would not go so far as to claim that this strategy can lead to the extreme of a right-libertarianism, that is, a strategy that combines promarket positions with opposition to hierarchical authority, support of unconventional political participation, and endorsement of feminism and of environmentalism. Moreover, the conditions under which right-libertarian appeals are more successful than right-authoritarian appeals are clearly constrained. In contrast, the "right-libertarianism" hypothesis advances the following more general hypotheses:

> *Rival Hypothesis 4.* Successful extreme-rightist parties are for the capitalist marketplace and support libertarian views of personal freedoms to choose lifestyles, women's equality and unique desires, environmentalism, and a broadening of political participation to unconventional forms of political action.

The contemporary Right in the fascist legacy. A third rival hypothesis to our own argument places the contemporary European Right in the context of earlier fascist movements that tapped a populist anticapitalism of the "common man" against the elite of large organizations in state, corporate, and labor union bureaucracies and invoked an authoritarian-corporatist vision of social order as the alternative to liberal market society. Contrary to the "right-libertarian" interpretation of the extreme Right, this view would expect right-wing extremist parties to emphasize authoritarian and racist political and cultural themes but not to endorse a distinctly procapitalist, promarket economic program. It would also entail that extreme-rightist parties rally a mass following that encompasses all social groups and may even overrepresent white-collar and businesspeople, as did fascist parties of the past. The main rival hypotheses of this perspective, therefore, are the following:

Rival Hypothesis 5. The contemporary extreme Right combines anti-capitalist with authoritarian appeals.

Rival Hypothesis 6. The contemporary extreme Right assembles a cross-class alliance in which middle-class professionals are at least not underrepresented.

The contemporary Right as protest politics. A final possibility is to interpret the extreme Right as an issueless protest against the political establishment, as a general sign of the political malaise in an era when political ideologies have decayed and voters are overcome by cynicism about what democratic politicians are able to accomplish. The hypotheses that could be derived from the protest hypotheses primarily concern the political opportunity structure but would otherwise agree with much that was already said about the single-issue hypothesis. Voters supporting the extreme Right should be ideologically amorphous and only united by their dissatisfaction with the democratic "system." The unique rival hypothesis that follows from the interpretation of the contemporary right as protest politics is the following:

Rival Hypothesis 7. The new extreme Right will be electorally powerful wherever the existing parties have become similar in their electoral appeals and government policies. The substantive appeal of the extreme Right makes no difference for its electoral chances and its electoral coalition is diffuse.

One suggestion that has been made throughout the presentation of our theoretical framework, as well as in the introduction of rival hypotheses, is that the contemporary extreme Right is most likely different from the fascist or national socialist Right of the interwar period. Having specified various ways to interpret the contemporary Right, the last task in this chapter is to refer back to the interwar period and explore the extent to which contrasts between the historical and the contemporary extreme Right may be justified.

Contrasting the NRR to the Old Fascist Right

Debates about the concept of fascism have continued since the emergence of the phenomenon in the early 1920s (cf. Eatwell 1992a). This study has no ambition to provide an exhaustive analysis of these debates, let alone to contribute an entirely new definition and explanation of fascism that pretends to resolve existing scholarly disputes. Nevertheless, the various academic analyses of the phenomenon usually suffer from an epistemological problem that has to do with the relationship between definition and explanation of political phenomena. One group of scholars engages in "essentialist" conceptual discussions to define the phenomenon of fascism in a semantically clear fashion but then does not explore whether a coherent explanation for the timing and the strength or weaknesses of fascism so defined can be supplied. Another group explores causal explanations of fascism but relies on intuitive lists of cases and implicit notions of fascism rather than an explicit theoretical definition of the explanandum. In most instances, scholars divorce the definitional and explanatory tasks from each other and thus render the entire debate about fascism rather sterile.

In our discussion of the contemporary extreme Right, we have introduced the ideal type of the NRR as an empirically grounded theoretical concept that corresponds to a sufficient number of empirical referents in contemporary democracies to be explained in coherent ways. We have then introduced additional hypotheses to account for contemporary rightist strategies that diverge from the NRR "master case" in a systematic way. Populist antistatist strategies are electorally profitable in patronage-based political economies; xenophobic welfare chauvinism prevails where the extreme Right is hampered in its strategic mobility by activists who are steeped in the fascist tradition. In other words, only one of the limitational cases of the contemporary extreme Right is historically and ideologically linked to the fascist extreme Right in a straightforward way.

Fascist Ideology and the Contemporary Extreme Right
The definition of fascism that allows us to highlight its difference from the NRR "master case" emphasizes ideology and movement practice. Following the advice of a number of scholars, fascist movements must be distinguished from fascist regimes (Payne 1980, 200–204; Sternhell 1976, 318). Whatever ideology fascist movements may have expressed, the historical realities of national institutions limited their ability to implement fascist visions, even where fascist movements took over the state apparatus. For example, fascist parties rarely reorganized the economy to the extent their rhetoric and ideology had called for. The specific ideology and organizational practice of fascism thus stands out much better in fascist movements than in fascist regimes. Moreover, present-day NRR parties have not established political regimes and can therefore be compared only to fascist movements.

Fascist movements and mass parties were antiliberal, antisocialist, and anticonservative (cf. Linz 1976, 15–23; Nolte 1966, 21; and Sternhell 1976, 345–50). They called for the reassertion of a communitarian spirit and in this vein supported a new "fraternalism" (Brooker 1991). Fascism opposed the dominance of markets and bureaucracy and instead advocated an authoritarian, hierarchical, and communitarian order under the leadership of charismatic individuals. This community was expected to provide "salvation through unity" (Weber 1964, 36), an achievement that requires clear-cut external boundaries separating friends from foes of the community. In this sense, fascism was *exclusionary and particularist*. Whether that exclusionary momentum was expressed by nationalist, racist, or imperialist sentiments, however, is a matter of historical contingency. Racism was not a constitutive element of fascism although a number of fascist movements expressed racist beliefs. Central to all fascist movements was the effort to establish boundaries between insiders and outsiders and to institutionalize a particularist vision of community.

The fascist effort to (re)draw the boundaries of social order went against a conservative clinging to status quo institutions. Instead, it called for an activist construction of a new society that was based on authoritarian principles. Although fascism expressed a hierarchical and organic vision of society, its belief that political action can reshape the entire social order betrayed a hypermodern trust that social organization is essentially at the disposal of political "engineers," whereas reactionary and antimodern thinking conceives of society as an immutable or incrementally growing organic entity not accessible to conscious social planning. The activist, authoritarian political creativity in fascism also implied a deeply antifeminist thrust that glorified decisive male action, particularly in war, and condemned gender equality.[24]

The fascist communitarian and authoritarian spirit involved an anticapitalist thrust. In contrast to Marxian socialism, which was primarily concerned with property rights, fascist anticapitalism left private property rights alone but attacked the primordial governance structure of the capitalist system: the competitive marketplace and its behavioral correlates, individual self-reliance and the tolerance for a diversity of personal tastes and opinions. Fascism intended to substitute market exchange by state-regulated resource allocation, especially in the financial and the raw materials sectors, and by state-led hierarchical corporatist interest intermediation. Fascists expected a statist, corporatist economy to create political harmony between different economic classes and thus to overcome the socialist challenge.

The fascist vision of communitarian, corporatist anticapitalism also sheds light on the contingent role of race in fascist rhetoric. Where Jews represented a significant share of the educated urban professional and bourgeois classes, as was the case particularly in Central and Eastern Europe, fascist anti-Semitism combined an ethnically coded anticapitalism with the quest for drawing boundaries around a particularist community that defined Jews as foes and outsiders. In contrast, where Jews were not popularly perceived as an important social group, such as in Italy, anti-Semitism did not play a role in fascist mobilization.

To sum up, the rhetoric of fascism is distinct from the rhetoric of the NRR in at least three respects. First, fascism expresses an anticapitalist, corporatist thrust, whereas the NRR endorses free market capitalism with a strong, but small, state. Fascism and the NRR share, however, the propensity to mobilize individuals around collective friend/foe divisions and particularist conceptions of social collectivities. Within the contemporary extreme Right, therefore, only welfare chauvinist appeals come close to incorporating the fascist heritage. Populist antistatist appeals, in contrast, are furthest removed from the fascist legacy.

Second, the NRR and fascism are both authoritarian, but each authoritarianism has different sources and implications for social organization, particularly market capitalism. The NRR's authoritarianism derives from its defense of capitalist governance structures, not the fascist rejection of a free market economy, and therefore at least implicitly draws on the thinking of conservative apologists of liberal market capitalism. Such theorists of the free market understood, but rarely articulated on an explicitly theoretical level, that the basic unit of capitalist society is not the individual but the traditional multigenerational family with clearly distinct sex roles. The defense of capitalism therefore calls for a protection of paternal authority that is instrumental for the preservation of the traditional family (Schumpeter 1950). If the time horizon of economic decision making is the continuity of the multigenerational family, incentives for accumulation reach beyond each individual's life span and capacity to consume. The capitalist ethic of work and accumulation is undermined by feminism and individualism because they cultivate a hedonistic ethic and limit the time horizon of economic choices to that of the individual decision maker's biography. Capitalism may call not only for cultural but also for political authoritarianism. Although capitalist competition contributes to a decentralization of political power, market liberals call for imposing limits on political democracy to prevent the latter from disturbing the operation of the market (Hayek 1979). In an individualist and hedonistic culture, democratic demands for redistribution may undermine capitalist mechanisms of accumulation.

Third, whereas racism and ethnocultural parochialism were contingent phenomena in fascism that were in some movements replaced by militarism and nationalism, they are central components of the NRR appeal. While racist dispositions probably are always present in certain population groups, they become politically virulent for the contemporary NRR precisely because of the historical conjuncture of a rapidly changing occupational structure and an increasing international vulnerability of economic sectors in industry and services. On the level of direct economic interests, they are fueled by the fear of less skilled workers and marginal small producers that they will be displaced by immigrants and foreign competitors producing with cheaper labor. On a deeper level, the multiculturalization of European societies offends individuals whose authoritarian dispositions and experiences harbor little tolerance for cultural and ethical difference and nonconformism. European fascist movements emerged before the advent of European multicultural societies; the NRR is in part the product of this process of multiculturalization.[25]

Fascist Movement Practice and the NRR
In addition to contrasts between the ideological appeals of fascist movements and the NRR, it may also be possible to identify differences in the organizational practice of these two forces. Given the recent appearance of the contemporary extreme Right and the rather novel institutional settings and historical circumstances in which they have begun to mobilize, clear-cut hypotheses about a lasting contrast between the organizational modes of the fascist "old" and the "new" extreme Right are on somewhat shakier ground.

Nevertheless, wherever fascist movements gained strength over an extended period of time before coming to power or subsiding, they created mass organizations that subjected members to the authority of a charismatic leader. Most importantly, fascist parties usually organized paramilitary units that provided the violent shock troops in their efforts to establish the political boundaries between friend and foe and to take over political power from their adversaries. Paramilitary mass organization is a practical expression of an authoritarian, communitarian, anticapitalist, and anti-individualist ideology.

In contrast to fascist paramilitary mass organizations, the organizational efforts of the NRR tend to focus on the construction of modern "framework parties" that rely on a few highly visible individuals and a staff of professional managers, together with a rather limited following of party activists. One might therefore predict that the member/voter ratio of NRR parties will remain much lower than that of fascist movements in the interwar period. Only parties with a clearly welfare chauvinist appeal in the contemporary Right have a tendency to associate a rather large number of activists with the organization and to entertain the affiliation of paramilitary wings within the limits that the democratic state sets on their mode of operation.

Both fascist and NRR parties, however, share in common the prevalence of charismatic leadership and the relative absence of formal-rational bureaucratic internal party structure. Such organizational features are bound to fuel feuds among subleaders that can be exploited by the hegemon of the party to consolidate his power. In the contemporary extreme Right, where the power of the charismatic leader is not backed up by absolute control over a paramilitary organization and where the main arena of politics is the electoral campaign, the absence of a clear bureaucratic chain of command generates often highly divisive and publicly visible internal factional battles that endanger the cohesiveness of the parties and sometimes damage their electoral fortunes. It thus appears that the contemporary Right faces rather different organizational challenges than the interwar fascist Right. Again, we admit, however, that it may still be too early for conclusive judgments.

Fascist and NRR Social Constituencies
So far we have almost entirely avoided the contentious issue of the socioeconomic and demographic backing of fascist movements and parties and a comparison to the social constituencies supporting the contemporary radical Right in its right-authoritarian, populist antistatist or welfare chauvinist modes of operation. The number of studies on fascist electoral constituencies is legion, although the evidence remains empirically ambiguous, given that European fascism precedes the age of opinion surveys. Ecological analyses of voting patterns and changing party fortunes as well as investigations of the parties' membership records constitute the main indirect empirical indicators for shedding light on this question. What appears clear, however, is that where established socialist, Catholic, or bourgeois parties had organizationally encapsuled a large proportion of the electorate, they lost relatively few voters to fascist movements. Fascism thrived among voters who lacked firm bonds to political organizations.

In occupational and class terms, such established party-constituency ties were particularly strong among skilled blue-collar workers in core industries who were organized in unions affiliated with socialist parties and among members of the Catholic middle and working class closely linked to Catholic parties. Fascism made strong inroads among politically less attached groups such as marginal workers in industry and agriculture, the new white-collar salariat, independent family farmers and small businesspeople, but also the professions, intellectuals, and the bourgeoisie. Fascist parties thus very nearly reflected the overall socioeconomic division of the population, although the working class remained underrepresented and the independent small middle class was overrepresented. The petite bourgeoisie may have been the fascist hard core (de Felice 1977, 183–86; Lipset 1981, chap. 5), but it constituted only one of many groups in the entire fascist coalition and could not provide the bulk of the fascist electorate.[26]

Also, the electorate of the contemporary extreme Right quite clearly reflects a broad range of groups in the occupational structure of advanced industrial democracies. The fuzziness of rightist support is in part a consequence of the imprecise conventional class and stratification schemes employed in run-of-the-mill opinion surveys. They do not satisfactorily reflect the special sectoral and occupational experiences we have hypothesized to be associated with support for the various expressions of the extreme Right. Nevertheless, even a crude comparison of occupational support patterns shows that contemporary extremist right-wing parties over- or underrepresent different groups and socioeconomic regions compared with European fascism in the interwar period. Today rightist parties overproportionally gain votes in large industrial metropolitan areas, not in small towns and urban middle-class areas, where fascists were strong. In contrast to fascist movements, blue-collar workers—even when they are unionized—are not underrepresented in rightist electorates but tend to be overrepresented, particularly among the youngest age cohorts. Just as in fascist movements, the independent middle class (farmers, shopkeepers, craftspeople) still has an overproportional tendency to support the extreme Right, but they represent a quantitatively much less important electoral constituency than at the time of the fascist movements in the 1920s and 1930s.

Most importantly, groups for whom fascist parties proved attractive in the interwar period now provide precious little support to the NRR, even though they have grown tremendously in the modern occupational structure: educated white-collar employees, professionals, and intellectuals. The anti-intellectualism of the NRR is much more pronounced and electorally consequential than that of earlier extreme-rightist movements who could build on the disaffection of preindustrial elites with liberal democracy. Also the character of late twentieth-century intellectuals and professionals is different than that of their precursors in previous generations and makes today's highly educated groups less available to right-wing appeals. The share of academics and professionals, particularly women, working in public-sector social service and cultural occupations is rather high in the late twentieth century. Citizens with such market locations and occupational experiences tend to be oriented toward the libertarian Left rather than the authoritarian Right. In contrast, the fascist Right could count on considerable support from intellectuals and professionals. A good example of this tendency were the 1928 elections to the German university student representative organs. At a time when the Nazi party collected not even 3 percent of the vote in national elections, the Nazi student organization emerged as the strongest political group on German campuses. Such a success would be inconceivable in contemporary universities.

Table 1.1 summarizes the differences between the electorates of the old fascist Right and of the various modes of the contemporary Right. For simplicity's sake, we have left out the electorally minuscule upper bourgeoisie and the nonparticipants in labor markets (students, homemakers, pensioners, the unemployed). We should also restate again that the occupational categories in table 1.1 are not ideal, though empirically measurable, for comparisons of right-wing parties among each other and to other party electorates. The table shows that the electorate of the fascist Right is quite different than that of any contemporary extreme-rightist party. Whereas fascist parties typically underrepresented blue-collar constituencies, this is not the case for any of the modes of contemporary right-wing extremism. Moreover, whereas the fascist Right overrepresented the new middle strata, this is clearly not the case for welfare chauvinist and mainline NRR tendencies and may be so for the populist antistatist Right only because it is anyway questionable whether this current is still adequately captured under the umbrella of the extreme Right. Only small

TABLE 1.1.   Old and New Extreme Right: The Electoral Coalitions

	Electoral Constituencies		
Party Type	Small Business and Agriculturalists	Blue-Collar Workers	White-Collar Employees and Professionals
Fascist parties	Overproportional support	Underproportional support	Overproportional support
Welfare chauvinist parties	Underproportional or proportional support	Overproportional support	Underproportional support
New radical Right: Right-authoritarian parties	Overproportional support	Overproportional support	Underproportional support
Populist, antistatist parties	Proportional support	Proportional support	Proportional support

business and farmers tend to be overrepresented both in the fascist and the contemporary extreme Right.

*Explaining Fascist Movements versus Explaining the
Contemporary Extreme Right*
The fascist Right has not only a different physiognomy than the three modes of the contemporary extreme Right but also a different etiology. The phenomenon of fascism can be as little accommodated by a monocausal explanation as that of the NRR. Instead, different social demand and political supply conditions must be brought into play. Drawing on a range of theories of fascism, a combination of three forces appears to be most important in accounting for the strength of fascist movements in the interwar period: (1) intermediate levels of industrialization; (2) the persistence of precapitalist elites, particularly in the state apparatus, and the recent introduction of liberal democracy; and (3) a sharp economic crisis of industrialization dislocating a large segment of the citizenry especially in traditional employment sectors.[27]

1. Intermediate socioeconomic modernization. To oversimplify matters, fascist movements appear only in the transition from agricultural to industrial society, whereas NRR movements emerge in the transition from industrial to postindustrial society. For modernization theories, this socioeconomic periodization of fascist movements is the centerpiece of the explanatory account (e.g., Organski 1968). Fascist movements have a backward-looking, antimodern and a forward-looking, modern face. They try to embrace the modern technical and organizational implements of an industrial market society but reject the cultural correlates of economic modernization, the decline of collective identities, and the rise of individualism. This is why fascist movements attract particularly those who are not fully anchored in industrial society: small businesspeople, intellectuals, higher civil servants, the military and professionals who experience a status decline, but also first-generation, often unskilled peasant workers who are not yet fully assimilated into the working-class organizations.

Although purely socioeconomic modernization theories, taken by themselves, provide an insufficient base for explaining the strength of fascist movements, they nevertheless highlight the *content* and *ideological thrust* of fascism. With the decline of normative and "mechanical" solidarity in the transition from a status-based social order to a market-based competitive and individualist system with formal bureaucracy in private corporations and public agencies, economically dislocated producer groups develop a yearning for a new community that would reconstitute normative integration under the changed conditions of industrial production.[28] Unlike simple reactionary movements, fascism aims at an "antimodern modernism" that combines visions of an organic, hierarchical, communitarian socioeconomic order with an affirmation of the operational capabilities of modern industry, synthesized through political mass mobilization based on the latest technologies of human manipulation and organizational control.[29]

In postindustrial capitalism, in contrast, few people long for a new encompassing solidary community and the different modes of the contemporary extreme Right therefore cannot thrive on a strong communitarian revulsion against modernity, a sentiment that is now confined to some rightist fringe sects. Both historical and contemporary extreme Right strive to draw lines between friends and foes, but such efforts are placed within different contexts. At the end of the twentieth century, racism and authoritarianism feed on different sources than communitarian antimodern modernism. In fact, the boundary-drawing efforts of the contemporary extreme Right are focused on the preservation of a particular image of capitalist modernity opposed to the further cultural transformation and pluralization of Western societies. If anywhere, a communitarian and antimodern spirit, but in an antiauthoritarian fashion, has migrated to a libertarian-anarchist Left that celebrates community through voluntary association among autonomous individuals situated outside market and bureaucratic institutions.

2. Organization and political process. Sophisticated modernization theories realize that economic change at best provides a necessary, but not sufficient, condition for the advent of powerful fascist movements. In addition, the specific configuration of political divisions and coalitions among different socioeconomic groups and classes must be taken into account to explain the strength of fascist movements. In general, fascist movements are particularly likely when two conflicts over the allocation of scarce resources coincide in the process of industrial capital accumulation. On the one hand, the urban and rural elites struggle over the distribution of the cost and the pace of industrialization.

On the other, the urban elites are already simultaneously challenged by socialist working-class movements insisting on a redistribution of resources from the capital owners to workers. The new bourgeois elites, faced with a battle on two fronts against reactive agricultural and proactive working-class movements, then cannot instate liberal democracy as the institutional form to assert their own political hegemony and to resolve the redistributive conflicts. Instead, they are compelled to resort to authoritarian political management. In this context, fascism is a "second-best" alternative to pacify and demobilize the working class and to organize a compromise between urban and rural elites (Organski 1968, 29–30).

In practice, fascist parties may have gained a slightly overproportional share of the vote in the countryside, but urban groups, such as small business, white-collar employees, and also dislocated elements of the unorganized working class, really dominated the politics of fascist movements (Poulantzas 1974, 281, 288). Needless to say, fascist *regimes* in fact privileged industry over agriculture and continued the modernization of industrial capitalism, though in a corporatist rather than a liberal free market framework (Forgacs 1986, 8; Schoenbaum 1967).[30] In this sense, it may be difficult to maintain that fascism expressed a compromise with the landed elites. Nevertheless, fascism crafted a particular *balance of socioeconomic groups* that undercut the hegemony of a liberal-democratic bourgeoisie (Andreski 1968; Poulantzas 1974).

Fascist movements thus gained strength only where, in addition to intermediate socioeconomic modernization, (1) elements of premodern agrarian elites still controlled important political institutions, such as the military, the bureaucracy, or the judiciary; (2) agrarian and bourgeois elites were unable to organize firm ties to broad mass constituencies through clientelistic or mass parties; and (3) liberal democracy had been recently introduced. In such settings, weak and divided bourgeois and right-wing parties, hampered by a state apparatus that resisted liberal democracy, quickly eroded citizens' confidence in the viability of parliamentary democracy. The crisis of democracy was exacerbated when strong socialist movements challenged the new regime at the same time.

Linz (1976) has emphasized the importance of late democratization together with weak associative linkages between elites and masses for the rise of fascist movements. Moore (1966) has highlighted the importance of the survival of tenacious agrarian elites who had colonized the state apparatus and prevented the emergence of stable liberal democracies early on in the process of industrialization and thus created a key precondition for fascism in a later period. Among the democratic latecomers of the era immediately following World War I, it is quite striking that only tightly organized subsocieties, such as Catholic and socialist parties together with their surrounding economic and cultural networks, successfully resisted the electoral progress of fascist movements, whenever other conditions favored the surge of the extreme Right. The failure of social democratic or Catholic mass parties to incorporate the small independent peasantry into the framework of mass politics may have facilitated the spreading of fascism in the countryside (Linz 1976, 29; Luebbert 1991, 277–85). In contrast, where the small family peasantry was tied into the progressive social democratic coalition, as in Scandinavia, or where urban and rural elites had organized elaborate clientelistic networks to the lower classes, such as in much of Latin America, fascist movements could not become dominant in the countryside. One should add, however, that the organizational encapsulation of the urban middle classes, for example, through Catholic or Protestant parties in Belgium and the Netherlands, in Switzerland, and even in Austria, were just as important for increasing a polity's resilience to fascism as the organizational penetration of the countryside.

Elite organization and dominance of the state also had an international aspect that highlights the role of nationalism and militarism so often associated with fascist movements. As Hagtvet and Rokkan (1980, 146–47) observe, fascist movements became strong in countries that had belonged to the core of the sixteenth-century world system but had subsequently entered a period of peripheralization within the geoeconomics of capitalism. In such late industrializers, deliberate military-industrial alliances employed fascism as one strategy to reestablish their international position.

The political and institutional forces that affected the career of fascist movements do not play the same role in the rise of the contemporary extreme Right. Fascism grew out of the crisis of liberal parliamentarism in transition to mass democracy (Sternhell 1976, 348). "Twentieth century Fascism is a by-product of disintegrating liberal democracies" (Weber 1964, 139). But by the end of the twentieth century, when NRR and lesser extreme-rightist parties have begun to appear, premodern elites have by and large vanished and democratic regimes have proved to be lasting and economically effective. Whereas fascist mass movements thrived on their linkages to antidemocratic economic, bureaucratic, and cultural elites, the contemporary extreme Right lacks such points of access to the social and political power structures of postindustrial society almost entirely. While fascist movements drew strength from a synergism between elite and mass discontent with liberal capitalist democracy, contemporary rightist parties are almost invariably supported by powerless constituencies that have lost access to scarce resources and ties to the political elites. One similarity between the "old" fascist and the "new" Radical Right, however, remains, and this is the importance of crises as a catalyst of mobilization.

3. Economic and national crisis. Even in countries where structural and institutional conditions were most favorable to fascist movements, their sudden surge would have been inconceivable without the severe and sudden economic and political disruptions of depression, inflation, and war. Fascist movements leaped forward only under economic crisis conditions, as the Italian and German cases quite clearly demonstrate. In Germany, over a period of four years of economic stabilization, the Nazi party fell from 6.6 percent in May 1924 to 2.6 percent of the popular vote in the 1928 parliamentary election. In the subsequent four years of the Great Depression, it shot up to 37.3 percent in the July 1932 parliamentary election. In other countries as well, the extreme volatility of the fascist electorate, together with that of the fascist party and movement membership, illustrates the importance of crisis conditions. Fascist success was made possible by structural and institutional arrangements, but it was directly determined by economic crisis conditions.

The contemporary extreme Right develops in an era of socioeconomic dislocation due to a structural change in production systems, the internationalization of economic competition, and the crisis of the welfare state. Yet the human suffering caused by these dislocations is mild compared to the economic and social catastrophes of the interwar period. Moreover, whereas the crisis of the 1920s and 1930s was a generalized phenomenon affecting all social groups and regions, the crisis of the 1980s and 1990s has very uneven effects sectorally and geographically. While some occupational groups, sectors, and regions continue to thrive, others within the same countries are caught up in a structural crisis. This stratification of economic and social pain restricts the share of the electorate that may be available for rightist appeals.

Table 1.2 partially operationalizes the three sets of variables that influence regime outcomes in the interwar period. The share of the active population working in agriculture serves as an operational measure for modernization theories of fascism.[31] The age of democracies by the 1930s is an indicator of the Barrington Moore-type hypothesis postulating a linkage between elite coalitions and the institutional infrastructure of democracy. Finally, the severity of the economic crisis in the interwar period operationalizes the conjunctural force of the Great Depression in bringing about antidemocratic movements.

Economic modernization is high when the agricultural share of the labor force has fallen below 25 percent, intermediate when it ranges from 25 to 50 percent, and low when it exceeds 50 percent.[32] In fact, all countries with strong fascist mass movements and later on fascist regimes fall into the middle tier, but far from all countries with a medium-sized agriculture became fascist. Industrial modernization was a necessary, but not a sufficient, condition for fascist mobilization. Where competitive democratic regimes had already been in existence for twenty years or more at the time of the most critical fascist challenge, fascist movements never could rise beyond a fairly modest level.

TABLE 1.2. Conditions for the Mobilization of Fascist Mass Movements

Share of the Active Population Employed in Agriculture	Competitive Democracy Older than 20 Years		Competitive Democracy Younger than 20 Years	
	Mild Economic Crisis, 1929–32[a]	Severe Economic Crisis, 1929–32[a]	Mild Economic Crisis, 1929–32[a]	Severe Economic Crisis, 1929–32[a]
Less than 25 percent	Britain (A: 6; E: −17)[b] Switzerland (A: 21; E: Moderate)	Belgium (A: 17; E: −31) Netherlands (A: 21; E: −38)		
Between 25 and 50 percent	Denmark (A: 35; E: −9) Sweden (A: 35; E: −11) Norway (A: 36; E: −7)	France (A: 37; E: −31)	Japan (A: 45–50; E: Mild) Spain (A: 46; E: Mild)	Czechoslovakia (A: 26; E: −36) Germany (A: 29; E: −42) Austria (A: 37; E: −39) Italy (A: 49; E: −33)
More than 50 percent	Ireland (A: 50; E: Mild)		Portugal (A: 57; E: Mild) Finland (A: 68; E: −16) Yugoslavia (A: 76; E: N.D.) Rumania (A: 80; E: −11) (Bulgaria: N.D.) (Greece: N.D.)	Hungary (A: 51; E: −23) Poland (A: 65; E: −46)

Source: Merkl (1980, 776–78), except estimate of agriculture for Japan (based on Beasley 1990, 121) and agricultural occupations in Sweden (based on Flora et al. 1987, vol. II).

[a]Cutoff point is a decline of industrial output of 20 percent from 1929 to 1932.

[b]"A" refers to the percentage of the labor force working in agriculture; "E" to the economic decline from 1929–32 measured by industrial production.

This linkage remains true, regardless of how severe the economic dislocations of the early 1930s were. In stable democracies, party systems had sufficiently consolidated elite-mass linkages that reduced the free-floating electorate available to fascist mobilization.

Regardless of the severity of economic crisis, European countries with a small share of agriculture always remained democratic in the interwar period. Countries with a very large agricultural population, in contrast, always developed traditional semiauthoritarian regimes, with the partial exception of Finland. In these semiauthoritarian agricultural polities, the traditional incumbent elites preempted mass mobilization by coopting challenging groups into the regime, for example, through new elite positions in the state bureaucracy or by isolating and undercutting the emerging fascist movements through strict repression. As a consequence, none of the East European countries developed fascist mass movements or fascist regimes at least until the commencement of World War II and German military supremacy in the area (cf. Luebbert 1991, 261–63).

Within the intermediate tier of economic development, fascist mass movements occurred only in countries with severe economic disruptions. Moreover, the interaction between levels of economic development and severity of economic crisis may explain the *extent* to which antidemocratic movements and regimes assumed a fascist character. Countries with a comparatively mild interwar crisis and a still relatively large agricultural sector at the very upper bound of the intermediate development tier (45 to 50 percent agrarian labor force) engaged in only very limited democratic experiments and eventually created military-authoritarian regimes. Fascist mass movements, preceding the installation of an authoritarian regime, did not manage to exceed a relatively small size in these countries (Japan, Spain). It is hence questionable whether Spain and Japan's modernizing military dictatorships can be called fascist at all.[33]

In contrast, in countries suffering a severe economic crisis, the level of fascist mass mobilization increased only where democratic regimes were fragile and the elites were still divided over the merits of democracy. Germany, the most advanced country in this group, was characterized by a broader fascist mass mobilization than Austria or Italy and eventually built a regime that established a more tightly knit totalitarian governance structure than the latter two. In Austria, the existence of close and polarized elite-mass linkages in the dominant Catholic and socialist subcultures reduced the level of fascist mobilization, and Catholic semidictatorship preempted a fascist strike until 1938. In Italy, the fascist movement grew around and against Mussolini (Payne 1980, 55) and never fully developed a fascist state (Kogan 1968, 16; Payne 1980, 101). Particularly in the least-developed predominantly agricultural South, fascism was no mass movement but turned into a new form of local state to which the old ruling class and local notables adapted (Forgacs 1986: 6).

An interesting country where the absence of fascism at first sight appears to defy explanation in terms of economic development, democratic institutionalization, and economic crisis is Czechoslovakia. In terms of economic modernization, age of democracy and economic crisis, it had conditions that closely resembled the German situation, yet it remained democratic until the Nazi state crushed it between September 1938 and March 1939. Closer analysis, however, reveals that Czechoslovakia did not have a homogeneous political regime. The Czech part of the country was economically as advanced as the most industrialized areas of Western Europe and built a stable democracy with close party-mass linkages. In more agrarian Slovakia, in contrast, the authoritarian and then increasingly clero-fascist Hlinka party received 25 to 40 percent of the vote and eventually set up a fascist puppet regime under Hitler's tutelage (cf. Jelinek 1980).

The comparative analysis of fascist movements and regime formation in the interwar period by no means suggests that fascism is a historical phenomenon confined to a particular epoch in Western Europe. Fascist or protofascist regimes may emerge in other areas of the world that exhibit a similar configuration of conditions as countries with strong fascist movements in the interwar era. In this vein, some of the more agricultural new democracies in Eastern Europe as well as some Middle Eastern industrializing countries that attempt to make the transition to competitive democracies may encounter rather strong quasifascist mobilization.[34] Both the historical fascist movements and the contemporary fascist potentials, however, involve a very different dynamic of political mobilization than the contemporary extreme Right in Western Europe under conditions of an advanced capitalist democracy.

Conclusion

The task of this chapter has been to identify the appeals of the contemporary extreme Right in the context of a theory of preference formation (demand for rightist politics) and a theory of party competition (supply of rightist alternatives) in advanced capitalist democracies. Three variants of the extreme Right have been highlighted. First, the "master case" of the NRR combines economic promarket and political authoritarian and xenophobic messages. The NRR has a considerable potential to attract an electorally significant coalition that overrepresents workers and small business. Second, the marginal case of welfare chauvinist and authoritarian mobilization is less successful because it appeals primarily to blue-collar groups. Finally, there is populist antistatist politics that is a borderline case of the extreme Right, especially where it is electorally successful. Against this backdrop, the variants of the contemporary extreme Right have been compared to the "old" European fascist Right of the interwar period. The old Right was fueled by different ideological appeals, brought together a different support coalition, and was propelled by different social, economic, and political conditions than the contemporary extreme Right in Western Europe.

On the phenomenological level, there are certainly some striking rhetorical resemblances between the fascist and the contemporary extreme Right, but important contrasts remain.[35] Both the old and the contemporary Right share an exclusionary view of citizenship, a willingness to subscribe to conspiracy and scapegoat theories, a call for strong leadership and law and order, an intolerance of political disagreements and pluralism of ideas, and a rejection of democratic competition. But these appeals occur within contrasting contexts and discursive universes that are shaped by the unique experiences of economic and political transformation in different episodes of capitalist industrial and postindustrial development. Fascism is a matter of recently founded volatile liberal democracies still faced with a large agricultural sector, whereas the contemporary extreme Right flourishes in stable competitive democracies faced with the transition to a postindustrial or Post-Fordist economic structure.

The NRR and the populist antistatist Right have given up on corporativist economic solutions and advocate the free market. Most NRR parties accept, at least for tactical reasons, parliamentary democracy and refrain from paramilitary mobilization; and racist beliefs are now by and large divorced from nationalist and imperialist visions but primarily originate in economic fears and cultural intolerance toward the emerging multicultural world society, which is reflected in an increasing pluralization of national societies as well.

The NRR is the offspring of the postindustrialization of advanced capitalist economies, of changes within the patterns of competition within democratic party systems, and of political entrepreneurs finding new electoral "market niches" they are able to exploit with racist, authoritarian, and procapitalist slogans. In contrast, the European fascist Right of the interwar period originated in the problems of rapidly industrializing societies with weak democratic institutions, strong antidemocratic elites, and severe economic crises. The fascist rhetoric was authoritarian, communitarian, and anticapitalist, a rather different blend of appeals than that of the NRR.

These schematic and somewhat oversimplified contrasts between fascism and the NRR, as the main manifestation of the contemporary extreme Right, may help to clarify the historical uniqueness of each phenomenon. As we said in the opening pages of this chapter, there is little analytical or political mileage to be gained by insisting on the sameness of the old and the new extreme Right. Also situating both political forces on the "right" does not mean much, because the meaning of "right" and "left" has remained contested terrain from the time of the French Revolution when these categories first entered the political discourse (Eatwell 1989, 33–34).

The propositions and materials presented in this chapter illustrate why the left/right semantics has continued to be controversial and confusing in political debates. First of all, the meaning of the spatial metaphor has varied over time and is closely intertwined with the historically changing social and political organization of industrial societies and competitive democracies. Second, the spatial metaphor, by itself, may have no symbolic or substantive content. American attitudinal research has found that citizens associate the liberal/conservative continuum, the American equivalent of "left" and "right," with party preferences for the Democrats or the Republicans, but less with policy issue positions and views of society (Conover and Feldman 1981). A study of European issue opinions and party preferences, however, concludes that issue positions are a much better predictor of left/right self-placements than party preferences (Huber 1989). At least in Western Europe, "left" and "right" do have a substantive content for a fairly large proportion of the population.[36]

The third and most difficult problem in the interpretation of spatial metaphors in politics is that their issue content may be multidimensional. In the historical environment of the French Revolution of 1789, for example, the Left stood for a complex cluster of positions. In political terms, it supported republicanism against monarchy; in cultural terms, it defended a secular order against the Catholic Church; and in economic terms, it called for a protection of the poor and an abolition of privileges derived from status and property (Eatwell 1989). But cultural, political, and economic conceptions of left and right may vary independently from each other. The issues that divide the Left and the Right are linked in ways contingent upon time and place.

The problems of historicity and multidimensionality make it impossible to fashion an "essentialist" definition of left and right that would provide a strict and invariant conceptual linkage between substantive issue positions and the spatial imagery. Instead, concrete historical configurations of social order and political institutions shape the cognitive process by which actors construct the linkage between issue positions and project them onto the left/right metaphorical space. As we have argued in this chapter, the critical question, then, is to develop a theory that explains the use of left and right in varying historical contexts.

An example may serve to illustrate the difference between essentialist conceptions seeking an invariant meaning of the Right, and the pragmatic, historical, and contextual approach advanced in this book. Eatwell (1989, 47) reports contemporary definitions of the political Right that single out (1) moral conservatism, (2) political authoritarianism, and (3) economic liberalism as constitutive properties of rightist beliefs. Eatwell then goes on to criticize these definitions because certain political currents most scholars intuitively locate "on the right" do not exhibit all the elements of this definition. Fascism at least fails to include market liberalism (element 3), whereas laissez-faire market liberalism has nothing intrinsically to do with moral conservatism or political authoritarianism. Eatwell correctly concludes that we need a typology of different rightist aspirations and belief systems, but the combination of authoritarian and promarket beliefs, that is, what we have introduced as the most important incarnation of the extreme Right in advanced postindustrial democracies, does not even appear in his proposed typology.[37] The search for general conceptions of the Left and the Right and the design of typologies, divorced from historical and contextual analysis, miss the historical specificity of left/right spatial metaphors and yield essentialist definitions of political alternatives that have little relevance for contemporary party and power relations. The worst consequence of the ahistorical mode of analysis is to lump all forms of authoritarian extremism under the label of fascism and thus create more confusion than enlightenment about the nature of the contemporary extreme Right.[38]

2

The Authoritarian Right against the Libertarian Left: Variations in West European Right-Wing Extremism

Extreme-rightist parties have appeared in most European countries in recent years. It is an open question, however, whether such parties appeal to a distinct cluster of political beliefs and policy issues that goes beyond the mobilization of a pure sense of uneasiness with and resentment against the incumbent political elites. We have hypothesized that such a set of beliefs and orientations does exist and right-wing strategies are electorally only successful where the parties appeal to these beliefs. Successful rightist parties combine a commitment to capitalist markets with an emphasis on social order, authority, stability, and cultural homogeneity. This is the "master case" of the NRR that attracts an electoral coalition that overrepresents blue-collar workers and small business but underrepresents more educated white-collar and professional occupations. In the especially favorable circumstances of "partocratic" regimes with highly politicized economies penetrated by relations of patronage and clientelism, the NRR appeal can be submerged in a broader populist antistatist message that emphasizes market liberalism more than authoritarian themes and rallies a much more encompassing social coalition than the master case of the NRR. Regardless of how favorable the opportunity structure is, however, right-wing parties in postindustrial economies that appeal to the beliefs of the "old" fascist Right, a blend of authoritarianism with corporatist or anticapitalist visions of economic organization, are destined to fail electorally because they can draw only on narrow electoral coalitions that primarily consist of marginal groups at the fringes of the working class.

This chapter is designed to provide a first round of comparative evidence to substantiate these hypotheses and compare them to rival arguments. The analysis proceeds on two levels. In the first section, we will discuss the broad macroinstitutional background conditions that shape the opportunity structure of NRR and populist-antistatist mobilization. But this analysis, by itself, cannot reveal whether successful extreme-rightist parties also issue the "winning appeal" that attracts significant segments of the electorate. Therefore, in the second section, we will offer some comparative evidence on the programmatic stance of the extreme Right in a number of Western European countries and the ideological and sociodemographic character of its electorate. It is unlikely that the electorate exactly reflects the issue appeals of the party leaders. Numerous studies have explored the extent to which party activists and even party leaders may take more "radical" positions on the issues than their average sympathizers in the electorate.[1] Nevertheless, leaders' positions "pull" the electorate in a certain direction and, in this sense, electoral sentiments can serve as tracers of leaders' issue positions.

The analysis of the contemporary extreme Right in this chapter has a comparative-static character. It emphasizes differences and similarities between countries but ignores dynamic change in each country's rightist mobilization over time and the actual process of getting a new political party under way. Moreover, it boils down differences and similarities of extreme-rightist electorates to a few highlights without examining the competitive space in which the extreme Right is situated and the political relations between mainline moderate conservatives, social democrats, and left libertarians. These elements of a more detailed reconstruction of the actual political mobilization on the extreme Right, including that of the trial-and-error process by which right-wing political entrepreneurs seize on opportunities and articulate the message of the emerging rightist political camp, will be relegated to the case study chapters. The final section of this chapter will outline the nature of the data and the modes of analysis that will be employed in each of the case studies to follow.

Conditions for the Rise of the Contemporary Extreme Right

The parties of the extreme Right that harness success with right-authoritarian or populist antistatist messages appear only in the most advanced postindustrial democracies. Even in these advanced democracies, however, opportunities for an electorally influential extreme Right are limited to those competitive configurations where moderate left and right parties have converged toward centrist positions and may even have cooperated in government coalitions. Where rightist parties in such circumstances *fail* to be successful, according to the theory proposed in this study, the only possible reason can be that they have not found the winning appeal to right-authoritarian or populist antistatist sentiments. Before exploring these hypotheses in greater detail, it is worth drawing up a list of "candidates" of political parties in Western democracies that may qualify as members of the broad extreme-rightist political sector. We will then later explore which issue appeals such parties have actually chosen in given circumstances of party competition.

In Western European polities, there are two plausible indicators to identify members of the extreme Right and potential right-authoritarian or statist-populist parties. Determining which of these candidates for membership in the

NRR "club" are actually NRR parties and which other parties not included in this initial list may also qualify to be subsumed under that label is a matter of empirical research on party leaders and voters. For the purposes of creating the list of candidate parties, it is useful to start with a fairly restrictive set of parties.

The two criteria to identify the contemporary extreme Right and candidates for right-authoritarian appeals are (1) whether a party's competitors perceive it to be located "on the right" and not a viable coalition partner, and (2) when the party appeared on the political scene. First, new rightist parties typically have been unable to participate in government alliances with moderate to conservative coalition partners because the latter deem them to be too extremist. Although moderately conservative coalitions have in some instances relied on the direct or indirect parliamentary support of parties they perceive as further to their right, the far rightist parties described in the paragraphs below have not been invited to hold cabinet positions. Whether these excluded parties actually do or do not belong to the authoritarian Right, of course, is a matter to be scrutinized by empirical analysis.

Second, the *timing* of an extremist right-wing party's appearance may distinguish potential members of the NRR party family from other parties. If NRR parties are polar counterparts to the libertarian Left, it is plausible to expect that NRR parties appear in the same general time period as their antagonists. The first successful left-libertarian parties began to make electoral inroads in Denmark, Norway, and the Netherlands in the late 1960s. For this reason, aside from these parties, the list of NRR candidates includes rightist parties that have been founded since the second half of the 1960s.

All northern European countries, with the exception of Finland, now have parties represented in their legislatures that meet the two empirical criteria of NRR candidacy, namely, exclusion from government alliance and comparatively recent party formation. Since the early 1970s both Denmark and Norway have seen the rise of virulently antisocialist Progress parties (FP and FRP) that have never been able to join nonsocialist government coalitions. In Sweden, in the 1991 parliamentary election a novel party, the recently founded New Democracy (ND), managed to surmount the 4 percent hurdle of legislative representation for the first time. The bourgeois government bloc did not control a majority of parliamentary seats without the new party, yet its members were unwilling to accept New Democracy as a coalition partner. Only in Finland, is there no obvious candidate for the NRR. The Finnish Rural Party, founded already in the 1960s, may come close to being perceived as a right-wing populist party, but it has participated in several governments throughout much of the 1980s and significantly toned down its message (Arter 1992).

On the European continent, there are a number of parties that meet both empirical criteria for NRR candidacy (exclusion from government, founding since 1965) and have been electorally successful. Most prominent is the French National Front (FN), capturing about 10 percent of the electorate in each of the

1986 and 1988 legislative elections and over 14 percent for its candidate in the first round of the 1988 presidential race. Most recently, it gained over 12 percent in the 1993 parliamentary election. Excluded new parties of the extreme Right have also won considerable success in Belgium and Switzerland. The Belgian Flemish Block (VB) surged in the 1987 and 1991 elections in Flanders, particularly in the Antwerp region. In Wallonia, a National Front won parliamentary representation in 1991. At the same time, the earlier incarnation of a right-wing challenge, the Democratic Union for the Respect of Work (RAD/UDRT) faded electorally. In Switzerland the National Action (NA) began to collect votes in 1961, was reconstituted as the Swiss Democrats in 1990, and more recently has been supplemented by the Swiss Automobilists' Party (SAP).

Germany is a borderline case for successful new right-wing parties. The National Democratic Party (NPD) has almost disappeared since its short-lived electoral breakthrough in the 1960s, although it has seen a few recent local successes, such as in Frankfurt am Main. More important has been its more recent spin-off, the German People's Union (DVU), a party that has been a marginal vote-getter in national elections but has performed sufficiently well in several recent northern German state elections to send representatives to the state legislatures. Most important, however, are the German Republicans (REP), a party founded only in 1983. The party made spectacular inroads in state and European elections between 1986 and 1989 and again in 1991-92 but failed to get even close to the 5 percent threshold of electoral representation in the 1990 federal parliamentary election.

The most recently founded candidate for the European NRR has gained ground in the 1991 Italian elections. It is an alliance of Northern Italian "leagues" that was obscure in the 1987 parliamentary elections (0.5 percent) but won a spectacular 8.7 percent of the national vote in the May 1992 legislative election, corresponding to one-sixth of all votes in northern Italy. Italy, of course, also has an old right-wing party excluded from government coalitions, the Italian Social Movement (MSI), a party that has won between 5 and 8 percent of the electorate since the 1950s. It will be interesting to see whether one, both, or none of the Italian parties qualify for membership in the NRR club. If theoretical expectations are correct, the MSI should experience significant difficulties in finding an attractive electoral appeal that resonates with voters drawn to the extreme Right elsewhere.

We will ignore in our investigation the developments of Italian politics in 1993–94 at the time of the breakdown of the old party system when the key players—particularly the Italian socialists (PSI) and the Christian Democrats (DC)—were submerged in a flood of political scandals that led to their dissolution. Both the Northern League as well as the MSI were short-term beneficiaries of this system breakdown, but it is unclear what—if any—political appeals of their leaders, beyond wholesale attacks on the compromised political establishment, contributed to the success of the rightist parties in this situation.

There is one further electorally successful European party that may be a candidate for membership in the NRR club although it does not unambiguously meet either of the two empirical criteria of candidacy, the Austrian Freedom Party (FPÖ). This party and its precursor have contested every Austrian election since 1949. But in the mid-1980s, the FPÖ underwent a dramatic reversal in its programmatic message and its leadership personnel, which led to its exclusion from Austrian government coalitions. If we consider this shift as sufficiently profound to qualify the FPÖ in the late 1980s as a "new" party, it is clearly a candidate for membership in the NRR club.

Disregarding small countries with less than one million inhabitants, all remaining European countries have only tiny right-wing factions that have remained incapable of collecting even 1 percent of the national vote. This applies to Britain's National Front and the Dutch Center Party until 1990, but also to a myriad of right-wing sects in Greece, Portugal, and Spain. In Spain, some might argue that the major opposition party, the post-Francist Popular Alliance, now called Popular Party, may belong to the NRR, but, overall, the party looks increasingly like a mainstream Western European conservative party.

Table 2.1 lists all candidates for inclusion in the set of parties that express NRR beliefs. With the exceptions already mentioned, all of these parties have been founded since 1965 and have been excluded from government coalitions. Among these parties, the present study will focus on the electorally more successful cases in order to determine whether they actually express right-authoritarian or populist antistatist messages and draw the electorate we have hypothesized in chapter 1. Since the explanandum of this study is the success of NRR parties, not the mere existence of small rightist sects, the electoral breakthrough of the extreme Right is key. In order not to sample on the dependent variable, in chapter 7 we will turn to a negative case and discuss the British National Front as an example that sheds light on the trajectory of failed rightist parties.

Before considering the actual messages and electoral coalitions of the extreme Right in each country, let us first analyze the conditions under which we would not expect electorally powerful NRR or populist antistatist parties because external constraints prevent rightist political leaders from gaining electoral influence, no matter what their programmatic message is. As a baseline, countries in which right-authoritarian or populist antistatist parties appear should be advanced industrial democracies. We do not expect such parties in countries where the main features of postindustrial welfare states are not present. For that reason, it is not by chance that the more recently developing Mediterranean democracies of Greece, Portugal, and Spain lack significant

TABLE 2.1.   Candidates for the European New Radical Right

Country	Party Name	Exclusion from Government?	Party Founded Since 1965?	Average Electoral Performance[a] (percent)	
Austria	Freedom Party (FPÖ)	N/Y	N/Y	10.4/13.2[b]	(16.6)
Belgium	Democratic Union for the Respect of Work (RAD/UDRT)	Y	Y	1.5	(—)
	Vlaams Blok (VB)	Y	Y	2.3	(6.6)
	National Front	Y	Y	—	(1.1)
Britain	National Front (NF)	Y	Y	less than 1	
Denmark	Progress Party (FP)	Y	Y	6.5	(6.4)
Finland	(Finnish Rural Party)	N	N	6.9	(4.8)
France	National Front (FN)	Y	Y	10.7	(9.7)
Germany	National Democrats/ German People's Union (NPD/DVU)	Y	Y	less than 1	
	Republicans (REP)	Y	Y	2.3	(2.1)
Greece	National Political Union & Successors	Y	Y	less than 1	
Italy	Italy Social Movement (MSI)	Y	N	5.9	(5.1)
	Northern League (NL)	Y	Y	4.5	(8.7)
Netherlands	Center Party (CeP)	Y	Y	less than 1	
Norway	Progress Party (FRP)	Y	Y	7.1	(13.0)
Portugal	Christian Democratic Party (PDC)	Y	Y	less than 1	
	Independent Movement for National Reconstruction (MIRN)	Y	Y	less than 1	
Spain	various Falange parties, National Front	Y	Y	less than 1	
	(Popular Alliance, Popular Party)	Y	Y	25.9	(26.0)
Sweden	New Democracy (ND)	Y	Y	6.7	(6.7)
Switzerland	National Action (NA)/ Swiss Democrats	Y	Y	3.2	(3.0)
	Swiss Automobilists' Party (SAP)	Y	Y	3.4	(5.1)

Source: Author's calculations from the official election results.

[a]Average performance in national parliamentary elections contested by the party since 1980–92. In brackets: Performance in the last national election before the end of 1992.

[b]Second value for the FPÖ refers to the party's performance since its right-wing turn in 1984–85.

right-authoritarian parties. The same applies to the Republic of Ireland.[2] Of course, in all but the Irish case, other political mechanisms have worked against a powerful extreme Right in these nations. Since the three Mediterranean countries became democracies only in the 1970s after previous unsuccessful efforts to institutionalize party competition in the 1920s, 1930s, or 1950s and 1960s, the population still has a very good recollection of the nature of the old regime and its many disadvantages. What may count more, however, under the democratic successor regimes, all three countries experienced significant economic growth and rising standards of living that made a return to the predemocratic state of affairs desirable only to a minute fraction of the electorate.

Among the remaining highly advanced countries, the opportunities for extreme-rightist mobilization depend on the convergence between moderate left and moderate right parties. If the distance between these parties is relatively small, political entrepreneurs have a chance to create a successful electoral coalition with a right-authoritarian agenda. Where "partocracy" in a country's political economy prevails, such entrepreneurs should be able to broaden their electorate beyond the right-authoritarian core through populist antistatist messages and actually build a very strong "cross-class" alliance against the established parties.[3]

The empirical measure of party distance we will employ here is derived from a study by Laver and Hunt (1992) in which they asked political scientists in almost all established democracies to rate the position of the relevant domestic parties on 20-point scales for eight issues: taxes versus social services, sympathies with the Soviet Union, nationalization of industry, permissive moral policies, environmental protection, government decentralization, urban/rural divisions, and church relations. Hunt and Laver's factor analyses of these issue positions show that most of the time, a single dimension explains a large share of the variance, although at times a second, much less prominent dimension loads on items such as government decentralization and (in part) environmental protection. I have taken the two issues most clearly related to the traditional economic left/right division, taxation/social services and nationalized industries, and added the scores on both dimensions for each country's major conservative party as well as for each country's major leftist party. The most procapitalist stance (low taxes, no nationalized industry) has a maximum score of 40, the most prosocialist stance (high social services, much nationalized industry) has a score of 0. The difference between the scores for the major rightist and leftist parties serves as a measure of the parties' relative convergence or divergence in political appeals. The results, represented in table 2.2, are essentially robust against further changes in the index of party positions, for example, by incorporating libertarian/authoritarian items (permissive moral policies, environmental protection) into the analysis.[4]

In table 2.2, countries have been divided into five groups. The first group includes advanced industrial countries that have no strong extreme-rightist parties: Britain, the Netherlands, and Sweden. We see here that with the partial exception of Sweden, the distance between the most conservative and the most leftist major party is significantly higher than in the overall sample (22.6 and

TABLE 2.2.   Distance of the Major Parties on the Economic Left-Right Axis and Performance of the Extreme Right

		Score of the Major Rightist Party	Score of the Major Leftist Party	Difference Between Rightists and Leftists
I. Countries without	Britain	35.39 (CONS.)	12.79 (LAB.)	22.60
Significant Extreme	Netherlands	34.28 (VVD)	14.10 (PvdA)	20.18
Right	Sweden	34.44 (M)	17.05 (SAP)	17.39
	Average Score	34.70	14.65	20.06
II. Countries with Some	Belgium	35.90 (PVV+PRL)	13.6 (PS+SP)	22.30
Extreme Right	Finland	29.36 (KOK)	9.29 (FPDL)	20.07
	Average Score	32.63	11.45	21.19
III. Countries with a	Denmark	32.0 (KF)	17.95 (SD)	14.05
Significant Extreme	France	30.07 (RPR)	14.40 (PS)	15.67
Right	Germany	27.09 (CDU)	14.66 (SPD)	12.43
	Norway	30.15 (H)	14.54 (DNA)	15.61
	Average Score	29.83	15.39	14.44
IV. Countries with a	Austria	26.23 (ÖVP)	19.78 (SPÖ)	6.45
Populist–Antistatist	Italy	21.38 (DC)	8.88 (PCI)	12.50
Mobilization				
	Average Score	23.81	14.33	9.48
V. Countries without	Greece	30.67 (ND)	15.13 (PASOK)	15.54
Societal Preconditions	Ireland	28.66 (FINE GAEL)	12.62 (LAB.)	17.43
for a Strong Extreme	Portugal	27.83 (PSD)	4.57 (PCP)	23.26
Right	Spain	31.20 (AP)	16.00 (PSOE)	15.20
	Average Score	29.59	12.08	17.51

Source: Calculations based on data provided by Laver and Hunt (1992).

Note: The parties (in brackets) are the major moderate left or right parties with a minimum electoral support level of 15 percent (average in the 1980s). The economic left/right scores sum the expert judgments of party positions on two items in Laver and Hunt's (1992) investigation: (1) increasing versus cutting taxes (1–20); (2) for public ownership of industry versus private ownership (1–20). High scores indicate rightist positions, low scores leftist positions.

20.18 compared to the average of 16.99 in all countries). In Britain, the polarization between Conservatives and Labour from the second half of the 1970s onward preempted a hemorrhage of voters moving from the established parties to an extreme-rightist party. In the Netherlands, the very pronounced leftism of the Dutch Labor Party and the equally determined economic liberalism of the liberal Party for Freedom and Progress also made it difficult for the extreme Right to gain more than fractions of one percentage in national parliamentary elections.[5]

The Swedish scores show a less clear-cut pattern because of the timing of Laver and Hunt's survey. It was taken in 1989-90 at a time when the Swedish social democrats were rapidly revising their economic policy toward fiscal austerity. For that reason, the Swedish difference score between social democrats and conservatives (17.39) may somewhat understate the true distance that prevailed throughout much of the 1980s. Of course, the convergence between conventional left and right may be reflected in the rise of New Democracy in the September 1991 election, a party that drew voters both from social democrats and conservatives and especially the pool of new and nonvoters. Although some analysts have placed New Democracy in the same category as the other Scandinavian rightist Progress parties with promarket and racist appeals (Husbands 1992c, 272), it may be too early to draw that conclusion. Of course, the theoretical framework advanced in this study would predict that a rapprochement of the Swedish social democrats and the conservatives would enable right-wing extremists to consolidate blue-collar and small business support around just the appeals that Husbands sees already articulated in the new party.[6]

The second group of countries has borderline cases of extreme rightist mobilization. In Belgium, the Flemish Block clearly has strong support but builds on an ethnoregional division. Voter flow analyses show that the party attracted substantial numbers of voters from all other parties, although the relatively greatest losses were sustained by the moderate Flemish regionalist party "Volksunie" (People's Union).[7] In Flanders, part of the Flemish Bloc's success may have to do less with a general right-authoritarian appeal than with the renewed salience of ethnoregional problems in a time of economic stagnation and the willingness of the Volksunie to compromise with the Walloons on questions of regional autonomy, a political move that alienated vigorous Flemish regionalists from that party. Nevertheless, empirical studies show overall that the Vlaams Blok support is not only Flemish nationalist, but also subscribes to law and order, free enterprise, and a retrenchment of immigrants' rights (Swyngedouw 1994). At the same time, in Wallonia and even Brussels, the National Front has not managed to collect a large share of the votes, most likely because the polarization between liberals and socialists has still remained fierce in that region and the liberals have taken on some of the new rightist agenda. For example, in 1991 the liberal parliamentary election list in Brussels featured a former mayor of a Brussels suburb, Roger Nols, an outspoken opponent of immigration.[8] In Finland, the Finnish Rural Party by the 1980s was no longer an outcast party but participated in a center-right coalition government and therefore cannot be counted as a clear right-extremist party, although it made efforts to dissociate itself from moderate conservatism in the late 1980s (Arter 1992). Overall, both in Finland and Belgium the distance measures between the major leftist and rightist parties are significantly above the average for the entire universe of European democracies listed in table 2.2. In Finland, the higher polarization drove the populist opposition into the conservative camp. In Belgium, it is the unique issue of regionalism that has helped right-wing parties, particularly in Flanders, even though the overall opportunity structure of party competition is not particularly favorable for the extreme Right.[9]

The third set of countries—Denmark, France, Germany, and Norway—all display distance scores between major conservative and leftist parties that fall somewhat below the average for all European countries. Three members of this group, but not Germany, developed significant extreme-rightist parties since the 1970s or early 1980s. In these countries, we expect that the appeal of the extreme Right is consistent with the NRR master case combining political authoritarianism with strong support of market capitalism that gathers an electoral coalition in which workers and small businesspeople are overrepresented. The German "outlier" would fully count as evidence against our theory, if the German rightist parties would (1) subscribe to an NRR appeal, but (2) not receive a substantial electoral support. The German outlier does not disconfirm the theory, however, if the rightist parties have not tried the correct NRR strategy of authoritarian rightist appeals and therefore could not assemble a critical electoral mass. In that case, we have to search for reasons for the parties' failure to adopt electorally profitable stances.

The fourth group of countries includes those where the distance between the main conventional left and right parties is minimal, Austria and Italy. In this configuration, it is likely that a "partocratic" political economy makes it impossible for both the conventional Left and Right to dissociate themselves from the institutional economic status quo of patronage politics and clientelism. The immobility of the conventional parties opens vast regions of the electorate to the conquest by new rightist parties. In this instance, my theory would anticipate the rise of broad populist antistatist parties with a less occupationally and class-specific electorate than that of NRR parties.

The fifth group lists those cases in which insufficient postindustrialization and/or a limited development of welfare states undercut political opportunities for the contemporary extreme Right. Here the relative convergence of conventional Left and Right is irrelevant for the capacity of rightist entrepreneurs to create a new electoral force. As can be seen from table 2.2, the relative distance of large conservative and leftist parties varies randomly around the mean for the entire country set, although all four countries in this group—Greece, Ireland, Portugal, and Spain—lack significant extreme-rightist parties. To sum up, table 2.2 shows clearly that the convergence of moderate leftist and rightist parties makes a difference for the mobilization of the extreme Right.[10] Whether this mobilization is associated with the hypothesized ideological appeal (right-authoritarianism or antistatist populism), however, must be explored with different data.

Complementary and Rival Hypotheses

Before moving from the macrocomparison of institutional and strategic settings of the contemporary extreme Right to the microanalysis of elite appeals

TABLE 2.3. **Rightist Parties As a Backlash against the Libertarian Left in the 1980s?**

		Left-Libertarian Success in the 1980s		
		Average > 6%	Average > 2%	Average < 2%
Rightist Party Success in the 1980s	Average > 6%	Denmark, Italy, Norway, Switzerland	Austria, Finland	France
	Average > 2%	Belgium	—	—
	Average < 2%	Germany Netherlands Sweden	—	Britain, Greece, Ireland, Portugal, Spain

Source: Authors' calculations from official election results.

Note: Extreme-rightist and left-libertarian party performance is measured in national parliamentary elections 1980–90.

and electoral followings, it is worth considering three complementary or rival hypotheses that have been floated in the literature. As already reported, a number of analysts have interpreted the contemporary Right as a materialist, authoritarian backlash against the postmaterialist, libertarian Left. The former insists on production, industry, and economic growth as the lead regulative of sociopolitical developments, whereas the latter emphasizes consumption, quality of life, and political participation. Table 2.3 shows that, in most instances, the structural configuration confirms that hypothesis. Often where left-libertarian parties have been electorally successful since the 1980s, we also find extreme-rightist parties. Conversely, in most instances without an influential libertarian Left, we also find a weak extreme Right. The structural symmetry between libertarian Left and authoritarian extreme Right, however, says little about causal sequence. Did the left-libertarian mobilization occur before the rise of the extreme Right and can the latter be seen as a response to the former? In cases with a powerful extreme Right, only in France did the electoral mobilization of the extreme Right precede that of the libertarian Left. The same may be true for Finland, provided we count the borderline case of the Finnish Rural Party as a true representative of the contemporary extreme Right. In all other cases, the electoral mobilization of the libertarian Left preceded that of the extreme Right.[11]

Nevertheless, the time sequence between libertarian-leftist and authoritarian-rightist electoral success suggests that the backlash hypothesis is not perfect. In Sweden, Belgium and the Netherlands, early and strong left-libertarian political mobilization has not prompted a right-authoritarian response. Even if we count the 1991 rise of New Democracy in Sweden and the

1991 breakthrough of the Flemish Block as true instances of extreme-rightist mobilization, these parties appeared with a much longer time lag after the strengthening of the libertarian Left than did rightist parties in other countries. Conversely, in France, the rise of the authoritarian Right in the early 1980s did not significantly boost the electoral chances of the libertarian Left for much of the 1980s. Only in the early 1990s, with the disintegration of the socialists, did the French libertarian Left pick up electoral support. These outliers show that the structural backlash hypothesis is incomplete, unless we take into account the strategic positioning of political parties on the moderate Right (or Left) that operate as "gatekeepers" for the emergence of a new extreme Right (or Left). As we have seen, in Sweden and the Netherlands conservative free market parties took stances quite divergent from that of the moderate Left throughout much of the 1980s and thus preempted the extreme Right. In France, the libertarian Left had been coopted by the socialists and only gradually distanced itself from that party, as the socialist governments of the 1980s pursued increasingly centrist policies with little left or libertarian content. Overall, then, the right-authoritarian backlash hypothesis can be accepted as a "friendly amendment" to the main thrust of our theoretical argument. Causally driving the backlash process, however, are political opportunity structures that are created by the strategic divergence or convergence of moderate leftist and rightist conventional parties.

A run-of-the-mill alternative to the macroinstitutional and strategic explanations of party formation insists on the significance of electoral laws: it matters how votes are converted into seats. Where plurality systems (first past the post) prevail, new parties have little chance to mobilize and gain a significant share of the vote.[12] Conversely, systems of proportional representation facilitate the proliferation of new parties. Duverger (1954) who originally formulated propositions about the relationship between electoral systems and party system format, as well as his followers, however, have been careful enough to qualify their arguments.[13] In proportional representation (PR) systems, electoral laws are not constraining the articulation of political cleavages, but they do not necessarily promote a multitude of parties, where few cleavages divide the electorate. Moderate thresholds of representation in PR systems cut both ways: they discourage splinter parties, but they encourage the formation of new parties that can reckon to represent significant voter constituencies. The constraining effect of electoral laws really applies only to first-past-the-post plurality laws because even in a majoritarian system with runoffs party proliferation may be encouraged if parties treat the first round of voting as a show of relative party strength that then influences the bargaining between parties before the runoff among the lead contenders.

Table 2.4 shows that there is only a modest correlation between electoral laws and strength of the extreme Right in Europe. True, Britain, as the only

TABLE 2.4. Electoral System and Extreme-Rightist Performance

	Proportional Representation Threshold below 4 Percent	Proportional Representation Threshold at 4 Percent or More	Majoritarian or Plurality System
Rightist Party Success in the 1980s			
Average > 6%	Denmark France (1986) Finland Italy Norway Switzerland	Austria	France (1988 and 1993)
Average > 2%	Belgium	—	—
Average < 2%	Netherlands	Germany, Greece, Ireland, Portugal, Spain, Sweden	Britain

Source: Authors' calculations from official election results.

Note: Extreme-rightist party performance is measured in national parliamentary elections 1980–90.

TABLE 2.5.   Share of the Foreign-Born Population and Rightist Party Performance

		Percentage of the Population Foreign-Born (Mid-1980s)		
		Less than 5 Percent	Between 5 and 10 Percent	More than 10 Percent
	Average > 6%	Austria (3.9), Denmark (3.1), Italy (2.1), Norway (2.4)		France (11.1)
Rightist Party Success in the 1980s	Average > 2%	—	Belgium (8.9)	—
	Average < 2%	Netherlands (4.2) Spain (1.7)	Britain (4.7) Germany (7.4) Sweden (7.9)	—

Sources: For the immigration statistics: United Nations, *World Population Policies.* 3 Vols. (New York: United Nations, 1987). For the Netherlands: *Annual Abstracts of Statistics.*

Note: Extreme-rightist party performance is measured in national parliamentary elections 1980–90.

country on the list with first-past-the-post laws, has no significant party. But, as we will show in chapter 7, this does not explain the varying performance of the British extreme Right over time nor the ability of other new British parties to overcome the disincentives voters face in supporting emerging competitors to the two lead contenders. Moreover, the countries with systems of proportional representation display rather starkly contrasting rightist party performance. Finally, in France, the switch from PR in the 1986 legislative election to a majoritarian runoff system in 1988 and 1993 appears not to have damaged the extreme Right, although it deprived the party of representation in the National Assembly. While electoral laws have a nonnegligible impact on party forma-tion and the fragmentation of party systems taken by themselves, they explain very little about the actual dynamics of competition.

Aside from the role of electoral laws, at least one of the three major rival theories that challenge our own explanation and interpretation of the new authoritarian Right can be tested with macrocomparative data. This is the idea that the contemporary Right is a set of "single-issue" parties with very little broader programmatic identity beyond its common rejection of accelerated immigration from regions outside Western Europe (Middle East, North Africa, Eastern Europe). The other two rival hypotheses—the contemporary extreme Right as right-libertarian or as neofascist phenomenon—can be tested only with attitudinal data on party elites and electorates.

According to the single-issue hypothesis, one would expect a strong right-wing mobilization whenever the level or the change rate of the foreign-born population is high. Table 2.5 provides data on the foreign born population as a percentage of the total population and the strength of right-wing parties. It is clear that there is very little association between the two measures. Strong right-extremist parties appear both in countries with a small foreign-born population as well as in those with a large immigrant population. In a similar vein, measures such as the change rates of immigration between 1983 and 1988 and the share of political refugees in the population in 1988 show little association with the strength of the extreme Right.

Table 2.6 represents subjective evaluations of immigrants in opinion surveys (columns 1 and 2), objective measures of immigration (columns 3 to 5) and the relative strength of the extreme Right in the 1980s (column 6). The figures show that there is a rather high correlation between subjective evaluations and objective measures of the foreign population. Where the share of the foreign population is great, more respondents believe there are too many people of other races in their country and respondents are typically more disturbed by the presence of people of other races than in countries where the number of foreigners is smaller.[14] At the same time, attitudes toward people from other races show very little association with the growth rate of the foreign-born population in the mid-1980s and the share of political refugees.[15] What is most important for our study, however, is the virtual absence of any systematic relationship between the success of the extreme Right in the 1980s and objective or subjective measures of societal "stress" imposed by immigration and ethnocultural pluralization.[16]

These highly aggregated results are obviously more suggestive than conclusive. First of all, they should be supplemented by a regional analysis of the relationship between the share of immigrant populations and the extreme Right, a subject too complicated for this book, although we draw on some ecological analyses of right-wing party support in the case study chapters. The single-issue hypothesis appears plausible, if electoral support for the extreme Right is confined to poorer quarters with high immigrant populations or situated close to such neighborhoods. The single-issue hypothesis is refuted if also more affluent areas or areas without much immigration turn out for the extreme Right. At the same time, a weak performance of rightist parties in residential areas with a middle and upper-middle white-collar population—particularly in cities that are centers for personal service professionals (higher education, health care, business services) even if such areas are located close to high immigrant neighborhoods—may signal that something else is going on with the extreme-rightist vote than a pure single-issue protest. Next, we must explore the decisiveness of ethnocentrist or racist attitudes and perceptions for the act of voting at the individual level through survey analysis. Finally, even if ethnocentrist attitudes are not decisive, it is still possible that the immigration issue can serve right-authoritarian parties with a much broader ideological appeal to focus their slogans and to employ ethnocentrism or racism as a catalyst for the initial mobilization of a right-authoritarian electoral coalition.

TABLE 2.6. Perceived Threat by the Presence of Other Races

	(1) Respondent believes there are too many people of other races in the home country (percent)	(2) Respondent feels disturbed by the presence of other races in the home country (percent)	(3) Foreign-born population as percentage of the residents in a country	(4) Growth of the foreign-born population (percentage per year, 1983–88)	(5) Refugees as percentage of the overall population in 1989	(6) Average level of electoral support for extreme Right in the 1980s (percent)
France	44.1 (N = 961)	18.5 (N = 975)	11.1	9.0	0.33	6.6
United Kingdom	37.9 (N = 1273)	11.4 (N = 1260)	8.7	7.5	0.18	<1.0
Germany	35.5 (N = 1022)	19.2 (N = 995)	7.4	39.2	0.25	<2.0
Denmark	34.9 (N = 951)	13.7 (N = 967)	3.1	42.5	0.53	6.6
Italy	32.4 (N = 1005)	12.5 (N = 1030)	2.0	38.0	0.19	6.4
Netherlands	28.9 (N = 948)	8.8 (N = 946)	4.2	30.0	0.19	<1.0

Sources: Columns 1 and 2: Eurobarometer 30; column 3: see table 2.5; columns 4 and 5: Betz 1990, 71; column 6: see table 2.1.

In this process, ethnocentrism may provide the ideological glue that under the umbrella of the extreme Right unites two different socioeconomic groups that have discordant economic-distributive positions but agree on authoritarian and ethnocentric points of view: namely, small independent businesspeople and farmers with strictly procapitalist attitudes and those elements of the working class that are losing out in the industrial modernization process and defect from conventional parties of the Left to NRR parties because of the latter's ethno-centrist, authoritarian, and progrowth appeal but only to a lesser extent because of the new Right's promise to dismantle the welfare state. These possibilities will be explored in depth in the individual case studies.

The Appeal of the Contemporary Extreme Right:
A Preliminary Comparative Analysis

So far, the macroinstitutional analysis has only identified party systems in which the argument laid out in chapter 1 would lead us to expect the growth of parties with right-authoritarian or populist antistatist appeals. We have not yet examined any evidence that the parties in fact do send such messages to their electorates and gather different social coalitions corresponding to the specific kind of appeal they have chosen. In this section, we will engage in a first effort to explore this argument in a comparative mode while we postpone the more refined analysis to the case study chapters.

It is difficult to explore the appeal of political elites directly and particu-larly that of right-wing extremists. In Europe, activists in such parties typically reject social science research because they tend to view this field as committed to leftist politics. Moreover, the anti-intellectualism that pervades right-extremist parties fuels resentment against any kind of systematic investigation conducted by academics.[17] If interviews and surveys are difficult to imple-ment, another method to determine the parties' political appeal is the content analysis of parties' election manifestos. This method has been employed with mixed results for a comprehensive set of European mainstream parties (cf. Budge, Robertson, and Hearl 1987), but such investigations typically do not include most of the extreme right-wing parties nor is the validity of their data collection method beyond doubt.[18] It is not clear whether the issues that are most extensively discussed in manifestos are actually those that are highlighted by the parties in their efforts to reach out to voters through the media or whether they represent nothing but more or less accidental results of the intraorganizational process by which these manifestos were produced.

Another method to explore the political appeals of party elites at least indirectly is to ask political science experts to judge parties' positions on a number of scales. Such experts do not rely on any single source of information but on a wealth of different streams of data that range from campaign speeches and newspaper reports, via manifestos and leaflets, to the activities of right-wing parties inside and outside the legislative arena, maybe even including courtroom battles and public demonstrations. Because they are based on multiple sources, such synthetic judgments may have greater external validity, although the measurement reliability is obviously limited because of the lack of unambiguously observable facts and figures. Nevertheless, on balance, such judgments are a good second-best source of information about party elite appeals.

We will draw again on the data set assembled by Laver and Hunt (1992), who asked political scientists in most advanced democracies in 1989-90 to rate all parties in their home countries on a number of issue scales with values ranging from 1 to 20. Table 2.7 represents the absolute issue positions of the rightist parties in six countries on a range of these scales. Unfortunately, no ratings for the Italian Northern League or the German Republicans are included. Their leaders' issue positions, therefore, will have to be derived entirely from other materials presented in the case studies and indirectly from their voters' opinions. Given the migration of German right-wing activists from the NPD to the Republicans (see chapter 6), it may be reasonable to presume in the German case that there is considerable ideological continuity between the two parties, although the Republicans are probably more moderate than the NPD.

If our theory is correct, the electorally successful rightist parties in France, Denmark, and Norway should combine procapitalist with authoritarian appeals. In the partocratic Austrian and Italian democracies, the Austrian Freedom Party and the Northern League not included in table 2.7 should engage in populist antistatism with a strong promarket bent, but mild authoritarian or even slightly libertarian positions. The two "old" rightist parties that were unable to increase their vote in the 1980s, the German NPD and the Italian MSI, are likely to express shades of fascist thinking that range from a workerist (and now welfare chauvinist) "social fascism" (authoritarian, but for economic redistribution) to a "corporatist capitalism" that endorses private property, but inside a politically coordinated, hierarchical governance structure of the economy and outside a competitive liberal market setting.

In the table, the first row for each issue item provides the mean judgment of the country experts for each party on the scale from 1 through 20. The second row for each issue item shows the difference between the values for each rightist party and the position of the most conservative large conventional party in the party system the acronym of which is given in brackets. A positive sign means that the contemporary rightist parties are more extreme than the next significant conservative party by the positive amount shown; a negative sign means that the rightist party is not the most extreme party on the scale, but some other conventional party receives that rating. In order to facilitate the

TABLE 2.7. The Ideology of Rightist Parties
Issue Positions of Extreme Right Parties and Comparison to the Next Most Radical Parties[a]

	Average Value for All Extreme Rightists	New Radical Right			Populist-Antistatism		Welfare Chauvism
		France (National Front)	Denmark (Progress Party)	Norway (Progress Party)	Italy (MSI)	Austria (FPOe)	Germany (NPD)
1. Privatize state property (fully endorse = 20)	16.87 +2.78	18.47 +2.40 (RPR)	19.25 +3.25 (KF)	19.12 +3.25 (H)	14.88 +4.50 (DC)	15.78 +3.11 (OeVP)	13.71 +0.15 (CDU)
2. Cut taxes (fully endorse = 20)	16.51 +2.71	18.00 +4.00 (RPR)	19.40 +3.00 (KF)	18.39 +4.07 (H)	14.57 +3.57 (DC)	15.44 +1.88 (OeVP)	13.25 -0.28 (CDU)
3. Economic growth should have priority over environmental protection (fully endorse = 20)	14.99 +1.35	16.17 +1.17 (RPR)	15.38 +1.75 (KF)	17.86 +3.58 (H)	14.25 +1.25 (DC)	12.56 -0.55 (OeVP)	13.71 +0.93 (CDU)
4. Antagonism to the Soviet Union (fully endorse = 20)	15.81 +5.37	18.86 +7.72 (RPR)	13.34 +2.19 (KF)	14.63 +2.81 (H)	19.57 +9.71 (DC)	12.00 +3.25 (OeVP)	16.36 +6.35 (CDU)
5. Against social permissiveness (fully endorse = 20)	15.66 +2.04	19.36 +4.89 (RPR)	14.00 +2.44 (KF)	11.18 +1.24 (H)	19.50 +2.00 (DC)	11.89 -1.89 (OeVP)	18.00 +3.58 (CDU)

Source: Laver and Hunt (1992), appendix.

[a]Scores are situated on a scale from 1 (complete rejection of position) to 20 (complete approval). The first value in each category refers to a party's absolute position as rated by experts in Laver and Hunt's (1992) survey on European parties; the second value with a positive or negative sign indicates difference between the extreme Right and the next most extreme party. Positive values indicate greater extremism by the radical Right, negative values that another party is more radical.

comparison among rightist parties, the first column of each row provides the average value of all extreme-rightist parties in the six countries on a particular issue and their distance from the closest large conventional parties.

The first two issues listed in table 2.7 on privatization of state property and tax cuts measure the economic-distributive dimension of politics, with low scores indicating a socialist antimarket position and high scores a capitalist promarket position. Here, the rightist parties in all countries but Germany are the most radically procapitalist in their own party systems. We will later see that survey results of the German Republicans also show that their voters are relatively less procapitalist than those of the other parties listed in the table. The German extreme Right appears not to follow the "winning formula" of right-authoritarian and populist antistatist politics to embrace market capitalism and free enterprise. Consistent with the theory presented above, German rightist parties are therefore less electorally successful than their counterparts in other countries.

The next three items in table 2.7 in varying ways load on questions of economic distribution and the libertarian versus authoritarian sociopolitical divide. Here we expect the NRR parties in France, Denmark, and Norway, but also the "old" Right in Germany and Italy, to be clearly more authoritarian than their mainstream competitors in these countries. At the same time, the party for which a populist, antistatist appeal appears electorally most beneficial, the Austrian Freedom Party, should take an ideological stance closer to the center of the libertarian/authoritarian position and thus manage to build broader electoral coalitions. The results for rows 3 (environmental protection versus growth), 4 (antagonism to the Soviet Union) and 5 (social permissiveness) show that these expectations are generally borne out.

The third item in table 2.7 measures the parties' positions on the trade-off between environmental protection and economic growth. It has both a distributive aspect (intervention into private rights to capital accumulation or not) and a libertarian/authoritarian connotation (capitalist elite decision making or participatory politics including environmental action groups). In that instance, the three parties for which NRR appeals are electorally beneficial distinguish themselves from their national competitors, as well as from the other three rightist parties in Italy, Austria, and Germany, by supporting the most extreme antienvironmentalist and antiparticipatory positions. These assessments suggest that the NRR parties are a spearhead of the defense of industrial society against the advocates of a hedonist consumer society. In contrast, the Italian MSI and the German NPD are more disposed to considering environmental protection. They are only marginally more proindustrial on this count than the Italian or German Christian Democrats. The postfascist German and Italian parties may thus reveal an undercurrent of "blood and soil" ideology that at times predisposes these older right-wing parties to embrace nature as a value and point of orientation against industrial capitalism, a sentiment that is absent from the true modern NRR parties in France, Denmark, and Norway.

In Austria, finally, where we expect the FPÖ to take a populist antistatist rather than an NRR position, the rightist party actually is not at all the most antienvironmental party, but is in fact more sympathetic to environmental protection than its competitor on the moderate Right, the Austrian People's Party. This configuration indicates that the FPÖ indeed expresses certain libertarian tendencies that are absent from the other more consistently right-authoritarian parties.

The fourth issue concerns anticommunism, a foreign policy question that does not directly relate to the ideological dimensions we have examined in this chapter but that can nevertheless be considered as an indirect proxy for tolerance to political disagreement and for the willingness to accept the right to free speech for people with political convictions fundamentally opposed to the institutions of Western capitalist democracies. The fifth issue in table 2.7 is a direct measure of libertarianism because "social permissiveness" is intended to tap a party's willingness to accept women's choice of abortion, liberal divorce laws, and other items that directly relate to gender equalization, but also the acceptance of gender differences and cultural minorities in society. The data show that five of the six parties are considerably more authoritarian on both the communism and permissiveness scales than their moderate conservative competitors. Note that the Danish and Norwegian Progress parties are the most authoritarian parties *within their respective party systems,* but that they look quite moderate when their absolute scores are compared to those of their French, Italian, or German counterparts. This cross-national pattern of issue scores suggests the interpretation that the Scandinavian Progress parties are a "diluted" extreme Right, an interpretation also borne out by the survey data analysis in chapter 4.

The one exception to the general pattern on the fourth and the fifth issue scale is the Austrian Freedom Party, which in absolute terms is almost in the middle of the scale, certainly not at the authoritarian extreme, and which is more libertarian on social permissiveness than the Austrian People's Party. Also this result closely conforms to the theoretical expectation that populist anti-statist parties avoid strong authoritarian appeals. If we had equivalent data for the Italian Northern League, we would expect it to score closer to the Austrian Freedom Party than to the Italian Social Movement. In contrast, had we data on the German Republicans, we would expect the party to be situated closer to the German NPD (authoritarian, but not particularly capitalist) than to the NRR in Denmark, France, and Norway or the populist antistatist parties in Austria and Italy. Again, we can explore this hypothesis only indirectly through voter data, which will be presented in subsequent chapters.

Laver and Hunt's data set includes three other scales on which values for rightist parties are not represented in table 2.7: government (de)centralization, secular/religious affinity, and urban/rural preferences. On none of these scales do extreme rightist parties display an interpretable pattern, and it is unlikely that these issues play an important role in party competition in the late twentieth century. Government decentralization is an important but most of the time a rather technical and obscure issue. Both NRR parties and populist antistatist parties tend to endorse more decentralization, a reflection of their commitment to market allocation. The traditional rightist parties (NPD, MSI) do not take a clear stance on this dimension. Rightist parties tend to be moderately secular in all countries. Religious affiliation, however, is no longer a highly contested dimension of party competition, although religious devotion continues to remain a rather reliable predictor of moderately conservative voter sympathies. In the same vein, the urban/rural division has lost much of its importance as an independent division relevant for party competition and therefore does not yield pronounced positions on the part of the extreme Right.

We indicated above that a direct assessment of the appeals of party elites would rely on surveys with party leaders rather than expert judgments. While we do not have a recent survey of right-wing parties revealing their leaders' and activists' stances on relevant strategic issues, there is one older data set that sheds some light on the trajectory of these elites. This is the European Political Parties Middle Level Elite (EPPMLE) survey of 1978–80 in which questionnaires were circulated at the party conventions of fifty-five major European parties. For our purposes, this survey has two drawbacks and all interpretations of the data have to be placed in that perspective. First, it excludes the Austrian and Norwegian parties, as well as the then nonexistent Italian Northern League and German Republicans, and thus does not give us the full set of comparisons. Second, as of this writing, the data are fifteen years old and were gathered at a time when many countries had unfavorable opportunity structures for the rise of the extreme Right. Moreover, some of the already existing new right-wing parties had not (yet) worked out their full NRR appeal, as will be shown in the analytical reconstruction of the development of the Danish Progress Party and the French National Front in subsequent chapters. For that reason, we can employ the results of the elite surveys only as a rough approximation of early differences within the European extreme Right that were later articulated more clearly.

Table 2.8 presents the mean positions of three groups of parties on five-point scales covering seven issue items related to the capitalism/socialism and to the libertarian/authoritarian dimensions. A low value (=1) always indicates approval of the item, a high value (=5) disapproval. We display average scores on the seven issues for activists of the extreme-rightist parties that existed at the time, the average value of the issue positions expressed by activists of the moderate left and right parties, and the positions of the left-libertarian extreme parties.

TABLE 2.8. Political Preferences of Party Activists in 1979-1980

	Extreme Right[a]				Middle of the Road[b]				Left-Libertarian Parties[c]		
	Denmark	France	Italy	Germany	Denmark	France	Italy	Germany	Denmark	France	Italy
1. Reducing the public control of enterprise	1.32	1.90	2.35	2.69	2.37	2.68	2.13	2.82	4.72	4.57	3.41
2. Equalize incomes	3.28	2.58	2.00	2.70	2.76	1.75	1.96	2.52	1.27	1.32	1.02
3. Equal opportunities for women	3.08	2.58	1.93	2.15	1.85	1.58	1.74	1.73	1.10	1.05	1.32
4. Women permitted to decide on abortion	1.62	4.18	3.10	3.87	2.07	2.58	2.80	2.61	1.15	1.30	1.67
5. Consider national interest in Third World assistance	1.78	1.75	1.82	1.63	3.34	2.73	2.61	3.09	4.38	3.23	3.37
6. Develop nuclear power	1.76	1.88	2.58	2.75	2.19	2.08	1.96	2.14	4.79	3.44	4.79
7. Fight terrorism	1.15	1.09	1.73	1.38	1.74	1.31	2.12	2.44	3.47	3.46	3.37

Source: European political parties middle level elite surveys, 1979

Note: average values on a four-point scale ranging from being strongly in favor (=1) to strongly opposed (=5), average values for respondents in parties of the extreme Right, middle-of-the-road parties, and the libertarian Left

[a]Denmark: Progress Party; France: National Front; Italy: Italian Social Movement; Germany: National Democrats.

[b]Average value for the mainline liberal, conservative, Christian democratic and social democratic or socialist parties in each country.

[c]Denmark: Socialist People's Party; France: Unified Socialist Party; Italy: Democratic Proletarian Union (PDUP)

For the extreme Right, we have two incipient NRR parties—the Danish Progress Party and the French National Front—and two "old" rightist parties, the Italian MSI and the German NPD. On the first two economic items (public enterprise, income equalization), the Danish and French rightist parties were already in 1979 the most extremely procapitalist among all of their competitors. Their positions are sharply set apart from the respective positions of the "middle-of-the-road" parties, let alone the left-libertarians at the time. In contrast, the Italian and German extreme-right parties are only marginally more procapitalist than the middle-of-the-road parties in these countries but less procapitalist in comparison to the positions of the Danish and French extreme Right. A similar picture emerges when we examine two issues that have economic distributive and libertarian/authoritarian connotations, women's equality (item 3) and nuclear power (item 6). In 1979, the Danish and French extreme Right was most militantly for nuclear power and against women's equal rights, again projecting a staunch NRR image of defending a paternalist industrial society. In contrast, the German and Italian extreme Right was considerably more antinuclear than the middle-of-the-road parties, yet not as antinuclear as the left-libertarians.

Items 4 (abortion), 5 (Third World assistance), and 7 (fighting terrorism) represent issues that tap the libertarian/authoritarian dimension more than problems of economic distribution and property rights. With one exception, we find the Danish and French extreme Right again in the most extreme positions nationally as well as internationally. This exception is the rather libertarian position of the Danish Progress Party on rights to abortion.[19] We have to keep in mind, however, that in 1979 the Progress Party had not yet fully evolved to its later NRR position.

In general, these early data from 1979 help us to trace differences among parties of the extreme Right back to a time before the surge in mobilization in the 1980s. These data suggest that history does matter in the positioning of extreme-rightist parties, an argument we have already made with respect to the "older" branch of the extreme Right, represented here by the MSI and the NPD. The issue positions of old Right activists in 1979 indeed show a generally greater distance from the NRR syndrome of procapitalist authoritarianism than those of the Danish Progress Party or the French National Front. The difference in positions is not accounted for by the varying electoral success of the parties. In 1979, one of the emerging NRR parties, the Danish Progress Party, and one of the older rightist parties, the MSI, were electorally relatively successful, but not their counterparts. Only since that time have political opportunity structures evolved that made right-authoritarian positions fully rewarding for political entrepreneurs in the electoral arena.

A final method for measuring the elite appeal of extreme-rightist parties is to examine the parties' organizational structure. The form of party organization

**TABLE 2.9.   Power Gap between Leaders and Rank-and-File Activists in
European Parties in Setting Party Policies
rank order of parties in six European countries with extreme-rightist parties**

1. Progress Party, Denmark	+12.83
2. Socialist Party, Italy	+12.00
3. National Front, France	+11.94
4. Progress Party, Norway	+10.29
5. Christian Democrats, Italy	+9.40
6. Italian Social Movement	+9.37
7. National Democrats, Germany	+8.87
8. Socialist Party, Austria	+8.55
9. Conservatives, Denmark	+8.38
10. Freedom Party, Austria	+8.22
.	
.	
.	
43. Socialist People's Party, Norway	−2.44
44. United Greens, Austria	−3.00
45. Greens, Italy	−3.37
46. Socialist People's Party, Denmark	−3.65
47. Greens, Germany	−4.05
48. Ecologists, France	−7.33

Source: Expert survey conducted by Laver and Hunt (1992).

Note: Positive values indicate the extent of leader control over activists. Negative values indicate greater say over policy by rank and file.

has not only instrumental significance for voter mobilization, it also sends a programmatic message to voters and party activists about the kind of society that party is willing to realize. The medium of political mobilization itself is a message conveying the party's objectives (Kitschelt 1989, chap. 2). In Laver and Hunt's expert study (1992), political scientists were invited to assess the relative influence of party leaders and rank-and-file activists over party policy. Table 2.9 reports the power differential between leaders and followers. A plus sign indicates that leaders prevail; a minus sign that followers have more say. The table includes only scores for those parties of the 48 covered in the six countries in our study that are ranked at the extreme ends of the power distribution.

The table clearly shows that all right-extremist parties are among the top 10 parties with the most lopsided power distribution in favor of the party leadership. Among these parties, the Austrian Freedom Party, with a populist antistatist message and the relatively least emphasis on authoritarian politics, receives the relatively lowest score. As one might expect, at the other extreme of the distribution, the parties with the most diffuse power structures tend to be left-libertarian parties, whether they are left-socialists or ecology parties. The organizational form is thus yet another signal of how party elites structure their voter appeal. The concentration of power around the often charismatic party leaders in extreme-rightist organizations is a way of appealing to authoritarian sentiments and longings in the electorate. It is a subtle message that does not even need to be accompanied by explicit authoritarian appeals.

We conclude from our fragmentary evidence on the appeals of party elites that there is considerable differentiation within Europe's extreme-rightist party spectrum with respect to the nature of political opportunity structures, enabling electorally successful rightist entrepreneurs to adopt either right-authoritarian (NRR) or populist antistatist appeals, and considerable differentiation in the historical legacy of parties that constrains their strategic flexibility to seek out new electoral niches. The mechanism that brings about this strategic paralysis is based on the patterns of intraparty decision making and the political social-ization of the activists into a fascist or national socialist tradition. This problem has also been encountered by the now completely marginalized extreme Right in postauthoritarian countries such as Greece, Spain, and Portugal. The ex-treme Right still fights the old battles of the past and has so far proved incapa-ble of overcoming its electoral insignificance by experimenting with new issue appeals.[20]

Our next task is to supply a set of empirical evidence that explores the extent to which the different appeals of political parties may be reflected by their electorates. Based on the elite data we have just examined, we would expect that the voters of the French, Danish, and Norwegian extreme Right express right-authoritarian inclinations, whereas the voters of the Austrian Freedom Party and the Italian Northern League are middle of the road on authoritarian appeals but display to a strong antistate and promarket affect. Followers of the rightist parties in the fascist tradition may tone down the procapitalist commitment where social-fascist legacies prevail. This may be the case with the NPD as well as the *Republikaner,* its electoral successor on the extreme Right. Where fascism is associated with more traditionalist defenses of the status quo, as in the (southern) Italian strongholds of the MSI, the neofascist party will endorse property and hierarchy as well as authoritar-ianism but remain less supportive of market competition. As a consequence, the German *Republikaner* should draw on a more working-class electorate, whereas the Italian MSI attracts an electorate in which blue-collar voters are underrepresented.

The central empirical source on voter opinions on which our investigation will draw in the subsequent comparative analysis is the 1990 *World Values Survey* (WVS), which was conducted in all advanced industrial countries, most postcommunist countries, and a range of less developed countries. The survey consists of national random samples ranging in size from about 1,000 to 2,000 respondents. We will first present some responses of right-wing sympathizers to questions that operationalize orientations toward capitalist markets, authority, nation, race, and gender. These orientations tap the critical dimensions of politics expected by our theoretical argument to discriminate extreme right-wing voters from the followers of other parties. Because we are dealing here with a very preliminary analysis, we omit information about sample size and missing values. Table 2.10 first lists the responses of those who indicate they would vote for one of the three French, Danish, and Norwegian parties whose elite appeal is right-authoritarian (NRR), next the respondents close to the two Italian and Austrian parties where the elites appeal or are presumed to appeal to populist antistatism, and finally the supporters of the two "old Right" German and Italian parties steeped in fascist traditions. For each survey item, the table provides the difference value between the percentage of extreme-rightist voters supporting a view and the percentage of the entire survey population supporting that view. For example, in the first row, 13.3 percent *more* of the French National Front's voters approve of capitalist competition than does the entire French sample. The difference values thus do not reveal the absolute level of support for an item in each country, but only the relative position of the extreme right supporters compared to the overall national sample. It should be kept in mind that extreme right-wing voters represent no more than 4 to 9 percent of the entire national samples. In the case of the German Republicans, less than 2 percent of the sample indicates it would vote for that party were elections held at the time of the survey. Therefore, for the German party especially the results have to be taken with a grain of salt, as there are fewer than 30 Republicans in the entire national sample.

The first three items in table 2.10 measure voters' commitment to capitalism. As expected, the voters of the three NRR parties are strongly procapitalist. They endorse competition and believe that owners (and not workers or some cooperative arrangement between owners and workers) should run firms and that more income equalization is undesirable. The Austrian Freedom Party, as a main representative of the populist antistatist position, comes close to the same pattern of views. The Italian Northern League also subscribes to private property and more inequality, but not to more competition. The two rightist parties organizing against the backdrop of a strong fascist legacy provide an interesting contrast to the historically less constrained contemporary rightist political creations. Both German Republicans and Italian MSI endorse a hierarchically stratified society with income differentials. But the German Republicans take a moderately anticapitalist stance on business governance and market competition, while the Italian MSI respondents endorse capitalist socioeconomic organization only marginally more than the overall population. These results suggest that for the Right in formerly fascist or national socialist countries social hierarchy is less tied to free markets than to property and authority. It is

TABLE 2.10. Economic Rightism and Politico-Cultural Authoritarianism

	New Radical Right			Populist Antistatism		Old Right	
	France (FN)	Denmark (FP)	Norway (FRP)	Italy (NL)	Austria (FPÖ)	Germany (REP)	Italy (MSI)
I. Capitalism							
1. Capitalism is good (endorsement)	+13.3	+18.5	+16.2	-1.1	+17.8	-4.3	+4.6
2. Owners should govern business (values 1–3)	+19.5	+20.1	+13.1	+15.8	+4.5	-12.1	+6.7
3. More income equality (values 1–3)	-12.0	-5.3	-10.2	-3.9	-3.3	-13.4	-16.6
II. Quality of Life							
4. Index of support for environmentalism (high)	-26.1	-16.6	-14.6	+4.0	-3.7	-11.3	+0.4
5. Less emphasis on money (endorsement)	-13.5	-16.7	-14.4	-8.8	-4.5	-19.6	-20.4
III. Authority							
6. More respect for authority (high)	+22.7	+10.5	+7.9	-9.4	-3.6	+10.0	+16.2
7. Postmaterialism	-8.3	-4.0	-4.4	-3.2	+4.4	-18.5	-18.0
8. Unconventional participation (high: 4–7)	-6.6	-4.3	-8.6	-3.5	+0.5	+7.1	-2.0
9. Confidence in the army (high)	+14.2	+5.2	+2.2	-0.5	-2.0	+14.4	+3.6
10. Confidence in the press (high)	-25.4	-3.0	-2.1	+2.8	-0.9	-15.6	+12.0
IV. Nation and Race							
11. Against neighbors of a different race	+26.1	+25.3	+9.3	+5.5	+1.8	+15.1	+4.7
12. Job priority for own nationals	+33.8	+38.4	+23.8	+16.5	+5.3	+27.2	+4.8
13. National pride (high)	+9.9	+12.8	+12.8	-4.6	-8.6	+19.7	+13.3
V. Gender							
14. Males among voters	+14.1	+26.5	+10.3	+23.4	+7.7	+23.1	+8.4
15. Housewife is a fulfilling role	+2.8	+6.7	-1.3	+4.2	+0.2	+9.4	+16.3
VI. Sociodemographics							
16. Low education (completed before age 17)	+21.0	+5.0	-4.5	0.0	-9.0	+16.7	-4.0
17. White-collar or professional employment	-7.7	-12.3	-13.0	-0.8	-5.6	+1.9	+9.7

Source: World Values Survey 1990; values are difference values between the percentage of rightist voters who support a statement and the population average in support of the statement.

therefore difficult for these parties to seize on the opportunities offered by the strategic configuration of contemporary party systems in which new extreme-rightist parties may attract voters with a resolutely market-liberal stance.

The next three sets of questions—on the quality of life, authority, nation, and race—should yield similar patterns of support among the voters of the NRR parties and also of the old-rightist successor organizations in Germany and Italy. If our theory is correct, the voters of NRR parties should show a distinct distaste for environmental protection, emphasize money over other goals (group II), favor more respect for authority and the army, but less "postmaterialism," and display less willingness to participate in unconventional forms of political action (demonstrations, etc.) as well as less confidence in the press as an arena of open and critical debate (group III). "Materialism" is an indicator of authoritarian attitudes because it signals that extreme-right orientations give priority to law and order and economic stability over freedom of speech and more citizens' participation in policy making. Finally, right-authoritarians should want to avoid neighbors of a different race, give priority to citizens over foreigners in labor markets, and express more national pride than the rest of the population (group IV). In contrast, the voters of populist antistatist parties should exhibit all these authoritarian and particularist views to a relatively lesser extent than the supporters of NRR parties or parties in the fascist legacy.

Table 2.10 shows that with very few exceptions the data confirm these patterns.[21] The authoritarian propensities are pronounced in the French National Front, the German Republicans, and the Italian MSI. Authoritarian patterns are generally somewhat less extreme, but still visible, in the Danish and Norwegian Progress parties. Authoritarian penchants are generally the least pronounced among the two populist antistatist parties, the Northern League and the Freedom Party. The supporters of these two parties exhibit only marginally higher tendencies toward ethnocentrism than the Italian or Austrian population at large (rows 11 and 12), and they show distinctly less pride in the nation or one of its symbols, the military, than the supporters of the other parties. Also, on all other measures, supporters of populist anti-statist parties are not much different from the overall population in their countries.

The final two groups of questions (V and VI) examine sociodemographic background as well as objective and subjective aspects of gender and politics. Everywhere, women are much less inclined to vote for the extreme Right than men. Moreover, the extreme Right has a tendency to endorse traditional gender roles. This tendency is rather sharply articulated among the parties steeped in the fascist tradition, but rather mild among the other parties.

In terms of sociodemographics, an area we will also explore with more sophisticated methods in the case studies, our theory hypothesizes that white-collar employees and professionals are underrepresented in the NRR, but not in populist antistatist parties. Rows 16 and 17 lend some support to this hypothesis, although the educational level of the Norwegian Progress Party voters is inconsistent with the overall argument. The German Republicans, with a less procapitalist and more authoritarian electorate, should appeal to less educated individuals and an overproportional share in the working class. Here, the occupational breakdown (row 17) is inconsistent with the theory, but we should keep in mind that less than 2 percent of the survey respondents signaled support for the Republicans. More so than is the case with any other party, sampling error is a likely cause of this inconsistency. Finally, the Italian MSI draws on individuals with somewhat lower education but generally more employment in the salariat. As we will see, this reflects the traditional entrenchment of the party in small cities of the Italian South, a traditional electorate beyond which the party could not expand until it gathered protest votes from former Southern Christian Democrats in the course of the breakdown of the Italian party system in 1993-94.

The sociodemographic findings of the *World Values Survey* can be cross-validated with Eurobarometer data analyzed by Niedermayer (1990). With respect to occupation, white-collar employees and professionals are everywhere underrepresented in the electorate of rightist parties, but the proportion of workers in these parties' constituencies varies substantially (see table 2.11). It is highest in the German Republican party, which has the least procapitalist orientation. In contrast to the *World Values Survey*, the Eurobarometer data thus remove the anomaly of overrepresented white-collar sectors and professionals in the Republicans' electorate. Blue-collar overrepresentation is less pronounced in the mainline NRR parties where businesspeople and farmers are at least as overrepresented as the working class. As expected, the populist antistatist Austrian Freedom Party has no distinctive occupational composition of its electorate, but represents all groups equally. In a similar vein, everywhere except Austria and Italy—the countries with populist antistatist parties or traditional neofascist parties—the educational profile of rightist supporters is skewed toward the low end. This tendency is clearest in the case of the German Republicans. Finally, in all countries men are overrepresented in the rightist electorate with a 60–40 to 70–30 margin. This pattern underlines the importance of the authoritarian antifeminist thrust in the contemporary extreme Right.

The comparative data on party elites, voter attitudes, and sociodemographics also allow us for the first time to evaluate the two rival hypotheses we have not yet been able to test at all, namely, that the new extreme-rightist parties represent right-libertarian or neofascist types of mobilization. Our evidence provides little support for either hypothesis. None of the parties we have examined at the elite or voter level ever engages in explicit politico-cultural libertarian appeals. What we find is a more or less authoritar-

TABLE 2.11. Social Structure Supporting Extreme Right-Wing Parties (in percentage of each social group)

	Germany (REPs 1989)	Denmark (Progress 1989)	France (FN 1989)	Italy (MSI 1989)	Austria (FPÖ 1989)
1. Occupation					
1.1. Self-employed, farmers	5.2	10.4	3.7	3.7	15.0[a]
1.2. White-collar/state officials	3.3	6.5	2.4	3.0	9.0
1.3. Blue-collar					skilled 11.0
workers	6.3	9.4	3.3	2.3	unskilled 8.0
2. Education					
2.1. Low education	5.8	8.2	3.3	2.3	6.0
2.2. Medium education	5.1	10.7	3.1	3.7	11.0
2.3. Higher education	1.0	5.7	2.0	3.9	14.0
3. Gender					
3.1. Men	5.8	9.2	3.5	4.2	12.0
3.2. Women	3.1	6.1	2.2	1.9	7.0

Source: Niedermayer (1990), except Austria; Austria: Plasser and Ulram (1989), 74.
[a]includes liberal professions.

ian bent that is most clear-cut among the French National Front and the three extreme-rightist parties steeped in a fascist legacy (MSI in Italy, NPD and Republicans in Germany). The Scandinavian parties show the same pattern, but in a milder form. The populist antistatist parties in Italy and Austria are slightly authoritarian, but close overall to the population mean on many issue items.

In a similar vein, there is no support for the hypothesis that the contemporary extreme Right is a reincarnation of the old fascist extreme Right. If fascism is defined as the ideological program of establishing an authoritarian and economically corporatist social order, only the German NPD and the Republicans and the Italian MSI remotely resemble fascist parties, based on the empirical evidence about leaders' appeals in the judgment of political scientists, where available, or voter attitudes as revealed by the *World Values Survey.* Further, the overrepresentation of blue-collar workers in most parties of the contemporary extreme Right is inconsistent with patterns known from the old fascist Right.

The data presented in this section also cast some light on the third rival hypothesis: that the contemporary extreme Right is a single-issue response to immigration and multiculturalization. It is true that questions of race, immigration, and nation distinguish the supporters of the extreme Right from other voters (rows 11 through 13 in table 2.10). But the extreme Right also stands out from the fold on a number of other issue dimensions, both at the elite as well as the electoral level. It is not a "cross section" of the population that has been rallied around the new right-wing parties by nothing other than their ethnocentric and xenophobic appeal. In subsequent chapters, with the aid of more sophisticated statistical methods we will check how large the "net effect" of ethnocentrism and racism is in accounting for voters' decisions to support the extreme Right. At this stage of the investigation, it is still possible that extreme-rightist voters are right-wing on a number of issues but are distinct from the supporters of other conservative parties on only one item, namely, ethnocentrism.

Finally, the idea that the new extreme Right is an issueless protest vote of those who generally feel cynical about democratic systems in which all the parties appear to say the same thing is groundless in light of the preliminary data we have presented. Both elites and their electoral followers on the extreme Right have very definitive opinions that diverge quite sharply from the population mainstream in numerous respects. The extreme Right, of course, expresses protest against the prevailing policies and institutions but with a rather specific thrust and with a vision of a different order that goes far beyond a general feeling of uneasiness about the practice of democracy in advanced capitalist democracies.

The Case Study Strategy and the Methodology of Quantitative Analysis

Although in this chapter we have outlined the general argument of this investigation as it applies to specific country cases and have provided some preliminary evidence supporting the validity of the underlying theory, much remains to be done in subsequent case study chapters. In this final section, we will sketch the strategy for the case study analysis and describe the empirical procedures that will be employed to test the main hypotheses in competition with their rivals—namely, single-issue protest, disaffection with elite democracy, right-libertarianism, and neofascist mobilization as driving forces of the contemporary extreme Right. In the case studies, more empirical evidence must be supplied to explain the origins and the elaboration of the party elites' political appeals. At the same time, we will subject the mass surveys of right-wing support to more sophisticated analysis than is presented in this chapter.

With respect to the appeals of right-wing party elites, it is vital to illustrate the dynamic interaction among right-wing political entrepreneurs in the appropriation or rejection of the historical legacy of extreme-rightist political mobilization in a country as well as the interaction between such entrepreneurs and their adversaries in conventional political parties, particularly those with moderately conservative programs. Each chapter will therefore begin with a brief review of the historical development of the country's extreme Right and the ideological appeals it has left behind. We will then turn to the emerging political opportunity structures for the formation of new right-wing parties at the time of their recent revival. In the third section of each case study, we will examine the actual techniques and tactical moves that made new parties successful. Beyond the general structural and strategic conditions necessary for rightist party success, two elements have particular importance for the micromanagement of the rise of a new political party: access to the mass media and the choice of the appropriate elections in which the new parties first compete. Reif and Schmitt (1980) pointed out that the successful launching of new parties typically takes place in "secondary elections," which have less political weight than national legislative or presidential elections. Such secondary elections can be local, regional, or supranational (European) elections. Because voter turnout in such elections is lower than in national parliamentary or presidential elections, small highly committed groups of voters are more likely to make a difference and lend visibility to a new party. Further, because the stakes in secondary elections are more modest, marginal supporters of other parties might be tempted to experiment with a new party to teach the establishment a lesson. In most cases, extreme-rightist parties, but not only those, could overcome the costs of entry into party competition only if in addition to a favorable opportunity structure in the arena of party competition they also managed to choose the appropriate sequence of electoral contests to maximize their chances of early national political visibility, particularly through access to the media.

The next issue is the right-wing parties' electoral entrenchment. The critical questions here follow directly from the theoretical framework of this study. First, do voter attitudes reveal that new rightist parties are located at one extreme of a dominant dimension of competition ranging from left-libertarian to right-authoritarian views? The location of the parties in the competitive space permits us to decide which of the competing hypotheses is correct: are rightist voters (and by implication, political elite appeals) right-authoritarians, right-libertarians, populist antistatists, or left-authoritarians? Second, which elements in the beliefs of extreme-rightist voters are decisive for their party preference and set them off from the voters of the moderate-conservative or even moderate-left parties? If ethnocentric opinions are decisive for voter choice, a "single-issue" hypothesis of right-wing mobilization would be plausible. Third, what is the electoral coalition surrounding each right-wing party? We will explore the extent to which occupational experience can help us to predict the issue orientations that further right-wing electoral choice.

The general idea behind our empirical investigation is to examine the issue opinions of party sympathizers as indirect tracers of the party leaders' strategic appeals themselves. The underlying assumption is that a critical subgroup of voters behaves rationally in the sense that it supports the party that is most in agreement with its ideal political program. In a competitive democracy, a large number of voters may support a party purely on the basis of party identification and habit. Even if their opinions vary independently of what the parties they support stand for, each party will have a different overall distribution of voter opinions as long as there are critical minorities who base their electoral decision not on habit but on the deliberate commitment to a party's programmatic appeal. The profile of issue positions that each party's supporters exhibits thus reflects the party leaders' strategic appeals as they are voiced in parliamentary debates, in the presentation of the party in the mass media, and in direct face-to-face interactions with voter constituencies.

The voters and profiles of issue support for each party can be placed in political spaces that allow us to estimate the relative proximity and distance between competing parties. Such spaces are *issue-defined spaces,* constructed on the basis of voters' preference distributions over a wide range of themes. We do not rely on *party-defined spaces* constructed from respondents' sympathy rankings of individual parties because it is difficult to interpret the "meaning" of party-defined spaces without already having access to information about the distribution of voters' issue positions. Party sympathies may shape voters' issue positions when their preferred parties assume "issue leadership." Issue-defined spaces, however, provide a much clearer sense of the policy content of the voter-party linkage and the resulting strategic options for parties than do party-defined spaces.

The issue space according to which voters' opinions are distributed is likely to be multidimensional. The multidimensionality of voter beliefs, however, does not necessarily imply that parties compete in a multidimensional space as well. First, some of the issues that divide voters may not be reflected by positions of political parties. In Sani and Sartori's (1983) terminology, the space of voter identification may be more complex than the space of party competition. Voters may be divided by religion, ethnic feelings, and a host of other orientations, yet parties do not systematically compete on issues where they know voters are hard to move. If parties ignore a particular issue division that structures the electorate, their voters' position on this issue should vary randomly, signaled by an average value close to the population mean and a very high standard deviation.

Second, competitive party spaces may have fewer dimensions than voter identification spaces because parties systematically link positions that are situated on several statistically independent dimensions of voter opinion. For example, voter opinions might vary on independent economic left/right and politico-cultural authoritarian/libertarian dimensions. But party competition remains unidimensional if each party's position on the first dimension also predicts its position on the second dimension. In this instance, parties collapse two dimensions of voter identification into a single competitive dimension.

A critical empirical problem in the construction of voter spaces of identification and party spaces of competition is the availability of data covering a wide range of issue positions and thus *permitting the unconstrained clustering of issues around a variety of imaginable dimensions.* In other words, the selection of issue items on which respondents' positions are measured should not predetermine the issue dimensions on which voters and parties are situated. Therefore, in the statistical analysis, great care has to be taken in combining issue items that permit the appearance of dimensions of voter identification and party competition *not* predicted by the theory of right-authoritarian politics we are obviously favoring.

Ideally, the same indicators of citizens' issue positions should be measured in a wide range of countries to assure the cross-national comparability of the dimensions of voter identification, party competition, and appeals of the individual parties.[22] One possible data source is the biannual Eurobarometer survey conducted in all EC countries. These data sets, however, are of limited use for a number of reasons. They do not include some countries with important candidates for inclusion in the family of right-extremist parties, such as Austria, Norway, and Switzerland. Furthermore, the Eurobarometer surveys typically incorporate a very limited range of issue positions that do not allow for a full test of the theoretical model. As a consequence, a previous study by the senior author of this book with Eurobarometer data (Kitschelt 1994) had to rely on a few general indicators of ideological orientation and on sociostructural proxies expected to be associated with left-libertarian versus right-authoritarian issue positions, such as age, education, and profession, in order to determine spaces of voter identification and party competition. Although there are two fairly recent Eurobarometers that have batteries of questions exploring racism and xenophobia, there is little else. We have employed these surveys in order to explore the uniqueness of right-wing voters, but we will not present these data for three reasons. First, they do not yield any surprising results that would contradict the findings derived from the data we will actually employ in this study. Second, there are too few issue items on authoritarianism/libertarianism as well as pro- or anticapitalist attitudes in the Eurobarometers to explore their linkage to racism and xenophobia. Finally, the Eurobarometers do not supply data on two of the countries on which we focus in this book—Austria and Norway.

The most useful comprehensive cross-national data source to explore the relationship between attitudes toward economic organization, libertarian or authoritarian views of politics and culture, and racist or xenophobic resentments is the *World Values Survey* of 1990. The questionnaire incorporates complex issue batteries that allow us to operationalize the theoretically expected main dimensions of voter identification and party competition as well as to explore the existence of alternative spaces. While the *World Values Survey* of 1990 data set promises to yield much more accurate results than the Eurobarometer survey, it should be pointed out that a comparison of the voter identification and party competition spaces generated with this data set do not differ much from the more limited Eurobarometer data. This is clear by comparing the results reported below with the spaces generated with Eurobarometer data from the second half óf the 1980s (cf. Kitschelt 1994, chap. 4).

The *World Values Survey* 1990 yields at least 20 issue items and ideological scales that bear on the rival theories about the nature of the extreme Right in postindustrial societies. Table 2.12 lists these items and proposes possible configurations of factor loadings on dimensions of voter identification and party competition that may be revealed by statistical analysis. The first column indicates that if there is a dominant left-libertarian versus right-authoritarian dimension to voter division that combines views on market economics with politico-procedural and cultural attitudes, then *all 20* variables should load on that dimension. Right-authoritarians are expected to be procapitalist in that they approve the management of businesses by capital owners rather than by the employees or the state, call for more income inequality, and wish to increase competition (items 1 through 3). They do not find ecology to be an urgent policy issue, would not welcome environmental taxes, and would not participate in protests against nuclear plants (items 4 through 6).

Left-libertarians and right-authoritarians also have pronounced positions on the items that measure tolerance for cultural diversity in society. Right-authoritarians have great national pride, dislike neighbors of a different race, and believe that nationals should be preferentially treated in the labor market (items 7, 8, and 9). Quite obviously, the two groups are at loggerheads on issues of authority and political participation. Right-authoritarians call for more respect for authority, have greater confidence in the army, are less likely to participate in demonstrations (even if they are lawful), and would not participate in disarmament protests (items 10 through 13).

Finally, the left-libertarian versus right-authoritarian dimension is also expected to discriminate between different positions on the rights and the status of women in society. Right-authoritarians are likely to object to women's choice over abortion and women's equal rights to a job, but they are more inclined to believe that the role of homemaker is satisfying for women (items 14 through 16).

The 16 issue items that distinguish left-libertarians from right-authoritarians may also be related to several broader ideological dispositions and points of orientation. The first of these is left/right self-placement (item 17). It is plausible that the notion of "left" and "right" has been increasingly associated with political and cultural issues of participation and individual autonomy rather than only economic questions of distribution and governance. In a similar vein, the divide between "materialists" and "postmaterialists" (item 18) may directly relate to the left-libertarian versus right-authoritarian dimension. Postmaterialists value participation and individual autonomy and tolerate more intervention in markets for the sake of other goals than economic efficiency, whereas materialists put more emphasis on social order and individual compliance with norms while also placing greatest emphasis on economic production. Postmaterialists are operationalized as those respondents who rank highest (1) free speech and (2) more citizens' participation in policy making and rank lowest (3) fighting inflation and (4) maintaining law and order as goals of public policy. Materialists have the inverse preference order. Those who have as their top two policy priorities (1) *or* (2) *and* (3) *or* (4) are classified as mixed. Inglehart (1977; 1990) has emphasized that "postmaterialists" put less emphasis on economic production and material affluence than on self-realization. We favor a somewhat different interpretation according to which prioritizing free speech and more citizens' participation, while giving little emphasis to law and order signals a libertarian attitude. The fourth item of Inglehart's scale, fighting inflation, also has less to do with the relative emphasis on material values than with left/right stances on economic distribution. Many citizens realize that monetary and fiscal austerity policies to fight inflation hurt the less affluent through rising unemployment, at least in the short run,[23] and thus such priorities express a rightist stance. Leftists, in turn, will always favor fighting unemployment over fighting inflation. Therefore, "materialists" on the left will appear like "postmaterialists" in Inglehart's index because they cannot give priority to fighting inflation. In our interpretation, then, what is labeled postmaterialism really measures a politically libertarian *and* an economically leftist commitment, not primarily a lower appreciation of high and rising standards of material affluence.

The two remaining general ideological dispositions included in table 2.12 have been thrown into the general analysis to guarantee that traditional cleavage dimensions in European politics are represented. One item is designed to tap religious cleavages, operationalized by the frequency of church attendance (item 19). The other item is residence in rural, town, or metropolitan areas (item 20). This variable is not strictly an attitudinal item, but it represents the only way to explore the significance of the urban/rural division for contemporary politics.

Where a factor analysis of the more specific 16 issue items reveals a clear economic and political left-libertarian versus right-authoritarian dimension, we would expect that it is rather strongly correlated to left/right self-placements and postmaterialism and somewhat less strongly to religious practice and urban/rural divides. Where separate authoritarian/libertarian and

TABLE 2.12. Possible Political Issue Dimensions in Western Publics

1	Economic Distributive Issues 2	Procedural Libertarian Authoritarian 3	Ecology versus Industry 4	Morality and Family 5	Exclusive Conceptions of Citizenship 6
Economic Issues					
1. Business management	yes	no	no	no	no
2. Income inequality	yes	no	no	no	yes
3. Competition	yes	no	no	no	no
Ecology and Industry					
4. Environmental taxes	yes/no	no	yes	no	no
5. Urgency of ecology	yes/no	yes/no	yes	no	no
6. No nuclear plants	yes	yes	yes	no	no
Race and Nation					
7. Objections to neighbors of different race	no	no	no	no	yes
8. Priority for own nationals in labor markets	no	no	no	no	yes
9. National pride	no	no	no	no	yes
Authority and Participation					
10. More respect for authority	no	yes	no	yes	no
11. Confidence in the army	no	yes	yes	yes/no	no
12. Would participate in lawful demonstration	no	yes	yes	no	no
13. Would participate in disarmament protest	no	yes	yes	no	no
Women and Family					
14. Choice over abortion	no	yes	yes/no	yes	yes
15. Women as homemakers	no/yes	yes	no	yes	no/yes
16. Women's right to a job	yes	yes	no	yes	no/yes
General Ideological Dispositions					
17. Left/right self-placement	yes	yes	no	yes/no	no
18. Postmaterialism	no/yes	yes	yes	yes	yes
19. Secularism/church attendance	no	no	no	yes	no
20. Urban/rural residence	no/yes	no	no	yes	no
Number of Variables Expected to Load on a Dimension	8.5	10.5	7.5	8.0	7.0

capitalist/anticapitalist attitude dimensions appear, each dimension should separately and in a statistically significant way contribute to left/right self-placements and possibly even to postmaterialism and religious practice.

The wide variety of issues employed to construct spaces of voter identification and party competition makes it possible that statistical explorations will reveal rather different dimensions of political attitudes in the electorate and rather different linkages between issue dimensions and general ideological orientations than the theoretically predicted division between left-libertarians and right-authoritarians. In table 2.12, columns 2 through 6 specify how the individual issue items are expected to relate to rival dimensions of political division that compete with the hypothesis of a dominant left-libertarian versus right-authoritarian space.

First, if there is a pure economic left/right divide over distributive issues (column 2), then the economic items (1 through 3), perhaps the ecology items (4 through 6), those items on women's status that relate to female labor market participation (15 and 16), and the left/right self-placement should be related to an economic-distributive factor. Postmaterialism should also correlate with that dimension, though more weakly, if the interpretation of postmaterialism as a libertarian, but also redistributive, commitment is correct (item 18). Finally, the urban/rural split (item 20) may be associated with property relations in that rural residents are less likely to be wage laborers and therefore prefer pro-capitalist market positions. A purely distributive dimension of politics will exhibit no relationship to the remaining 10 issue items. At the bottom of table 2.12, we have listed a counter of how many items in the factor analysis are expected to tap a dimension. Where an item is expected to load strongly on a dimension, it is counted as a whole point; where it should show a more limited loading (yes/no entry in the table), it is scored as a half point. According to this counter, a pure economic left/right dimension has a fair chance to appear as a strong, independent factor because 8.5 items potentially load on this dimension.

Second, in column 3, we have specified expectations for a purely procedural authoritarian/libertarian dimension. Libertarians are likely to want more participatory inputs to further environmental causes (items 4 through 6), although they may be somewhat less concerned about the specific policy tool of taxation (item 4). They are cosmopolitans (items 7 through 9) and anti-authoritarians (items 10 through 13), and they are likely to endorse the cultural and economic autonomy of women (items 14 through 16). A libertarian position is also likely to lead to leftist self-placements and to endorse postmaterialism (items 17 and 18). Altogether, a pure authoritarian/libertarian dimension could load on as many as 10.5 items of the scale.

Third, some authors have postulated that there is a separate ecological dimension in contemporary politics that is unrelated to distributive concerns and to procedural liberalism (cf. Rüdig 1989). This separate "deep ecology" dimension (column 4) is likely to combine a commitment to postmaterialism (item 17), an insistence on the urgency of the environmental issue (including that of taxes [item 4]), a disposition to participate in demonstrations against hazardous military and civilian technologies (items 6, 12, and 13), and maybe a rejection of abortion because it devalues the sacredness of life (item 14). Overall, an ecology versus industry dimension is tapped by at least 7.5 items under consideration.

Fourth, a further possible dimension is concerned with family and morality (column 5). At one extreme, it may rally "moral fundamentalists" who place little emphasis on material well-being (item 18), are religious (item 19) and tend to live in small towns (item 20), and have great respect for authority (item 10) and the army (item 11). They also endorse traditional roles for women in society (items 14 through 16). At the other extreme, there are "moral relativists" who are secular materialists in large metropolitan areas, express little respect for authority or the army, and emphasize tolerance for the equality and individual autonomy of women. The morality and family dimension thus may load on up to eight of the twenty items.

Finally, racism, ethnocentrism, and nationalism may constitute a separate dimension with items 7 through 9 as the core issues (column 6). Racists, however, may also endorse income inequality, especially among different races (item 2) and call for law and order rather than participation (item 18) to suppress the purported "disorder" created by ethnic pluralism. Both moral fundamentalists as well as racists may place themselves on the right (item 17). Racists and nationalists may also be opposed to the legalization of abortion (item 14) because they wish to promote population growth. They therefore may also endorse disadvantages for women in the labor markets in order to make mothering a more attractive alternative to gainful employment (items 15 and 16). Altogether, the race and exclusive citizenship dimension may load on as many as seven items in table 2.12.

Overall, the rivals to the expected left-libertarian versus right-authoritarian dimension are rather well represented in the exploratory factor analysis to which voters' opinions are going to be subjected in each country. In general, where the left-libertarian versus right-authoritarian dimension does *not* emerge as the strongest dimension of voter identification and party competition, the proposed theory is in trouble, provided a second-best result fails to emerge as well: there are separate economic-distributive and cultural-libertarian dimensions, but the mean positions of each party's voters on the two dimensions are strongly associated with each other, at least for all the major parties. For example, if the electorate of party A is on the antimarket side of the economic dimension, we expect to find it on the libertarian side of the authoritarian/libertarian dimension.

We will use two statistical techniques to represent the clustering of the respondents' issue opinions in each country and the mean position of the parties' supporters: first a simple exploratory principal components analysis on the entire set of attitude measures and then a confirmatory factor analysis on representative issue items that forces the appearance of three separate factors, namely, an economic left/right factor relating to distributive views, a libertarian/authoritarian factor relating to procedures of collective decision making and individual cultural autonomy, and a cosmopolitan/parochial factor measuring ethnocentrist, racist, and nationalist conceptions of citizenship.[24]

The exploratory principal components factor analysis of voters' opinions and the calculation of party supporters' mean positions on the revealed factors is only the first of four empirical steps in each case study analysis. We report principal components because they can be interpreted in a straightforward manner, although they are cross-nationally less comparable because the components slightly vary from country to country.[25] Moreover, the exploratory principal components typically yield an interpretable two-dimensional space in which we can visually represent the mean position of each party's supporters on the two main components to identify the parties' likely ideological appeal and competitive strategic situation. Here, as well as in the later confirmatory analyses, we do not report the standard deviation of the party supporters' mean positions on the factors, unless they are outside the ordinary range of 0.70 to 1.00. These standard deviations indicate that there is considerable overlap among the electorates of the various parties because only a fraction of each party's electorate actually votes on programmatic concerns rather than party loyalty. This fraction, of course, is critical for our analysis as well as for politicians' competitive strategies.

The principal components analysis allows a first assessment of the clustering of issue opinions and a visual representation of relations. It has serious disadvantages, however. It often does not sharply identify opinion dimensions. Moreover, the dimensions may vary somewhat across countries (in our study particularly, second principal components vary) so that the parties' locations cannot be easily compared across countries. Further, we might find that none of the principal components yields a separate cosmopolitan versus parochial dimension. In order to increase the comparability of our analysis across countries and to explore the independent impact of ethnocentrism and racism on voter alignments, we then performed a confirmatory factor analysis. As an alternative to that second step, we also estimated varimax rotated factors. Varimax rotation does tend to separate economic left/right and authoritarian/libertarian issue factors, but the party supporters' mean positions on each dimension remain substantially correlated, at least for the major parties in each system. The results of the varimax rotation thus do not differ significantly from the principal components. The varimax analysis also yields an important third factor, typically an ecology/social movement supporters versus opponents factor on which party supporters' mean positions also correlate with the two other economic and political factors.[26] But the varimax rotation nowhere yields a separate xenophobia/ethnocentrism factor. While the varimax rotation provides more sharply defined factors than the principal components analysis, it does not allow for a simple two-dimensional representation of the results (the strength of principal components) nor the exploration of the significance or insignificance of race and ethnical issues for the structuring of party competition (the strength of a confirmatory factor analysis). We therefore report the results of the varimax rotations only in endnotes.

In order to further probe the relevance of immigration, race, and ethnocentrism and also deliver a sharper definition of the other relevant issue dimensions (markets/redistribution; authority/liberty), we performed a confirmatory factor analysis using unweighted least squares (ULS). Unlike maximum-likelihood estimations of confirmatory factor models, ULS does not assume that the values on the variables are normally distributed, a requirement several of our variables do not meet because they provide only dichotomous or trichotomous values. The greater robustness of ULS, however, comes at the price of standard goodness-of-fit measures that are not available for our estimation technique.

As in the case of the exploratory factor analysis, we report party supporters' mean positions on the three factors but standard deviations only if they are outside the typical range of roughly 0.5 to 0.7. The confirmatory factor analysis facilitates cross-national comparison because it generates closely similar factors in each country. Moreover, it will assist us in determining whether the supporters of competing parties actually endorse different positions on the critical dimensions. Next, it will determine whether the mean positions of each party's supporters on the three dimensions are correlated in the ways we have postulated. In other words, we expect supporters of successful rightist parties in Denmark, France, and Norway to be in the market-liberal, authoritarian, and ethnocentric field of the three-dimensional space. In contrast, the supporters of populist, antistatist parties in Austria and Italy should emphasize market liberalism and be more moderate on authoritarianism and ethnocentrism. Finally, the German postfascist Right should have followers who are not particularly market-liberal but are clearly ethnocentric nationalists with authoritarian predilections.

After establishing the general dimensionality of voter and party positions, in two further steps we explore how they are related to voters' social background in order to shed light on the coalitional structure of rightist party support. In particular, we would like to know whether parties with a right-authoritarian appeal underrepresent more educated voters who work in white-collar and professional employment. Conversely, we wish to explore whether small business and working-class voters are overrepresented among such parties. Cross-national variations in the extreme rightist parties' electoral coalitions should be correlated to the parties' relative emphasis on procapitalist or on authoritarian and racist appeals, with populist antistatist parties showing the least overrepresentation of workers and welfare chauvinist, but social-fascist parties the most. In a final analytical step, we employ multivariate estimation techniques to examine the association between the respondents' party preferences, their issue positions on the three dimensions constructed in the confirmatory factor analysis (capitalism/socialism, authoritarianism/libertarianism, and parochialism/cosmopolitanism), and sociodemographic background characteristics. If our theory is correct, electoral support for the extreme Right should not be primarily determined by the single issue of ethnocentrism but also by a mixture of authoritarian and procapitalist beliefs. It is quite possible that sociodemographic determinants of the right-wing vote wash out once issue dimensions are entered as predictors of right-wing party preferences.

As a final analytical step, we then predict the vote for extreme-rightist parties in a subsample that includes only voters for the extreme Right and the moderate Right. In that case, we expect that race/parochial constructions of citizenship make a greater difference on the decision to support the new Right than economic liberalism and political authoritarianism, an orientation that is likely to be shared also by other parties of the Right. Given that authoritarianism goes with rule compliance, it may even be possible that extreme-rightist voters are less authoritarian than the supporters of some traditional conservative parties and therefore undertake the unconventional step of supporting a highly controversial party. In other words, parties of the NRR are right-authoritarian, but, at least in some instances, racist and ethnocentric politics set them apart from the other parties of the Right.

Conclusions

The main advantage of our approach compared to its rivals is that it does not establish a single "syndrome" of the extreme Right but explores the conditions under which different variants of the contemporary Right appear: right-authoritarianism, populist antistatism, or welfare chauvinism. These variations are introduced not in an ad hoc fashion but within a theory of party competition. Other authors, who have undertaken interesting efforts to compare the European extreme Right, such as Betz (1993; 1994), Minkenberg (1993), or Taggart (1993), tend to downplay differences that reveal the different strategic possibilities and choices of the various parties. In a worst case scenario, everything is subsumed under the label of "populism," without appreciating the substantial distance between the German Republicans, the Danish Progress Party, and the Italian Northern League. Some authors do draw distinctions among right-wing parties, but these specifications remain ad hoc and unrelated to an explanatory account of the rise and performance of right-wing parties. In this vein, Husbands (1992c) talks about populist-nationalist and neofascist parties as the most important division of the contemporary extreme Right but does not provide a clear logic for explaining what makes these parties different and why they vary in programmatic appeal and electoral success. In contrast, our study accounts for similarity and differences on the extreme Right in terms of three variables: (1) economic affluence and the comprehensiveness of welfare states as a baseline precondition for the rise of the contemporary extreme Right; (2) the convergence of moderate-left and -right government parties or their partocratic symbiosis with the political economy; and (3) the political legacies of the historical extreme Right, especially the strength of fascist movements in the interwar period.

The parties with right-authoritarian appeal include the French National Front, the Danish and Norwegian Progress parties (with a somewhat more restrained authoritarianism), and also most likely the Swiss extreme-rightist parties (Automobilists and National Action/Swiss Democrats) and the Belgian *Vlaams Blok* (Flemish Block), parties we cannot examine here for want of comparable data. Next, the Freedom Party in Austria and most likely the Northern League in Italy cannot be clearly classified as right-authoritarian parties, but belong to the populist antistatist category. Both parties are radically free market procapitalist, but they do not express generalized authoritarian orientations to the extent found in all other parties of the extreme Right. The Austrian Freedom Party in particular does not fit the pattern of run-of-the-mill rightist parties. In 1990, the Northern League was situated somewhere between true NRR parties and the FPÖ, but by 1992–93 its greatest electoral boost came from the general breakdown of the Italian party system that overwhelmed the League's rightist residues, as we will discuss in chapter 5. Finally, there are the welfare chauvinist parties, such as the German Republicans, or the neofascist parties, like the MSI, which is itself divided into a more traditional and a more social-fascist wing. These parties have generally made fewer inroads in the electorates in recent years than one would expect given the rise of right-authoritarian or populist and antistatist parties elsewhere.

3

France: The National Front As Prototype of the New Radical Right

In the 1980s and 1990s, the French extreme Right that was organized by Jean-Marie Le Pen in the National Front comes close to an ideal-typical realization of what we have characterized as the "New Radical Right" or new right-authoritarianism in previous chapters. The National Front combines an appeal to vigorous state authority and paternalism in the family with an endorsement of free market capitalism in the economy. The state should be strong but limited; the family and the marketplace are complementary institutional forms that maintain order and stability in society.

While the endorsement of state authority and paternalism in the family belongs to the heritage of the French Right, the approval of market competition represents an ideological departure unique to the development of Le Pen's National Front within the broad field of French rightist political organizations. It is the result of a political entrepreneurism that had to dissociate itself from important earlier currents on the extreme Right. The new ideological appeal, however, could flourish electorally only once the configuration of the existing party system created an ideological space and an electorate available for the slogans of the National Front. These conditions arose in France when the conventional French Right began to unravel in its last years of government preceding François Mitterrand's victory in 1981 and particularly after the new socialist government's turn to a policy of *rigueur,* the French version of economic austerity policy in 1983. In a number of "secondary elections" since 1983, the National Front then thrived on the strategic dilemmas revealed by the established government and opposition parties. In the legislative elections of 1986, the National Front succeeded in becoming an important player in the parliamentary arena and in developing a characteristic profile and geographic ecology of voter support that bears out its characterization as a right-authoritarian party. As a consequence of this consolidation, however, the party has begun to encounter its own internal problems of strategic choice that mirror those of the moderate Right.

Currents in the French Extreme Right and the Emergence of the National Front

It is important to note from the very beginning that the realignment of the French extreme Right was not driven by the theme of immigration and race, but actually preceded the rise of this issue to high popular salience. While undoubtedly of critical importance for Le Pen's spectacular electoral success, this topic is embedded in a broader set of ideological propositions and interpretations of French society. It is precisely this web of meaning that makes the themes of race and immigration so potent an electoral appeal in French party competition.

The French extreme Right has always been a multifaceted political sector with a very large number of groups, clubs, sects and semiorganized political tendencies. Before World War II, monarchism in a number of variants, often linked to ultramontanist Catholic corporatism, and Bonapartism with a populist and antiparliamentary thrust found their place on the extreme Right, as did quasifascist elements that combined the call for authoritarian order with anticapitalist, antimarket sentiments. Bits and pieces of these currents influenced the Vichy regime established under Pétain after France's defeat by the Nazi armies in 1940. Critical experiences of the extreme Right after 1945 were the Poujadist movement and party, which peaked in the 1956 legislative election, and the movement of French settlers and military officers around the Algerian Liberation Front (FNL) to keep Algeria as part of France's national territory. These efforts led to the attempted military coup in Algiers in 1961. Nevertheless, it would be wrong to single out the Poujadist movement as the only relevant strain of the historical French extreme Right. What is characteristic, and theoretically relevant, is precisely the plurality and diversity of rightist movements in France, which make it a "complex mosaic" (Hainsworth 1992b, 30) of currents constantly able to adapt and redefine its message. Because the extreme Right in France was not characterized by the hegemony of a single fascist strand with limited variations in the same way as the German or Italian extreme Right in the post–World War II period, it became easier for emerging political entrepreneurs like Le Pen to experiment with new issue appeals and to craft innovative political coalitions. The legacy of the past did not cut down on the innovativeness of efforts to seize upon new electoral opportunities in the same way as in countries with past fascist regimes or at least authoritarian militarist governments, such as in Spain and Portugal.

To put Le Pen's National Front into sharper relief, a comparison with Pierre Poujade's "Union de Défense des Commercants et Artisans" (UDCA) is instructive. While the Poujadist movement began as a populist defense of the "little people"—agriculturists, artisans, and small retail shopkeepers—against the process of capitalist industrialization and more rigorous taxation of the petite bourgeoisie, it quickly acquired a broad nationalist, anti-Semitic, and antimodernist appeal (cf. Eatwell 1982, 76–77). When the established parties remained impervious to these sentiments, Poujade set up a political party, the "Union et Fraternité Française" which promptly won 11.6 percent of the national vote in the 1956 legislative elections. With De Gaulle's meteoric rise, based on a populist and nationalist cross-class appeal during the Algerian crisis of the Fourth Republic, the Poujadists, however, began to crumble quickly and disappeared.

It is critical to note that Poujade's movement had an *antimodernist* thrust that did not conceal its hostility to free market capitalism. While the National Front in many ways has assimilated the authoritarian and populist appeals of the Poujadist movement, it avoided the Poujadist anticapitalism that contributed to the latter's demise.[1] In the aftermath of the 1956 episode, this program lost its social and political viability. On the one hand, the rapid modernization of French social structure and the decline in numbers, but increase in wealth, of the French petite bourgeoisie made that group less predisposed to support antisystem groups. Later efforts to organize small business, such as Gérard Nicoud's "Comité d'Information et de Defense - Union Nationale des Travailleurs Independents" (CID-UNATI) voiced more specific grievances and operated as a special-interest pressure group to extract selective favors from the state, some of which were granted by the Pompidou government. Social change and government policy made the independent middle class unable to formulate a coherent program of political demands (Berger 1981). On the other hand, many of Poujade's former supporters were absorbed by the new Gaullist camp in French politics. As a consequence, the candidate of the far Right in the 1965 presidential election, Jean-Louis Tixier-Vignancour, abandoned a radical rightist stance in order to become palatable to a significant electorate, a strategy that yielded 5.3 percent of the vote in the first round of the presidential contest. In 1968, Tixier-Vignancour in fact joined the de Gaulle-Pompidou camp in the legislative elections (Hainsworth 1982, 148) and later supported Pompidou's bid for the presidency.

In addition to these developments on the Right, the leftist student movement of 1968 served as the catalyst for the emergence of a new "modernist" right that manifested itself first in 1967 in the "Rassemblement Europeén de la Liberté," and then in 1968 in "Groupe de Recherche et Etudes de la Civilisation Europeén" (GRECE) under the intellectual inspiration of Alain de Benoîst. Contemporary right-wing intellectuals in France share the tradition of rightist clubs in French history of creating sectarian and almost private spaces of political debate but also their eagerness to trigger intense public controversies and debates, something normally attributed to the French Left (Jaschke 1990, 55). While GRECE and similar intellectual groups, such as the "Club de l'Horloge," always kept an arms-length relationship to political parties, these new rightist thinkers showed politicians the viability of a New Right ideology that would dissociate itself from the traditional extreme Right without buying into the perspective of the dominant parties of the moderate Right. GRECE postulates the superiority of the Occident over the Orient and thus defined a parochial, particularist ethnic view not as a conflict between nation-states, but as a cultural conflict between regional civilizations. The rallying point of the Right here is transformed from the nation to the European cultural civilization that constitutes the boundary between friends and foes. Moreover, the new rightist intellectuals assert the natural inequality of individuals and peoples and attribute only a limited role to state authority in the economic sphere. These neo-Darwinian ideas about Western civilization and the uniqueness of capitalism in that context began to exert their influence on the National Front in the late 1970s (Camus 1989, 31). While Le Pen and the National Front never bought into the quasi-Gramscian strategy of the new intellectual Right to reestablish the "hegemony" of a rightist discourse on the ideological terrain (Hainsworth 1992b, 34), particularly the paganism and Eurocentrism invoked in the publications of GRECE, the intellectual new Right set a critical example of how rightist currents could become ideologically mobile and dissociate themselves from traditional rightist appeals and programmatic conceptions.

The National Front was founded in October 1972 as a result of the confluence of a number of right-wing sects and clubs with rather varied ideological orientations. Participants at the founding of the National Front were impressed by the 1972 electoral success of the Italian Social Movement (MSI), which at the time appeared to create a broad umbrella for the entire Italian Right and to focus its mobilization against the leftist student and workers' movements. In France, this attempt to create a unified rightist alternative to the challenge of the New Left brought together right-wing student organizations around the "Ordre Nouveau," founded in 1969, former supporters of Poujade and Tixier-Vignancourt, such as Le Pen, and a variety of other rightist groups (Gordon 1991, 24–25). The initial political compromise of the new party revolved around national-revolutionary and conservative ideas, seeking a "third way" between capitalism and communism, but promising a withdrawal of the state from the economy while also calling for a strong defense of small business (cf. Camus 1989, 20). This confused program that, among other things, also remained ambiguous on immigration did not offer a realistic prospect for welding together a new stable right-wing party formation. Indeed, over the ensuing 10 years the National Front stayed in the political wilderness, with one electoral defeat after another. The Front experienced a continuous coming and going of right-wing splinter groups (Camus 1989, 22–28). Most importantly, "Ordre Nouveau" split off in 1974 and set up a more moderate "Parti des Forces Nouvelles" (PFN) that embraced the more "modernist" wing of the far Right for whom the campaign of the National Front's presidential candidate in 1974, Jean-Marie Le Pen, was too wedded to the themes of the traditional Right, such as the reestablishment of order, security, and moral values.

In the 1979 European election, the PFN received 1.3 percent of the vote and a mini-Poujade party, with participation of Pierre Poujade, 1.4 percent. Le Pen's National Front called for abstention from the vote. Le Pen's party reached its nadir in 1981 when he failed to receive the 500 signatures from local notables necessary to run as a candidate in the presidential elections. By that time, however, Le Pen had already refurbished his party's appeal to take advantage of the coming opportunities that were to present themselves from 1983 on.[2] First of all, he had broken with the anticapitalist Poujadist heritage and in an unambiguous way made a commitment to popular capitalism. Le Pen began to espouse an extremely market-liberal, antistatist program with populist-authoritarian supplements: lower taxes, reduction of state intervention, and dissolution of the bureaucracy (Calderon 1985, 203). The model of the Thatcherite and Reaganite New Right in Britain and the United States left its mark on the development of the French extreme Right. One could go even further and claim that the FN's 1978 program was "Reaganite before Reagan" (Hainsworth 1992b, 48). At the same time, Le Pen gave up the anticlericalism of important currents in the traditional French Right, including his personal distaste for the church, and seized on the new Catholic fundamentalism represented by Bishop Lefevre, a dissident in the Catholic Church intent on preserving the Roman Catholic mass and opposing all liturgical reforms of the Second Vatican Council. "National Front rallies begin with a Latin mass, but its leader would not have a crucifix in his home" (Vaughan 1991, 220).[3] Already in 1979, a clear stance against women's choice on abortion and feminism highlighted the political appeal of the extreme Right and its compatibility with Catholic fundamentalists (Dumont, Lorien, and Criton 1985, 165). Finally, the entry of the "Union solidarité," headed by Jean-Pierre Stirbois, in 1978, brought the theme of racism and the exclusion of non-European immigrants from France into the party, a topic that gained increasing prominence in the early 1980s. At the same time, the anticapitalist national-revolutionary Right left the party. In contrast to the traditional Right in France, Le Pen thus prepared a new "catchall" extremism that appealed to bourgeois elements on anti-statist, free market themes, and Catholic authority but also to more secularized groups, particularly in the working class, on its racist rhetoric. This new programmatic mix was to be tested electorally in the early 1980s when the existing party system underwent critical changes.

The Convergence of the Established Left and Right
Parties in French Politics

With the reform of the Socialist Party in 1971 and the advent of the left opposition parties' Popular Front alliance strategy in 1972, the established French party system was divided into two sharply defined blocs located at polar opposites of the competitive space, at least as far as political rhetoric was concerned. This polarization reached its peak in the 1973–78 period and then crumbled and disappeared in the ensuing five years until 1983–84. In the era of intense polarization, clear-cut ideological competition between the two major party blocs and the sense in the electorate that they offered real political alternatives explain why a new extreme Right had no chance to achieve an electoral breakthrough. Because the two blocs were sharply defined, sympathizers of an extreme Right faced the full force of the "wasted vote" argument: support of a marginal New Right party might have withdrawn that critical increment of votes from the moderate Right that made the difference between victory over or defeat by the Left. The closeness of the competition between the two blocs was highlighted by the hard-fought 1978 parliamentary elections in which the government parties—the Gaullist "Rassemblement pour la Republique" (RPR) and the more liberal "Union pour la Démocratie Française" (UDF)—barely prevailed over the leftist opposition parties, the socialists and the communists.

The first signs of the dissolution of the two major party blocs already became evident in the late 1970s, but fully developed only around and after the 1981 presidential and legislative elections. On the side of the conservative-liberal government coalition, cracks in the alliance between UDF and RPR began to surface during the prime ministership of the Gaullist Jacques Chirac in the mid-1970s, whom President Giscard d'Estaing replaced by the liberal UDF economist Raymond Barre in 1976. From that time on and well into the 1980s, personal rivalries between Chirac and Giscard reinforced the political and strategic differences between Gaullists and the UDF.[4] The relative ineffectiveness of the Giscard administration in combating inflation and unemployment was a critical bone of contention. While the Gaullists in the 1960s had pursued a more state-interventionist economic policy than the hands-off monetarism and austerity policy implemented by Raymond Barre and the UDF, Jacques Chirac gradually moved to the economic Right and began to project himself as a Reagan-style market liberal in the 1980s. The indecisiveness and division of the conservative-liberal coalition throughout this period of time, however, as well as the government's mixed policy record, clearly dampened voter enthusiasm and eventually induced those voters on the Right who could never see themselves voting for the popular front parties to search for novel alternatives. In 1981, before Le Pen appeared to offer a viable political vehicle to voice their dissatisfaction with the incumbent government, such voters indirectly helped Mitterrand to come to power by abstaining in the presidential and parliamentary elections.

At the same time as divisions on the Right intensified, the Left also began to experience its own internal tensions. In many ways, these divisions were even more intense than those of the Right, but because the parties were in opposition rather than in government and were not obliged to make tough policy choices the Left was not damaged electorally by these internal divisions as much as the Right. In some respects, the socialists at least drew electoral benefits from their conflict with the communists because it showed the party's ability to contain communist radicalism and thus to make itself more attractive for centrist voters seeking political change, but without increasing the influence of the communist party.

In 1977, the PCF withdrew from the popular front alliance with the argument that the socialists had become "social democratized." Without returning to a common program agreement, the cooperation between socialists and communists was temporarily patched up in the run-up to the second round of the 1978 legislative elections. But when these elections confirmed the communists' suspicion that the Socialist Party was gradually gaining ground at the expense of the PCF, further chances for a renewed programmatic alliance between the two parties vanished. At the same time, however, the communists were a prisoner of Socialist Party strategy because they had no opportunity to form an alliance other than with the socialists. Thus, in 1981, when the socialists won the presidency and proceeded to conquer the absolute majority of seats in the National Assembly in the ensuing parliamentary elections with less than 38 percent of the popular vote, the PCF willy-nilly joined a coalition government in order to break out of the opposition ghetto for the first time since 1947.

The alliance between socialists and communists, however, lasted only until 1984. It began to crack in 1983 when Mitterrand's socialists engaged in a dramatic reversal of economic policy that led the government from a left-Keynesian demand-side strategy to a monetarist austerity and supply side policy akin to that of conservative and centrist governments elsewhere in advanced capitalist democracies. The coalition finally ruptured in 1984, when Mitterrand appointed a young technocrat, Laurent Fabius, as prime minister who proceeded to orient his government program toward the modernization of the French economy rather than the redistribution of resources from the better- to the worse-off.

After the differentiation of the moderate-right camp into followers of Chirac, Giscard, and Barre, the collapse of the united Left and the essentially centrist policy of the socialist government removed the last intellectual obstacle for rightist voters to consider a new alternative to the moderate-conservative parties. Whereas before the moderate Right could project itself as a "lesser evil" that would provide a barrier to the ascent of a united and radical Left, the socialists' centrist policies made them appear to be just another version of status quo politics. The pinnacle of this convergence was probably reached at the time of the 1984 European elections, the first national breakthrough of the National Front. In that election, the conventional conservative opposition parties fielded a joint list headed by a centrist politician, Simone Veil, who had made her reputation with a liberalization of the abortion law in the mid-1970s when serving in the cabinet under president Giscard d'Estaing. Because-right wing voters could no longer see a clear difference between the record of the moderate-conservative government until 1981, the centrist Veil list in 1984, and the socialist government since its turnabout in 1983, their quest for a policy alternative began to turn to new competitors. Cynicism with the conventional parties assembled in the "gang of four" (Safran 1993, 35) and disaffection with politics became widespread (Fysh and Wolfreys 1992, 312).

Two related developments enhanced the opportunities for a new rightist party in the wake of the disappearance of a clearly contoured leftist bloc. First, some leftist voters, especially among blue-collar clienteles, were disappointed with the performance of the socialist government and began to search for alternatives (Charlot 1986). Since they, like many former rightists, also had little confidence in the traditional parties of the Right, they became available for the appeal of new parties. In this sense, France experienced a generalized crisis of confidence in the established parties in the mid-1980s (cf. Schain 1987).

Second, the communists, in their desperate quest to find an electoral niche and to rebuild their electoral base in areas protected from socialist competition, had in 1981 already begun to play with the fire of the immigration issue in their electoral campaign appeals. The influx of immigrants from the Maghreb countries imposed strains particularly on blue-collar municipalities with cheaper housing where often communist mayors had to cope with the new fiscal, social, and cultural challenges imposed on these towns by the influx of foreign workers. In this situation, the PCF engaged in an ambivalent strategy. On the one hand, the party employed the immigration issue to demonstrate the need for better social protection and services for all poor in French society and accused the central government of ignoring the plight of the municipalities. On the other, however, in subtle ways communist politicians played on the racist and xenophobic predispositions of those voters in vulnerable labor market positions who could feel most threatened by the immigrants. The event that symbolizes the ambivalent PCF policy most clearly was the order of the communist mayor of Vitry-Sur-Seine to remove immigrant squatters by employing bulldozers to destroy their makeshift housing (cf. Plenel and Rollat 1984, 159–65). The ambiguity of the national communist party leadership on race and immigration, however, may have backfired in the 1981 electoral campaign because it divided the party's own electorate between more xenophobic authoritarians and more multiculturalist libertarians, particularly among the intellectual strata sympathetic to the party (cf. Schain 1988, 604–7).

In a sense, changes in the dynamics of party competition among the four dominant French parties of the late 1970s and early 1980s thus created an opening for the National Front both in negative and in positive terms. In negative terms, the waning of left/right polarization allowed voters to begin to experiment with new parties without having to fear that, as a consequence, a government could come into office that would be much worse than their second-best party preference. In positive terms, the established parties in their own ways introduced the themes on which the National Front could thrive later on because it could present them in a more credible way than representatives of the old parties. The Gaullist Chirac moved from a more statist economic policy to Reaganite free-marketeering, but, given his past record, was obviously less credible with this new approach than a fresh contender. In a similar vein, on the Left, the communists began to toy with the immigration issue but failed to deliver a clear message, given their own internal divisions on this issue. Also, when the conventional conservatives tried the same theme in the second half of the 1980s, they lacked credibility and only helped to improve the legitimacy of the National Front. Thus, radical market reforms and ethnocentrism were placed on the political agenda by established parties, but in rather unconvincing ways. It now required only the appropriate "trigger mechanisms" to give an authoritarian, ethnocentric promarket party its electoral momentum.

Secondary Elections and the Mobilization of the NRR

Even if structural conditions are favorable, new parties take off only if a number of precipitating conditions encourage voters to experiment with new electoral choices. Here, "secondary elections" and the mass media play a critical role. For new and unproven parties, local elections have the particular advantage that they mobilize nationally unrepresentative distributions of voter preferences and may revolve around salient issues that allow a new party to make a breakthrough in a bounded arena of party competition that would be impossible at a higher level of territorial voter aggregation. Once maverick parties have succeeded in local secondary elections, their accomplishment is amplified and disseminated by the selective attention of the mass media. Always in search of the spectacular and often playing on populist antiestablishment resentments of the "common man," outsider parties are the darlings of media attention. Those who successfully challenge the political establishment can count on the media to highlight and talk up their success quickly. Thus, at least for a certain period of time, national attention is drawn to a locally successful small new party. In this window of opportunity, the new party must quickly act to broaden its challenge to the political system and keep the attention of the mass media and the voters. This is most easily achieved by a chain of secondary elections that draw in ever wider electoral constituencies and eventually climax in a national election bout. In this process, the new challenger gradually becomes the object of strategic controversies within the established parties about whether or not to coalesce with the new contender where this may be possible or necessary to prevent a government of established rival parties. Such debates lend credibility to the new party and contribute to its growing prominence and acceptance by the electorate. Moreover, extremist right-wing parties in particular may prompt left-wing counteractions, such as demonstrations and public campaigns warning against a new threat of fascism. Such activities actually contribute to the new party's "underdog" status. Thus, left-wing efforts to stop a rightist party unintentionally may reinforce its growth because such activities prompt those people who always felt deep antipathy to its leftist opponents to rally around the new flag.[5]

The French National Front went through this exact sequence of events and media-induced amplification of its appeal. The secondary local election that triggered initial national interest in the National Front took place in the small dormitory town of Dreux on the outskirts of the Paris region. By the 1970s, about half of Dreux's population lived in public housing, and unskilled laborers accounted for 64 percent of the residents. From the 1960s onward, immigrants had moved into the area and represented about 30 percent of the residents by the 1980s.[6] In 1978, LePen's close associate Jean-Pierre Stirbois moved into this community and began to organize support for the National Front based on racist and antiimmigration appeals. In the cantonal elections of March 1982, when the National Front received only 0.2 percent nationwide, it garnered 12.58 percent in Dreux West and 9.58 percent in Dreux East.

In the 1970s, the town of Dreux was governed by an alliance of the Left, so that the moderate rightist parties had every incentive to rally all opposition forces in a joint effort to topple the local municipal administration. As a consequence, after the FN had repeated its 1982 performance in the first round of the 1983 municipal elections and the Left had failed to win an outright majority, local RPR and UDF politicians entered an alliance with the FN for the runoff election. The second round of the local elections was narrowly lost by this coalition against the candidate of the Left, but, the outcome was in fact so close that new elections were required to determine a clear-cut winner in September 1983. In the first round of that election, Stirbois, the candidate of the National Front, received no less than 16.7 percent of the local vote. Between rounds, the RPR-UDF again chose to team up with the Front National, and Stirbois defeated the candidate of the left alliance. "The victory of Dreux liberated a political space for the extreme Right" (Charlot 1986, 43).

With the by-election of Dreux the National Front achieved several objectives at once. First, it accomplished an electoral success in a "secondary" (or even "tertiary") election at the local level at a time when no bigger electoral news could overshadow it. Second, it triggered a vigorous strategic debate within the moderate-conservative parties because their local affiliates had been enticed into joining hands with the new extreme-rightist force. Over night, this made the National Front a plausible electoral alternative for many conservative voters but also raised questions about whether mainstream conservatism could hold on to more centrist voters who definitely disapproved of any alliance with the extreme Right. Third, the National Front's local success and its impact on intraparty controversies in the moderate-conservative camp stirred up tremendous media attention for the new party. This helped to publicize its goals and at least indirectly contributed to the reputation and credibility of the National Front, even though much of this publicity was openly hostile to the objectives of the party. The mere fact that the party was talked about was probably more important than the media's assessment of its political motives and objectives. After Jean-Marie Le Pen appeared on the television interview program *L'heure de verité* on February 13, 1984, four months after the success of Dreux, the National Front's ratings in opinion polls shot up from 3.5 percent to 7.0 percent (Ignazi 1989, 65). Fourth, the success of the National Front triggered counterdemonstrations by the radical Left wherever Le Pen was scheduled to speak (cf. Dumont, Lorien, and Criton 1985, 204–5), providing even more publicity to the new party and thus unintentionally aiding its growth. Many of those who definitely did not want to be associated with the extreme Left and disliked its intellectualism and bohemian style now began to perceive the National Front as a plausible political alternative. The Left's attention to the extreme Right contributed to the latter's political standing and facilitated the success of the National Front's antiintellectual, populist appeal.

The next electoral opportunity for the French radical Right offered itself in a nationwide secondary election, the European election of June 1984. Some claim that the proportional representation format of that election, with a 5 percent threshold, further helped the National Front, but the Dreux experience shows that a majoritarian system with second-round runoffs also allows for the growth of new parties. Duverger (1954; 1986), the initiator of the modern debate about the relationship between electoral laws and party system formats, had always been keenly aware of the fragmenting effect of a two-round majoritarian system that allows a multitude of parties to run in the first round and then bargain over parliamentary representation through second-round coalitions with other parties. Thus, it is unclear whether the proportional format of the European election in fact helped or hurt the National Front.

The National Front was aided in the 1984 contest by the internal division of the moderate Right into a centrist list made up of UDF and RPR candidates headed by Simone Veil and a more rightist, dissenting Gaullist list. This division yet again demonstrated the indecisiveness of the pre-1981 government parties as well as their inability to offer a clear alternative to the socialist government. Media attention, leftist mobilization, and divisions within the moderate Right are likely to have contributed to the National Front's spectacular result of 11.2 percent nationwide in the European election. In Dreux, its initial point of success, the party collected no less than 19.1 percent.

The rise of the National Front first rallied the old sympathizers of the radical Right but also bourgeois elements dissatisfied with the moderate-rightist parties. This is suggested by the flow of voters and the ecological pattern of National Front support in the 1984 European election. At least initially, in 1984 the FN was overrepresented among conservative independent professionals, petite bourgeois, and farmers—not just among lower-income Frenchmen living in depressed suburban areas with a high proportion of immigrants from Maghreb countries. It was also obvious that the new party attracted voters primarily at the expense of the moderate-bourgeois parties. In 1984, 18 percent of those who supported Jacques Chirac's bid for the French presidency in 1981 voted for Le Pen, 22 percent of those who voted for the hard-line Gaullist Debré, but only 6 percent of Mitterrand's and 2 percent of Marchais' voters did the same (Charlot 1984, 40).

The National Front's strength in the bourgeois quarters of Paris shows this pattern of rather dispersed socioeconomic support impressively. The party did not perform well only in urban blue-collar areas. The ecological pattern of National Front support began to change in the 1986 election when workers and small businesspeople became more prominent in its electorate and when professionals and the white-collar salariat clearly became the underrepresented electorates inside the new extremist party's voter coalition (Mitra 1988, 55; Hainsworth 1992b, 45).

The year 1984 constituted the breakthrough of the National Front onto the national political scene in France. Much has been made of the socialists' change of the French electoral law to proportionality before the 1986 legislative elections as an important statutory reform making it more attractive for conservative voters to support the extreme Right. The socialists, it is argued, in their zeal to prevent a solid moderate right-wing majority in the parliament, created a new extremist monster that split the Right into two factions expected to be too deeply divided to form a viable coalition. While it is undeniable that the "mechanical effect" of proportional representation in 1986 was to weaken the center-right majority by converting votes into seats without giving a great advantage to the larger parties, it is an entirely different question whether the "psychological effect" of the new electoral law was to induce such people to vote for the National Front who otherwise might have supported the center-right parties. As we have said, two-round majoritarian systems encourage party fragmentation. Moreover, the return of French parliamentary elections to the two-round majoritarian voting system in 1988 did not bring about a dramatic decline of National Front support. The party's electoral yield fell by only 0.1 percent from 9.9 percent (1986) to 9.8 percent (1988).[7]

Electoral Entrenchment of the French NRR

The critical question in the entrenchment of New Right parties is whether they represent "single-issue" concerns that stand and fall with the salience of the immigration question or whether they assemble a distinct social constituency around a broader programmatic appeal that has been characterized by right-libertarian or right-authoritarian themes. It is clear from the programmatic statements and the appeals issued by Le Pen and his candidates in the 1980s that the party tried to place itself on the authoritarian Right. Unlike much of the traditional French extreme Right, the National Front is not anticapitalist, but "Reaganite" (Safran 1993, 21). Moreover, there was no "objective" crisis in immigration that could have triggered the attractiveness of the single-issue appeal. In fact, the proportion of immigrants in the workforce did not change in the 1970s and 1980s, and there was no additional "problem load" that could have triggered the violent reaction to the single issue of immigration (Fysh and Wolfreys 1992, 321). The ethnocentric anti-immigrant rhetoric served as a catalyst that was associated with a broader web of ideological orientations. We will now report some French electoral studies both at the ecological and the individual level that tend to confirm this interpretation. This does not exclude the fact, however, that a critical minority of New Right voters in France is singularly motivated by racism and immigration when it enters the voting booth to cast its ballots in favor of the National Front. We will then turn to the *World Values Survey* in order to present a more rigorous test of rival theories of extreme-rightist electoral entrenchment.

Perrineau (1989) found rather strong evidence that at least initially, in the 1984 European Election, the immigration issue may have been decisive for Le Pen voters because there was a rather striking correlation between urbanization, the proportion of immigrants in a community, and electoral support of Le Pen's party at the ecological level.[8] The problem, however, is that this relationship is apparently not very robust across levels of geographic aggregation and over time. Mayer (1989, 249) highlights the puzzle that a reasonable correlation between the proportion of immigrants in the residential population and National Front support can be found at the departmental (county) level, whereas it is very weak at the local municipal level. The ethnic mix appears to have an electoral "halo effect" beyond the immediately concerned communities. In contrast, the diverse ethnic composition of communities with large proportions of immigrants is not directly reflected in an extraordinary success of the National Front. A detailed analysis of the Paris region yields only a rather unimpressive correlation between right-extremist success and the presence of foreigners in the parliamentary elections (1986: $r = 0.51$; 1988: $r = 0.47$). Moreover, in the elections preceding 1988, the tendency to vote National Front is most pronounced in areas with many Mediterranean immigrants, yet not in the areas with a strong presence of (mostly poor) immigrants from the Maghreb countries (252).

This finding is consistent with the observation reported earlier that initially, in 1984, the National Front excelled in the most bourgeois quarters of Paris, and its electorate appears to have been better educated than the average citizen (Mitra 1988, 56). It was not simply the economic threat of North African immigrants that scared lower-income blue-collar workers into supporting a racist party. Instead, the opportunity to support an electorally effective extreme-rightist party that would cater to a range of demands not represented by the moderate Right attracted many voters, and particularly bourgeois voters, who were predisposed to a more general extremist right-wing. As the National Front grew, however, the initial overrepresentation of the well-educated and the liberal professions and the underrepresentation of the working class vanished and gave way to a blue-collar/small-business dominance propelling the success of the new party. The right-wing constituency among educated strata may be small, but it could be mobilized quickly. When this support pool was fully exploited, further growth of the National Front could come only from breaking into those groups and strata particularly amenable to authoritarian and ethnocentric appeals. In all elections since 1984, there is a strong negative correlation between the proportion of intellectual-professional jobs in an electoral precinct and the electoral success of the National Front (Mayer 1989, 265).

Although workers are overrepresented in the National Front electorate, there is little evidence of a direct transfer of votes from the Communist Party to Le Pen's National Front. Such a transfer would indicate in a dramatic way that workers who were staunch leftist supporters of economic redistribution suddenly might vote on political and cultural questions and be swayed by the racist slogans of the National Front. But at the individual and the ecological level, studies disconfirm that former communists are especially likely to vote for the National Front (Platone and Rey 1989). From the beginning, the National Front was weakest in cities whose municipal government was dominated by the communists, but strongest where the center-right government parties controlled government majorities (Penel and Rollat 1984, 118).

How does this finding jibe with the observation that the National Front recruits an overproportional share of its electorate from young, male, working-class, and nonelite voters? In 1988, for example, 21 percent of industrial workers, 20 percent of farmers, and 27 percent of independent businesspeople supported the National Front, but only 11 percent in the managerial and professional occupations (cf. Cole 1988; Perrineau 1989, 56). A possible explanation is that younger workers in particular who have not been "encapsuled" by the parties of the Left and who are not immersed into a tightly knit leftist working-class subculture are prone to vote for the far Right. For them, the attractions of economic leftism were never strong, and they could more easily shift to voting on ethnic and political issues where their sentiments are close to parochial and authoritarian positions (Hainsworth 1992b, 45).

Individual-level studies illustrate that the National Front draws on a rather varied electorate, only a limited segment of which is primarily drawn in by the party's ethnocentrist and even racist appeal. According to Mitra's analysis of the 1984 European election, the primarily racist electorate amounted to less than 40 percent of the National Front's voters and was distinctly working class (Mitra 1988, 58). It is outweighed by a traditional rightist group rooted in the Gaullist party and more concerned with free markets as well as by Catholic fundamentalists who abandoned the centrist RPR/UDF list headed by Simone Veil. A further small group amounting to less than 10 percent of the party's electorate consisted of young workers without clear-cut political affiliation (Mitra 1988, 59).

Immigration is definitely a salient issue for National Front voters, but it is rivaled by general law-and-order concerns (Lagrange and Perrineau 1989, 229). National Front voters stand out in their high valuation of authority (245). The proportion of National Front voters who endorse the statement that France has too many foreigners distinguishes the party much less from its competitors than the proportion that emphasizes the need for law and order. In 1990, 68 percent of the entire population endorsed the proposition that there are too many foreigners, especially farmers (84%), pensioners (74%), workers (72%) and small businesspeople (67%), but less so lower white-collar employees (65%), intermediate professionals (56%) and advanced managerial and professional occupations (50%). Among political parties, 98 percent of the National Front endorsed the statement, but so did 84 percent of the sympathizers with the Gaullist RPR and 76 percent of the UDF supporters. At the other extreme, the same opinion was shared by only 52 percent of the Communist Party's voters, 53 percent of ecologists, and 62 percent of socialists (LeGall 1991, 121). In a similar vein, Lewis-Beck and Mitchell (1993) conclude that a complex interaction of "materialist" values of law and order and economic well-being, including the threats of crime, immigration, and unemployment, taken together distinguish National Front voters from the electorate of the moderate-rightist parties.

The ideological proximity of National Front and moderate-Right voters is evidenced by voter flow analyses. In the 1988 presidential elections, 54 percent of those supporting Le Pen in the first round supported Chirac in the second round, while only 17 percent cast their vote for Mitterrand. The remaining 29 percent stayed home (Perrineau 1989, 50). In the 1988 parliamentary elections, socialists and communists lost about 4 percent of those voters who had supported them in the 1986 legislative elections to the National Front, whereas the moderate Right lost about 13 percent of its 1986 voters to Le Pen according to exit polls (Boy and Dupoirier 1990, 181). Moreover, 91 percent of first-round National Front voters proceeded to cast their vote in the second round for an RPR or UDF candidate, but where a National Front representative was ahead, moderate-bourgeois voters did not transfer their votes to him (56).

Let us now see whether the 1990 *World Values Survey* can cast further

TABLE 3.1. Ideological Divisions in France: An Exploratory Factor Analysis

	Factor I (Left-)Libertarian versus (Right-)Authoritarian	Factor II Capitalist Right versus Socialist Left	Factor III Capitalist Ecology versus Socialist Production
Economic Issues			
1. Business management	−.35	+.45	+.35
2. Income Inequality	−.14	+.57	+.19
3. Competition	−.19	+.34	+.50
Ecology and Industry			
4. Environmental taxes	+.28	−.11	+.41
5. Urgency of ecology	+.29	+.17	+.31
6. No nuclear plants	+.35	−.50	+.45
Race and Nation			
7. Objections to neighbors of different race	−.29	−.02	−.26
8. Priority for own nationals in labor markets	−.53	−.13	−.02
9. National pride	−.50	−.03	+.30
Authority and Participation			
10. More respect for authority	−.55	−.18	+.18
11. Confidence in the army	−.58	+.07	+.24
12. Would participate in lawful demonstration	+.52	+.28	−.04
13. Would participate in disarmament protest	+.45	−.50	+.34
Women and Family			
14. Choice over abortion	+.48	+.31	−.11
15. Women as homemakers	−.30	−.31	+.09
16. Women's right to a job	+.50	+.29	+.27
Eigenvalues	2.77	1.60	1.27
Party Factor Scores			
Ecologists (N = 70)	+.54	+.11	+.38
Communist Party (N = 19)	+.39	−.82	−.87
Socialist Party (N = 156)	+.40	−.07	+.01
Union for French Democracy (N = 73)	−.49	+.41	−.01
Rally for the Republic (N = 33)	−.84	+.44	+.13
National Front (N = 22)	−.69	+.82	−.40

Source: World Values Survey 1990. Own calculations.

light on the emerging picture of a broad right-authoritarian political appeal issued by the National Front. Table 3.1 reports the results of the principal components factor analysis of issue positions whose design was explained in chapter 2. The results are sufficiently clear-cut to skip a varimax rotation of the factor axes. At first glance, the statistical results only partially confirm the theoretical argument outlined in chapter 1. The most powerful factor discriminating among people's issue opinions loads strongly on almost all of the libertarian versus authoritarian indicators (items 7 through 16). It pits libertarians who want less respect for authority, have little confidence in the army, oppose racial discrimination, are not particularly proud of being French, and have no objections to neighbors of a foreign race, but would participate in lawful demonstrations (such as those for disarmament) against authoritarians with racist and nationalist inclinations. At the same time, the libertarians subscribe to an egalitarian role for women in labor markets and would give them the right to choose an abortion, whereas authoritarians oppose such views.

The authoritarian/libertarian divide also loads on the six issue items that directly or indirectly concern capitalist governance structures (items 1 through 6). But these loadings are comparatively weak. Libertarians tend to be slightly anticapitalist and environmentalist, but this tendency is not pronounced. Instead, capitalism and ecologism load on the second and the third factor in table 3.1. Judged by the eigenvalues, these factors have much less power to structure popular opinions than the authoritarian/libertarian divide. Nevertheless, there is a capitalism versus socialism second factor that also loads on gender relations and disarmament, and there is an independent ecology versus production dimension that actually associates procapitalist positions with environmental protection (factor III).[9]

This configuration of major and minor factors would become a problem for the theory of left-libertarian versus right-authoritarian political competition if the parties took positions on each dimension independently of their positions on the other dimensions, particularly if mean party positions on the first and second dimension were unrelated. However, an inspection of the average position of each party's voters on the three factors, reported at the bottom of table 3.1, reveals that with the exception of the French ecologists there is a strong correlation between each party's position on the first and the second factors. The third factor distinguishes antienvironmental communists and National Front supporters, at one extreme, and ecologists, at the other, but none of the major parties.[10] The division between ecology and production is thus a minor independent competitive dimension that underlines a distinctiveness of PCF and FN in the electoral space but is also illuminated in different ways by the parties' positions on the first two dimensions. The third dimension suggests that the two productionist parties shape the working class electorate that expresses strong antienvironmental sentiments.

Figure 3.1 visualizes the relations among party positions on the two strongest factors. The vertical axis represents the left-libertarian versus right-authoritarian dimension, the horizontal the socialist versus capitalist economic

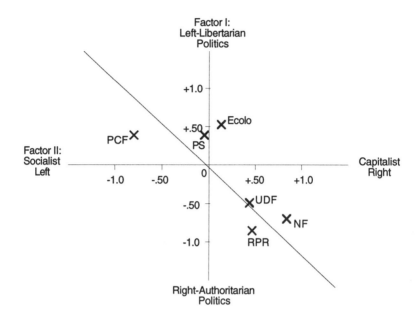

Fig. 3.1. The political space of European democracies: France

options. The figure clearly reveals the strong correlation between the parties' mean factor positions on the first and the second factors. What is particularly important for our concerns is that the supporters of the National Front are indeed located at the right-authoritarian pole of the first dimension, as well as in the most capitalist position on the second dimension. They occupy a distinctive ideological space with a coherent political appeal. The mean ideological position of the FN sympathizers thus closely mirrors the ideological appeals of the party leadership that we discussed above and in chapter 2 with respect to Laver and Hunt's expert judgments of party stances.

The ideological constraint between the first and the second factors can also be demonstrated by employing respondents' factor scores as predictors of general ideological orientations (table 3.2). Left/right self-placements are best predicted by the authoritarian/libertarian factor, but also by the pure capitalist/socialist factor, and marginally the ecology factor. Postmaterialism is primarily

TABLE 3.2.   General Ideological Dispositions Predicted by Voters' Issue Positions (Factor Scores of the Exploratory Factor Analysis) in France

	Constant		Factor I (Left-)Libertarian versus (Right-)Authoritarian		Factor II Capitalist Right versus Socialist Left		Factor III Capitalist Ecology versus Socialist Production		adj. R^2
	PE	t	PE	t	PE	t	PE	t	
Left/Right Self-Placement	4.98	64.4	-.99	-12.89	+.38	4.94	+.18	2.14	.30 *** (N = 488)
Postmaterialism	2.06	83.17	+.25	9.98	+.10	4.04	+.03	1.82	.16 *** (N = 573)
Church attendance[a]	6.36	79.83	+.58	6.80	-.02	-.24	-.14	-1.62	.08 (N = 571)

Source: World Values Survey 1990. Own calculations.
Note: PE = parameter estimate; t = t ratio.
***significant at the .001 level
**significant at the .01 level
*significant at the .05 level
[a]Scale inversed: high values indicate infrequent or no church attendance.

due to libertarian orientations, although more socialist leanings contribute as well. Church attendance, finally, relates only to the authoritarian/libertarian factor.

Combined into a single competitive dimension, the party sympathizers' mean positions on factors I and II are sufficient to establish the uniqueness of the National Front in the French electoral space. Curiously, however, the racial question (item 7) plays only a minor role in this picture. Its factor loadings are weak on all three factors. Is there perhaps a hidden weak dimension that really explains how voters of the moderate-conservative camp are distinguished from the extreme-rightist FN voters? It is very possible that beyond the general procapitalist and authoritarian location of the FN the party's particular position on immigration and race tips the balance among right-authoritarian voters whether they will affiliate with the FN or with RPR and UDF.

The opinion data reported by LeGall (1991, 121) on the French public's aversion to immigrants tend to disconfirm this speculation. We already saw that Gaullist voters are almost as ethnocentric as Le Pen voters. Also, a French survey study that employs rather different measures of voters' issue positions generates a dimensionality of the French electoral space strikingly similar to the 1990 *World Values Survey* analyzed here and finds only weak evidence for the independent influence of ethnocentrism and racism on the Le Pen vote. Based on a survey conducted during the French presidential campaign of 1988, Chiche (1990) measured 10 scales, including ethnocentrism, traditionalism, sexual permissiveness, authoritarianism, support of the market economy, and economic liberalism, to name only the most important. The first and second factors are almost identical to those found in the present analysis and account for 24 percent of the variance. In the same vein, the ideological profile of the supporters of presidential candidates reflects the same configuration as that reported in figure 3.1, with the candidates of the National Front, Jean-Marie Le Pen, and of the conservative RPR, Jacques Chirac, being located closely together on the authoritarian Right with strong procapitalist views, whereas Mitterrand was positioned in a moderate left-libertarian and socialist position. Chiche (1990, 223) found only a weak separate Le Pen factor that explains 3.5 percent of the variance and extracts a well-defined subpopulation of ethnocentric authoritarians who are favorable to the market economy and to economic liberalism.

To explore this matter a step further, we have run a confirmatory factor analysis that forces the appearance of a racist-xenophobic factor, in addition to separate authoritarian/libertarian and capitalist/socialist factors (table 3.3). From this analysis, it is clear that the National Front, followed by the RPR, is the party with the most racist electorate. These two parties are quite clearly set apart from the organizations belonging to the moderate Union for French Democracy and the political Left. The National Front is situated within a

TABLE 3.3.   Ideological Divisions in France: Confirmatory Factor Analysis (missing values set equal to zero)

	Capitalism versus Socialism	Authoritarianism versus Libertarianism	Parochialism versus Cosmopolitanism
A. Economic Distribution			
1. For more income inequality	+.37	—	—
2. For private business ownership	+.63	—	—
3. For more competition	+.47	+.03	—
4. For owner-managed business	+.52	+.17	—
B. Libertarian versus Authoritarian Issues			
5. Postmaterialism	—	−.51	—
6. Respect for authority	—	+.52	—
7. Participation in lawful demonstration	—	−.54	—
8. Women's right to abortion	—	−.47	—
9. Role of housewife fulfilling	—	+.29	—
C. Cosmopolitan/Particularist Dimension			
10. Acceptance of a neighbor of different race	—	–	+.64
11. Acceptance of a foreigner as a neighbor	—	–	+.86
12. Members of one's nationality have priority in the labor market	—	+.45	+.25
Average Factor Scores of Party Followers			
Communist Party ($N = 21$)	−.82	+.19	−.58
Socialist Party ($N = 250$)	−.15	−.25	−.10
Ecologists ($N = 97$)	+.02	−.35	−.19
UDF/Center Democrats ($N = 39$)	+.32	+.02	−.01
UDF/Republicans ($N = 72$)	+.30	+.26	+.19
RPR/Gaullists ($N = 58$)	+.60	+.39	+.53
National Front ($N = 24$)	+.34	+.18	+.74

Source: World Values Survey 1990. Own calculations.

Note: The confirmatory factor analysis was estimated using unweighted least squares (ULS).

crowd of conservative parties located in the procapitalist and authoritarian area and does not even clearly distinguish itself in terms of ethnocentrism from at least one segment of that moderate Right, the Gaullist RPR. How, then, could Le Pen mobilize voters at all successfully? The explanation is likely to be found in the strategic history of the moderate French Right and the RPR in particular. While the RPR electorate is staunchly right-wing, the party elites have vacillated between rightist and moderate positions because they are forced to work with the UDF. As a consequence, they have lost credibility among many formerly conservative voters or could never earn it among young ethnocentric working-class authoritarians.

The evidence presented so far does not yet allow us to estimate the "net effect" of procapitalist, authoritarian, or racist views on party choice. Before we explore this relationship, let us first make one further detour that will allow us to introduce some controls for the final analysis of party choice. We have hypothesized that right-authoritarian parties, such as the FN, rely on a particular coalitional structure of their electorates that overrepresents workers and small businesspeople, but underrepresents the professions and white-collar employment. These occupational differences are driven by levels of education and a number of unobserved variables, such as the occupational task structure and the sector of employment. In order to determine the National Front's coalitional structure, we have analyzed these four occupational categories, together with a residual group of those not active in the labor force, in two complementary ways (see table 3.4). First, we report the percentage of respondents within each occupational group who support selected opinions connected to beliefs about the economy, political process and individual autonomy, and citizenship. Workers and independent producers (businesspeople and farmers) are clearly more authoritarian, antifeminist, racist, and nationalist than professionals and white-collar employees.

The second section of table 3.4 then analyzes the occupational support for different parties. It clearly shows that workers and small business are overrepresented in the National Front electorate, a configuration that is quite different in the mainstream conservative French parties. We infer from these data that the National Front builds a *social coalition* that relies primarily on small businesspeople and farmers, who are motivated by strong procapitalist and authoritarian preferences as well as xenophobic resentments, and on elements of the working class whose decisive criterion of affiliation with the National Front is authoritarianism and racism, yet not procapitalism. The socioeconomic attribute both of these occupational groups have in common is lack of high formal education. National Front voters, but also those of the Gaullists and Communists, have much lower levels of educational achievements than the Republicans, the Socialists, or the Greens. Only 13 percent of National Front supporters finished their education at age 20 or later, about the same as in the RPR (13 percent) and the PCF (16 percent). In contrast, 53 percent of ecology party supporters, 38 percent of UDF supporters, and 34 percent of Socialist Party sympathizers belong to that group.

To summarize the linkage between party preference, on the one hand, and sociodemographic attributes, general ideological orientations, views of capitalism, authoritarian/libertarian politics, and racism, as measured by the three confirmatory factors, on the other, multiple regressions may be instructive in helping us isolate the political punch of ethnocentrism (table 3.5). The first

TABLE 3.4. Occupation, Ideological Dispositions, and Party Preferences in France

	Professions (percent)	White Collar (percent)	Nonactive in the Labor Force (percent)	Workers (percent)	Independent Business and Farmers (percent)
A. Issue Positions					
1. For business-managed enterprises	23.9 (117)	20.7 (396)	29.8 (151)	12.7 (165)	47.7 (86)
2. Endorse stronger authority	36.9 (122)	55.2 (393)	73.4 (158)	67.9 (165)	66.3 (92)
3. Against women's choice of abortion	23.6 (127)	22.0 (414)	30.2 (169)	36.2 (174)	44.8 (94)
4. Against neighbors of different race	6.9 (130)	7.4 (422)	8.1 (174)	14.4 (180)	14.6 (96)
5. Proud to belong to one's nation	26.3 (118)	27.6 (388)	41.5 (164)	46.4 (166)	44.6 (92)
N for occupational group	92	295	100	122	68
B. Percentage of Occupational Group Supporting a Party					
Communist Party	3.4	4.4	4.1	11.3	3.3
Socialist Party	44.9	45.6	34.0	45.3	23.3
Ecologists	19.1	22.2	16.5	9.4	5.0
Union for French Democracy	20.5	15.5	26.1	12.3	35.0
RPR/Gaullists	5.6	5.6	16.5	8.5	23.3
National Front	4.4	4.0	3.1	8.5	10.0

Source: World Values Survey 1990. Own calculations.

TABLE 3.5. Determinants of Political Orientations and of Party Preferences in France

A. Determinants of the French National Front Vote, Entire French Sample
(Maximum likelihood estimates)

	Parameter estimate	Standard error	Probability	Percentage of voters supporting the rightist party if all other variables are held constant but value on the focal variable is at its—	
				Minimum	Maximum
Intercept	−5.15	3.31	.12		
Market Liberalism (Factor I)	+.65	.28	.02	0.3	3.1
Authoritarianism (Factor II)	−.08	.31	.80	1.3	1.0
Parochialism/Racism (Factor III)	+.45	.15	.003	1.1	4.2
Gender (Female = 2)	−.30	.42	.47	1.5	1.1
Age	+.001	.01	.94	1.1	1.1
Education	−.13	.09	.15	2.2	0.7
Business or Farmer	+.67	.72	.35	1.1	2.2
Professional	+.27	.95	.78	1.1	1.5
White-Collar	+.47	.67	.48	1.1	1.8
Worker	+.76	.70	.30	1.1	2.4

Note: Percentage of concordant cases: 72.9; Cases N: 933 (missing values on the independent variables were assigned mean values); Missing cases M: 79.

B. Determinants of Vote: Extreme Right Versus Moderate Right Voters

	Parameter estimate	Standard error	Probability	Percentage of voters supporting the rightist party if all other variables are held constant but value on the focal variable is at its—	
				Minimum	Maximum
Intercept	−2.83	3.30	.39		
Market Liberalism (Factor I)	+.23	.28	.43	4.3	9.2
Authoritarianism (Factor II)	−.45	.38	.24	15.0	3.6
Parochialism/Racism (Factor III)	+.10	.18	.60	6.5	8.6
Gender (Female = 2)	−.32	.46	.48	8.9	6.6
Age	−.02	.02	.29	9.3	3.4
Education	−.28	.11	.01	22.1	2.3
Business or Farmer	+.50	.74	.50	6.6	10.4
Professional	+.41	1.00	.68	6.6	9.6
White-Collar	+1.04	.71	.14	6.6	16.7
Worker	+1.26	.73	.09	6.6	20.0

Source: World Values Survey 1990. Own calculations.
Note: Percentage of concordant cases: 70.4; cases N: 194.

logit regression shows the net impact of each independent variable on preference for the National Front. The logit parameters were used to estimate the probability of voting for the National Front when all independent variables were set at their mean level. The probability was then recalculated taking one independent variable at a time and setting it to its minimum and its maximum observed level, while all other variables were set to their means. The difference in the probability of voting for the National Front when the independent variable is set to its upper and lower extreme values provides a measure of the degree to which that variable influences the vote for the extreme Right.

The data reveal that procapitalist orientations and racist-xenophobic orientations are significant predictors of National Front voting in France. Further, low education is almost a significant predictor of extremist support. Authoritarianism, but also the occupational variables, wash out in the multiple regression.

The second part of table 3.5 is a regression in which support of the National Front is predicted based on the subsample of right-wing voters only. In other words, this equation pits supporters of UDF and RPR against National Front voters. Interestingly, none of the ideological variables set the National Front voters apart from the rest of the French Right. Only less education and being a worker is a predictor of support for Le Pen. This equation suggests that while racism and xenophobia clearly make a difference that separates the National Front from voters of the Left, it is certainly not a "single issue" that determines the vote among rightist parties. The strategic movements of the moderate Right and its lack of credibility on core right-wing issues contribute to the strength of the National Front in France.

We have now reached the point at which we can step back and reconsider the key hypotheses of this study and its rivals in light of the French data. One of the rival hypotheses postulates that the contemporary extreme Right is a single-issue response to the problems of immigration and multiculturalization of advanced democracies. The evidence we have assembled suggests that the FN builds on a far broader ideological foundation than racism alone. There are systematic linkages of other issues to voting behavior for the extreme Right, as well as between such issues and racism itself, although they are not as strong as one might expect (see table 3.1). It is also not true that the extreme Right draws on a cross-class coalition in which no occupational group is overrepresented, as the single-issue hypothesis might imply.

An alternative rival hypothesis is that the contemporary extreme Right expresses procapitalist and libertarian sentiments that are directed against an interventionist state. This hypothesis is also not borne out by the facts in France. There is no evidence that Le Pen's appeals or his voters are libertarian on *any* of the conceivable range of issues and dimensions that come to mind. They tend to be nationalist, authoritarian, paternalist, and opposed to more environmental protection and unconventional political participation. These are not the trappings of a libertarian movement.

The third rival hypothesis, that the contemporary Right is neofascist, finds little support in the French data, *although* its authoritarianism would associate it with fascist historical precursors. What speaks against this linkage is the militant promarket capitalism that characterizes not only the National Front's leadership but also its following, particularly those sympathizers who are not blue-collar workers. It would therefore be misleading to see the National Front as just another incarnation of fascism, a conclusion that Fysh and Wolfreys (1992, 313) are inclined to draw from the authoritarian and anti-Semitic rhetoric of Le Pen and other party leaders. Politically speaking, our analytical judgment does not imply that the National Front is harmless for contemporary democracy. After all, it does mobilize authoritarian resentments, but in a rather different overall program and societal context than the fascist Right of the past.

Taking all considerations together, the weight of the evidence in our own and in other studies favors the hypothesis that the contemporary French radical Right represents a case of right-authoritarian mobilization. National Front voters constitute a diversified coalition, in which workers and small business-people are overrepresented, and which is configured around law and order, xenophobia, Catholic fundamentalism, and its correlate, rejection of feminism. On top of this, sentiments of political alienation, together with strategic voting to punish the parties of the moderate Right and teach them a lesson are likely to contribute to the National Front's success as well.[11] Spatial analyses of the ideological positions endorsed by FN voters in French survey analyses confirm that the right-wing electorate evolves from broader ideological predispositions than pure ethnic resentment. Employing somewhat different methodologies, Chiche's (1990) and Grunberg and Schweisguth's (1990) investigations appear to arrive at similar interpretations of French party preferences and their relationship to the substantive political demands and divisions among voters.

We do not deny that racism and immigration are important catalysts for the growth and entrenchment of the French radical Right in the mass electorate in the 1980s and 1990s. Nevertheless, in light of these findings, it would be shortsighted to predict that the National Front stands and falls with the established parties' handling of immigration alone. The electoral strength of the new parties is anchored in a broader web of concerns and appeals.

Strategic Dilemmas of the French Right

The rise of the National Front in the arena of French party competition has created strategic dilemmas both for the conventional parties of the moderate Right as well as for the new extreme Right itself. These problems parallel similar strategic conflicts between social democratic parties and the New Left configured around various left-socialist and ecology parties. For the established parties of the moderate Right, the main question is whether a "centrist" strategy, rejecting any affiliation with the National Front, is more advantageous than a more centrifugal "polarizing" strategy that attempts to entice the National Front into a broad rightist bloc. As the mirror image of these options, the National Front must choose between cooperation with the moderate Right, which may compromise its unique appeal, or a radical antisystem strategy, which may marginalize the party once its novelty value has worn off and many right-authoritarian voters return to parties with better prospects of government participation. Within each political camp, there are thus mixed incentives that pull and push politicians into different strategic directions.

The moderate French Right has been deeply divided about coalition strategies vis-à-vis the National Front. Most UDF politicians have categorically rejected any association with the National Front, whereas RPR politicians have addressed that issue with multiple and contradictory voices. In 1983, when the National Front celebrated its first minor success in the Dreux local by-election, a survey showed that 56 percent of those who supported the RPR politician Jacques Chirac as candidate for the French presidency also welcomed an alliance with the National Front (Plenel and Rollat 1984, 105). A survey in November 1984 found sympathy with Le Pen reaching far into the moderate-rightist camp. Forty-six percent of RPR voters and 37 percent of UDF voters signaled such inclinations, whereas the same feeling was shared by only 12 percent of socialist voters and 17 percent of communist voters (Schain 1987, 135).

The strategic predicament of the moderate Right became more complex by the determined centrist strategy of the French socialists in the late 1980s to restrict the range of maneuverability for the UDF and the RPR (Ysmal 1990). The linchpin for the moderate Right's strategic choice has clearly been the RPR. If it teams up with the UDF in favor of a more centrist strategy, the two parties, taken together, always have a chance to win the pivot of the party system and thus executive power against a weakened socialist party, increasingly embattled by a new ecologist competitor and a gradually declining communist Left. The success of this strategy is made more likely by the two-round majoritarian electoral system, which magnifies the parliamentary representation of the party alliances that win a plurality of the votes and which may encourage Le Pen voters in the first round to support a conservative candidate in the second. Due to the extraordinary decline of the socialists in the spring 1993 National Assembly elections, the moderate Right has gained temporary relief from its strategic dilemmas. It managed to win a landslide victory in terms of National Assembly seats, although its electoral support fell to the lowest level ever (39% of the vote) and the National Front excelled with over 12 percent of the vote. If there will be a restructuring of the Left, however, the strategic dilemma of the moderate Right could become virulent again, perhaps as soon as the next presidential election.

In this context, a persistently centrist strategy by the moderate Right runs the risks of alienating increasing numbers of staunchly conservative voters from the established government parties, reinforcing the electoral entrenchment of the far Right that has in fact made headway in the 1993 election, and thus, in the long run, undermining the viability of a moderate strategy to capture the pivot of the party system. Moreover, the moderate-rightist parties may have to take the sentiments of their activists into account, although their leaders enjoy considerable autonomy from rank-and-file pressure. Among middle-level party activists in the RPR, there has been a distinctive shift to the right that has been documented by a comparison of delegates' ideological dispositions at the 1978 and 1984 party conventions (Ignazi 1989, 69). It remains an open question whether party activists would tolerate a persistently centrist strategy, particularly in regional strongholds besieged by an increasingly vocal extreme Right. The moderate Right thus may face a severe trade-off between a more centrist "office-seeking" strategy, intent on capturing the state executive, and a more radical "vote-seeking" strategy that keeps the National Front at bay, possibly by adopting some of its objectives and cooperating with the National Front in subnational governments. The latter strategy, however, risks losing the electoral plurality to the socialists, if they are able to rebuild their electoral constituency in cooperation with new ecology parties.

The National Front, as well, has to weigh incentives and disincentives of cooperation with the moderate Right. Unlike the established Gaullist Right, where the wavering between moderate and radical strategies is common to its electoral constituencies, party activists, and party leaders alike, the situation on the extreme Right is characterized by a split between radical party activists and the party's more moderate average voters.[12] Whereas most National Front voters do support an alliance with the moderate-right parties in the runoff elections among lead candidates in the majoritarian electoral system, a 1990 survey showed that 71 percent of the National Front's party activists who were delegates at the party's national convention would abstain in the second round if the choice was between a candidate of the moderate Right and a socialist. A similar proportion saw no chance for participation in a coalition with the moderate Right (Ysmal 1991, 189–91).

In order to attract more voters, the National Front's members and candidates for the National Assembly have taken more moderate positions than the party activists, thus opening a gap that is likely to generate intraparty frictions.

In the party's executive board, the "old fighters" who were loyal to the party even when it was in the electoral wilderness still dominated in the second half of the 1980s. Yet at the same time, Le Pen tried to find "presentable" candidates for electoral positions who usually were not drawn from the ranks of long-time members. In the party's 35-strong caucus in the 1986 National Assembly, only 15 had joined the party before 1984 (Birnbaum and Bastien 1989, 87). Whereas the party activists constitute a "petite bourgeoisie déclassée" (Ysmal 1991, 183), electoral candidates and parliamentarians are primarily drawn from the liberal professions and the ranks of former politicians. It is these people who try to give the party a more moderate image in order to make further inroads into the electorates of RPR and UDF.

Since the economic downturn of 1991–92, Le Pen has put more emphasis on unemployment as a political issue. But it would be wrong to interpret this as a rapproachment to moderate voters and a step toward abandoning his resolute free market liberalism. In fact, his preferred policy measures to reinvigorate employment markets—lower taxes and social welfare cuts that would reduce the social wage bills of private enterprise and boost profits—are out of the textbook of what conservative market economists would recommend if labor markets do not clear (Betz 1994, 129). Needless to say, a repatriation program for foreign workers figures prominently in Le Pen's employment program.

Internal rifts and divisions between voters, activists, party executives, and parliamentary candidates of the National Front will not threaten the precarious alliance between these tendencies as long as the moderate Right refrains from overtures to include the National Front in political alliances or does not steal its political positions. Particularly after the defeat of the socialists in the 1993 National Assembly elections, Le Pen has been able to continue his game of projecting an image of restraint to national television audiences, while indulging in extremist rhetoric in speeches to the party faithful. If the RPR changed its strategic approach and sought to embrace its right-wing competitor, however, such an opening to the extreme Right—either through coalition overtures or an even stricter anti-immigration policy than that pursued by the post-1993 conservative government—could wreak havoc within the ranks of Le Pen's party and seriously diminish its voter appeal. In 1993, the efforts of the RPR interior minister, Charles Pasqua, to enact and implement a more restrictive immigration law clearly pointed in that direction.

The consequences of an opening by the moderate Right to its new competitors within the NRR party family can be illustrated by Scandinavian party politics, which we will examine next. In France, institutional incentives, particularly the mechanical consequences of the majoritarian electoral system to inflate the legislative representation of the party bloc winning a plurality of the votes, work against a convergence between extreme Right and RPR. While these institutional rules keep the National Front on the margins of the political system, they also give the party a lease on life because they preserve an electoral space protected from invasion by the moderate Right.

Conclusion

The National Front in France displays an almost ideal-typical pattern of right-authoritarian mobilization and voter appeal. Moreover, the development of the party since the early 1980s illustrates the "micrologic" of right-wing mobilization in a favorable political opportunity structure. The dynamic of secondary elections and media attention, together with clumsy strategic responses by the established parties, provided significant boosts to the still fledgling new competitor. Once the NRR party achieved a breakthrough, however, not only its moderate competitors but also the extreme Right itself had to face up to difficult strategic tradeoffs. Unless voters' preference distribution radically shifts to the right, this opportunity structure constrains the electoral potential of any viable extreme-rightist voter coalition. Under present conditions in advanced capitalist democracies, it is quite possible that the extreme Right tops out in the neighborhood of 10 to 15 percent of the electorate, the same level the libertarian Left has itself never exceeded.

4

Scandinavia: A Milder Version of the New Radical Right

Although Scandinavian countries lack a legacy of strong right-extremist movements, in the late 1980s the Danish and Norwegian Progress parties, *Fremskridtspartiet* (FP) in Denmark or *Fremskrittspartiet* (FRP) in Norway, articulated political viewpoints that are fairly close to the ideal-type of the NRR sketched in the first two chapters of this study and already illustrated by the French case. In Sweden, the appearance of New Democracy in the 1991 election pointed toward a similar development,[1] but this political phenomenon was too vaguely articulated to go beyond a diffuse "flash" protest party[2] and become a lasting political formation in Swedish politics.[3]

At the same time, even where the Scandinavian New Right has experienced success, it differs in some respects from the rightist party family's "ideal-type" that is so closely approximated by Le Pen's National Front. The Progress parties express a more subdued authoritarianism than the FN, although it would be far from accurate to characterize them as market-liberal *and* politically libertarian parties. Nevertheless, on a number of issues concerning democratic institutions and cultural evaluations the web of attitudes and dispositions expressed by voters of the Scandinavian New Right and the appeal of their political leaders is closer to the moderate conservative mainstream than that of the French National Front. Within their own party systems, the Denmark and Norwegian Progress parties represent extreme positions, but they are unlikely to be viewed as extreme by the standards of continental European politics.

It is instructive to retrace the steps by which the Danish and Norwegian rightist parties arrived at strategic appeals that enabled them to win a substantial share of the electoral market in national parliamentary contests in the late 1980s. In the 1970s, both parties started out as protest parties that were not clearly located on the extreme Right. Their political stances in the late 1980s resulted from drawn-out, trial-and-error learning through electoral defeats and organizational reform, including leadership turnover, in which the parties gradually inched toward more right-authoritarian political appeals that were revealed as the winning formulas for attracting voters. Along that path, but also at the point of success on their political learning curve in the second half of the

1980s, the parties faced strategic dilemmas that make it questionable whether they would ultimately continue to succeed in drawing a large following.

We will first argue that the absence of a significant prehistory of right-wing activism made it harder and at the same time easier to construct contemporary NRR parties. Political entrepreneurs lacked the input from past authoritarian mobilization but also the constraints that might have prevented them from finding an electorally profitable appeal. We then discuss the opportunity structure for right-wing mobilization that demonstrates the linkage between moderate party convergence in the 1970s and then again in the second half of the 1980s, and the success or failure of the New Right. We will then turn to the party leaders' issue appeals in order to explain their electorates' issue preferences and socioeconomic coalition. We conclude with a discussion of the parties' strategic options.

Prehistory of the New Scandinavian Right

Unlike France and a number of the other European countries discussed in later chapters, the Scandinavian Right could not build on organizational precedents and the skills and memories of politicians involved in earlier episodes of extreme-rightist mobilization. Instead, the Scandinavian parties had to be created from scratch. Andersen says about the situation in Denmark on the eve of the Progress Party's founding:

> When Mogens Glistrup launched his anti-tax Progress Party in 1972, he did not draw upon any Danish tradition of right-wing extremism, let alone populism or collective tax evasion. Like most other countries, Denmark had a small Nazi party in the 1930s. This was certainly an extremist organization, but was supported by only 2.1 percent of the voters even during the German occupation. (1992, 193)

After World War II, rightist formations essentially failed to mobilize any significant electoral support in Denmark and Norway. A report on right-wing radicalism in Europe for the European Community identified extreme-rightist groups and sects with fascist sympathies in Denmark and Norway, but they command no popular support beyond a small hard core of activists (Ford 1992, 11–13, 41–43).

The absence of a strong historical lineage provided incipient political entrepreneurs like the tax lawyer Mogens Glistrup in Denmark and the dog-kennel owner and member of the Conservative Party Anders Lange in Norway with an opportunity and a constraint. The opportunity was to define the new parties' appeals without being forced to relate to older incarnations of right-wing protest in positive or negative ways. The constraint was the absence of intellectual, personnel, and organizational resources that could speed the growth of a new rightist party. Both opportunity and constraint explain (1) the parties' ability to learn new political appeals in a relatively short time period as well as (2) the necessity to define the parties' appeals in interaction with potential voters rather than to build on an established image of the extreme Right.

Both Denmark and Norway had small fascist movements in the 1930s, yet they remained without political influence. In other European countries where fascist movements became strong, they thrived on support from a broad coalition of rural smallholders, urban industrial elites, and the petite bourgeoisie, but could attract only an underproportional share of the working class. In Scandinavia, in contrast, rural smallholders stayed away from the extreme Right and could be coopted into an alternative coalition that also included the labor movement and elements of the industrial bourgeoisie (cf. Luebbert 1991; Swenson 1991). This alliance became possible because of the unique political mobilization of the countryside and the strategy of the emerging working-class parties. In Norway and Sweden, and to a lesser extent in Denmark, independent freeholders had persisted throughout the period of feudalism elsewhere in Europe. In the nineteenth century they began to develop their own political representation first in alliance with or directly through liberal parties, and later as independent agrarian parties in the early twentieth century. In Denmark, the liberals were the political representatives of independent farmers and later spun off a new party, the Radical Liberal Party (RV), supported by smallholders who often were peasant workers. In other words, whereas a politically and economically subordinated peasantry could be coopted into the conservative, antidemocratic coalition organized by rural and urban elites in countries where later on fascist movements thrived, the politics of the Scandinavian countryside expressed a distinctly democratic and antielitist thrust that enabled these political forces to enter an alliance with working-class parties. This coalition was also made possible by the strategies of the Scandinavian social democrats. The working-class parties did not attempt to compete with the agrarian parties for rural votes and did not organize landless laborers in a way that would have created a political antagonism to the agrarian interests of the smallholders.[4]

In addition to the particular political alignment of socioeconomic groups, fascism in Scandinavia was also undercut by the consolidation of long-standing institutions of party competition, even though a full democratization of elections and the parliamentary responsibility of government in Scandinavian countries was accomplished only at the beginning of the twentieth century. In contrast, countries with strong fascist movements were characterized by semicompetitive or authoritarian regimes antedating World War I. As a consequence, in Scandinavia, there was little basis for a strong antidemocratic fascist mobilization in the Great Depression of the late 1920s. The German occupation of Norway and Denmark during World War II and the puppet regimes set up by the Nazi state further discredited right-wing mobilization after the war and prevented any kind of extremist mass appeal.

As data on the share of agricultural employment in Scandinavia in the 1930s show (see table 1.2 above), Scandinavian urbanization and industrialization were not really more advanced in the 1920s and 1930s than in the countries where fascist movements were able to mobilize a large share of the population. The critical difference between Scandinavia and continental Europe was the pattern of political-institution building and political-interest articulation. The fascist and national socialist Right in Germany or Italy operated in an environment of unconsolidated democracies and relied not only on urban votes but also excelled in small towns and rural areas among small businesspeople, craftspeople, and farmers who were caught up in a deep structural crisis at that time. On the other hand, the continuity of democratic competition and particularly the unique political organization of the countryside prevented the rise of a strong fascist movement in Scandinavia, although its independent middle class suffered in the Great Depression.

If there is any sociostructural factor that made fascism less likely here than in Germany or Italy, it is the relative insignificance of small industrial producers. In Scandinavia, the quantitative weight of these groups had been reduced by a process of industrialization that favored very large corporations. This removed the petite bourgeois constituency that fueled extreme-rightist and populist movements in some European countries after World War II, such as Poujadism in France and the MSI in Italy.[5] All these conditions, then, must be taken into account in order to understand the absence of an extreme-rightist political legacy in Scandinavia. As a consequence, the new parties that emerged in the early 1970s at first could not be unambiguously located "on the right." Only through the exposure to party competition could they undergo an evolution that eventually turned them into right-wing parties by the mid-1980s.

Political Opportunity Structures: The Narrowing of the Competitive Space in Scandinavian Politics

A critical condition for the emergence of any kind of new party that draws a large share of its voters from the existing bourgeois parties in Scandinavia was the gradual convergence of the policies and programs supported by the social democrats and their bourgeois opponents. Under these circumstances, rightwing voters became inclined to abandon their customary party choice and experiment with new maverick parties.

In Scandinavia, the fragmentation of the bourgeois party camp undercut its ability to stake out political positions clearly distinct from those of the social democrats. As Castles (1978) has shown, the growth of the social democratic welfare state depended less on the sheer electoral strength of social democratic parties than the relationship between a by and large united moderate Left and a fragmented bourgeois party camp. In this configuration, bourgeois parties had an incentive for "product differentiation" in the arena of electoral competition in order to attract a loyal following. Such electoral strategies, however, complicated the formation of coalitions among the nonsocialist parties. The most "centrist" bourgeois parties in particular were always tempted to defect and to support a social democratic minority government to prove their distinctiveness and indispensability in policy making and government formation. As a result, even where bourgeois coalition governments were formed, they were internally divisive and rarely able to alter public policy significantly beyond the social democratic status quo. This dynamic prevailed in Denmark and Norway in the 1960s and early 1970s before the emergence of new tax-protest parties that later acquired a New Right profile (cf. Aimer 1988). With some cyclical oscillations, the same pattern continued to characterize these countries throughout the 1970s and especially the second half of the 1980s.

Before 1973, when the Progress parties first appeared on the Danish and Norwegian political landscape, both countries had experienced episodes of bourgeois coalition government. In Denmark, a bourgeois coalition replaced a social democratic minority government in 1968. Previously, the social democrats had governed for two years with the selective support of the far left Socialist People's Party (SF), but this coalition collapsed due to strategic conflict in both parties. A minority of the SF insisted on strict opposition and founded the Left Socialists Party (VS). A minority of the social democrats, in turn, opposed any kind of cooperation with the far Left and eventually founded the Center Democrats (CD) in 1973. Efforts to polarize Left and Right failed not only within the leftist camp, but also in the bourgeois camp. In the 1960s, in parliamentary decisions, the opposition voted more than 80 percent of the time with the government parties (Damgaard 1974, 112). The 1968 bourgeois government found it difficult, therefore, to engineer a radical departure from the dominant social democratic policies. In 1971, it was replaced by a renewed social democratic minority government that sought selective policy support on the Left in the SF and among the centrist bourgeois parties, especially the Radical Liberals (RV), by then representing the culturally libertarian and economically moderate end of the bourgeois party spectrum.

In a similar vein, Norwegian bourgeois coalition governments were disappointing to voters who sought a dramatic departure from social democratic consensus policies. In 1965, after several decades of social democratic government hegemony, a bourgeois coalition collapsed within months and gave way to a renewed period in which centrist parties were willing to endorse social democratic minority governments. The bourgeois parties won the 1969 parliamentary election, but the ensuing coalition government did not embark on a profoundly different policy course than its social democratic predecessor. Both in Denmark and Norway, many voters perceived a lack of substantive policy alternatives among the established parties on the eve of the rise of new tax-protest parties.

Even after the emergence of the Progress parties, the pattern of convergence between established left and right parties in Scandinavia was only marginally modified because the bourgeois parties did not lose their incentive to engage in "product differentiation" of electoral appeals and strategies. Although the Progress parties declined in the second half of the 1970s and early 1980s for reasons to be discussed shortly and although the conventional conservative parties pursued some modicum of political polarization against the social democrats particularly in the early 1980s, the opportunities for staunch rightist parties never entirely vanished throughout the entire time period and were finally seized upon by rejuvenated Progress parties both in Denmark and Norway in the late 1980s.

In Denmark, the 1973 electoral earthquake in which the newly founded Progress Party instantly harnessed 15.9 percent of the vote and became the country's second-strongest party precipitated the formation of a centrist minority government that was later replaced by social democratic minority governments drawing on centrist legislative support. It is true that the Danish conservatives began to back away from the social democratic welfare state beginning in the late 1970s, but they never went as far as Reagan's or Thatcher's rhetoric or policies in the same time period. Even when the conservatives came to power in Denmark in 1982, they could craft only policy modifications that, from an international comparative perspective, amounted to a rather small incremental change of the status quo, although, within Danish politics, these reforms constituted the first real effort to modify the social democratic welfare state by injecting neoliberal free market policies into the political economy. The key constraint on conservative reform zeal was coalition politics. In order to create policy majorities in parliament, the conservatives had to rely on the centrist parties, particularly the RV, for legislative support or even on social democratic endorsement. Nevertheless, the Danish conservatives at least made an effort to polarize party competition more than had been the case in previous decades.

The overarching pattern of centripetal competition was reinforced by the strategy of the Danish social democrats who abstained from programmatic polarization when the conservative government was elected in 1982 but pursued a centrist policy in order to recapture the median pivotal voter in the party system and deprive the bourgeois parties of the opportunity to govern without social democratic party support (cf. Bille 1989). Thus, the centripetal opposition stance, together with the policies of the conservative government, which became increasingly moderate as the 1980s went on (cf. Borre 1988, 77), created for the second time an opening for a new right-wing party to harness disappointed voters who would have welcomed a radical departure from the policy status quo in Denmark.

The situation in Norway was roughly parallel. In the late 1970s, the conservative party also began to pursue a more strictly market-liberal course and targeted what it thought were excesses of the social democratic welfare state. This strategy paid off in elections and the conservatives gradually increased their support to about 30 percent of the electorate, thus becoming the hegemonic party within the bourgeois camp. Nevertheless, the conservative-led nonsocialist government formed in 1981 was weakened in its policy resolve by the presence of at least three quarrelsome coalition partners—the agrarian Center Party (C), the Christian Democrats (KRF), and the Liberals (V)—all of which only on rare occasions endorsed the clear-cut political polarization advocated by the conservatives. The Liberals eventually attempted to depart from the common ground of the coalition and sought to stake out a new position with libertarian cultural and political themes that moved the party closer to the ecologists, but this strategy was an electoral failure. After the 1985 election, strategic problems inside the bourgeois coalitions were exacerbated because they had to rely on the representatives of the right-wing Progress Party to win legislative majorities over the social democratic and left-socialist opposition parties. But several coalition parties were unwilling to tolerate the de facto inclusion of the Progress Party in the government coalition through the backdoor of parliamentary decision making. As a consequence, the conservative government fell in 1986 and gave way to a social democratic minority government that relied on selective support from the center. Efforts to rebuild the nonsocialist coalition in 1987 and again after the 1989 election failed due to strategic disagreement among the conventional nonsocialist parties and a dispute over the alliance strategy with the Norwegian Progress Party (cf. Strom 1994).

If conservative governments in the late 1960s and in the second half of the 1980s disappointed many of their supporters by their moderate policies and eventually lured significant numbers of voters into the camp of the Progress parties, why did not the same process take place in the aftermath of six years of nonsocialist rule in Sweden? The Swedish nonsocialist government coalition did little to depart from the social democratic status quo and was characterized by high internal divisiveness and government instability. Nevertheless, voters did not seek a new nonbourgeois alternative in the early 1980s. The difference between Sweden, on the one hand, and Norway and Denmark, on the other, is that the nonsocialist governments in the latter two countries, particularly in the 1980s, were led by their conservative parties, whereas in Sweden the electorally and politically dominant force from 1976 to the early 1980s was the

TABLE 4.1.   The Electoral Performance of the Danish and Norwegian
Progress Parties

	Denmark	Norway
1973	15.9	5.0
1975	13.6	—
1977	14.6	1.9
1979	11.1	—
1981	8.9	4.5
1984	3.6	—
1985	—	3.7
1987	4.8	—
1988	9.0	—
1989	—	13.0
1990	6.4	—
1993	—	6.0
1994	6.4	—

Source: Official election data.

Center Party, a socially and economically moderate party that featured many libertarian themes, such as more citizens' participation and environmental protection. In this coalition, the conservatives did not yet "taint" their record sufficiently to persuade those who were discontented with the welfare state to search for completely new political alternatives (Aimer 1988, 7–8). In fact, the Swedish conservatives were able to dissociate themselves from the Liberals and the Center Party in the last phase of the non-socialist government and join the opposition to the Liberal-Center cabinet. This is highlighted by the accord on tax reform struck between social democrats, Liberals, and Center Party in 1981, an agreement bitterly opposed by the Swedish conservatives.[6]

Thus, both in Denmark and Norway, but not in Sweden, in the 1970s and 1980s strategic opportunities existed for launching new nonsocialist parties that would fight against the centripetal convergence of the major political parties. In the two countries with Progress parties, these opportunities were greatest in the 1970s and then again in the second half of the 1980s, when this convergence between the conventional party camps was particularly striking. These changes in the opportunity structure are reflected in the distribution of Progress Party electoral support over time in both countries (table 4.1). After initial successes in the first half of the 1970s, they soon began to experience an electoral "trough," particularly in the early 1980s. The parties were able to overcome this low point in the later 1980s and hang on to about 6 percent of the electorate in the 1990s.

At the same time, the absence of a right-wing tradition in Scandinavian politics made it more difficult than in France to find a policy appeal that would rally voters around a new program. At least in part, the trough of the early 1980s is due to the waning of the protest theme of the Progress parties' early years—taxation—and the difficulty of finding new themes that would dissociate them from the dominant parties, while still appealing to a significant reservoir of potential voters.

Protest Mobilization: Building New Party Alternatives

Unlike all the other new right-extremist parties discussed in this book, the Danish and Norwegian parties experienced their first major breakthrough *not* in secondary elections but in national parliamentary elections. Their phenomenal rise was in part due to the sudden salience of a new issue that divided the existing socialist and bourgeois parties internally, the question of whether or not to join the European Community. The European issue, however, was superimposed on a deeper conflict over the development of the Danish and Norwegian welfare states, which had antagonized significant electoral constituencies without being represented by the bourgeois parties and which revolved around an increasingly explosive issue: income taxes. The convergence between bourgeois and socialist parties in support of an expanding welfare state had led to a dramatic increase of income taxes that made many middle- and lower-middle-income families move up in the progressive tax brackets. In the perception of many citizens, this mode of taxation was particularly offensive because it was more visible to individual taxpayers than indirect taxes on consumption or payroll taxes shared with employers. Visible tax structures generating revenue through income taxes are most prone to trigger tax revolts (Hibbs and Madsen 1981), particularly among middle-income groups belonging to skilled labor, white-collar employees, and small business.

The political significance of income taxes and of conditions for tax revolt demonstrates a critical difference between Sweden, on the one hand, and Denmark and Norway, on the other. Whereas the potential for tax revolt was high in Denmark and Norway, it remained relatively low in Sweden, although Sweden had an overall tax burden equivalent to or greater than that of its Scandinavian neighbors. But unlike its neighbors, Sweden relied on a mix of income, sales and payroll taxes that decreased the visibility of taxation levels and growth rates.

Within this favorable environment for the mobilization of political dissatisfaction, both in Denmark and Norway political entrepreneurs rose to the occasion and politicized the taxation and European Community issues that were poised to disorganize the established parties and thus to destabilize electoral party alignments. In Denmark, the new challenging party was created by the successful tax lawyer Mogens Glistrup who never had been active in politics and who initially wanted to run on the conservative party's ticket in

1973 rather than form his own party (Harmel and Svasand 1993, 82–3). In Norway, Anders Lange, a small businessman who had retired from running his dog kennel, was a member of the conservative party until he felt the party catered too little to the growing antitax sentiment within the rank and file and the electorate at large. When Glistrup founded his party in August 1972, barely 16 months before the decisive parliamentary election in which it received 15.9 percent of the national vote, he named it "Progress Party." Anders Lange labeled it very modestly "Anders Lange's Party for a Strong Reduction in Taxes, Rates, and Public Intervention." After Lange's death in 1974 and the decline of the remaining organization, his successor, Carl Hagen, renamed it "Progress Party" at a time when Glistrup's Danish party was sufficiently successful to serve as a model for rebuilding its Norwegian counterpart.

As illustrated in the case of the French National Front in the previous chapter, new political entrepreneurs thrive on structural weaknesses and sudden opportunities in the competitive electoral arena only if the mass media serve as a catalyst for disseminating their messages. In Glistrup's case, he put his name on the political map through a provocative television interview in early 1971 in which he, a wealthy lawyer, explained how he evaded Danish income taxes and how he encouraged his clients and every other citizen to do the same. The uproar and political outrage this 118-second interview triggered among the established politicians and the popular approval he received elsewhere motivated Glistrup to pursue his antitax crusade further and eventually decide to found a party to promote the cause of tax cuts. He single-handedly wrote a party platform that focused on only three issues: income taxation, bureaucracy, and regulatory policies.

In a similar vein, in Norway Anders Lange's eccentric and electrifying personality, brought into every home by television, enabled a political entrepreneur without mass organization to reach out to a national political audience and establish himself as a serious political competitor. Lange wrote a one-page campaign program consisting of 10 policies he was against and 10 policies he was for, such as shrinking the welfare state, lowering taxes, cutting back on foreign aid, making it harder to misuse social security funds, and stopping the government's meddling in the use of alcohol and tobacco. Lange had a gift for expressing his ideas through simple language and striking anecdotes. At the same time, he as well as Glistrup were opposed to building regular party organizations. Both Glistrup and Lange wanted to run their political campaigns as personal affairs, inspired by spontaneous action rather than the coordinated mass campaigning of a party machine (cf. Harmel and Svasand 1993, 78 and 83).

Issues dividing the established parties and media exposure of new political entrepreneurs set the stage for a major electoral shake-up. In the electoral campaigns of 1973, the new political entrepreneurs were aided by the highly egalitarian regulations on the access of all competing parties to the publicly controlled television networks, which were obliged to provide air time for campaign advertisements for parties without a past record of electoral support.

In the 1973 Danish election, both the socialist block and the bourgeois camp each lost about 15 percent of the national electorate to new parties (Borre 1974). Previous voters for the left parties split three ways. They voted for the small anti-EC Danish Communist Party, supported the new Center Democrats—a party founded by former social democrats dissatisfied with the party's leftist alliance with the SF—or threw in their lot with Glistrup's Progress Party. With 7.8 percent of the vote, the Center Democrats in fact might have been the greatest beneficiary of left party losses. Glistrup's Progress Party, however, benefited most from the decline of the nonsocialist parties, among whose voters the campaign against income taxes and for the preservation of national political autonomy struck a strong chord.

In a similar vein, in the Norwegian election of 1973, the Labor Party lost votes primarily to an anti-EC election alliance under whose umbrella the entire radical Left was assembled for that single election and which received no less than 11 percent of the vote. Anders Lange's party drew most of its voters from the nonsocialist parties, but its success, at 5 percent of the vote, fell far short of Glistrup's 15.6 percent in Denmark.

While the sudden electoral rise of the tax-protest parties did shake up the established party systems, these jolts were soon dampened by the internal political ambiguities and contradictions of the new parties. Because the Progress Party and Anders Lange's party could not fall back on rightist intellectual traditions and organizations, which would have provided a "semantic web" of interpretations for all relevant policy themes but were initially single-issue protest parties against taxation and an overgrown state, the political entrepreneurs and their lieutenants at the helm of these new parties and did not know how to position themselves on other issues on which they now had to take a stand to reinforce the commitment of their first-time electoral constituency.

It was unfortunate for the parties that they began to publicize issue positions that were certain to be inconsistent with the general political worldview of those voters who had supported the new parties because of their antitax appeal. Glistrup, for example, proposed to scrap the Danish military and replace it with an answering service that would signal the message "we surrender" to the Russians in case of an attack. Within the broader ideological landscape, this pacifist, antimilitarist position would be typically associated with the libertarian political Left, although, of course, it is consistent with an antitaxation appeal and a zeal for reducing government spending. But antitaxation voters were really inclined toward an all-out defense of capitalism, and that included a strong military, even in an era of detente between capitalism and communism.

Moreover, there are empirical indications that the Progress Party's electorate had authoritarian leanings that were not adequately reflected by the leadership's libertarian escapades. Surveys in 1973 and 1975 found that a much larger share of the Progress Party's electorate was willing to endorse the statement that a strong man should seize power in a situation of economic crisis than that of the overall population (Nielsen 1976, 149). These discrepancies between the electorate and the leadership of what was initially a protest party may illustrate the difficulties Glistrup faced in assembling a cognitively coherent program that would permanently bind a group of voters ready to defect from the existing parties to the Progress Party.

The evolving struggles over the issue positions of Progress parties on other than taxation issues were intertwined with "growing pains" that are part of the normal development of large organizations.[7] Parties, just like business firms, may require visionary leadership to open up new markets and find new consumer or voter appeals, but once they have discovered such opportunities they are compelled to develop efficient organizations that exploit the benefits to be reaped. In party politics, this typically requires the construction of formal organizations that coordinate party activists and party representatives in municipal councils and legislatures. Both Glistrup and Lange resisted facing up to this task. In Lange's case, a pro-organizational faction, including the later chairman Carl Hagen, left the party shortly before his death and returned in 1977 when the party was in shambles and needed to be rescued by politicians who would find a new style and method of reaching out to the voters. In Glistrup's case, a fundamentalist, spontaneist faction continued to battle with a more moderate group of organization builders, while the party went into gradual decline from the 1970s to the early 1980s. When Glistrup was finally jailed for tax fraud in 1983, the moderate faction under the interim chairperson Pia Kjaersgaard steered the party onto a new course that catered to the organization builders. After Glistrup's release from jail in 1988, he did not manage to regain control of the party and eventually was forced to withdraw when the moderate majority on the party executive effectively took over control of the nomination process of parliamentary candidates for the 1990 election. Glistrup then founded his own party, which he called "Well-Being Party." The new party was unable to collect a sufficient number of signatures to be placed on the ballot. He then teamed up with the workerist and anti-immigrant "Common Cause" party, which had won a modest share of the votes in previous elections, but this alliance failed to attain the 2 percent threshold of electoral representation (Andersen 1992).

The problem of the antitax parties was not only that, once pushed into the parliamentary arena, they had to build electoral organizations, and take positions on a variety of issues for which they were not prepared but also that their core issues, by themselves, proved insufficient for securing a permanent share of the electoral market. Questions of taxation went through an issue attention cycle that could be weathered only if the party's issue positions were linked backward to some kind of broader ideological framework in which voters could place the Progress parties. Given the absence of such a framework, the parties' parliamentary actions and public statements on other policy questions began to undermine their reputation and credibility among their own voters. The parties would not articulate coherent positions on a wide range of issues that would make them calculable for voters and enable the latter to draw a clear linkage between their own preferences and the political appeals of the party leaders. For this reason, after their initial electoral successes in 1973, both the Danish and the Norwegian parties declined in subsequent elections. In the Norwegian case, the party drifted entirely into the electoral backwater with Anders Lange's death.

Glistrup's efforts to accompany the antistatist free market economic message with a culturally libertarian-individualist and politically antiauthoritarian party appeal, such as his ideas about national defense, were self-defeating. While support for free markets and a libertarian-individualist cultural and political message may be cognitively coherent, the Progress Party soon found that it was impossible to build an electoral coalition around this configuration of programmatic messages. A stable segment of the electorate outside the domains occupied by the established parties could be assembled only at the "right-authoritarian" extreme of the political spectrum. A number of years in the political wilderness with marginal electoral returns taught the Danish and Norwegian Progress parties that this formula was the only approach that promised substantial electoral payoffs.

In Norway, Anders Lange's party had the good fortune to find a new charismatic and telegenic leader, Carl Hagen, who began to change its political image. From the late 1970s onward, with increasing effectiveness, he complemented the party's antistatist market liberalism with an authoritarian appeal to law and order and the containment and eventual reduction of the proportion of foreigners in Norway, particularly political refugees from Third World countries such as Pakistan. After winning barely 4 percent of the vote in the 1985 national election, in the 1987 municipal elections this appeal allowed his party to attract a considerable chunk of former conservative party supporters (3% of the electorate; about 10% of conservative voters), but also a significant share of the social democrats (1.4% of the electorate). Voter flows from other parties were comparatively minor (Björklund 1988). In the 1989 parliamentary elections, Hagen's party surged from 3.7 percent (1985) to a spectacular 13 percent of the electorate (Valen 1990). Most of these gains were made at the expense of the bourgeois parties, although the social democrats also suffered some losses to the Right in large cities.[8] Hagen's strategy very clearly shows that the Norwegian Progress Party is not a "single-issue" mobilization that happened to move from questions of taxation to immigration. When the Norwegian government tightened immigration rules in 1988, Hagen quickly switched to more general law-and-order appeals in 1989 (Arter 1992, 364). The party generated salient issues against the backdrop of a broader ideological appeal that allowed it to extend messages to its potential electorate contingent upon the political situation. This is exactly what our theory of party competition in a left-libertarian versus right-authoritarian space would predict. If racism and immigration—as one issue at the right-authoritarian end of the competitive space—no longer command sufficient attention, another issue, such as law and order, may still do the trick.

In a similar vein, the Danish Progress Party revised its voter appeal and put more and more emphasis on immigration and law-and-order slogans (cf. Harmel and Svasand 1989). The party enjoyed its greatest gains in 1988, moving it up to 9 percent of the electorate, after several years in which the initial polarization between the conservative-led government that had entered office in 1982 and the leftist opposition parties had gradually given way to a more centrist consensus politics. The Progress Party's gains came at a time when the conventional parties had already passed a tough new immigration law that reduced the flow of immigrants by 90 percent (Borre 1988, 78). This fact suggests that opposition to immigration may be only a symbol that certain electoral constituencies decode as an indicator of the Progress Party's broader commitment to an authoritarian policy agenda. Closer analysis of the Danish Progress Party's message in fact shows that it has developed a general populist appeal that chastises overregulation by the state. This antistatism, together with the party's anti-immigrant stance, has promoted an approach Andersen (1992, 197) calls a "neo-liberalism of the lower strata." This neoliberalism attacks big government but wishes to engineer a socially fair reduction of public expenditure. Rather than calling for lower income tax rates, the Progress Party advocated larger basic deductions that particularly benefit lower-income earners. Rather than increasing energy taxes with a regressive effect on income distribution, the party called for expenditure cuts in areas unpopular with the lower strata, such as culture, aid to less developed countries, and social funds for refugees and immigrants. This appeal may be intertwined with the changing electoral coalition of the party, which we will explore in the following section. If the party appeals to authoritarian, anti-immigration, and racial sentiments, it potentially draws on a significant lower-class electorate. This electorate, however, cannot be easily won over if the party at the same time professes to support an unrestrained market liberalism that helps the economically strong. In this situation, a successful electoral coalition requires the party to craft an appeal that moderates its market liberalism with social and economic policies designed to attract the xenophobic electorate.

Overall, after a period of electoral crisis, the "learning process" of new electoral appeals, has not turned the Danish or Norwegian Progress parties into full-blown NRR parties. Nevertheless, as Andersen (1992, 196, 198) points out, the Danish party is distinct from other NRR parties by its low emphasis on nationalist themes, and its anti-immigrant stance is motivated more by welfare chauvinism than biological racism. Moreover, neither the Danish nor the Norwegian Progress parties have harbored activists who openly call for the abolition of liberal democracy. This may explain why representatives of the Danish Progress Party refused to participate in a meeting of extreme-right groups in Copenhagen in May 1990 that featured such leaders as Le Pen from the French National Front and Schönhuber from the German *Republikaner* (Ford 1992, 56).

To sum up, both the Norwegian and the Danish Progress parties went through a trial-and-error period of electoral defeat and renewal to find a new winning electoral formula in the second half of the 1980s. This winning formula is much closer to the right-authoritarian perspectives that have also inspired parties of the New Right in other countries than to their initial appeal in the 1970s. At the same time, however, there are specific Scandinavian modifications and restraints on the articulation of NRR demands. We will now explore whether the electorates of the Progress parties mirror what can be learnt from the party leaders' programmatic appeals.

Right-Authoritarianism within the Bounds of Competitive Democracy

Based on the party elites' political appeal, we will explore the contention that a change of Progress Party electorates has taken place over time, transforming them from a bourgeois tax-protest to a NRR authoritarian electorate in which the working class and small business are overrepresented. On average, supporters in the new electorate support both economically rightist promarket policies as well as authoritarian appeals. All of these tendencies, however, should be less pronounced than in the electorate of the French National Front. Moreover, the Scandinavian right-wing electorates clearly support liberal democracy, whereas in countries with stronger extreme-rightist legacies there are more outright advocates of totalitarian nondemocratic regime forms.

The analysis of trend changes in Progress Party support is confined to the Danish case, which can be analyzed by Eurobarometer surveys taken from the early 1970s to the late 1980s. Because Norway is not a member of the European Community, it is not included in the Eurobarometer surveys.

When the Danish Progress Party established itself as a tax- and EC-protest party in the early 1970s, its electorate in general consisted of voters with above average education and income, primarily drawn from the salariat and business. In terms of left/right self-placements, these voters situated themselves close to the center. Followers of the Progress Party in no way constituted an extreme-rightist camp sharply contoured in social and ideological terms. The party merely happened to attract voters who were critical of the welfare state and its costs, had some subterranean authoritarian leanings, and distrusted the incumbent politicians.[9] The Danish Progress Party thus really revolved around a "dual-issue" concern that was bound to fade with a policy resolution of the taxation and EC questions. Over time, however, the Danish Progress Party attracted more and more rightist voters. Whereas the average self-placement of Progress Party sympathizers on a 10-point scale, ranging from extreme leftism (=1) to extreme rightism (=10), was 6.21 in the 1974 Eurobarometer 2, in which almost 10 percent of the respondents expressed a voting preference for the Progress Party (N = 95), in ensuing years self-placements of those who indicated they would vote for the Progress Party became more rightist. The four 1976–77 Eurobarometer surveys yield an average left/right self-placement of 6.76 for Progress Party sympathizers, with roughly 7 percent of the respondents indicating their intention to vote for this party (N = 272). By the mid-1980s, support for the Progress Party had dwindled to about 1 to 2 percent of the survey respondents, and the average self-placements of Progress Party supporters for the five surveys from the first half of 1984 to the first half of 1986 had now moved to 7.22 (N = 55). The rightist shift, however, is not simply due to the fact that the party was reduced to its hard-core supporters, as is evidenced by Eurobarometers 30 through 32 from the second half of 1988 through the second half of 1989. In that time period, support for the Progress Party surged to over 8 percent of the respondents (N = 256) and left/right self-placements moved to an extreme 7.77, more rightist than any measure of Progress Party electorates taken in earlier time periods.

It should be emphasized that the shift of the Progress Party's electorate is not simply the correlate of a general movement of Danish voters to the right. On the contrary, Progress Party supporters moved from the center-right to an extreme-rightist position, while the overall distribution of Danish voters on the left/right self-placement scale stayed relatively stable throughout the almost two decades in which Eurobarometer surveys have been gathered. Although we do not have the data, we are confident that future research will find a similar trajectory for the Norwegian Progress Party electorate from 1973 to the late 1980s.

In the early 1970s, Progress Party electorates were primarily attracted by a market-liberal message. But what about the imputed authoritarianism that follows from the theory we have presented above? And what about changes in the sociodemographic composition of Progress Party electorates that we have hypothesized? Before we analyze the *World Values Surveys*, let us briefly review some findings from other studies and sources.

Eurobarometer surveys provide some evidence that the Danish Progress

TABLE 4.2.   View of the Political System and Right Extremism

	Liberty valued more than equality (percent approval)		Democracy is the best political system under any circumstance (percent approval)	
	All respondents	Respondents intending to vote for the extreme Right	All respondents	Respondents intending to vote for the extreme Right
Denmark	69.1 (N = 825)	74.0 (N = 77)	93.1 (N = 855)	87.0 (N = 77)
France	45.8 (N = 836)	40.0 (N = 30)	79.4 (N = 839)	36.7 (N = 30)
Germany	39.0 (N = 958)	25.0 (N = 8)	83.9 (N = 985)	12.5 (N = 8)
Italy	37.0 (N = 701)	34.3 (N = 35)	75.0 (N = 730)	36.1 (N = 36)

Source: Eurobarometer 30.

Party taps a broad authoritarian disposition. In 1989, Eurobarometer surveys 31 and 32 asked a variety of questions about participation in and tolerance for political protest behavior. Progress Party supporters consistently placed themselves within an extreme group that was least inclined to participate in citizens' initiatives and legal demonstrations and that would most welcome police measures against demonstrators and the bringing in of troops to fight strikers. In a similar vein, Progress Party supporters were most willing to mark the identification papers of AIDS patients or even to confine them to closed institutions. Other Eurobarometer surveys consistently show that Progress Party supporters are the least inclined to support the causes of the libertarian Left—disarmament movements, ecology movements, and movements to stop the construction of nuclear power stations. In these respects, the Progress parties resemble the French National Front.

In one area, however, the Scandinavian Progress parties may be clearly distinct from extreme-rightist parties on the European continent, which are steeped in stronger right-wing legacies and which have experienced episodes of authoritarian or totalitarian government in the twentieth century. Whereas the supporters of extreme-rightist parties on the continent have great reservations about the democratic process and whereas upwards of a third of their supporters challenge the institutions of competitive democracy, a parallel tendency cannot be detected in Scandinavia. Eurobarometer data on the Danish Progress Party show that support for competitive democracy is not much lower among its voters than among those of its competitors. Eighty-seven percent of Danish Progress Party voters in Eurobarometer 30 (N = 77) supported democracy as the best political system, compared to 93.1 percent of all respondents who indicated a party preference (N = 855). Table 4.2 compares the ranking of liberty relative to equality and the overall endorsement of democracy of all respondents and of right-wing respondents in Denmark as well as three countries with significant rightist legacies. Not only is the overall endorsement of liberty and of democracy higher in Denmark than in any other country, the Danish supporters of the Progress Party are much more willing to support democracy and equality than rightist voters in France, Germany, and Italy.

Nevertheless, we expect that in Denmark and Norway, the strategic move of Progress parties to a right-authoritarian appeal attracts a general sociodemographic voter coalition that looks quite similar to that encountered in France. Progress parties in the late 1980s are likely to draw on a significant working-class constituency that has responded to the parties' new xenophobic and authoritarian appeals and on small businesspeople with authoritarian and ethnocentrist dispositions rather than the white-collar and professional electorate. Several surveys illuminate the working-class bases of extreme right-wing support in Scandinavia. Workers are not attracted to the extreme Right because of its free market appeal but because of its insistence on restricting the access to the welfare state to nationals, thus expressing a certain "welfare chauvinism." The welfare state protects workers from the vicissitudes of the labor market, but in the universalistic Scandinavian welfare states, many workers object to the right of nonproducers and noncontributors, such as immigrants, to draw benefits from the system. Moreover, the welfare state is seen as financing an increasingly large sector of public employees who burden private corporations and endanger industrial jobs in the private sector by reducing the international competitiveness of domestic firms. Andersen and Björklund (1990) demonstrate that over time the support of workers for the Danish and Norwegian Progress parties has increased. Simultaneously, the Progress parties position themselves at one extreme of what these authors call a cleavage between production and consumption spheres that involves sharply polarized attitudes about the welfare state. Voters of the extreme Right support a rollback of the welfare state, presumably in order to exclude noncontributors, and endorse materialist and antienvironmentalist stances as well. At the opposite extreme on this cleavage dimension are the socialist people's parties, environmentalists, and public-sector employees. It is not difficult to see that Andersen and Björklund's indicators of voter positions tap what we have called the left-libertarian versus right-authoritarian dimension of party competition. Workers who support the Progress parties are slightly more favorably disposed to the welfare state than middle-class sympathizers of these parties, although less than voters of the conventional or the libertarian Left. The workers' stance against the welfare state is primarily a "welfare chauvinist" appeal to the exclusion of immigrants from benefits of the system (cf. Andersen 1992).

Consistent with these findings, other studies show that public-sector employees, the ideal-typical incarnation of the left-libertarian constituency, have the lowest propensity to support Progress parties (Hoel and Knutsen 1989, 294). In Norway, the social structure of support for the Progress Party is almost a mirror image of support for the left-libertarian Socialist People's Party. Whereas the latter attracted 21 percent of all public-sector employees, but only 11 percent of the workers, the Progress Party attracted only 4 percent of the public sector employees, but 14 percent of the workers (Lane et al. 1993, 205). Workers are not on the "postmaterialist" Left, but rather on the materialist Right (Togeby 1990).[10]

In light of these data, it is misleading to refer to the Scandinavian Progress parties as manifestations of a right-wing libertarianism (Harmel and Gibson, 1991). This characterization may have been partially true in the 1970s, as Glistrup's extravagant position on defense issues has illustrated, but it definitely does not apply to the position of Progress parties in the 1980s. While the Danish and Norwegian Progress Parties' electoral profile is most clearly governed by ethnocentric, anti-immigrant, and law-and-order appeals, blended with market liberalism, other secondary themes that relate to authoritarian political dispositions surface as well. In this respect, opposition to the regulatory and participatory demands of environmentalists, but also to the claims of cultural minorities, has played a certain role. Such slogans go over well particularly among the growing blue-collar constituencies of the new political Right.

At this point, we will turn to the *World Values Study* for Denmark and Norway and explore whether these data yield findings that correspond to the theoretical hypotheses and the results of other studies we have reported. Tables 4.3 and 4.4 display the results of the exploratory factor analysis of the 16 items we have selected to measure economic left/right and political as well as cultural authoritarian/libertarian orientations. The results are almost identical for the two countries. In both of them, the strongest factor structuring voter opinions is a left-libertarian versus right-authoritarian factor that—in contrast to France—combines economic and noneconomic issue items rather clearly. Only perceptions of women's role in society loads quite weakly on this factor. The second factor combines capitalist and antixenophobic (cosmopolitan) positions at one extreme and anticapitalist and xenophobic (particularist) views at the other. A third factor links endorsement of capitalism with a commitment to environmental protection, at one extreme, and against a socialist "productionism" at the other.[11]

The eigenvalues for each factor in both tables show that the first factor has about as much or more power to organize the voters' beliefs as the two other factors taken together. Moreover, an inspection of each party's voter means on the three factors at the bottom of the tables demonstrates that it is really the first factor that most structures the party competition. The second and third factors generate only "noise" that is more or less difficult to interpret and does not differentiate the parties significantly.[12] This interpretation is also confirmed by the overwhelming power respondents' scores on the first factor have as predictors of their overall ideological dispositions, as captured by left/right

TABLE 4.3. **Ideological Divisions in Denmark: An Exploratory Factor Analysis**

	Factor I	Factor II	Factor III
	Left-Libertarians versus Right-Authoritarian	Capitalist Cosmopolitans versus Anticapitalist Parochials	Capitalist Ecology versus Socialist Production
Economic Issues			
1. Business management	−.49	+.27	+.41
2. Income inequality	−.53	+.31	+.40
3. Competition	−.39	+.33	+.36
Ecology and Industry			
4. Environmental taxes	+.38	−.08	+.36
5. Urgency of ecology	+.45	+.13	+.43
6. No nuclear plants	+.59	−.25	+.35
Race and Nation			
7. Objections to neighbors of different race	−.28	−.27	+.07
8. Priority for own nationals in labor markets	−.38	−.39	−.06
9. National pride	−.28	−.41	+.27
Authority and Participation			
10. More respect for authority	−.34	−.34	+.20
11. Confidence in the army	−.34	+.04	+.08
12. Would participate in lawful demonstration	+.58	+.19	−.10
13. Would participate in disarmament protest	+.55	−.41	+.37
Women and Family			
14. Choice over abortion		No data	
15. Women as homemakers	−.19	−.40	+.01
16. Women's right to a job	+.32	+.45	+.12
Eigenvalues	2.68	1.44	1.19
Party Factor Scores			
Socialist People's Party (N = 109)	+1.00	−.03	−.19
Greens (N = 12)	+1.11	+.11	+.02
Radical Liberals (N = 26)	+.27	+.21	+.04
Social Democrats (N = 188)	−.20	−.15	−.07
Center Democrats	−.33	+.31	+.19
Christian People's Party (N = 14)	−.28	+.47	+.08
Liberals (N = 72)	−.60	+.27	+.11
Conservatives (N = 88)	−.55	+.29	+.32
Progress Party (N = 34)	−.58	−.02	+.16

Source: World Values Survey 1990. Own calculations.

TABLE 4.4. Ideological Divisions in Norway: An Exploratory Factor Analysis (Principal Components)

	Factor I Left-Libertarians versus Right-Authoritarian	Factor II Capitalist Cosmopolitans versus Anticapitalist parochials	Factor III Deep Ecology versus Industry
Economic Issues			
1. Business management	−.40	+.35	+.13
2. Income inequality	−.30	+.44	+.24
3. Competition	−.31	+.33	+.40
Ecology and Industry			
4. Environmental taxes	+.34	−.10	+.40
5. Urgency of ecology	+.35	+.06	+.30
6. No nuclear plants	+.61	−.28	+.43
Race and Nation			
7. Objections to neighbors of different race	−.31	−.31	−.27
8. Priority for own nationals in labor markets	−.42	−.40	+.05
9. National pride	−.34	−.16	+.41
Authority and Participation			
10. More respect for authority	−.45	−.20	+.24
11. Confidence in the army	−.48	+.12	+.38
12. Would participate in lawful demonstration	+.51	+.15	−.10
13. Would participate in disarmament protest	+.55	−.42	+.31
Women and Family			
14. Choice over abortion	+.30	+.37	−.21
15. Women as homemakers	−.24	−.36	+.03
16. Women's right to a job	+.33	+.49	+.20
Eigenvalues	2.61	1.57	1.31
Party Factor Scores			
Socialist People's Party (N = 102)	+.98	+.01	−.23
Norwegian Labor Party (N = 246)	+.22	−.14	−.03
Liberals (N = 30)	+.47	+.20	+.13
Center Party (N = 48)	−.10	−.19	+.29
Christian People's Party (N = 56)	−.28	−.30	+.39
Conservatives (N = 158)	−.30	+.54	+.18
Progress Party (N = 100)	−.57	+.31	+.03

Source: World Values Survey 1990. Own calculations.

self-placements, postmaterialism, and church attendance (table 4.5). The concentration on the first factor is stronger in Denmark than in Norway, where church attendance in particular is also explained by the second and third factors.

We have visualized the competitive space in Danish and Norwegian politics in figures 4.1 and 4.2. In Denmark, the left-authoritarian versus right-authoritarian factor overwhelmingly structures party competition. Indeed, the Progress Party is at the right-authoritarian extreme of the scale. At the same time, as parties move toward right-authoritarian positions, they also tend to become more capitalist-cosmopolitan on the second dimension and more capitalist-ecologist on the third. Even though voter beliefs are structured in a multidimensional way, this is not necessarily the case for the parties' mean positions, which plausibly reflect the elites' political appeal. A partial outlier to this strong association between the parties' values on the first, second, and third factors of voter opinion is the Danish Progress Party. While it is at the right-authoritarian extreme on the first factor, it is situated in the center on the comparatively weak primarily economic and antiracist second factor. Moreover, it does not take a pronounced position on the third factor where only the conservatives are clearly in procapitalist territory. These results are likely to reflect Andersen's (1992) contention that the Progress Party articulates a "neoliberalism of the lower strata." Workers are not likely to endorse an unqualified market capitalism, and this is reflected in the party supporters' mean values on the second factor.

In Norway, the dimensionality of the competitive space is slightly more complicated than in Denmark. In addition, here, the major parties, amounting to 82 percent of the respondents with a party preference (N = 606), can clearly be located on a single competitive dimension that combines party positions on the first and the second factors of issue opinions. The Socialist People's Party and the Norwegian Labor Party are most left-libertarian on the first factor and in the center of the second economic left/right factor. In contrast, the conservatives and the Progress Party are more right-authoritarian on the first and promarket on the second factor. Crosscutting this dimension is a second dimension on which three minor parties are located. The Liberals combine a more left-libertarian position with promarket economics on the second factor. In light of our theory, this is an awkward combination with limited voter appeal. This may be one reason why the Liberals have declined in Norway and have not been represented in parliament since 1985. At the other extreme of the subordinate competitive dimension, we encounter the Center and the Christian People's parties with mildly right-authoritarian, but also distinctly anticapitalist, positions on the second factor. It is possible that these parties appeal to a rural and smalltown niche electorate that is not located on the main competitive dimension.

TABLE 4.5. General Ideological Dispositions Predicted by Voters' Issue Positions (Factor Scores of the Exploratory Factor Analysis) in Denmark and Norway

A. Denmark

	Constant		Factor I Left-Libertarians versus Right-Authoritarian		Factor II Capitalist Cosmopolitans versus Anticapitalist Parochials		Factor III Capitalist Ecology versus Socialist Production		adj. R^2
	PE	t	PE	t	PE	t	PE	t	
Left/right Self-Placement	5.72	93.76	-1.00	-16.32	+.07	+1.14	+.24	+3.79	.30*** (N = 654)
Postmaterialism	2.02	105.37	+.21	+11.07	+.07	+3.59	-.01	-.33	.16*** (N = 698)
Church attendance[a]	6.37	92.10	+.27	+3.84	+.06	+.79	+.03	+.70	.02* (N = 697)

B. Norway

	Constant		Factor I Left-Libertarians versus Right-Authoritarian		Factor II Capitalist Cosmopolitans versus Anticapitalist Parochials		Factor III Capitalist Ecology versus Industry		adj. R^2
	PE	t	PE	t	PE	t	PE	t	
Left/right Self-placement	5.70	96.11	-.89	-15.14	+.52	+8.54	+.23	+3.85	.28*** (N = 864)
Postmaterialism	1.83	99.07	+.17	+9.19	+.05	+2.80	-.02	-1.26	.09*** (N = 913)
Church attendance[a]	6.07	92.34	+.33	+4.98	+.24	+3.54	-.37	-5.58	.07** (N = 907)

Source: World Values Survey 1990. Own calculations.
Note: PE = parameter estimate; t = t ratio.
***significant at the .001 level
**significant at the .01 level
*significant at the .05 level
[a]Scale inversed: high values indicate infrequent or no church attendance.

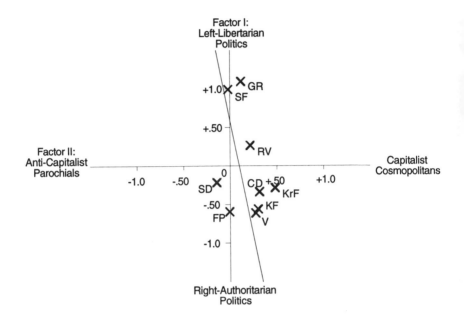

Fig. 4.1. The political space of European democracies: Denmark

As in the French case, the factor analyses do not reveal that race and xenophobia provide a strong dimension that discriminates voters of the Progress parties. To test the robustness of this conclusion, we have engaged in the same statistical operations we already described for the French case. First, we completed a confirmatory factor analysis that forces the appearance of a cosmopolitanism versus parochialism race/xenophobia factor, along with separate economic and politico-cultural factors (tables 4.6 and 4.7). The mean party scores on each factor show that parties that are more socialist on the economic factor also tend to be more libertarian on the politico-cultural factor. The Danish and Norwegian Progress parties, in contrast, are both strongly market-oriented and authoritarian on these scales. With respect to race-xenophobia, an interesting finding emerges. Only the Danish Progress Party clearly caters to voters with parochial-ethnocentrist orientations, whereas in the Norwegian case the voters are somewhere in the middle of the scale. We thus have a rather

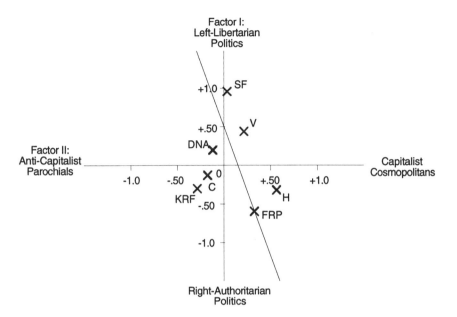

Fig. 4.2. The political space of European democracies: Norway

strong indication that, at least in the Norwegian case, racist appeals are far from decisive for the support of the Progress Party. In the Danish case, we must proceed with further tests to determine the "net impact" of racist attitudes on electoral preferences.

But let us first introduce sociodemographics as a set of control variables and explore the parties' social support coalitions. Tables 4.8 and 4.9 present the familiar occupational group breakdown and its relation to select issue opinions and the percentage of each group supporting a specific party. As in the French case, workers and small businesspeople, together with those inactive in labor markets, have the greatest propensity to voice national and xenophobic sentiments, as well as to endorse stronger authority (rows 2, 4, and 5 in the tables). At the same time, of course, workers are much less procapitalist than independent businesspeople and farmers, although not by a wide margin compared to the professions and to white collar sectors (row 1).

TABLE 4.6. Ideological Divisions in Denmark: Confirmatory Factor Analysis (missing values set equal to zero)

	Capitalism versus Socialism	Authoritarianism versus Libertarianism	Parochialism versus Cosmopolitanism
A. Economic Distribution			
1. For more income inequality	+.58	—	—
2. For private business ownership	+.63	—	—
3. For more competition	+.47	+.11	—
4. For owner-managed business	+.53	+.28	—
B. Libertarian versus Authoritarian Issues			
5. Postmaterialism	—	−.54	—
6. Respect for authority	—	+.39	—
7. Participation in lawful demonstration	—	−.57	—
8. Women's right to abortion	—	−.26	—
9. Role of housewife fulfilling	—	+.15	—
C. Cosmopolitan/Particularist Dimension			
10. Acceptance of neighbor of different race	—	—	+.66
11. Acceptance of foreigners as neighbors	—	—	+.88
12. Members of one's nationality have priority in the labor market	—	+.45	+.32
Average Factor Scores of Party Followers			
Socialist People's Party (N = 143)	−.65	−.67	−.15
Greens (N = 17)	−.65	−.72	−.22
Social Democrats (N = 277)	−.21	+.02	−.01
Radical Liberals (N = 32)	+.06	−.21	−.15
Center Democrats (N = 49)	+.19	+.13	−.10
Christian People's Party (N = 17)	+.10	+.33	+.19
Conservatives (N = 126)	+.53	+.27	−.08
Liberals (N = 109)	+.51	+.21	−.02
Progress Party (N = 52)	+.43	+.28	+.97

Source: World Values Survey 1990. Own calculations.

The electoral coalitions of the Progress parties in both countries can be characterized rather unambiguously. Workers and independent businesspeople are overrepresented (in Denmark, together with the economically inactive respondents), whereas the professions and white-collar employees are underrepresented in the Progress Party electorates. The latter groups, in turn, are

TABLE 4.7. Ideological Divisions in Norway: Confirmatory Factor Analysis (missing values set equal to zero)

	Capitalism versus Socialism	Authoritarianism versus Libertarianism	Parochialism versus Cosmopolitanism
A. Economic Distribution			
1. For more income inequality	+.46	—	—
2. For private business ownership	+.57	—	—
3. For more competition	+.40	+.11	—
4. For owner-managed business	+.43	+.21	—
B. Libertarian versus Authoritarian Issues			
5. Postmaterialism	—	−.47	—
6. Respect for authority	—	+.43	—
7. Participation in lawful demonstration	—	−.51	—
8. Women's right to abortion	—	−.27	—
9. Role of housewife fulfilling	—	+.21	—
C. Cosmopolitan/Particularist Dimension			
10. Acceptance of neighbor of different race	—	—	+.76
11. Acceptance of foreigners as neighbors	—	—	+.91
12. Members of one's nationality have priority in the labor market	—	+.45	+.28
Average Factor Scores of Party Followers			
Socialist People's Party (*N* = 130)	−.41	−.59	−.26
Labour Party (*N* = 343)	−.28	−.01	−.04
Liberal Party (*N* = 35)	.00	−.53	−.06
Christian Party (*N* = 78)	+.04	+.42	−.11
Center Party (*N* = 60)	+.14	+.04	+.20
Conservatives (*N* = 197)	+.44	+.04	−.05
Progress Party (*N* = 128)	+.45	+.20	+.43

Source: World Values Survey 1990. Own calculations.

most heavily overrepresented in both countries' left-libertarian parties at the other extreme of the competitive dimension, the Socialist People's Parties.[13] The Scandinavian Progress parties thus assemble the electoral coalitions we would expect to find in successful NRR parties.

We can now conclude with a fuller analysis of voting patterns for the extreme Right in Scandinavia in order to test the main hypotheses of this study and its rivals (tables 4.10 and 4.11). The first equation in table 4.10 shows that,

TABLE 4.8. Occupation, Ideological Dispositions, and Party Preferences in Denmark

	Professions (percent)	White Collar (percent)	Nonactive in the Labor Force (percent)	Workers (percent)	Independent Business and Farmers (percent)
A. Issue Positions					
1. For business-managed enterprises	46.3 (41)	43.8 (432)	57.4 (108)	42.2 (325)	73.2 (82)
2. Endorse stronger authority	30.8 (39)	31.3 (434)	36.6 (112)	39.5 (332)	34.6 (78)
3. Against neighbors of different race	0.0 (41)	5.4 (428)	7.0 (114)	8.3 (350)	13.1 (84)
4. Proud to belong to one's nation	40.0 (35)	37.9 (427)	48.2 (118)	45.7 (427)	42.7 (82)
B. Percentage of Occupational Group Supporting a Party					
Socialist People's Party	17.9	9.5	6.1	17.7	5.6
Social Democrats	25.0	26.9	33.7	48.0	15.3
Radical Liberals	10.7	5.4	1.0	2.6	1.4
Center Democrats	7.2	6.2	10.2	4.4	2.8
Christian People's Party	7.1	0.8	2.0	2.6	4.2
Liberals	17.9	12.9	19.4	6.6	29.2
Conservatives	14.3	17.5	18.4	7.0	27.8
Progress Party	0.0	4.9	5.2	6.6	11.1

Source: World Values Survey 1990. Own calculations.

TABLE 4.9. Occupation, Ideological Dispositions, and Party Preferences in Norway

	Professions (percent)	White Collar (percent)	Nonactive in the Labor Force (percent)	Workers (percent)	Independent Business and Farmers (percent)
A. Issue Positions					
1. For business-managed enterprises	25.8 (151)	30.1 (196)	35.5 (214)	28.5 (506)	52.9 (121)
2. Endorse stronger authority	26.7 (150)	27.7 (202)	37.2 (222)	33.1 (528)	32.3 (124)
3. Against women's choice of abortion	37.3 (150)	28.0 (201)	36.0 (220)	35.3 (527)	36.6 (120)
4. Against neighbors of different race	4.0 (151)	9.4 (203)	16.9 (225)	13.6 (536)	14.5 (120)
5. Proud to belong to one's nation	30.9 (149)	44.5 (200)	49.8 (219)	47.8 (525)	40.2 (122)
B. Percentage of Occupational Group Supporting a Party					
Socialist People's Party	21.1	15.0	13.5	13.5	8.3
Labour Party	21.9	32.7	35.9	42.8	19.6
Liberal Party	7.8	0.8	2.9	2.4	2.0
Christian Party	8.6	5.9	7.6	7.4	13.4
Center Party	4.7	4.6	4.9	5.0	17.5
Conservatives	25.8	25.5	23.4	13.5	25.8
Progress Party	8.6	9.2	15.8	14.7	12.4

Source: World Values Survey 1990. Own calculations.

TABLE 4.10. Determinants of Political Orientations and of Party Preferences in Denmark

A. Determinants of the Danish Progress Party Vote, Entire Danish Sample
(Maximum likelihood estimates)

	Parameter estimate	Standard error	Probability	Percentage of voters supporting the rightist party if all other variables are held constant but value on the focal variable is at its—	
				Minimum	Maximum
Intercept	23.41	2.28	.0001		
Market Liberalism (Factor I)	+.54	.23	.02	0.9	5.6
Authoritarianism (Factor II)	+.48	.27	.07	1.1	5.1
Parochialism/Racism (Factor III)	+.67	.11	.0001	2.4	18.7
Gender (Female = 2)	−1.20	.41	.003	2.7	0.8
Age	−.02	.01	.06	4.0	1.2
Education	−.12	.07	.08	5.2	2.4
Business or Farmer	+.35	.66	.59	2.7	3.7
Professional	−25.14	—	—	2.7	0.0
White Collar	+.57	.57	.32	2.7	4.6
Worker	+.38	.56	.49	2.7	3.8

Note: Percentage of concordant cases: 82.
Cases *N*: 1010 (missing values on independent variables were substituted by mean values).
Missing cases *M*: 20.

B. Determinants of Vote: Extreme Right versus Moderate Right Voters in Denmark
(Maximum likelihood estimates)

	Parameter estimate	Standard error	Probability	Percentage of voters supporting the rightist party if all other variables are held constant but value on the focal variable is at its—	
				Minimum	Maximum
Intercept	26.81	2.56	.0001		
Market Liberalism (Factor I)	−.39	.29	.17	21.5	6.8
Authoritarianism (Factor II)	+.07	.35	.83	10.0	12.4
Parochialism/Racism (Factor III)	+.80	.14	.0001	10.0	61.4
Gender (Female = 2)	−1.21	.47	.01	11.3	3.7
Age	−.03	.01	.03	18.9	3.7
Education	−.15	.08	.07	23.3	9.9
Business or Farmer	+.01	.73	.99	11.3	11.4
Professional	−26.4	—	—	11.3	0.0
White Collar	+.45	.62	.47	11.3	16.6
Worker	+.98	.63	.12	11.3	25.3

Source: World Values Survey 1990. Own calculations.
Note: Percentage of concordant cases: 81.7.
Cases N: 296.

TABLE 4.11. Determinants of Political Orientations and of Party Preferences in Norway

A. Determinants of the Norwegian Progress Party Vote, Entire Norwegian Sample (Maximum likelihood estimates)

	Parameter estimate	Standard error	Probability	Percentage of voters supporting the rightist party if all other variables are held constant but value on the focal variable is at its—	
				Minimum	Maximum
Intercept	1.30	1.29	.31		
Market Liberalism (Factor I)	1.04	.16	.0001	1.5	39.1
Authoritarianism (Factor II)	.46	.17	.007	4.5	18.2
Parochialism/Racism (Factor III)	.35	.09	.0002	9.7	22.7
Gender (Female = 2)	−.28	.22	.20	10.0	7.8
Age	−.02	.007	.002	15.6	4.7
Education	−.006	.05	.99	10.1	10.0
Business or Farmer	−.81	.39	.04	10.0	4.7
Professional	−.60	.37	.11	10.0	5.7
White Collar	−.70	.36	.05	10.0	5.2
Worker	−.02	.26	.92	10.0	9.8

Note: Percentage of concordant cases: 75.0.
Cases *N:* 1191 (missing values on independent variables were substituted by mean values).
Missing cases *M:* 48.

B. Determinants of Vote: Extreme Right versus Moderate Right Voters in Norway (Maximum likelihood estimates)

	Parameter estimate	Standard error	Probability	Percentage of voters supporting the rightist party if all other variables are held constant but value on the focal variable is at its—	
				Minimum	Maximum
Intercept	2.82	1.43	.05		
Market Liberalism (Factor I)	+.47	.18	.01	12.1	42.0
Authoritarianism (Factor II)	+.16	.21	.45	19.7	29.6
Parochialism/Racism (Factor III)	+.43	.12	.0002	24.0	52.0
Gender (Female = 2)	-.14	.26	.60	24.8	22.4
Age	-.02	.01	.01	34.9	13.2
Education	-.13	.06	.01	45.9	22.4
Business or Farmer	-.69	.43	.11	24.8	14.3
Professional	-.59	.41	.15	24.8	15.5
White Collar	-.59	.40	.14	24.8	15.5
Worker	+.33	.30	.27	24.8	31.6

Source: World Values Survey 1990. Own calculations.
Note: Percentage of concordant cases: 70.1.
Cases N: 392.

compared to the entire Danish sample, Progress Party voters are more market-liberal, considerably more particularist, and somewhat more authoritarian. The occupational variables wash out, but voters tend to be younger, more male, and less educated, pointing toward a blue-collar and small business electorate. The second equation pits Progress Party voters against voters of the other Danish moderate-rightist parties (Conservatives, Liberals, Christians). In that case, procapitalism and authoritarianism no longer significantly distinguish the extreme-rightist vote, but particularism, male gender, youth, and less education and also—almost significantly—being a blue-collar worker survive as statistically significant predictors. Andersen's (1992) conception of a "neo-liberalism of the lower strata" may also be confirmed by the reversal of the sign on factor I, where less market allegiance is almost a significant predictor of Progress Party voters when pitted against voters of the conventional Right.

In Norway, the picture is rather similar to that of Denmark. Here, all three attitude factors, plus youth, predict support of the Progress Party (table 4.11, first equation). Unlike Denmark, the Norwegian Progress Party is market-liberal and particularist-racist even when compared to its conservative competitors (table 4.11, second equation). As in the Danish case, being male, younger, and having less education are significant discriminators of party preference on the extreme Right. Both the results for Denmark and Norway show that racism, xenophobia, and ethnocentrism do play a role in supporting extreme-rightist parties, but they are far from being a "single issue" that completely dominates support for Progress parties.

In light of these findings, we can now review our hypotheses. Other studies and our own data support the argument that the Progress parties are incarnations of right-authoritarian politics both at the elite level (party appeals) as well as the mass level (voter attitudes). These parties assemble social coalitions in which workers and independent business are overrepresented, whereas white-collar employees and professionals are underrepresented.

Our findings demonstrate that the Scandinavian Progress parties do not thrive on a "single-issue" appeal, whether this is conceived as liberal capitalism or ethnic particularism. Instead, a complex cluster of market-liberal, authoritarian, and ethnocentric orientations taken together is critical. The parties' followings express much greater respect for authority than the supporters of other parties and the population in general, as we have shown in chapter 2. Moreover, these right-wing electorates have a propensity to disapprove of unconventional political participation, ecological concerns, and pacifism. Only with respect to gender roles are our findings somewhat ambiguous. In Scandinavia, women's equality in labor markets and the family is more advanced than elsewhere in Europe, and compared to these other countries, the supporters of the Danish and Norwegian Progress parties might also appear to be mildly libertarian. Yet within the contexts of the two countries, Progress Party voters tend to be middle of the road or somewhat more sexist than the supporters of other parties.[14]

The net impact of the libertarian/authoritarian dimension on the vote for Progress parties in tables 2.10 and 2.11 undermines the rival hypothesis that the contemporary Right articulates a "right-libertarian" agenda. This agenda could not be verified at the level of leaders' appeals and has also now been refuted by an analysis of the parties' electoral support. In a similar vein, there is also no corroboration for the "neofascism" hypothesis. The parties are clearly pro-capitalist, not corporatist or anticapitalist. Moreover, it appears that the absence of an extreme-rightist tradition in Scandinavia also tames the ideological articulation of the New Right in the 1980s. This is most clear-cut with respect to the acceptance or rejection of the democratic order where no traces of a neofascist craving for a nondemocratic order can be detected. The comparatively greater moderation of the Scandinavian contemporary Right is also signaled by the more limited cultural and social traditionalism that is conveyed by the party supporters' positions on family and gender roles. In general, however, Progress Party voters would like to see a combination of free market economics with a more authoritarian social and political climate. It would be wrong, therefore, to describe these parties as single-issue mobilizations, right-libertarian parties, or neofascist mobilizations. In the 1980s, the Progress parties moved to the NRR, although they were situated in a less extreme position than comparable parties in other countries.

Strategic Dilemmas of the Scandinavian New Right

Since the emergence of the National Front as a serious vote-getter in France, its moderately conservative competitors found themselves in a dilemma: should they opt for an office-seeking "centrist" strategy to capture the median voter or should they compete with the extreme Right? The strategic dilemma poses itself in such sharp contours because the French moderate Right is comparatively united as a political bloc, and this unity is reinforced by the two-round majoritarian electoral system. The situation is different in Scandinavia. Here the nonsocialist parties are highly differentiated, and the proportional system of representation makes it unlikely that any single party's strategic change will have major consequences for the overall strength of the bourgeois and the socialist party camp. Most parties, except the social democrats, are too small to strive for the big prize of controlling the pivot of the party system that would enable them to control policy making and government formation, the key payoff derived from an office-seeking strategy. As a consequence, on the political Right, at least some of the nonsocialist parties are not exposed to a centripetal pull toward the median voter and therefore may be inclined to compete with more radical competitors, such as the Progress Party. This happened first after 1973 when the conservatives began to embrace one key issue highlighted by the Progress parties—that of income tax relief—and thus contributed to the ensuing decline of the new challengers in the following 10 years up to about 1985.

In Denmark and Norway, the strategic mobility of the nonsocialist parties to move against the Progress parties in a centrifugal competitive mode is most constrained, however, when a bourgeois coalition government is in power. For Progress parties, the best possible competitive situation is a bourgeois minority coalition that can be held hostage on critical issues by compelling it to seek support for a parliamentary majority either on the Right or the Left. In this configuration, bourgeois minority governments cannot go too far toward embracing Progress Party demands on issues such as immigration, law and order, defense, and taxation because some of the more centrist coalition members strictly refuse to join hands with the NRR. As a consequence, Progress parties can demonstrate their political distinctiveness to the electorate whenever bourgeois governments have to cater to centrist political demands. Not by chance, the big surges of the Danish and Norwegian Progress parties in the 1980s came on the heels of lengthy episodes of bourgeois government incumbency gravitating toward increasingly moderate, centrist policies and the seeking of compromises with the opposition social democrats. The Progress parties' electoral gains in the late 1980s, therefore, were won mostly at the expense of the conservatives (Svasand 1991, 22).

A related lesson can be drawn from episodes where nonsocialist parties are in the opposition but try to displace an incumbent social democratic minority government (Strom 1994). It may not necessarily be in the interest of Progress parties to see such maneuvers succeed. What is most important from the perspective of Progress parties is that the competing nonsocialist parties publicly compromise themselves by supporting policies that fly in the face of the free market credo and the right-wing insistence on law and order for which Progress parties claim to stand. The effort of the Norwegian Christian People Party, the Center Party (agrarians), and the Conservatives to replace the Labor Party minority government in 1987 is a good illustration. When the agrarians agreed to the joint effort to topple the government only after Conservatives and Christians had accepted new subsidies for farmers, the Progress Party had a field day exposing the antimarket policies of the aspiring new government parties and significantly benefited from their embarrassment in the 1989 election. In contrast, in 1993, after four years of rather clearly drawn battle lines between the core bourgeois parties and a social democratic minority government, the Norwegian Progress Party had to hand back much of the gain it had made in 1989 to the conventional rightist parties.

Bourgeois minority parties in government or aspiring coalitions, however, have still other advantages for Progress parties. By selectively supporting bourgeois coalitions, NRR parties can demonstrate their political sincerity, calculability, and respectability to the electorate. In this vein, Carl Hagen promised in 1987 that a government with Progress Party participation would rescind agricultural subsidies, thus showing his concern to project a consistent and credible market-liberal image to the voters.

Progress parties have also tried to reinforce an image of respectability by institutionalizing their party organizations and making them less dependent on individual charismatic leaders (Harmel and Svasand 1989). Given the absence of an antidemocratic, antisystem political tradition in Scandinavia, efforts to gain organizational respectability are probably more important for the Scandinavian New Right than for that of any other European country.

Moderate bourgeois governments are generally hostages to the Progress parties' game. Where they play the game and opt for selective parliamentary alliances with the NRR, Progress parties may win voters at their expense. But where they do not play the game and pursue a centrist political course, they are likely to lose even more. In contrast to Denmark, where the moderate bourgeois government made concessions to the Progress Party, such as a strict immigration law, the Norwegian nonsocialist minority government coalition refused in 1985-86 to honor the then small Progress Party's selective parliamentary support of the government with policy concessions. In return, Progress withdrew its support, and the government fell in 1986. Later, in 1989, Hagen's Progress Party almost quadrupled its electorate in the national election, with almost all of its new voters shed by the bourgeois parties. Svasand (1991) argues that in Norway the centrist parties—agrarians and Christian People's Party—prevented the conservatives from pursuing a government policy more accommodating to the Progress Party's demands. Yet again, the internal dilemmas of moderate bourgeois minority governments provide the conditions under which Progress parties can thrive.

The Progress parties' tendency toward a general moderation through selective support of conservative governments and organizational institutionalization in the late 1980s, however, creates strategic dilemmas inside the contemporary New Right. By moving toward a more consistent right-wing program with free market liberalism, more authoritarian views of the political process, an insistence on the boundaries of citizenship and Western culture as well as a greater emphasis on defense and law and order, the parties overcame the rapid factionalization and marginalization they had suffered in the aftermath of their initial successes in the early 1970s when they appeared on the political scene essentially as single-issue protest parties. Nevertheless, in the late 1980s, intraparty conflicts sometimes arose between activists supporting the more moderate strategy of selective accommodation to bourgeois minority governments and advocates of a radical, intransigent opposition course. This became particularly virulent in the Danish Progress Party. The exponent of the radical wing was the party founder, Mogens Glistrup, whose prison sentence allowed the moderate faction to crystallize around a new leader, Pia Kjaersgaard. The ensuing intraorganizational division was reinforced by the conservative government's skillful enticement of the moderate wing into political deals. While this strategy, in the short run, did not stop the Progress Party from increasing its voter share to 9 percent, subsequent elections showed that the right-wing challenge could be contained by selective incorporation of its demands into government policy.

In contrast, the greater polarization of politics since the mid-1980s between moderate bourgeois parties and NRR in Norway helped Hagen's Progress Party contain internal conflict and increase the party's share of the electorate considerably beyond the ceiling reached by its Danish counterpart. Yet the Norwegian Progress parties encountered similar strategic dilemmas between self-marginalization through radicalism or bourgeois cooperation and loss of distinctiveness, experiencing a small time lag in the early 1990s when its support sagged both in municipal elections and the 1993 parliamentary election.

Conclusion

In comparing the Danish and Norwegian Progress parties to the French National Front, the main message of this chapter is that the Scandinavian parties belong to the contemporary authoritarian-rightist sector in the competitive electoral arena of advanced capitalist democracies, yet with a qualification. More than in France, the general social democratic orientation as well as the prodemocratic and libertarian predispositions of most Scandinavian voters restrain the ability of political entrepreneurs to appeal to extreme-rightist and antidemocratic views. As a consequence, the Scandinavian Progress parties unambiguously endorse democratic politics, whereas their continental counterparts remain more or less noncommittal about their democratic loyalties and many of their activists and voters support authoritarian political regimes. Because an extreme-rightist tradition is absent in Scandinavia, the Progress parties do not draw on antidemocratic cadres who had already been involved in other extremist causes before they seized on the favorable political opportunity structure that led to the surge of the Progress parties.

A relatively nonviolent transition to democracy at the turn of the century and more than 50 years of social democratic hegemony have emasculated not only the conservative parties in Scandinavia. To a lesser extent, the same phenomenon can be observed inside their more extreme-rightist competitors who also have to appeal to an electorate that is willing to accept their programmatic message only in comparatively mild dosages. Thus, the Scandinavian Progress parties belong to the NRR, but they constitute a diluted version compared to their counterparts on the European continent.

5

Blending New Right Appeals into a Broad Populist Antiestablishment Strategy: Austria and Italy

Before the rise of the National Front in France and the Progress parties in Scandinavia, none of these countries had significant right-wing parties with an antidemocratic heritage from fascist interwar regimes that might have predestined them to incorporate the themes of the contemporary extreme Right and thus preempt the foundation of new unique rightist parties. The situation is almost the opposite in Italy and, to a lesser extent, in Austria. In both countries, right-wing parties in the 1980s had been represented in the legislature almost since the founding of the new republics after World War II, and they have drawn on distinctly antidemocratic rightist legacies and political constituencies. This continuity is most clear-cut in the case of the Italian Social Movement (MSI) whose precursor was established as a quasifascist party in 1946. The traditional linkage to an ultranationalist and antidemocratic political strand is more indirect in the case of the Austrian Freedom Party (FPÖ) which had a pronounced rightist rhetoric in the 1950s but then a decidedly liberal-democratic profile in the 1960s and 1970s, peaking in the party's admission to the Liberal International in 1979.

With increasing societal opportunities to reach out to new voter groups endorsing a market-liberal and politically rightist program in the 1980s, the Austrian Freedom Party undertook a second strategic reversal and managed to gather new constituencies under its umbrella. In contrast, the MSI failed to reach out to new voter groups and gradually declined in electoral significance, reaching its lowest support level in several decades in the 1992 national legislative election. Its apparent resurgence in the final crisis of the Italian postwar party system, under the umbrella of the National Alliance, may be due more to voter support by default—when the corrupt Christian Democrats ceased to be a viable electoral alternative for conservatives—than the ability of the party to renew itself and target new electoral groups. Time will tell whether the shock of 1993–94 also disrupted the continuity of the "old" extreme Right and breathed new life into a tired party or whether the Italian political Right has been subjected to a radical transformation that also eroded the underpinnings of the postfascist MSI.

In any case, in the political dynamic leading up to 1993–94, the MSI played only a subordinate role. Instead of affiliating with the MSI, voters disgruntled with and alienated from the established parties gravitated toward a new party formation, the Northern League (NL), composed of several regional leagues, the most important of which has been the Lega Lombarda. In a similar vein, the Austrian Freedom Party became the rallying point for frustrated voters in the second half of the 1980s. What both parties have in common is that they do not exclusively appeal to the NRR of authoritarian and ethnocentrist promarketeers, constituting an electoral coalition in which businesspeople and blue-collar workers are overrepresented. Instead, these parties express the sentiments of a "populist" antistatist segment of the electorate whose crucial common denominator is the alienation from the incumbent political elites in parties and public administration, and a generalized disaffection with the established channels of patronage-driven and clientelistic interest intermediation. Both in Italy and Austria, new rightist demands have thus been incorporated into old or new parties, but these parties have subordinated such demands to broader appeals that also reach out to "progressive" constituencies that call for "clean government."

In the social sciences, the notion of populism has been employed to denote a variety of economic and political demands that redistribute power and resources from what is perceived to be an organized elite to the masses, understood in varying and often only vague ways (Conovan 1981). For the purposes of examining the Austrian Freedom Party and the Italian Northern League, only the political meaning of populism is appropriate, not the insistence on redistributive economic policies. In political terms, populism signifies the effort to destroy established institutions of interest intermediation and elite control and to put in their place some kind of "direct" voice of the people, embodied in the leader of the populist party. Austrian and Italian populist parties attack the incumbent political elites, but unlike economic populism, they endorse free market institutions and thus directly oppose the major tenets of economic populism, namely, redistributive income policies that elevate the standard of living of the masses at the expense of the wealthy.

In this chapter, we will first argue that the different pathways of antistatist, market-liberal populism in Austria and Italy—renovation of an existing party in one country, displacement of the entrenched right-wing party in the other—involves the entrenchment of the historical Right in politics. It is precisely the depth of the MSI's rootedness in a variety of strands of ancient fascist politics that prevented it from recognizing and seizing upon the new political opportunities to revitalize the extreme Right. Because the MSI shares a direct historical continuity with the fascist movement of the 1920s and the regime governing Italy over the subsequent two decades, it proved unable to change its strategy and appeal in the same way as the Austrian Freedom Party with its more indirect historical roots in a fascist movement and regime.

The capacity of parties to synthesize different political appeals and constituencies results from the intellectual and organizational traditions of the extreme Right. In the Italian case, the existence of the MSI made some traditional right-wing electoral constituencies who otherwise might have supported a new rightist party unavailable to the latter. The MSI itself had become part of an establishment and of practices in southern Italian politics that became the target not only of new rightist currents, but also of a broader range of populist forces. Conversely, the Austrian Freedom Party, through its liberal-democratic turn in the 1960s and 1970s, was less caught up in a traditional rightist mold and could seize on the appropriate moment to craft a new antiestablishment coalition that would attract not only entirely new constituencies but also still maintain some continuity and linkage to previous and potential moderate FPÖ voters. Unlike the MSI, but similar to the Northern League in Italy, the FPÖ became the harbinger of voters who wished to register their protest against the tightly knit cartel within the Austrian political elite without having to support the more left-libertarian Alternative Austrian Green (GA).

As mentioned in chapters 1 & 2, the critical variable to explain the special new Austrian and Italian party configurations, in which right-authoritarianism is diluted and submerges into broader populist currents rather than finds its own articulation in distinctive parties, is the development of partocracy (or *partitocrazia*) in these two countries, a term used to indicate the fusion of state, party, and economic elites in politico-economic networks characterized by patronage, clientelism, and corruption. In quantitative terms, there can be little doubt that the key features of these networks have always had a much more intense presence in Italy than in Austria. Nevertheless, in qualitative terms, these institutional features have given rise to similar sentiments of dissatisfaction in both countries' political cultures. Comparing population surveys across Western Europe, Austrian and Italian respondents are much more likely to express high levels of political alienation, disaffection with the parties, cynicism, and low sense of personal political effectiveness than citizens of other countries (Plasser and Ulram 1992, 157).

Partocracy existed in both countries before populist political sentiments became virulent, but two interactive processes have made partocracy progressively less bearable for significant population groups. First, the advent of postindustrial society with an explosion of advanced education and instruction and related occupations has increased the share of highly trained, politically sophisticated citizens who demand a more transparent and participatory political process than is delivered by closed intraelite concertation in partocracies. To a considerable extent, the populist revolt against the incumbent elite is thus a white-collar "middle-class" revolt, whereas pure right-authoritarian parties draw more on petit bourgeois and working-class elements, as we have seen in the cases of France and Scandinavia. Second, the surge in demands for greater political participation and effectiveness occurred just at the time that a strategic convergence of the incumbent Austrian and Italian political elites on the symbolic and the substantive level—through government coalitions and policies—highlighted the powerlessness of the population and the absence of true democratic checks on the governing parties in the 1980s. In other words, an interaction effect of social change and political elite strategies brought about a political explosion. On top of all that, the final blow was handed to the partocratic structures by the collapse of communism that removed the old friend/ foe images in the domestic political competition that had concealed interelite collusion and motivated voters to remain loyal to the established political organizations.

If this theoretical sketch is correct, the facts should demonstrate that (1) the populist antistatist parties in Austria and Italy are less authoritarian relative to their intrasystemic competitors than the French and Scandinavian parties of the contemporary extreme Right and that (2) this difference in strategy is reflected in corresponding differences between the electorates of the two groups, both in terms of their respective issue positions and their socioeconomic composition. The leaders of the populist parties on occasion do cater to racist and xenophobic sentiments, but such appeals are calculated supplements to a much broader expression of dissatisfaction and disgust with the prevailing interpenetration of state, party, and economy in Austria and Italy. In fact, putting too much emphasis on an ethnocentrist, if not racist, message may be a positive danger to keeping the populist coalition together. This is something the leader of the Italian Northern League, Umberto Bossi, realized quickly in the early 1990s, whereas his colleague Jörg Haider in Austria had to learn this message the hard way through a failed referendum campaign for tough immigration laws in 1992. Populist parties have to maintain a careful balance between tirades against corruption and party patronage, on the one side, and xenophobic appeals on the other. A preliminary analysis of the 1994 Austrian election, for example, suggests that Haider's recent emphasis on antiforeigner slogans may have won him votes among the Vienna working class, but he lost votes among the progressivist electorate. The FPÖ's balance of voter movement may remain positive, however, as long as the pillars of the patronage system, the Austrian People's Party (ÖVP) and the Austrian Socialist Party (SPÖ), still govern together and fuel the misgivings of an increasing share of the electorate.

Historical Antecedents of the Contemporary Right in Italy and Austria

In order to understand the reasons why the MSI in Italy did not seize on new electoral opportunities, it is important to examine the party's historical entrenchment after World War II. With some simplification, one can generally say that the Italian fascist movement in the early 1920s was strong in northern

Italy among urban groups as well as among the rural elites and their clienteles. In contrast, the Italian South was dominated by traditional patronage networks of the entrenched older parties, particularly the liberals, and lent relatively little support to the fascist movement. With the seizure of power, Mussolini's party began to establish itself in southern Italy, but in that process the fascist party transformed itself into a new southern traditional, patronage, and clientelist party that differed sharply from the more modern hierarchical party of mass mobilization in the north of the country. Italian interwar fascism thus involved two partially crosscutting, partially reinforcing, internal cleavages. On the one hand was the territorial and organizational cleavage between North and South. On the other was the programmatic cleavage between (1) an antisystem movement whose features later reemerged in a transformed mode in the short-lived northern Italian "Social Republic" of Saló with socialist and antimonarchist leanings and (2) the traditionalist totalitarian regime from the mid-1920s to 1943, which was allied with the Catholic Church and the monarchy.[1]

The post-World War II extreme Right, however, could not be reconstructed in the North, where the labor movement and urban, moderately conservative religious and secular parties became dominant, but only in the South where traditional patronage networks prevailed well into the new republic. The extreme Right in the South established a clientelist network that very much parallels similar networks created by the parties supporting the republic, particularly that of the "Democracia Christiana" (DC). In other words, it is the traditional, conservative wing of the old fascist regime, which survived into the new republic and entrenched itself at the grassroots level in mass organizations encapsuling a loyal electorate. This traditional wing has always lent support to private property and political hierarchy. However, it was uninterested in the mass mobilization organized by the fascist state and never endorsed the socialist fascist Left that came to the fore in the Italian Social Republic of 1944. Moreover, this traditionalist extreme Right also rejected the dynamic forces of the competitive marketplace as an organizing principle of the economy. The organizational entrenchment of the MSI in patronage networks and the party's hostility to open market competition set it clearly apart from the contemporary rightist agenda of the 1980s with its emphasis on liberal economic ideas. Nevertheless, its insistence on property, hierarchy, and order may appear to make its voters belong to the new extreme Right although they do not share key ideas with the contemporary Right, such as the supremacy of free market competition or the significance of racial policies in a moral and cultural reform of society.

In spite of the traditionalist southern orientation of its majority wing, the MSI has always incorporated a minority current committed to the national socialist program of the Italian Social Republic of Saló. This strand of the extreme Right combines an authoritarian statism with a quest for socialist redistribution and thus comes close to the left wing of German national socialism of Gregor Strasser and his national socialist labor unionism. The national socialist minority current inside the Italian historical extreme Right is also inimical to the adoption of a New Right political agenda. Whereas the latter endorses free markets and unconstrained economic inequality, the former attacks it. Thus, both legacies of the fascist movement and regime in Italy, a southern clientelist traditionalism and the national socialist undercurrents of the fascist movements, have made it difficult for the MSI to adopt a new right-authoritarian political appeal.

The third difference between the traditional fascist Italian extreme Right and the contemporary authoritarian Right of the 1980s involves race and ethnocentrism. In contrast to German national socialism, racism and especially anti-Semitism, played no role in Italy before Mussolini came under Hitler's spell in the late 1930s. Italian fascism drew a line between the national community and outsiders, but this line between friends and foes was entirely nationalist and imperialist. If anything, the fascists' imperialist ambitions called for inclusion of different races and cultures in the process of modernization under Italian leadership. As a consequence, it has been difficult for the postwar fascist party in the 1980s to conceive of its struggle as one against foreigners and peoples of different ethnic and cultural origin, particularly those who actually or potentially were included in an Italian empire on the southern shores of the Mediterranean and in Africa.

It would be misleading to believe that the MSI represented the only organization of the Italian extreme Right in the postwar period. To the contrary, Italian politics has been characterized by the existence of numerous right-extremist sects, many of whose militants drifted in and out of the MSI. This extreme Right includes both terrorist organizations as well as an intellectual New Right that has modeled itself on the French example.[2] Nevertheless, the MSI has always been the hegemonic electoral organization on the Italian Right and was never seriously challenged in importance by any other groups in the arena of party competition. The effort of moderate MSI legislators after 1976 to form their own party, "Democrazia Nazionale," ended up in complete failure in the 1979 election. In this sense, it is appropriate to treat the MSI as the key rightist political actor whose fascist legacy and strategic choices in the arena of party competition have shaped the fortunes of the entire ideological sector until the late 1980s.

In contrast to Italy, in Austria the Freedom Party, which began to attract elements of the extreme Right in the 1980s, is historically and organizationally somewhat further removed from national socialist origins than the MSI is from Mussolini's fascism, although there are definite linkages between the FPÖ and extremist predecessors both with respect to personnel and programmatic ideas. But in the historical fund of right-extremist ideas in Austria, there are elements that can be directly brought to bear on the reconstitution of the contemporary

Right. In particular, racism and anti-Semitism, which were widespread in the interwar period, not only among fascist forces but also in the Catholic pillar of Austrian politics, could be revived and up to a certain level mobilized for xenophobic and ethnocentric purposes in the 1980s and 1990s when Austria again provided an opinion climate in which the new FPÖ leadership could attract at least some new followers based on such messages. The importance of racism and ethnocentrism in Austria has always been further reinforced by the fact that—unlike Italy—a nationalist appeal has been unavailable to the Austrian far Right. The Austrian Right never endorsed an Austrian nation and always sought a unification with Germany. With this option ruled out by the results of World War II, in right-wing efforts to draw particularist boundaries around collective identities the definition of friends and foes quite naturally has turned to differences in culture and ethnicity rather than territoriality. Nevertheless, one has to be cautious not to overstate the importance of racism for the rise of the FPÖ in the 1980s. As we will show below, the overall electoral performance of the party must be explained in different terms, even though xenophobia and anti-Semitism certainly appeal to a critical segment of its new followers.

A second difference between the impact of Italian fascism on the MSI and that of Austrian national socialism on the FPÖ involves the organizational position of the historical Right vis-à-vis other political forces. Whereas in the Italian South the fascist Right became the carrier of traditional clientelist politics, the Austrian Nazi movement, configured around a relatively modest party organization and limited support from some para-military *Heimwehr* groups, was wedged in between two vast socialist and Catholic organizational blocs and "subsocieties." The Austrian Catholics were strong primarily in the countryside and in western Austria where they were supported by quasi-fascist *Heimwehr* units and the socialists dominated Vienna and other industrialized areas of the country where they built their own para-military units. The fascist movement could target only groups that were not organized by these two major parties, primarily a secular urban middle class opposing both hegemonic politico-cultural pillars in Austrian society.

This configuration of political forces with two overpowering organized blocs and a small secular urban middle-class segment in between these giants continued after World War II. In this setting, novel political appeals may not invoke authoritarian ideas, but they may primarily thrive on populist anti-establishment resentments against the entrenched, hierarchical Catholic and socialist blocs. In the 1980s, the FPÖ became the prime political locus for articulating populist ideas, although they also played a role for the Austrian Greens. This appeal was reinforced by the FPÖ's efforts to embrace market-liberal doctrines that were not part of the extreme-rightist legacy but could now be connected to the party's national populist agenda. Nothing was more plausi-

ble than breaking up the hierarchical interlocking politico-economic networks
created by the hegemonic parties than by forcing economic actors to engage in
free market competition. The political populism of the traditional Right thus
provided an intellectual bridge between the demand for market liberalism and
the realities of a partocratic regime. Simultaneously, the combination of market
liberalism and political populism struck a responsive chord with a much
broader share of the electorate than that reached by the New Right in France
and Scandinavia. Even voters who do not care about authoritarian and
xenophobic positions may still support the FPÖ because of its emphasis on
breaking partocracy and substituting free markets in its place.

A somewhat simplified reconstruction of the intellectual, social, and organizational legacies of the Italian and Austrian Right thus brings to the fore
several critical differences that made it difficult for the established Italian
Social Movement to adopt the appeals of the NRR, but which facilitated a
strategic reversal of the Austrian Freedom Party in which it embraced critical
themes of the extreme Right yet subordinated them to a broader populist and
market-liberal message. The NRR tends to be promarket, antiegalitarian, and
racist. But the Italian MSI has always been ambivalent about market liberalism, although its traditionalist majority supports private property. Moreover,
the MSI and the fascist right have been nationalist and imperialist, but they
have not adopted racism. In contrast, the Austrian extreme Right and its undercurrents in the Freedom Party were always strictly opposed to the hierarchical
politico-economic corporatism of the two leading forces in Austrian politics—
Catholics and socialists. This stance allowed them to adopt a pronounced
market-liberal program in the 1980s combined with a populist attack on the
"powers that be." Moreover, the Austrian Right looks back on a legacy of
intense racist and ethnocentric resentment, all appeals that regained relevance
in the party's strategy in the late 1980s, though it remained partially submerged
in a populist program.

Strategic Opportunities for an Anti-Statist Populism in the 1980s

Both in Italy and Austria, the configuration of the dominant moderate parties of
the Right and the strategies of their leftist opponents offered unique opportunities for the construction of new populist antistatist parties in the late 1980s.
For the first time, both critical conditions fostering the growth of contemporary
rightist parties of different shades came together in these two countries. On the
sociological level, a shift of the voters' demand profile toward "clean," transparent, and more participatory politics occurred, particularly by voters in the
most economically advanced regions. On the political level, strategic positions
by both the socialist/communist party camp and the parties of the bourgeois

Right were moderated, a condition that had existed in Austria already in the 1950s and early 1960s, but without the sociological environment conducive to the contemporary Right. In Austria, the more recent political convergence was highlighted by the renewal of the Grand Coalition in 1986. In Italy, it was expressed first in the Historical Compromise between communists and Christian Democrats in the 1970s and then in the reconfiguration of the communist Left in the late 1980s, precipitated by the end of the Cold War. Each party system thus moved toward convergence on different pathways.

Both Italian and Austrian governments of the 1950s were products of the Cold War era. In Italy, it pitted a majoritarian centrist and moderate-right bloc against communists and socialists and a much smaller neofascist extreme Right. The governing Christian Democrats saw the threat to the new Italian Republic as coming primarily from the Left, a conception that initially included both communists and socialists. In this alignment, there was little room for the MSI to grow. Sartori's (1966) description of Italian democracy as "polarized pluralism" with two powerful extreme poles fighting against the middle was always incorrect in the sense that the relative strength of the extremes was lopsided in favor of the Left. The extreme Right could never gain the strategic weight it aspired to, a weight that would have forced the Christian Democrats to engage in centrifugal competition with the MSI. In the second half of the 1950s, the Christian Democratic government often relied on MSI votes in parliament and a DC representative was even elected to the presidency with rightist support. In order to encourage this process of integration into the conservative camp, the MSI moderated its strategic stance, a process that triggered the exit of the radical "Ordine Nuovo" current in 1956. The year 1960 marked the climax and watershed of DC-MSI cooperation (cf. Ignazi 1993, 80–81). The Christian Democrat Tambroni was elected as prime minister with MSI support but fell soon thereafter over the controversies that this rapprochement with the MSI stirred inside his own party. Forces within the Christian Democrats who sought an opening to the socialists then gained the upper hand (Chiarini 1991a, 31–33). The interlude of Christian Democratic cooperation with the MSI gave way to a new isolation and strategic irrelevance of the MSI in an essentially bipolar political system.

In Austria, a Grand Coalition of socialists and Catholics prevailed throughout the 1950s. Although this government commanded more than 90 percent of the parliamentary seats, it would be wrong to see it as an all-party centrist government that provided excellent opportunities for new leftist and rightist challengers. While the government had no serious internal political enemy, the division of Austria until 1955 between the Western and Eastern allies of World War II, and then Austria's precarious position as a neutral "frontline" state at the height of the Cold War, pitted the Grand Coalition against an external enemy. In this situation, it could rally broad-based domestic support without having to fear a strong populist counterforce. In this period, the extreme Left, organized by the Austrian communist party, declined, and the FPÖ was compelled to abandon its German-nationalist and antidemocratic overtones.

In the 1960s, both in Italy and in Austria, competition around the two major political camps intensified and thus prevented opportunities for new extremist parties to attract disaffected conservatives. In Italy, the governing Christian Democrats opened to the moderate Left and included the socialists in coalition governments. Yet at the same time, the Italian Communist Party (PCI) dramatically strengthened its electoral appeal and became the hegemonic opposition party. Moreover, with the communists' efforts to embrace democratic rules, this opposition increasingly looked like an alternative government party that eventually might put together a leftist majority coalition. Italian politics became a bipolar system with a moderately conservative and an initially radical leftist, but gradually moderating, opposition bloc (Farneti 1985).

In Austria, the Grand Coalition was marred by increasing tensions before and after the 1962 elections and was eventually abandoned. In 1966, the Catholic Austrian People's Party (ÖVP) formed a majority government that was replaced first by a social democratic minority government in 1970, then by a social democratic majority in 1971. In the brief interlude of the socialist minority cabinet, the SPÖ government was supported by the FPÖ, which then appeared to have become a mainstream European liberal party. From 1971 to 1983, the SPÖ won outright parliamentary majorities and pursued social reform policies that set the social democrats apart from the previous ÖVP government, although it is clear that on fundamental aspects of the Austrian political economy ÖVP and SPÖ supported almost identical policies.

In the period from 1966 to 1983, government alternation between the two major parties and their efforts to present differing visions on social and political reforms in Austria provided an incentive for voters to choose among the two major alternatives rather than support a third option. As a consequence, neither the FPÖ nor any other party running on antiestablishment sentiments could make serious electoral inroads. The situation began to change only in the late 1970s when the socialist government's capacity for reform began to decline, as more and more interests configured around the party insisted on the maintenance of the status quo. The first consequence of this development, however, was not a realignment on the political Right, because the People's Party was still in opposition to the SPÖ government and thus could rally right-wing voters, but a realignment on the Left, propelling various Green lists into the electoral arena that eventually consolidated around the United Austrian Greens. The Austrian Greens did gain some votes of conservative "deep ecology" fundamentalists from the People's Party, but the bulk of their support came from actual or potential SPÖ voters, particularly among the youngest age cohorts.

In contrast to Austria, the Italian configuration of party competition in the 1970s did create an opportunity for the extreme Right to make electoral advances, when the communists' strategy to entice the governing Christian Democrats into a "Historical Compromise" led the party from the opposition into a quasigovernmental role. If nothing else, this development showed that Italy had moved from "centrifugal" to "centripetal" competition among the major parties. This trend triggered the emergence of new extremist movements on the left of the communist party. On the right, the MSI had won an unprecedentedly high level of electoral support in the 1972 parliamentary election with 8.7 percent, but then it could not take advantage of the convergence of the major left and moderate-right parties. The 1972 success was primarily achieved on law-and-order slogans opposing the mobilization of the extraparliamentary New Left whose capacity to disrupt Italian politics had been manifested by the "hot autumn" of 1969. The MSI thus attracted the southern Italian lower classes and the "silent Northern middle class" opposed to student leftism (Chiarini 1991a, 35). But the MSI could not capitalize on this advance because the party itself supported a "double strategy" of seeking respectability within the framework of democratic competition but simultaneously tolerating right-wing street violence and even terrorist attacks (Caciagli 1988, 24). Due to this contradiction, the MSI's efforts to project itself as the counterweight to an unruly extremist Left collapsed and led to a decline of voter support. From a comparative perspective, what may have been equally important in explaining the MSI's failure to sustain its electoral breakthrough of 1972 is its inability to offer its actual and potential constituencies a new program beyond traditional authoritarian appeals. An entrenched player in a hierarchical and clientelist political system, it was an unlikely standard-bearer of populist resentments against partocracy.

The existing alignment of the established Italian political parties received a new lease on life with the collapse of the PCI's Historical Compromise strategy in 1979 and the eventual entry of the socialists under Bettino Craxi into the government. On the one hand, the new relationship among the parties reestablished a clear line between government and opposition that was highlighted by numerous conflicts between the two party blocs over economic and social policy. On the other, in the initial years of the socialists' participation in a five-party coalition until about 1987, Craxi's party and Craxi himself as prime minister appeared to provide the leadership to reform Italian "partocracy" from the inside rather than from the periphery of the political spectrum.

A renewed electoral opportunity for the extreme Right arose only when bipolar moderate competition among the established parties began to crumble in the second half of the 1980s. At that time, it became clear that Craxi's socialists could not and would not reform Italian "partocracy" to the extent desired by many voters. Externally, the socialists were constrained by a

Christian Democratic party entangled in numerous patronage scandals and allegedly linked to various southern Italian mafia groups. Internally, Craxi had never been able and willing to dismantle the locally entrenched mass party apparatus of the PSI that sought patronage and treated the state as a bounty. These practices were not confined to local politics but also reached into the highest ranks of the socialists' and Christian Democrats' leadership, as was revealed by scandals surrounding the parties' meddling with state-owned enterprises. The wave of scandals that shook the ranks of the socialists in the late 1980s and early 1990s, claiming Craxi himself, damaged the PSI's respectability as a party of institutional reform and contributed to a growing realization in the Italian population that political improvements could be sought only from the outside, by placing new parties and new politicians in responsible offices. The mass media and new political entrepreneurs contributed to this changing perception of the political situation.

It must be underlined that the antiparty affect in the Italian population has not been confined to voters who harbor racist and authoritarian predispositions not fully represented by the established parties, but has spread through a broad cross section of Italian society. Thus, a party could expect to become most successful that harnessed both right-wing protest as well as general antisystem resentment against the partocracy of the political establishment. In the early 1990s, it appeared that this combination of appeals had been engineered in Italian politics by the emerging Northern League. The anger against the political elite in general could be combined with parochial ethnocultural resentments against southern Italians who, in the eyes of many northern Italians, have inflicted the curse of partocracy on the entire country.

In the same vein, in Austrian politics the winning formula for a new challenger in the 1980s was to thrive on a general anger directed against the main parties' hold on the state apparatus and to a lesser extent on select specific extreme-rightist concerns, once a favorable political opportunity structure in which a populist party could thrive. In 1983, a still liberal-democratic FPÖ entered a government coalition with the SPÖ that had lost its majority in the preceding parliamentary election. Yet the growing frequency of patronage scandals in which the SPÖ was entangled and the lack of electoral rewards the FPÖ received in state elections for its alliance with the SPÖ led to a deep rift inside the Freedom Party that precipitated the replacement of its leadership in 1986.[3] In this process, the moderate liberal leaders were effectively cast aside by a new populist, antiestablishment, and sometimes ethnocentrist group led by a young entrepreneur, Jörg Haider, from Carinthia. Haider wasted no time antagonizing the social democratic coalition partner with his populist, anti-Semitic, and xenophobic rhetoric, a strategy that quickly led to the collapse of the government coalition.

In the ensuing early national elections, Haider's party could double its electoral support to almost 10 percent of the national vote, while both established parties suffered losses. Since none of the parties had an outright majority, the ÖVP was now faced with an unpleasant dilemma. On the one hand, it could form a narrow majority government with the FPÖ, a party that promoted not only highly contentious racist and nationalist divisions, but also assaulted the ÖVP's participation in Austrian "partocracy," thus raising anxieties among ÖVP beneficiaries of the established system. On the other hand, it could join the SPÖ in a new Grand Coalition to protect and only gradually modify the status quo of partocracy, but run the risk of reinforcing Haider's opportunities to thrive on antiparty sentiments and attacks against the "cartel" of the large Austrian parties. In this situation, the ÖVP chose the second strategy and paid a heavy price in the subsequent national election. In 1990, the party lost almost 10 percent of the vote, and the bulk of these defectors appear to have been won over by the FPÖ, which reached an unprecedented 16.6 percent of the electorate. The participation of the ÖVP in the partocratic regime maneuvered the party into a strategic trap between almost equally unpalatable and electorally costly coalitions with the SPÖ or the FPÖ, a trap from which the ÖVP has yet to escape liberation.

The entry of the People's Party into the Grand Coalition with the SPÖ not only reduced the ÖVP's public support base, but also led to a structural reassessment of party competition by the Austrian electorate. Whereas in the 1970s, voters saw the FPÖ as a party of the center, a view still prevalent in 1985, by 1992 the Austrian electorate located the Greens on the left, followed by the SPÖ, then the ÖVP on the center-right, and finally the FPÖ on the right. Austrian surveys that ask respondents to locate the parties on a five-point scale from left (=1) to right (=5) found that the FPÖ moved from 3.2 (1976) to 3.37 (1985) to 3.80 (1992). In the same time period, the ÖVP was rated at 3.86 (1976), 3.82 (1985), and 3.51 (1992). The SPÖ's location moved slightly to the center from 2.31 (1976) to 2.52 (1992), whereas the United Greens are seen on the left at 2.4 in 1992 (Plasser and Ulram 1992, 153).

Thus, by the late 1980s, both in Austria and Italy the established parties had created the settings in which new rightist appeals could thrive electorally. This potential was magnified by the "partocracy" penetrating the state apparatus with representatives of the major parties and giving rise to an endless slew of political scandals that entangled a growing proportion of the parties' top- and middle-level politicians. While qualitatively similar, these problems reached a much greater order of magnitude in Italy than in Austria and therefore have also left deeper marks on the Italian party system.

Strategic Choices on the Far Right

The Lombardian League was founded in 1982 by a young lawyer, Umberto Bossi, upon the model of the small Northern Italian "Union Valdotaine." In

1985, the party won 2.5 percent of the vote in local elections in Varese, and in 1987 2.7 percent in the Lombardian regional elections. It took off in 1989 with 6.5 percent in the European election and 16.4 percent in the regional election. By 1992, the unified list of the various regional leagues, the Northern League, won no less than 20.5 percent in Lombardy in the parliamentary election of that year and thus was close behind the leading party, the Christian Democrats, with 25.2 percent.

A critical factor in the meteoric rise of the regional leagues and then their umbrella and successor organization, the Northern League, has been the inability of the Italian MSI to benefit from the agenda of the NRR and of more broad-based populist antipartocratic sentiments. The MSI's southern Italian conservative traditionalism, deeply entrenched in local patronage networks, made it an unlikely candidate to represent an antipartocratic position with credibility. At the same time, its corporatist and social-fascist tendencies prevented it from invoking a market-liberal and antistatist appeal. Moreover, social fascism did not subscribe to racism but to a new version of imperialism. The history of the MSI is characterized by a wavering between right-wing traditionalism and social fascism, alternatives that were still highlighted by the intraparty controversies after the death of the party's long-time leader Georgio Almirante in 1988.

Almirante, a fascist cadre of the Salό Republic, led the MSI from 1946 to 1950, but was then shoved aside by more moderate forces who sought an understanding with the ruling Christian Democrats.[4] When this strategy failed in 1960, Almirante reemerged as the party leader with the task of revitalizing the organization by a more radical course, which led to the MSI's 1972 electoral success. At the same time, the radical strategy, with its ambiguous evaluation of right-wing terrorism that cost many lives in the first half of the 1970s, also constrained the party's appeal and eventually led to its decline. In the aftermath of the party's 1976 defeat, Almirante set the party on a more moderate course that attempted to lead the Right into the democratic order (cf. Ferraresi 1988, 93–98). In 1983, Almirante even tried to present himself as the Italian Ronald Reagan (Tassani 1990, 128). But the MSI could never liberate itself from its historical roots, the traditionalist and fascist legacy, image, and reputation transmitted by its activists and electoral constituencies. The range of political forces under the umbrella of the MSI is well captured in the following two quotations from historical analyses of the MSI:

> The fascist inheritance is, of course, a major factor, and it finds embodiment in a *legal* neo-fascist party (the fourth largest party in the country), which caters to the "nostalgics" of the past regime, to conservative notables, to "know-nothing," "ordinary men," malcontents and, finally, to self-styled revolutionary fringes. (Ferraresi 1988, 104)

Yesterday and today, the ideological universe of the Italian right has been out of step with the social and economic dynamics of Western capitalism. The right still gets worked up about the specters of the twenties: the soldierly, combative spirit of the veterans of World War I, including those who served in the Foreign Legion; a view of society which includes inequality, hierarchy, and organicism; and a view of politics which is anchored to the abstract and worn-out schemes of socialization and compulsory corporatism. The language of the right has remained "spiritual" and largely metapolitical. A negative bias, which holds that the economy is innately a carrier of moral infection and decadence for modern civilization, has never disappeared from the cultural universe of the Italian Right. (Chiarini 1991b, 13)

The MSI's critique of partocracy became increasingly insistent in the 1980s (Caciagli 1988, 29), but history—via the reputation a party acquires over time—explains why it had a hollow ring in the eyes of most voters. Moreover, the historically conditioned incapacity of the party's leaders and activists to understand the signs of the time and to recognize new voter alignments on which a rightist party might thrive was revealed by the political debates and competition for the party leadership after Almirante's death in 1988. A representative of the party's traditionalist and moderate wing, Gianfranco Fini, was pitted against a representative of a radical antiestablishment fascist wing, Pino Rauti. Fini won the first round of the competition and led the party as secretary until 1990, when he was replaced by Rauti (Chiarini 1991a, 39). But Rauti could not weld the party together or find a new electrifying appeal that would reestablish the MSI's hegemony over the emerging rightwing currents in Italian politics. During a visit by Le Pen in 1988, Rauti made it clear that the MSI would not play the xenophobic card (Tassani 1990, 137). In fact, Rauti experimented with a strange blend of "Third Worldism" that invoked solidarity with the poor countries against the capitalist centers as a neofascist strategy for fighting *against* racism and xenophobia (cf. Ignazi 1993, 89).

Both Fini's and Rauti's strategy also missed the chance to appeal to free market economics. Moreover, by ignoring a racist and xenophobic sentiment on the authoritarian political Right that was undoubtedly available in Italy and more specifically already widespread in the MSI's core electorate, its electoral support went into a free fall (Chiarini 1991b, 37–38). The blind spots of the Rauti strategy are all the more striking given that he aimed to make use of the antisystem sentiments of the subproletarian groups of southern Italy (Sidoti 1992, 158). Precisely these groups, however, might respond more to authoritarian, racist, and xenophobic appeals than to a nationalist anticapitalism. By the time Fini staged a comeback and replaced Rauti, and the party finally moved to a more ethnocentrist and intensely populist appeal, the Northern League had already established itself and barred the MSI from regaining lost electoral territory, let alone conquering new territory now occupied by the Northern League. Even in the 1994 parliamentary election, when the MSI, now submerged in an "Alleanza Nazionale," was handed an electoral windfall by the disintegrating Christian Democrats and collected 13.5 percent of the vote nationwide, its electoral support was concentrated in the south, whereas it made little headway against the Northern League in the latter's core region.

Racism and ethnocentrism in Italian politics differ from those of other countries insofar as they are directed not just against non-Italians but against the strangers within Italy. From the perspective of many northern Italians, this includes much of the southern region of the country. The resentment against southern Italians is based not only in the economic North/South differentiation, the disparity of productivity and wealth in the country, and the compulsory transfers of economic resources to the South, but also on the popular perception that most Italian politicians involved in the clientelistic political machines are recruited from the south. Southern Italy is seen as the land of partocracy, northern Italy as the land of business and commerce. Thus, liberal procapitalist and antipartocratic orientations in the North could be combined with ethnocentric biases, a fusion of political views engineered by the constituent members of the Northern League in Lombardy, Tuscany, and Veneto.[5]

It is critical to note that these leagues are not just reactionary and sentimental efforts to reestablish regional boundaries. To the contrary, these boundaries have to be crafted strategically because there is no historical precedent for political regionalism in Italy (cf. Schmidtke and Ruzza 1993). The possibility of a separate regional political mobilization was institutionally prepared by the emergence of regional governments in Italy in the 1970s, which made the differential economic productivity of the various Italian regions, the flow of transfers from the North to the South, and the glaring discrepancies in the political efficacy of regional governments more visible (cf. Putnam 1993, chap. 3). In fact, the League of Lombardy won its first big victory in an administrative regional election, a typical secondary election that provides maximum advantage for a new maverick party. Following the 1989 European elections in which the Lombardian League won a respectable share of the electorate, the great success in the regional elections of the same year instantly put the party on the political map. Media attention on the Lombardian League began to accelerate dramatically (cf. Schmidtke and Ruzza 1993, 13, 17). This apparently benefited the party, *although* almost all the publicity was negative and tried to ridicule the new political movement. It was sufficient that the media focused on the same themes on which the leagues were also thriving: political corruption, inefficient political management, wasted public resources, inadequate state services (Ruzza and Schmidtke 1993, 8).

Opinion polls indicate that it was not the racist and antisouthern Italian slogans that were most effective in making the Northern League attractive to a growing share of voters. Instead, it was primarily the overwhelming concern with the corruption and inefficiency of the partocratic state and party machines that rallied voters around the new party (cf. della Porta 1993, 62; Plasser and Ulram 1992, 160–61, Gallagher 1993). Northern League voters call for a liberal separation of public and private concerns absent in the Italian patronage and clientelist state more than for an exclusion of foreigners and southern Italians (Woods 1992, 58). The League's telegenic leader, Umberto Bossi, artfully combined market-liberal and xenophobic elements in his rhetoric. Numerous observers have found that the use of provocative arguments and imagery, the exploitation of the shock value of crude and idiomatic language in his attacks on partocracy have earned him public attention and a broad following (cf. Gallagher 1993, 618). Bossi's ethnoregional and xenophobic anti-immigration slurs have to be placed in this context. They are not expressions of a biological or cultural racism as much as new efforts to attack the establishment of corporate business, Catholic Church, and political parties who are said to dominate the average citizens in the Italian South and who create a new subproletariat of immigrants in the North. For this reason, a number of observers emphasize the fundamental differences between the Northern League and Le Pen's National Front in France. Whereas in the latter, racism and xenophobia are central elements of the party's appeal, in the Northern League they are tactical moves within a broader discursive pattern that targets the political elites. Moreover, the League is not nationalist, but pro-European, nor does it express any nostalgic sentiments about a past state of political affairs. Gallagher summarizes investigations on the Northern League's appeal:

> The League's policies—federalism, European integration, cutting back the state bureaucracy, privatization of public utilities and economic tasks coordinated by the state, coupled with defense of the environment— makes the attempt to categorize it an unrewarding one. What gives coherence to these policy goals is that they are mostly the reverse of those followed by the *partitocrazia* and are felt to amount to a counter-project designed to restore good government and normalize relations between the state and the citizen. (1993, 620)

As Bossi's leagues succeeded in elections, he gradually toned down the ethnocentrist appeal in favor of the broad antipartocratic message that helped his organization to move from strength to strength (Betz 1994, 122). In the national elections of 1992, the Northern League managed to win almost one tenth of the Italian electorate or more than one sixth of all Northern Italian voters. In the 1993 local elections, the Northern League became the strongest party in many municipalities and reached up to one half of all votes in some municipalities. The substantial levels of Northern League electoral support in 1990 and 1992 and especially the extremely high support levels of 1993 indicate that the party is a broad and complex coalition of social and political groups that are not confined to the extreme Right, but driven by an increasingly generalized protest against partocracy. It differs from NRR parties in France or Scandinavia by its ability to tap into electorates that are not genuinely moved by law-and-order authoritarianism and xenophobia. For the bulk of the party's electorate, its liberal anticentralist and antipolitical class slogans are more important. This, however, also made it vulnerable to rival antipartocratic political bids, such as Silvio Berlusconi's "Forza Italia," which stopped the League's electoral progress in the 1994 parliamentary elections. As will be shown momentarily, the difference between the message of the Italian Northern League and of pure NRR parties in other countries is also reflected in the structure and the issue opinions of its electorate.

Similar observations can be made about Jörg Haider's Freedom Party in Austria. It is undoubtedly true that both Haider personally and the party under his leadership have made anti-Semitic and racist remarks and have developed ties to extremist German-nationalist and anti-Semitic organizations (cf. Bailer-Galanda 1990; Knight 1992). Yet at the same time, it would be myopic to ignore the fact that the Freedom Party's success since 1986 is primarily based on its antiestablishment and antipartocracy appeal that is reinforced by the continued existence of a Grand Coalition of SPÖ and ÖVP. Electoral researchers have long detected in Austria a general disaffection with the party establishment, an increasing unwillingness to develop close ties to a party, and a rising tendency to abstain from party membership (cf. Plasser, Ulram, and Grausgruber 1987). This permitted the FPÖ to attract voters through a populist antiparty discourse that is much more important to Austrian voters than German-national, xenophobic slogans. For this reason, it is misleading to equate the FPÖ with the French National Front or other pure New Rightist parties (cf. Plasser and Ulram 1989, 159–61). In a 1990 survey that explored voters' motivations to opt for the Freedom Party, 62 percent of the FPÖ supporters mentioned their disaffection with the scandals and privileges of the big parties, 44 percent wanted to teach the major parties a lesson, 42 percent were attracted by Haider's personality, and only 39 percent also mentioned the question of immigration as a reason for their voting preference (Plasser and Ulram 1992, 160).

Haider, like his Italian counterpart Bossi, employs public rhetoric in order to draw attention, to shock, and to provoke. Racist slurs serve as calculated provocations of a political establishment whose traditional political cleavage lines run the risk of being disrupted by the topics of partocracy and immigration. Haider's form of delivering attacks on the incumbent political elites often takes precedence over their content to the extent that the political leader of the Right can afford to deliver contradictions and to gloss over them:

Haider is also a master of a popular pose of the extreme right—the flippant provocation. In all this he provides, in the words of a recent penetrating psychological study, a cure against boredom and melancholy. These gifts help Haider play two roles which are in theory contradictory—that of the anti-establishment new broom, to sweep away corruption and inefficiency, and that of the restorer of the safety and secure values of "community." (Knight 1992, 296)

The contradictions in Haider's message are testimony to the complexity of the electoral coalition he tries to craft together. On the one hand, his party intends to appeal to antipartocracy sentiments that reach far into the educated middle strata; on the other, he seeks the support of the petit bourgeois and blue-collar constituency that responds favorably to his ethnocentric message. In this bind, he tries to dissociate himself from national socialism (in a book published in 1993) yet embrace contempt for immigrants from different cultures. Yet when he puts too much emphasis on the anti-immigration theme, as in his 1992 referendum campaign, his party may be in danger of losing its growth momentum. This risk remains minimal, however, as long as the major system parties, ÖVP and SPÖ, continue their coalition government.

The appearance of new or refurbished rightist-populist parties in Austria and Italy, therefore, should not be set on a par with right-authoritarian parties in other countries, although both groups of parties may at times articulate racist and xenophobic resentments. The former also tap into the same electorate as the latter, but the particular national political opportunity structure in which they are situated allows them to cast their net much wider than pure right-authoritarian parties. The major condition for the success of such broad populist rallies is the existence of partocratic systems in which the established mass parties have penetrated the state apparatus through clientelist and patronage networks. The minor condition is that existing old right-extremist parties, such as the Italian MSI, are too deeply entrenched in fascist traditions to detect the new disgruntled electorate and to refashion their own electoral appeal in time to serve new constituencies.

Differences between the Voter Appeal of the NRR and of Right-Populist Parties in Austria and Italy

If the Northern League in Italy and the Freedom Party in Austria have a somewhat different and broader appeal than pure NRR parties, this should be evidenced by the composition of their voter support. These new parties should, on average, appeal less to New Right extremists than to a more general cross-section of the population. In particular, the tendency of pure NRR parties to be overproportionally supported by less educated small businesspeople and blue-collar workers should not apply to the Austrian and Italian populist, antistatist parties. Moreover, the antiestablishment and antipartocracy spirit of the Northern League and of the Freedom Party should make party supporters more inclined to challenge authority and question nationalism. On the other hand, racism and authoritarianism still should leave their trace at least in subsets of these parties' electorates.

Tables 5.1 and 5.2 provide the principal components exploratory factor analysis for Italian and Austrian voters included in the *World Values Survey* we have already presented for the countries discussed previously.[6] In both countries, the first factor is a pure libertarian versus authoritarian factor with almost no association to questions of capitalism or ecology issues. In Italy, the second factor is a muddled capitalism versus socialism factor that is dominated by the rejection of contemporary social movement activities against the arms race and against nuclear power. The third factor pits libertarian procapitalists who are open-minded about members of different races and citizens of different countries against welfare chauvinists who wish to extend income equality, limit competition, and avoid people from different races as neighbors and competitors in the labor market. This third factor thus taps "working-class authoritarianism" at one extreme.

In Austria, somewhat similar factors, but in different sequence, appear in the principal components analysis. The capitalism versus socialism factor is here weaker and appears in third place with an eigenvalue of only 1.27. Traditional divisions on property and distribution thus apparently have precious little capacity to structure the Austrian electorate. This is most likely a reflection of the policy convergence of SPÖ and ÖVP on questions of political economy essentially since the 1950s. In second place is a factor dividing "deep ecologists" from industrial modernizers. As in Italy, the strongest factor loadings are on the two items tapping willingness to join contemporary social movements (antinuclear and disarmament protests). These, in turn, are linked to other environmental, xenophobic, and nationalist attitudes.

How are voters' issue dimensions reflected in the distribution of respondents over political parties? Our theory of left-libertarian versus right-authoritarian politics is in trouble if the major parties do not combine libertarian (authoritarian) positions on factor I in both countries with anticapitalist (capitalist) positions on factor II in Italy and factor III in Austria. Inspection of the party supporters' mean factor scores in table 5.1 and the representation of the relationship between parties' mean positions on factors I and II in figure 5.1 reveals that in Italy the theoretical expectations are mostly borne out. Out of 959 Italian respondents, 736 support parties whose mean position is very close

TABLE 5.1. Ideological Divisions in Italy: An Exploratory Factor Analysis (Principal Components)

	Factor I	Factor II	Factor III
	Libertarians versus Authoritarians	Capitalists versus Socialists	Ecological Capitalism versus Welfare Chauvinism
Economic Issues			
1. Business management	−.16	+.38	+.19
2. Income Inequality	−.02	+.45	+.40
3. Competition	−.23	+.37	+.27
Ecology and Industry			
4. Environmental taxes	+.15	−.16	+.48
5. Urgency of ecology	+.35	−.08	+.33
6. No nuclear plants	+.17	−.75	+.11
Race and Nation			
7. Objections to neighbors of different race	−.26	−.13	−.41
8. Priority for own nationals in labor markets	−.37	.00	−.30
9. National pride	−.55	−.12	+.28
Authority and Participation			
10. More respect for authority	−.49	−.18	+.27
11. Confidence in the army	−.57	−.11	+.27
12. Would participate in lawful demonstration	+.45	+.12	+.09
13. Would participate in disarmament protest	+.29	−.65	+.21
Women and Family			
14. Choice over abortion	+.48	+.13	−.18
15. Women as homemakers	−.43	−.15	−.03
16. Women's right to a job	+.55	+.18	+.17
Eigenvalues	2.32	1.67	1.21
Party Factor Scores			
Demoproletarians (N = 9)	+1.42	−.09	−.97
Radical Party (N = 12)	+1.39	−.18	−.28
Greens (N = 133)	+.78	−.17	+.18
Communist Party (N = 166)	+.48	−.32	−.21
Socialist Party (N = 116)	+.08	+.10	.00
Liberal Party (N = 16)	+.05	+1.00	+.57
Republican Party (N = 29)	+.02	+.63	+.50
Social Democratic Party (N = 12)	−.20	−.36	−.10
Christian Democrats (N = 294)	−.50	+.01	+.25
Northern League (N = 55)	−.26	+.58	−.32
Italian Social Movement (N = 27)	−.49	+.49	+.41

Source: World Values Survey 1990. Own calculations.

TABLE 5.2. Ideological Divisions in Austria: An Exploratory Factor Analysis (Principal Components)

	Factor I	Factor II	Factor III
	Libertarians versus Authoritarians	Deep Ecology versus Modern Industry	Capitalism versus Socialism
Economic Issues			
1. Business management	−.11	+.21	+.55
2. Income Inequality	+.15	+.03	+.37
3. Competition	+.04	+.22	+.46
Ecology and Industry			
4. Environmental taxes	+.31	+.26	−.30
5. Urgency of ecology	+.31	+.34	+.13
6. No nuclear plants	+.28	+.65	−.05
Race and Nation			
7. Objections to neighbors of different race	−.29	−.03	+.04
8. Priority for own nationals in labor markets	−.29	+.31	+.40
9. National pride	−.44	+.31	+.15
Authority and Participation			
10. More respect for authority	−.58	+.12	−.03
11. Confidence in the army	−.49	+.11	+.20
12. Would participate in lawful demonstration	+.56	+.11	−.21
13. Would participate in disarmament protest	+.24	+.72	−.20
Women and Family			
14. Choice over abortion	+.45	−.18	+.31
15. Women as homemakers	−.49	+.27	−.30
16. Women's right to a job	+.60	−.07	+.03
Eigenvalues	2.43	1.56	1.27
Party Factor Scores			
Green Alternative (N = 60)	+1.39	+.10	−.09
Social Democrats (N = 225)	−.24	+.11	−.11
People's Party (N = 287)	−.10	−.04	+.05
Freedom Party (N = 109)	+.17	+.03	+.37

Source: World Values Survey 1990. Own calculations.

to a left-libertarian versus right-authoritarian continuum that runs from about the position of PCI and Greens (Verdi) at the left-libertarian pole to the Italian Social Movement at the opposite right-authoritarian pole. Twenty-one further respondents who support extremely radical libertarian positions expressed by the Radical Party (PR) and the Demoproletarians (DP) also belong to this axis. Overall, then, 79 percent of Italian respondents with party preference are unambiguously located in a single competitive dimension.

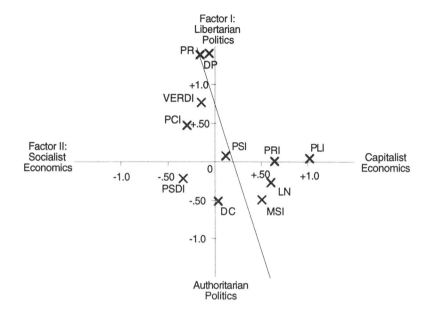

Fig. 5.1. The political space of European democracies: Italy

As we expected, the Northern League voters are distinctly promarket on the second factor and less authoritarian on the first factor than Christian Democrats or MSI. The populism of the Northern League is directed against the state and the establishment more than against libertarian politics. Nevertheless, table 5.1 reveals that on the weak factor III, the mean position of Northern League voters reveals a subterranean "welfare chauvinism" also shared by supporters of parties of the extreme Left, whereas the MSI, as a party with little racist or xenophobic appeals, as well as the secular bourgeois minor parties support a more cosmopolitan and ecological capitalism at the other extreme of this factor. The position of the Northern League on the two more powerful factor dimensions may still be viewed as close enough to the main dimension of competition to preserve the unidimensional conceptualization of Italian politics, pushing the share of voters on that dimension up to 95 percent. On the other hand, one could also see the Northern League as situated on a minor competitive dimension that is almost insensitive to libertarian versus authoritarian appeals but divides purely economic positions associated with opinions on social movements that interfere with business prerogatives over investment decisions (nuclear power) or the defense of capitalism against communism (disarmament in the 1980s). On that dimension, we have primarily the three small secular nonsocialist parties (PSDI, PLI, PRI), amounting to a little more than 5 percent of the respondents with party preferences and, if we so choose, the Northern League with a decidedly procapitalist view.

Overall, the Italian picture is thus quite consistent with the theoretical expectation that the Northern League, as a populist antistatist movement, would be more procapitalist than authoritarian and racist in its appeals. Nevertheless, one seeming inconsistency of the overall picture of Italian political competition with our theoretical argument should be addressed. We argued in the previous section that the MSI could not fully develop the New Rightist appeal to mix capitalist liberalism with authoritarianism, yet in the factor analysis the party appears to deliver just that. Why, then, did the party leave room for the electoral surge of the Northern League? At least three conditions may contribute to this picture, all of which have some plausibility. First, regardless of the MSI's issue appeal, Northern populist promarketeers or authoritarian racists would always be *inaccessible* to the party because the MSI is identified with the Southern clientelist establishment and northern xenophobes define southern Italians as a foreign element whose financial and social claims need to be fought off. Future empirical analysis may show that questions of credibility and reputation provide the strongest reason for the inability even of a strategically mobilized MSI to break into new electorates.

Second, the survey questions may not adequately reflect subtle variances in the meaning of the far Right that come into play when one attempts to assess the competition between the Northern League and the MSI. Both parties may support capitalist property and inequality, but Northern League followers may call for a more dynamic, liberal-competitive capitalism and system of economic inequality than the more corporatist and traditional MSI voters. This is suggested by the *World Values Study*'s finding that 43.3 percent of all Italian respondents believe that businesses should be run by private owners compared to 50 percent of MSI supporters, but no less than 59.1 percent of NL sympathizers. At the same time, however, both parties are equally firmly committed to the extension of private ownership (MSI: 65.7 percent; Northern League: 64 percent; population: 42.9 percent), and the MSI puts more emphasis on individual responsibility and competition than the Northern League.[7] This raises a third possible explanation for the discrepancy between the MSI's position, as revealed by its voters' preferences, and its strategic appeal. MSI voters may be intuitively supporting New Right positions on many questions of authority and capitalism, but the party did not explicitly combine them on its issue agenda until the early 1990s because it was controlled by activists and leaders with traditional fascist or social-fascist political conceptions. While the present supporters stick with the MSI for reasons of party identification and tradition, the lack of an explicit NRR message—for example on race and capitalism—made it impossible for the party to reach out to *new* voters. These electorates available to New Right appeals instead contribute to the broader rallying process around the populist Northern League.

The less authoritarian and more antiestablishment orientation of the Northern League compared to the MSI is evidenced by a number of indicators. The MSI, as a traditional right-wing party, attracts voters who are highly patriotic, whereas Northern League supporters are critical of the nation and the institutions it harbors. According to the *World Values Survey,* 41.4 percent of those who express a party preference are also proud to be Italian compared to 54.7 percent of MSI voters. Among Northern League voters, the same sentiment inspires only 36.8 percent of respondents. A similar difference between MSI and League voters appears in responses to the question whether respect for authority is good. For example, 48.8 percent of all Italian respondents with a party preference think authority should be respected; 65 percent of MSI voters subscribe to this view versus only 39.4 percent of Northern League adherents. In a similar vein, questions on gender and sex roles in the family and the economy reveal that while, compared to the population average, supporters of both parties have a tendency to endorse traditional female role definitions, this tendency is more pronounced in the MSI than in the Northern League. Finally, there are rather dramatic differences on the "postmaterialism" index that by and large measures attitudes toward state authority. As one might expect in rightist parties, both MSI and Northern League supporters show less enthusiasm for postmaterialism (antiauthoritarianism) than the population average (22.4 percent of those with party preference). But this percentage is much lower in the MSI (4.4 percent) than the Northern League (19.2 percent). Again, the League is closer to the mainstream of Italian society and appeals to a broader cross section of the population.

Consistent with the ideological tradition of the Italian extreme Right, but also the exigencies of a broad populist appeal, neither MSI nor Northern League voters are particularly racist and ethnocentric. Both MSI and Northern League supporters are only slightly more antagonized by neighbors belonging to a different race than the average of all Italian respondents.[8] In Italy, ethnocentrism plays a less important role in mobilizing the extreme Right than elsewhere in Europe. In a sense, *both* the neofascist MSI and the populist Northern League are *regionalist* parties with different constituencies, *some* of which can also be mobilized by right-authoritarian appeals. The MSI appeals to a southern Italian establishment in the fascist tradition. Therefore, at the ecological level, urbanization and economic underdevelopment are the best predictors of MSI support (Caciagli 1988, 22). In contrast, the League appeals to a

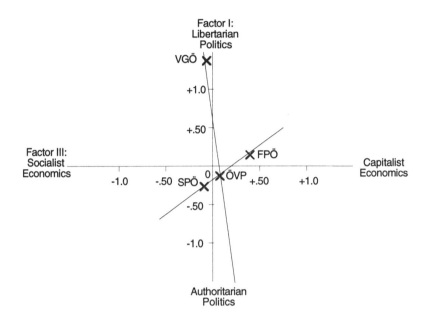

Fig. 5.2. The political space of European democracies: Austria

northern Italian electorate that is more concerned with partocracy and shattering the clientelist establishment in Italian politics than anything else. A survey showed that 63 percent of League voters first mention the inefficiency and bureaucratization of state agencies as their main reason for political protest against the establishment parties, 47 percent interpret their vote as opposition to the major parties, and only 38 percent really focus on the ethnocentric demand to keep northern Italy free from economic immigrants (Plasser and Ulram 1992, 160).

While, overall, the Italian findings are consistent with the theory developed in this study, the findings for Austria are at first sight more troublesome, but also intelligible in light of Austria's partocratic political economy. Factor II in table 5.2, which we labeled "deep ecology versus modern industry," has just about no power to distinguish among party supporters' positions. We therefore represent in figure 5.2 only the libertarian versus authoritarian factor I and the very weak capitalism versus socialism factor III. On both factors, SPÖ and ÖVP supporters' positions are virtually indistinguishable. In a country that has gone through grand coalitions of these two parties for two out of four decades between 1950 and 1990, the voters of the two parties are converging as well. Competition between the two major parties in Austria appears to have little to do with issues but is still primarily a matter of party identification. This inference can be drawn also from a striking finding delivered by table 5.3 where we regressed the three opinion factors in Austria and Italy on three general ideological dispositions—left-right self-placements, postmaterialism (antiauthoritarianism), and religiosity. In Italy, the configuration of coefficients is already familiar from equivalent equations in France, Denmark, and Norway. Left/right self-placements are driven mostly by libertarian/authoritarian views (factor I) and to a lesser extent by more economic assessments of capitalism and social movements (factor II) and even by the weak division between ecological and cosmopolitan procapitalists and welfare chauvinists (factor III). In contrast, in Austria, left/right self-placements are inexplicable in terms of issue opinions on *any* of the three issue dimensions (factors) that divide the Austrian electorate! Left/right self-placements are here purely due to issueless party preference. On the other hand, postmaterialism and religiosity are associated in both countries with the authoritarian/libertarian factor and in the case of religiosity also with the capitalism/socialism factors.

In Austria, however, the two major parties shrink because the two new (or strategically renewed) challengers—Greens and Freedom Party—do compete on issues that attract more voters, as organizational and sentimental bonds to the two big parties wane. But given that the left/right language is monopolized by SPÖ and ÖVP, other parties with issue appeals will stay away from it. They will directly appeal to libertarian (postmaterialist) or procapitalist themes in order to attract support coalitions. Only the minor parties will therefore exhibit a clear issue appeal of their following.

In figure 5.2, the Greens take an extremely libertarian and slightly leftist position, suggesting the emergence of a left-libertarian versus right-authoritarian competitive dimension. But the FPÖ is clearly not located at the other extreme of that dimension. Like its populist counterpart in Italy, the Northern League, the Freedom Party distinguishes itself from the established parties primarily on the (weak) capitalism versus anticapitalism dimension. Voter support therefore shows very clearly that the FPÖ is not a right-authoritarian NRR party but a populist-antistatist party that takes advantage of the unique opportunity structure of a partocratic regime. Voter positions and populist antistatist appeal by the party leadership are closely matched in Austria.

This lesson can be gleaned also from a brief review of FPÖ supporters' issue positions. Anti-Semitic and xenophobic sentiments surface in Haider's

TABLE 5.3. General Ideological Dispositions Predicted by Voters' Issue Positions (Factor Scores of the Exploratory Factor Analysis)

A. Italy

	Constant		Factor I Libertarians versus Authoritarians		Factor II Capitalists versus Socialists		Factor III Ecological Capitalism versus Welfare Chauvinism		adj. R^2
	PE	t	PE	t	PE	t	PE	t	
Left/right self-placement	4.82	84.08	−.80	−14.24	+.35	6.12	+.32	5.55	.21*** (N = 1089)
Postmaterialism	2.04	118.70	+.25	14.18	+.03	2.05	+.04	2.45	.13*** (N = 1354)
Church attendance[a]	3.99	69.90	+.84	14.73	+.14	2.42	−.42	7.24	.17*** (N = 1343)

Note: PE = parameter estimate; t = t ratio.

B. Austria

	Constant		Factor I Libertarians versus Authoritarians		Factor II Deep Ecology versus Modern Industry		Factor III Capitalism versus Socialism		adj. R^2
	PE	t	PE	t	PE	t	PE	t	
Left/right self-placement	6.30	97.50	−.12	1.80	−.11	−1.68	−.01	−.21	.004 (ns) (N = 780)
Postmaterialism	2.14	111.28	+.24	12.65	+.01	.57	+.01	.49	.16*** (N = 854)
Church attendance[a]	4.58	61.89	+.67	9.13	−.20	−2.79	+.50	6.79	.14*** (N = 854)

Source: World Values Survey 1990. Own calculations.
Note: PE = parameter estimate; t = t ratio
***significant at the .001 level
**significant at the .01 level
*significant at the .05 level
[a]Scale inversed: high values indicate infrequent or no church attendance.

speeches, but they are embedded in the broader populist antiestablishment message as a provocation more than as a central party plank. This interpretation is consistent with the findings that the FPÖ electorate is not clearly more racist and xenophobic than the overall Austrian population. Of the Austrians indicating a party preference in the 1990 *World Values Survey,* 8.2 percent object to neighbors of a different race. Among Freedom Party followers, this ratio is only insignificantly higher (9.9 percent). Further, 77.2 percent of Austrians believe nationals should have priority in the domestic labor market; among Freedom Party supporters this view is only slightly more frequent (+4.3 percent). It is true that Austrians, in general, are more xenophobic and protectionist on jobs than citizens of other countries. In comparison to Austria's 77.2 percent, population averages are 74 percent for Italy, 63 percent for France, 62 percent for Germany, 57 percent for Norway, and 52 percent for Denmark. Yet at the same time, upwards of 90 percent of New Right party supporters in these countries endorse the priority of nationals in the labor market, setting them apart more sharply from the overall population and signaling a generally higher absolute level of labor protectionism than the supporters of the Austrian Freedom Party.[9]

It is therefore plausible that the effectiveness of Haider's racist and anti-Semitic ruminations work on his electorate in two ways. First of all, an analysis of subgroups of FPÖ supporters in the *World Values Survey* shows that his electorate is quite clearly divided between a majority of market liberals, who are middle of the road on ethnicity and authority, and a minority with clearly racist and ethnocentric commitments. Second, for the majority of Haider's electorate, racist slurs are less impressive because of their substance than their symbolic meaning, indicating that Haider is willing to challenge taboos and offend the Austrian "partocracy" that is united in its condemnation of racism and anti-Semitism. In a subtle way, racist signals may here contribute to the Freedom Party's antiestablishment message, which is clearly the most important driving force of its electoral success.

As a consequence, taking the FPÖ electorate as a whole, authoritarianism does not prominently figure into its central tendency. In the 1990 *World Values Study,* Freedom Party supporters are less willing to respect authority than the average of all party supporters (43.8 percent to 47.4 percent), and they are less proud of being Austrian (44.4 percent to 53 percent). In all true NRR parties, the relationship is the reverse. Moreover, there is no tendency for Freedom Party followers to subscribe to a more traditional view of women's sex roles in family and labor market than the average Austrian respondent. In contrast to all true NRR parties we have discussed, there are also more "postmaterialists" among Freedom Party adherents than in the overall Austria survey (29.2 percent to 25.5 percent).

What we have learned is that the Northern League in Italy and the Free-

dom Party in Austria with a populist antistatist elite appeal indeed draw electorates that are more characterized by distinctly procapitalist attitudes than an
explicit authoritarianism. Even racism and xenophobia, sentiments the leaders
of both parties have played with, are subordinated to the general antipartocratic
message. As in the other countries, we will not take these results, gleaned from
a simple exploratory principal components factor analysis, at face value, but
rather explore the impact of libertarian, pro-capitalist, and racist issue stances
on the decision to support these parties more rigorously.

As a first step, we have produced a confirmatory factor analysis that
forces the appearance of separate libertarian versus authoritarian, procapitalist
versus anticapitalist, and cosmopolitan versus particularist factors (tables 5.4
and 5.5). These calculations yield no surprises when we examine the party
supporters' mean positions given at the bottom of each table. In Italy, there is a
rather strong linkage between the parties' mean positions on capitalism (socialism) and authoritarianism (libertarianism). In terms of ethnocentrism and parochialism, the Northern League does emerge as the most extreme party, but
given an extraordinarily large standard deviation of its voters' position on this
factor (S.D. = 0.99, compared to most parties' standard deviations in the range
of 0.50 to 0.80), there is little unity in the party following's rejection of
foreigners. Overall, the Northern League takes the most pronounced position
on market liberalism, where it is only surpassed by the tiny Liberal Party. Yet
the Northern League is only mildly and incoherently authoritarian and
ethnocentric.

The findings for the Austrian Freedom Party tell a similar story (table
5.5). Here, FPÖ supporters are the most procapitalist of all parties' electorates,
but even here only by a small margin. At the same time, they do not take a
distinct position on the libertarian versus authoritarian dimension, but are
generally rather closer to the libertarian than the authoritarian side. Finally,
there is a slight racist particularist tendency among FPÖ voters, but the mean
positions of all parties are again very close to each other, particularly given that
standard deviations of each party's mean position are in the neighborhood of
0.80.[10]

In tables 5.6 and 5.7, we examine the linkage between occupational
background, issue positions, issue factors, and party support. In both countries,
workers and businesspeople or farmers are distinctly more authoritarian, racist,
and nationalist than respondents in white-collar employment or professionals.
The only disconfirmation here is the Italian pattern on abortion where there is
no linkage to occupation. We might expect that workers are more anticapitalist
in both countries, but this does not show up in the Austrian workers' endorsement of private business. If FPÖ and Northern League were right-authoritarian
parties, we would expect an overrepresentation of workers and businesspeople
and an underrepresentation of the professions and white-collar sectors in their

TABLE 5.4. Ideological Divisions in Italy: Confirmatory Factor Analysis (missing values set equal to zero)

	Capitalism versus Socialism	Authoritarianism versus Libertarianism	Parochialism versus Cosmopolitanism
A. Economic Distribution			
1. For more income inequality	+.28	—	—
2. For private business ownership	+.62	—	—
3. For more competition	+.43	+.12	—
4. For owner-managed business	+.36	+.14	—
B. Libertarian versus Authoritarian Issues			
5. Postmaterialism	—	−.55	—
6. Respect for authority	—	+.38	—
7. Participation in lawful demonstration	—	−.46	—
8. Women's right to abortion	—	−.35	—
9. Role of housewife fulfilling	—	+.29	—
C. Cosmopolitan/Particularist Dimension			
10. Acceptance of neighbor of different race	—	—	+.82
11. Acceptance of foreign workers as neighbors	—	—	+.73
12. Members of one's nationality have priority in the labor market	—	+.32	+.16
Average Factor Scores of Party Followers			
Demoproletarians ($N = 14$)	−.45	−1.08	+.01
Communist Party ($N = 218$)	−.30	−.30	−.05
Radical Party ($N = 16$)	−.10	−.84	−.37
Greens ($N = 165$)	−.01	−.50	−.18
Socialist Party ($N = 151$)	−.03	−.13	−.08
Social Democratic Party ($N = 18$)	+.18	−.10	+.19
Republican Party ($N = 37$)	+.31	−.14	−.02
Christian Democrats ($N = 451$)	+.05	+.29	+.02
Liberal Party ($N = 20$)	+.62	+.04	−.30
Northern League ($N = 75$)	+.34	+.08	+.20
Italian Social Movement ($N = 32$)	+.27	+.25	+.10

Source: World Values Survey 1990. Own calculations.
Note: The confirmatory factor analysis was estimated using unweighted least squares (ULS).

TABLE 5.5. Ideological Divisions in Austria: Confirmatory Factor Analysis (missing values set equal to zero)

	Capitalism versus Socialism	Authoritarianism versus Libertarianism	Parochialism versus Cosmopolitanism
A. Economic Distribution			
1. For more income inequality	+.13	—	—
2. For private business ownership	+.57	—	—
3. For more competition	+.58	.00	—
4. For owner-managed business	+.20	+.13	—
B. Libertarian versus Authoritarian Issues			
5. Postmaterialism	—	−.50	—
6. Respect for authority	—	+.50	—
7. Participation in lawful demonstration	—	−.50	—
8. Women's right to abortion	—	−.37	—
9. Role of housewife fulfilling	—	+.39	—
C. Cosmopolitan/Particularist Dimension			
10. Acceptance of neighbor of different race	—	—	+.60
11. Acceptance of foreign workers as neighbors	—	—	+.74
12. Members of one's nationality have priority in the labor market	—	+.25	+.13
Average Factor Scores of Party Followers			
Green Alternative ($N = 90$)	+.09	−.86	−.27
Social Democrats ($N = 455$)	−.13	+.10	+.08
People's Party ($N = 344$)	+.07	+.19	−.03
Freedom Party ($N = 161$)	+.16	−.11	+.04

Source: World Values Survey 1990. Own calculations.
Note: The confirmatory factor analysis was estimated using unweighted least squares (ULS).

electorates. In other words, their occupational profile of electoral support should be a mirror image of that of the Austrian Green Alternative and of the Italian Greens in tables 5.6 and 5.7. But FPÖ and Northern League supporters are evenly spread over the entire occupational structure. This, again, shows that FPÖ and Northern League are not typical right-authoritarian parties, but populist antistatist parties with the capacity to attract a broad electoral coalition.

As a final step in our analysis, we can now probe the relationship between occupational background, issue positions, and party choice in order to determine the "net effect" of views on economic governance structures, political

TABLE 5.6. Occupation, Ideological Dispositions, and Party Preferences in Italy

	Professions (percent)	White Collar (percent)	Nonactive in the Labor Force (percent)	Workers (percent)	Independent Business and Farmers (percent)
A. Issue Positions					
1. For business-managed enterprises	48.9 (350)	38.5 (457)	49.8 (601)	38.7 (380)	47.8 (92)
2. Endorse stronger authority	40.2 (363)	43.3 (473)	51.6 (655)	48.9 (417)	54.5 (101)
3. Against women's choice of abortion	40.9 (362)	36.3 (468)	45.4 (651)	39.1 (467)	43.0 (100)
4. Against neighbors of different race	6.9 (364)	10.3 (476)	13.8 (658)	15.3 (419)	15.8 (101)
5. Proud to belong to one's nation	28.4 (356)	35.7 (457)	43.6 (653)	48.7 (417)	48.0 (100)
B. Percentage of Occupational Group Supporting a Party					
Demoproletarians and Radical Party	2.2	2.9	2.5	2.7	2.8
Communist Party	15.7	15.8	15.4	27.2	9.9
Greens	19.1	16.5	11.9	9.3	5.6
Socialist Party	11.7	13.6	11.1	13.2	11.3
Republican Party	4.8	3.2	2.8	1.2	4.2
Christian Democrats	30.9	33.3	41.4	34.2	49.3
Northern League	7.0	5.4	6.8	5.1	5.6
Italian Social Movement	2.2	2.9	2.5	3.5	0.0

Source: World Values Survey 1990. Own calculations.

TABLE 5.7. Occupation, Ideological Dispositions, and Party Preferences in Austria

	Professions (percent)	White Collar (percent)	Nonactive in the Labor Force (percent)	Workers (percent)	Independent Business and Farmers (percent)
A. Issue Positions					
1. For business-managed enterprises	46.6 (311)	42.4 (224)	50.4 (365)	51.0 (347)	73.8 (84)
2. Endorse stronger authority	36.1 (321)	49.6 (240)	43.3 (390)	57.4 (383)	55.0 (100)
3. Against women's choice of abortion	44.5 (319)	49.8 (239)	58.9 (389)	53.4 (386)	79.8 (94)
4. Against neighbors of different race	5.5 (326)	8.3 (241)	5.6 (396)	11.4 (394)	13.6 (103)
5. Proud to belong to one's nation	45.6 (307)	52.8 (233)	48.8 (373)	61.6 (375)	60.0 (100)
B. Percent of Occupational Group Supporting a Party					
Austrian Social Democrats	28.2	32.4	27.8	42.1	8.7
Austrian People's Party	24.9	19.1	24.0	16.0	57.3
Austrian Freedom Party	11.7	9.1	10.1	12.4	11.7
Austrian United Greens	8.6	7.9	7.6	3.3	0.0

Source: World Values Survey 1990. Own calculations.

and social authority, and multiculturalism (tables 5.8 and 5.9). For Italy, we have reproduced only the logistic regressions for the Northern League (table 5.8). MSI voters are both slightly more procapitalist and more authoritarian, but the effect of capitalism on voting behavior is far greater in the case of the Northern League, as the first equation in table 5.8 demonstrates. Northern League voters also tend to be more male and slightly more parochial than the voters of other parties, but the latter effect especially is rather subdued. If we compare Northern League voters to other voters of the political Right (MSI, Christian Democrats), then procapitalism and youth are the decisive distinguishing elements. At the same time, the League voters tend to be slightly more libertarian than other right-wing voters, whereas the effect of parochial-ethnocentric orientations is reduced to a level that is almost statistically insignificant. We conclude that the Italian Northern League is not a NRR party because it lacks a pronounced authoritarian and parochial electorate, but is rather a much broader right-wing populist and antistatist party.

A similar picture with even starker features emerges for the Austrian Freedom Party (table 4.9). Procapitalism and higher education set its electorate apart from all Austrian voters. There is also a slight, but insignificant, tendency for FPÖ voters to be more parochial, male, and younger than all voters. But the data show that racism and ethnocentrism certainly are not the main force that made the electoral coalition around the Freedom Party grow over the past decade. Only in the second equation, when FPÖ voters are pitted against ÖVP voters only, does ethnocentrism emerge as a significant force affecting the choice of voters. But the net effect of that variable is less pronounced than the more libertarian orientation of FPÖ voters compared to ÖVP voters, the higher education of FPÖ voters, and, net of these attributes, the greater propensity for blue-collar workers to support the Freedom Party.

Like the Northern League, the Austrian FPÖ tends to be a populist antistatist party for which ethnocentric parochialism plays a subordinate role. Most of its voters are distinguished by their preference for free markets and a more libertarian lifestyle, both attributes that set them apart from SPÖ and ÖVP. It would be wrong to lump the FPÖ into the same category of parties as the right-authoritarian parties in France or Scandinavia.

Overall, our analysis confirms that the sociodemographic coalition and the issue preferences of Freedom Party and Northern League voters are substantially different from those of right-authoritarian parties in Scandinavia and France. This result is consistent with what we know about the party elites' issue appeals (see previous section) and the findings of other studies. In particular, the "cross-class" character of electoral support for the populist antistatist parties has been highlighted by previous research. Thus, in contrast to NRR parties, the Northern League also attracts well-educated and younger voters (cf. Backes 1990, 7–8; Woods, 1992: 71). Moreover, ecological studies of

TABLE 5.8. Determinants of Political Orientations and of Party Preferences in Italy

A. Determinants of the Northern League Vote, Entire Sample
(Maximum likelihood estimates)

	Parameter estimate	Standard error	Probability	Percentage of voters supporting the rightist party if all other variables are held constant but value on the focal variable is at its—	
				Minimum	Maximum
Intercept	−.18	1.43	.90		
Market Liberalism (Factor I)	+.75	.19	.0001	0.6	6.5
Authoritarianism (Factor II)	+.10	.19	.61	2.0	2.7
Parochialism/Racism (Factor III)	+.24	.12	.04	2.3	4.7
Gender (Female = 2)	−.88	.27	.001	5.6	2.4
Age	−.002	.008	.84	2.5	2.3
Education	−.04	.06	.54	2.4	1.8
Business or Farmer	−.49	.56	.38	2.4	1.5
Professional	−.12	.36	.74	2.4	2.1
White Collar	−.47	.35	.17	2.4	1.5
Worker	−.52	.36	.16	2.4	1.4

Note: concordant cases: 69.6; cases *N*: 1995 (missing values on independent variables were substituted by mean values); missing cases *M*: 23.

B. Determinants of Vote: Northern League versus Moderate-Right Voters
(Maximum likelihood estimates)

| | Parameter estimate | Standard error | Probability | Percentage of voters supporting the rightist party if all other variables are held constant but value on the focal variable is at its— | |
				Minimum	Maximum
Intercept	2.55	1.62	.12		
Market Liberalism (Factor I)	+.61	.22	.006	3.2	19.1
Authoritarianism (Factor II)	-.42	.24	.07	17.8	5.2
Parochialism/Racism (Factor III)	+.23	.14	.09	9.0	16.6
Gender (female = 2)	-1.09	.29	.0002	23.2	9.2
Age	-.01	.01	.44	10.6	7.2
Education	+.02	.06	.79	9.2	10.5
Business or Farmer	-.78	.60	.20	9.2	4.5
Professional	-.43	.41	.29	9.2	6.2
White Collar	-.65	.39	.10	9.2	5.0
Worker	-.46	.40	.25	9.2	6.2

Source: World Values Survey 1990. Own calculations.
Note: concordant cases: 71.7; cases N: 545.

TABLE 5.9. Determinants of Political Orientations and of Party Preferences in Austria

A. Determinants of the Freedom Party Vote, Entire Sample
(Maximum likelihood estimates)

| | Parameter estimate | Standard error | Probability | Percentage of voters supporting the rightist party if all other variables are held constant but value on the focal variable is at its— | |
				Minimum	Maximum
Intercept	−.280	1.21	.02		
Market Liberalism (Factor I)	+.40	.13	.002	3.7	11.4
Authoritarianism (Factor II)	−.16	.13	.22	10.3	6.4
Parochialism/Racism (Factor III)	+.16	.11	.13	7.6	11.5
Gender (Female = 2)	−.26	.18	.14	9.8	7.7
Age	−.01	.01	.13	9.7	5.9
Education	+.09	.04	.03	5.1	10.7
Business or Farmer	+.09	.37	.28	7.7	11.1
Professional	+.12	.25	.63	7.7	8.6
White Collar	−.11	.29	.71	7.7	7.0
Worker	+.35	.26	.17	7.7	10.6

Note: concordant cases: 62.5; cases *N:* 1436 (missing values on independent variables were substituted by mean values); missing cases *M:* 24.

B. Determinants of Vote: Freedom Party versus Moderate Right Voters
(Maximum likelihood estimates)

	Parameter estimate	Standard error	Probability	Percentage of voters supporting the rightist party if all other variables are held constant but value on the focal variable is at its—	
				Minimum	Maximum
Intercept	-.91	1.38	.51		
Market Liberalism (Factor I)	+.21	.15	.16	16.7	27.3
Authoritarianism (Factor II)	-.51	.16	.002	44.7	13.6
Parochialism/Racism (Factor III)	+.27	.13	.04	22.4	38.4
Gender (Female = 2)	-.37	.21	.09	30.2	23.2
Age	-.01	.01	.23	27.4	18.6
Education	+.11	.05	.03	15.0	31.5
Business or Farmer	-.43	.40	.27	23.1	16.3
Professional	+.02	.29	.94	23.1	23.5
White Collar	+.01	.35	.97	23.1	23.4
Worker	+.69	.31	.02	23.1	37.5

Source: World Values Survey 1990. Own calculations.
Note: concordant cases: 68.3; cases N: 499.

voting show that the party stood to gain, especially in areas where the Christian Democrats had been strong, such as small towns, whereas the NRR in France or Scandinavia thrives especially in the big cities. In Austria, the socioeconomic position of Austrian party voters thus does not statistically explain Freedom Party support (cf. Haerpfner 1987, 264; Plasser, Ulram and Grausgruber 1987, 245; Plasser and Ulram 1989, 160). Just like the supporters of the Northern League, FPÖ voters tend to be younger and often more rather than less educated than the average voter. In the 1990 *World Values Study,* for example, 62 percent of the respondents who supported a party had completed their education before their eighteenth birthday compared to only 53 percent of Freedom Party sympathizers. All this reflects the fact that the Freedom Party draws on quite a different audience than the more sharply defined extremist right-wing parties we have discussed in earlier chapters.

Strategic Dilemmas of Challenges to Partocracy

The new populist antiestablishment parties in Austria and Italy confront the parties of the conventional moderate Right that have suffered the greatest hemorrhage of voters to the new challengers with a clear-cut strategic dilemma. Either these moderate-rightist parties will not respond to their new competitors and continue to lose votes, or they will give up partocratic privileges, dismantle their clientelist networks, and reduce political patronage, policies that would be extremely unpopular among entrenched party activists and core followers. Until the early 1990s, despite heavy losses of the Austrian People's Party and the Italian Christian Democrats, and in the 1994 Austrian elections the SPÖ as well, the intraparty forces of conservatism and defense of the patronage system prevailed. The question is how long moderately conservative parties can hold out in their resistance to "progressivist" efforts to depoliticize the civil service, professionalize the administration, and draw a clear border between private and public sector by denationalizing many of the state-owned companies that have been the cause of political scandals and economic losses in the 1980s.

   It is quite possible that moderately conservative patronage parties will experience increasing defections by disgruntled activists or by ambitious young politicians who sense that only a modernized, liberal conservatism without patronage affiliations can attract voters. The fortunes of the Italian Christian Democrats illustrate this process through the emergence of the "Rete," a political grouping of Southern Italian reform activists who were former DC politicians but felt compelled to extricate themselves from the swamp of corruption, patronage, and ties to the mafia in which that party has slid. The virtual collapse of the Italian party system under the impact of an avalanche of corruption scandals compromising all major parties in 1993–94 and its replacement by a still fluid set of successor organizations demonstrates that the old parties held out against reform for too long to save themselves.

As long as traditional conservative parties show few signs of cutting their ties to the patronage networks and dismantling partocracy, the new semirightist populist antiestablishment parties encounter few strategic difficulties. They must walk a fine line, however, so as not to overdo their racist and xenophobic messages because these messages are not central to the majority of their following and could in fact repulse an important segment of their potential electorate. A lesson in this matter was Jörg Haider's 1991-92 drive for a referendum on immigration policy in Austria that, in the final analysis, failed because all other parties mobilized against racism, and Haider could not bring together the broad political coalition he expected to assemble around the ethno-centrist appeal. In the 1994 election campaign, Haider again was able to weave together the two electorates of the party and to prey successfully on former SPÖ voters, particularly in the latter's stronghold, Vienna. Nevertheless, his more pronounced ethnocentric campaign may have contributed to the success of a new liberal antixenophobic party, the Liberal Forum, that entered parlia-ment with 5 percent of the vote.

More recent data than those collected in the World Values Survey show that the FPÖ in 1994 moved from an antistatist populism a step closer toward the New Radical Right. The relative share of authoritarian, disenchanted, but also extremely market-liberal voters has increased. The immigration problem rose among the issue priorities of Freedom Party voters and the party was perceived as even further to the right than in 1990 (Plasser and Ulram 1994, 12–29). With its changing appeal, the FPÖ made its main inroads into new segments of the less-educated working-class voters with authoritarian and ethnocentric dispositions. In this process, the SPÖ lost voters overpropor-tionally to the Freedom Party (Plasser and Ulram 1994, 34–39). Although this policy may be costly to the FPÖ in terms of more educated and libertarian, but antistatist voters, as long as partocracy remains in place and the established party cartel of SPÖ and ÖVP runs the government, the FPÖ may have con-siderable strategic freedom to modify its position without shedding too many middle class market-liberal voters in exchange for working-class authoritar-ians in marginal labor markets.[11]

The Austrian and Italian antipartocratic protest parties are likely to face difficult strategic problems only when the established parties open up to their message or collapse, and they are being displaced by a set of new parties all of which attack partocracy. In that case, the new populists could be invited to form governments with their competitors and would be compelled to show which elements of their message they are willing to implement or to trade off in public policy making. Moreover, their coalition partners would force them to reveal their positions on difficult matters of economic and social policy, thus unleashing intraparty conflicts within populist parties that are likely to strike observers as familiar to other episodes when new parties challenged the status quo as long as they remained in the opposition, but then had to change course as participants in executive office. It is plausible that with government participation the Italian Northern League or the Austrian Freedom Party will lose some of their luster. Moreover, they may be compelled to deal with the potential tension between those among their supporters who are primarily inspired by antiestablishment, liberal, and even libertarian ideas, and those groups that respond primarily to the parties' racist and xenophobic or even authoritarian pronouncements. The early experience of Umberto Bossi in the rightist Berlusconi government that was formed after the spring 1994 parliamentary elections in Italy appears to confirm these expectations.

Conclusion

It is unlikely that partocracy in Austria and Italy became worse from 1970 to 1990 or when compared to the more distant past. The rise of populist parties and the reform or collapse of partocratic systems is thus not a matter of increasing voter deprivation. What has changed, however, is the popular perception of partocratic practices because an increasingly educated and politically sophisticated population calls for a more transparent political process that permits more chances of mass participation. The antipartocratic challenge is thus caught up in the dissolution of the Catholic and socialist organizational "pillars" of industrial society that wane with the advent of postindustrial conditions (cf. Hellemans 1990; Schmidtke and Ruzza 1993, 10).

The message of the Italian and Austrian new "populist" parties to scholarly analysts of the European extreme Right, as well as to political activists, is clear: do not expand the universe of NRR parties by including Austrian and Italian political neopopulism without closely examining the parties' appeals and their electorates. A wealth of evidence demonstrates that it would be wrong to the lump the Freedom Party and the Northern League into the same group with the French National Front or the more moderate, but still new, rightist Scandinavian Progress parties. All of these parties may subscribe to similar racist and xenophobic symbolisms, but such appeals are integrated into rather different encompassing political programs. These programs, in turn, respond to different contexts of party competition and challenges to public authority.

What unites populist challengers of partocracy, such as the Austrian Freedom Party and the Italian Northern League, is the fact that they are new political departures that express themselves in an aggressive, provocative language, that draw simple lines between masses and elites, and that seek out taboos to break them, such as the question of immigrants and ethnic diversity

(Plasser and Ulram 1992, 159). Moreover, simple political dichotomies dividing the world into friend and foe may help populist parties to rally support as long as they are in opposition to the partocratic establishment and as long as they are therefore able to confine their actions to negative campaigns in which they express more what they dislike than what they like. It is questionable, however, whether the negative electoral coalition brought together by populist parties will stick together once these parties have to act on policy problems as governing parties. Given the role of the Austrian Freedom Party in the government of some Austrian states and the role of the Northern League in local politics after the 1993 municipal elections—let alone its role in the 1994 right-wing national Italian government—the issue of populist government competence can soon be examined empirically.

Because parties of the NRR express a different political thrust and assemble different electoral coalitions than populist parties in Austria and Italy, their conventional competitors in the camp of moderate conservative parties also have different strategic options at their disposal when confronting each type of new challenge. In the Italian and the Austrian cases with populist challengers, these alternatives are least palatable. The established parties eventually will be forced to reduce their partocratic entrenchment and patronage networks or permanently lose major electoral constituencies to the new competitors. In contrast, where "pure" NRR parties are the challengers, their appeal is less broad-based so that conventional parties may simply "write off" a rather limited right-authoritarian segment of the electorate without making strategic concessions. Here, conventional politicians also have reason to hope that the extremism of the NRR parties' activists may eventually embroil them in internal conflicts that drive the parties into a collapse. By comparison, the antiestablishment and antipartocratic appeal of the Italian and Austrian challengers may prove to be more fundamental and durable, as long as partocratic structures survive and populist parties maintain a negative coalition of mostly disgruntled voters. But even here, the long-term existence of such coalitions may be fragile. For Italian democracy, it may well be plausible that the populist antipartocratic assault destroys the existing party alignments, but is then unable to replace them with an alternative. The productive momentum of populist parties may reside more in the release of destructive forces than in the creative capacity to design viable alternatives.

6

The Legacy of National Socialism in the New Radical Right: Germany

In Austria and Italy, right-wing strength in the interwar period shaped the range of strategic possibilities open to successor organizations after 1945, particularly in the 1980s when they were faced with the opportunity of expressing a right-authoritarian appeal with some prospect of electoral success. The political legacy of the fascist Right has a generational and an intellectual component. Activists who were very young during the fascist and national socialist regimes, but shaped by its interpretation of society and political objectives, later on emerged as the cadre of parties promoting a revival of the extreme Right in post–World War II democracies. At least in the 1950s and 1960s, but even in the 1970s, the presence of such individuals left its stamp on rightist activities, as is demonstrated by the role Georgio Almirante played in the Italian Social Movement. The presence of "old fighters" from the fascist interwar regimes also provided intellectual continuity to the debates and the strategic deliberations of the new extreme Right. At the same time, however, this intellectual legacy reaches beyond the generation of the "old fighters." It is handed down not only via direct socialization of younger entrants into the extreme Right by the old cadres, but also more indirectly through books, journals, and other cultural artifacts produced by the fascist survivor generation and then absorbed by successor generations of younger extreme-rightist militants. These artifacts provide a web of meaning in which radical rightists place their cause.

In Germany, just as in Italy, the traditional extreme Right managed to transmit its interpretation of politics to successor generations of activists who then employed such cognitive frameworks to cope with novel strategic situations in which they sought to mobilize a significant public following. As a consequence, differences in the outlook and the organizational entrenchment of the traditional fascist and national socialist extreme Right in Germany and in Italy are reflected today in distinctive patterns of contemporary rightist extremism in each country. Whereas in Italy the MSI provided organizational and political continuity for the extreme Right and has been represented in the national parliament ever since the inception of the postwar republic, the German federal parliament has not seen legislators of a Nazi successor organization since its inception in 1949.[1] The most obvious reason for the parliamentary failure of the extreme Right is the 5 percent electoral threshold of legislative representation in Germany.[2] Had a similar electoral provision been enacted in Italy, the MSI would have most likely not been represented in parliament in several legislative terms as well.

The differences between the two countries that influence the contemporary career of the extreme Right, however, go deeper than electoral rules. Germany lacks the equivalent of a traditional southern clientelist political environment in which the MSI survived the postwar decades, although the party was politically marginalized in the northern heartland of the 1920s fascist movement. In German political geography, particularly after the loss of the eastern territories and the migration of more than 10 million people from eastern Prussia, Silesia, and later on the German Democratic Republic (GDR) to the Federal Republic of Germany, there was no such refuge in which the extreme Right could build a firm electoral base.[3] Most regions of industrial and Catholic western and southern Germany had not been strongholds of the Nazi party before 1933.

Most importantly, the atrocities and crimes against humanity committed by the German Nazi state far surpass anything the fascist Mussolini regime ever attempted. International vigilance against the recurrence of extreme-rightist politics in Europe therefore focused primarily on Germany. This obliged the new German democratic regime to exercise more political control when successor organizations of the Nazi party attempted to stage a comeback than the Italian postwar governments when facing neofascist movements. Thus, in 1952 the German Constitutional Court, upon request of the German federal government, outlawed a Nazi successor party.

Even though many former second-tier Nazi officials and functionaries found a new political home under the umbrella of the conservative Christian Democratic Adenauer administration, the new West German state could not afford to permit high-profile neo-Nazi party activities. In the cold war era, Adenauer's antagonists in the new East German state tried everything to boost their own legitimacy by insisting on the antidemocratic continuity between the national socialist regime and the politicians of the new Bonn Republic, which in the East German view discredited the Western state. A significant neofascist party tolerated by the new Western political elite would have been proof positive of the correctness of the East German allegations.

In addition to these political and institutional differences between the Italian and the German opportunities for right-wing activism in the post-World War II period, the ideological appeal of the traditional German extreme Right differed from that of its Italian counterpart. Whereas the Italian Right had always been nationalist and imperialist, from its beginnings in the nineteenth century the German extreme Right had also been racist and ethnocentric, a sentiment that strikes a strong chord among followers of the contemporary

NRR as well. In this respect, the Italian extreme-rightist tradition, configured around the MSI, encountered greater obstacles to absorbing the ethnocentric message of the NRR than its German equivalent.

Of course, Germany's extreme Right has also always been highly nationalist, especially in light of Germany's division and the expulsion of Germans from the former eastern territories of the German Empire. The post-World War II territorial settlement kept alive intense nationalist appeals that found resonance far beyond the extreme Right in the narrower sense of the word.

Both the Italian fascist and the German national socialist legacy made it difficult for the extreme Right in the two countries to embrace the other main plank of the NRR in the 1980s, namely, liberal market capitalism buttressed by a strong but small state. The German national socialists, like the Italian fascists, at best had an ambivalent relationship to capitalism. Most German national socialists accepted private property in the economy, but within the frame of a strictly regulatory authoritarian state that would coordinate economic activities, not within the frame of a liberal competitive market economy. A significant minority, particularly activists organized around the "laborist" wing of the Nazi party headed by Gregor Strasser, openly supported socialist redistributive policies as an objective of the national socialist authoritarian state. As a consequence of these various antiliberal strands in Nazi ideology, the postwar German extreme Right expressed hostility to liberal capitalism and searched for a "Third Way" beyond socialist plan and liberal markets. Up to the present, the vision of an economic order that is organized along corporativist lines and hierarchically subordinated to the state has stood in the way of adopting the NRR message of liberal market capitalism. Unlike Le Pen's extreme Right that sought to present itself as the French equivalent to Ronald Reagan in the United States, illiberalism and nationalism in the German Right always promoted anti-Americanism.

Just as the Italian fascist movement has left its imprint on the MSI, so the legacy of German national socialism has left its mark on the various German extreme-rightist efforts. At one end of the spectrum, there are quasimilitary and terrorist sects and groups that are so fundamentally opposed to the German postwar democratic regime that they resist any kind of participation in elections or in any rule-governed process of interest intermediation. Further, there are national socialist successor parties that participate in democratic competition, but openly declare antidemocratic objectives. Finally, there are extreme rightists, such as the German Republicans, who initially tried to free themselves from the legacy of the traditional extreme Right and to project a new image of the Right within the frame of competitive democracy. As the Republican Party's conferences and public declarations show, however, it could not maintain this posture in the 1980s and early 1990s and was soon engulfed by activists of the old fundamentally antidemocratic extreme Right. Although it would be wrong to see the Republicans as a direct national socialist successor organization, its voter appeal and programmatic message is sufficiently distant from the archetypical parties of the NRR in other countries to suggest that the national socialist past still articulates itself in the most influential manifestations of the extreme Right in contemporary Germany.

The German extreme Right in the 1990s shares authoritarian ethnocentric and racist resentments with NRR parties elsewhere. But such dispositions have a long history in German extremist politics. At the same time, the German extreme Right has not managed to absorb the NRR's market-liberal message. As a consequence, our theory would predict that its electorate is significantly more limited than that of NRR parties in France or Scandinavia, let alone populist antistatist parties in Austria and Italy, and exhibits a more constrained socioeconomic profile than that of any extreme-rightist party discussed so far.

At first sight, this argument flies in the face of opinion polls that, between mid-1992 and mid-1993, found about 7 percent of the respondents ready to vote for the Republicans in national elections (Falter 1994, 161). As Falter shows, the popularity of the Republicans is closely linked to the issue attention cycle on immigration and asylum-seeking in German politics. With the compromise among the major German parties to restrict the opportunities for immigration to Germany in 1993, the issue declined on the agenda and so did public support for the Republicans, with a few months of lag. In contrast, in other countries, such as Denmark and France, the extreme Right survived the enactment of even more restrictive immigration laws than those imposed by the German government in 1993.[4] We would argue that the vulnerability of the German Republicans to the issue attention cycle about political asylum and immigration is due to its inability to broaden its political agenda and—because of its national socialist legacy—its failure to reach out to market-liberal electorates who do not feel represented by the major parties. For historical reasons, the Republicans thus have been unable to find the winning formula of electoral appeals in a postindustrial capitalist democracy.

Our analysis of the German extreme Right focuses on the West German situation. After discussing the historical legacy, opportunities, initial mobilization and electoral entrenchment of the latest wave of German extreme Rightism, the *Republikaner,* in the concluding section on strategy we address the unique problem faced by the German extreme Right due to the unification of the country in 1990. The unification brought into the German polity 17 million citizens who still live in a socioeconomic regime that cannot be characterized as postindustrial capitalism. Even where new economic structures evolve in the new German states, political preferences and perceptions of the situation adjust with some time lag. For these reasons, we would not expect a dominant competitive dimension that links economic equalizers and libertarians at one pole and pits them against economic free marketeers and authoritarians at the other. In East Germany, as in other postcommunist countries, a defense of socialist principles of distribution may be unrelated to libertarian politics or in fact attract those who have the least chances to adjust to a capitalist market.[5] These, however, are typically citizens with less education and working in obsolete manufacturing industries, such as coal and steel plants, who also may express a preference for authoritarian and culturally exclusionary political programs. Therefore, in many postcommunist societies left-authoritarian positions may be pitted against right-libertarian programs. As a consequence, for the extreme Right in East Germany not a right-authoritarian but a left-authoritarian appeal may represent the winning formula. The revival of the postcommunist Party of Democratic Socialism (PDS) in German elections in 1993 and 1994, which appears to combine an odd coalition of left-libertarians and left-authoritarians in East Germany, united by their rejection of West German economic, political, and cultural hegemony, provides some evidence for such developments. The Republicans thus face at least two strategic problems. On the one hand, the fascist legacy prevents them from choosing the winning strategic appeal in West Germany. On the other, they are compelled to appeal to East and West German voters with different messages. These conditions explain the overall weak performance of the extreme Right in Germany, which has not managed an electoral breakthrough at the national level but only in a handful of state elections.

The German Extreme Right in the Federal Republic

In West Germany, practically from the time of the first competitive elections in 1946 and 1947, parties appeared on the scene that appealed to national-conservative or even to more or less thinly disguised national socialist proclivities.[6] The first of these parties that experienced some electoral success was the "Sozialistische Reichspartei" (SRP, Socialist Empire Party), which found sympathizers particularly in regions of northern Germany where many eastern expellees had taken up residence. This party was subsequently banned by the German Constitutional Court, because it was judged to be a successor organization of the Nazi party and thus prohibited by the West German constitution. The SRP's support was then transferred to the "Deutsche Reichspartei" (DRP, German Empire Party), which was founded by a variety of national conservative and neo-Nazi organizations in 1950 and received significant voter support in several northern German state elections in the late 1950s.

Throughout the founding decade of the Federal Republic, however, more moderate national-conservative organizations were electorally far more effective than the hard-core neo-Nazi Right. The most influential among them was a new party geared to the special needs and aspirations of the eastern German expellees, the "Bund der Heimatvertriebenen und Entrechteten" (BHE, Federation of Expellees and People Deprived of their Rights). The BHE was closely associated with the Christian Democrats, and the CDU even entered into an alliance with the BHE that enabled the latter to send representatives to the German legislature in 1953. The CDU called upon its followers to support BHE candidates in several safe conservative single-member electoral districts. According to the German electoral law, a party is entitled to full proportional representation in parliament if it wins at least three mandates in single-member districts, even though its national support level may fall short of the 5 percent electoral threshold. By embracing the BHE and catapulting it into parliament, the CDU eventually absorbed the party's more moderate activists, whereas the remainder moved on to the hard-core extreme Right.

Another mildly successful party of the national conservative Right was the "Deutsche Partei" (DP, German Party) which also appealed to nationalist sentiments longing for a reconstitution of the German Empire. Here as well, a mainstream party hastened the demise of this national-conservative organization. The DP initially was situated within the orbit of the German Free Democrats (FDP), until the DP's moderate wing abandoned its own party and joined the FDP, whereas the rest of the DP pursued a more radical nationalist appeal.

The affiliation of conservative-nationalist groups with the major German government parties in the 1950s signaled the latter's efforts to attract and include disaffected Nazis and Eastern expellees into the new Bonn Republic by selective alliances with elements of the right-wing political spectrum. In this era of Cold War hostilities between East and West, the conservative government parties combined this strategy with an intense rhetoric of German national unity and anticommunism. As a consequence of such appeals and the CDU's success in polarizing the German party spectrum between itself, as the focus of all nonsocialist political forces, and the German social democrats, the extreme Right failed to attract a significant independent voter bloc. Efforts to create a "nationalist rally," consisting of the remnants of BHE, DP, and DRP at the end of the 1950s failed to bear any fruit in this political climate. In the 1961 federal election, the "All-German Party" (*Gesamtdeutsche Partei*) failed to attract more than a tiny fraction of the electorate. According to the German Interior Ministry's monitoring activity, the organized extreme antidemocratic Right declined from 75,000 members in 1954 to 55,000 in 1959 down to about 20,000 in 1964 (Stöss 1989, 99).

The first real opportunity to revive the extreme Right emerged in the mid-1960s when economic and political conditions became more favorable for its revival. First, under the impact of Kennedy's and Johnson's detente policy, the conservative-liberal government parties found themselves increasingly embroiled in internal debates about a new foreign policy that would overcome

Cold War thinking and seek some kind of accommodation with the Soviet Union and with what until then was still called the "Soviet Occupied Zone" of Germany in the official West German political terminology. Strict nationalists thus could find themselves no longer unambiguously represented by the mainstream conservative government parties. Second, the domestic polarization between social democrats on the Left and Christian democrats and liberals on the Right gave way to a more open situation in which all parties became available for coalitions with each other. This development was evidenced in new state-level coalition agreements between SPD and FDP and CDU and SPD and peaked in the Grand Coalition of CDU/CSU and SPD at the federal government level in 1967–69. The two parties together commanded more than 90 percent of the seats in the German *Bundestag*. This prompted the formation of left- and right-wing opposition movements outside parliament because the centrist liberals, by themselves, were too weak and politically too narrow to represent popular objections to the policies of the Grand Coalition. On the Left, the "Außerparlamentarische Opposition" (APO, Extra-parliamentary Opposition), created by the student movement, began to mobilize for its demand to democratize German society and to create more opportunities for citizens' participation. On the Right, new organizations invoked the Cold War themes of national reunification and anticommunism, but also called for more emphasis on authority, law and order, and opposition to the new cultural libertarianism and permissiveness advocated by the APO. On top of these political developments, West Germany experienced its first serious postwar economic downturn in 1966-67, an event that added fuel to the flames of right-wing protest.

In 1964, a new rightist organization that combined many of the previously existing and electorally unsuccessful extremist splinter groups had been founded under the label of the "Nationaldemokratische Partei Deutschlands" (NPD, National Democratic Party of Germany).[7] In the changing economic and political climate of the Grand Coalition years, this party managed to enter state legislatures with 5 to 9 percent of the vote in elections held between 1966 and 1969 in Hesse, Bavaria, Lower Saxony, Rhineland Palatinate, Schleswig-Holstein, and Baden-Württemberg. It is important to recall the socioeconomic profile of the NPD's activists and voters in the 1960s because it was strikingly different from that of the extreme-rightist parties of the late 1980s. Older males with recollections of the Nazi period, refugees and members of the old ("petit bourgeois") middle class, particularly small-town residents, were prominent support groups, both in the party's electorate and among its activists. The party also gained a substantial working-class following, but blue-collar support represented a smaller proportion than what would have corresponded to the workers' share in the voting population.[8] In many ways, the NPD represented the last mobilization of the "old warriors" of the German Nazi Right (Jaschke 1990, 18). Two thirds of the members of the NPD's national executive board elected in November 1964 had been active Nazis before 1945 (Childs 1991, 72).

In contrast to the state elections held in the period of the Grand Coalition from 1966 to 1969, however, at the national level the NPD failed to overcome the 5-percent hurdle of legislative representation and received only 4.1 percent in the September 1969 federal election. Over the next several years, the NPD all but vanished from the electoral landscape, although its membership declined only moderately from a high of 36,800 (1968) to a low of 17,200 (1975) (Childs 1991, 74). The reason for the NPD's decline can be traced to the disappearance of the favorable conditions that permitted its rise in the mid-1960s. First of all, economic growth began to resume in 1968 and quickly reduced German unemployment below 1 percent of the labor force. What was more important, in the run-up to the 1969 federal election, the polarization between social democrats and Christian Democrats drew nationalist and right-wing voters back into the CDU's political orbit. The social democrats ran on a platform that highlighted themes of the New Left, such as political democratization and domestic social reforms, as well as support for a European detente policy to overcome the Cold War division. In contrast, the Christian Democrats began to reemphasize the importance of German unification, resistance to a recognition of the GDR, and opposition to the new cultural and political libertarianism that was promoted by the Left. In this situation, a sufficient number of NPD sympathizers could be persuaded to vote for the CDU to keep the NPD below the 5-percent threshold of parliamentary representation. The polarization between Christian Democrats and social democrats further intensified under the subsequent social-liberal government headed by Willy Brandt, which pursued a reconciliation with West Germany's eastern neighbors, including the GDR, that prompted the Christian Democrats to resort to intense nationalist rhetoric. This controversy climaxed in the 1972 federal election in which the Christian Democrats were defeated on their untimely foreign policy stance. At the same time, the 1972 election obliterated the remaining support for the NPD most of whose voters returned to the Christian Democratic camp.

The decline of the NPD, however, was not entirely due to changes in the party's political opportunity structure and competitive environment. It was also hastened by internal organizational processes that are instructive because they have reappeared inside the Republican party of the 1980s and 1990s. To be electorally successful, parties of the extreme Right must reach out beyond their core of fully committed zealots, an objective that requires a certain strategic moderation. As soon as a rightist party experiences electoral success, however, it becomes a magnet for a wide range of militants who had previously adhered to unsuccessful extremist splinter groups and right-wing sects. Such militants typically are more radical than the founding members of the now successful rightist party organization. Particularly in Germany, with a hard-core neo-Nazi infrastructure of sects and clubs, a rising right-wing conjuncture in electoral politics thus draws a large number of extremists into the party organization who then pull its strategy toward more extreme positions. Once the party becomes more extreme, the existing major conservative parties can more plausibly document their new competitor's neo-Nazi credentials and persuade more moderate conservative-national voters wavering between mainline and extreme Right not to support the new party. Eventually, the extremism of the new party contributes to a reversal of its electoral fortunes and its political demise.

Following this pattern, the NPD underwent a process of progressive right-wing radicalization from its inception in 1964 to the mid-1970s that contributed to its electoral decline. This change is symbolized by the succession of party chairmen beginning with the German nationalist Fritz Thielen who was subsequently replaced in 1966 by the more radical Adolf von Thadden, the offspring of a family of eastern Junkers. After the party's national electoral defeat in 1969, von Thadden, in turn, came into the cross fire of more extremist party activists and had to resign from his position in favor of Martin Mußgnug in 1971 (cf. Jaschke 1990, 75). At that time, a new equilibrium was reached between an extremely radical party chairman, a radical group of rank-and-file activists, and the remaining hard-core, but microscopic, electorate.

Overall, in West Germany extreme-rightist political organizations in the second half of the 1970s and in the first half of the 1980s were in the political wilderness. Nevertheless, the German Interior Ministry registered an increase of rightist political crime, peaking at 2,500 judicially prosecuted incidents in 1982, but then a decline to about 1,500 incidents in 1987 (Stöss 1989, 154). Membership in right-extremist youth organizations increased from about 500 in 1967 to about 2,500 in 1976–78, and then declined to about 1,000 in the 1982–86 period (157). In that era, a number of tiny national socialist, terrorist, and national-conservative organizations survived but could not gain political momentum (cf. Husbands 1991). It is significant that the conjunctures of right-wing sectarian activism are not entirely synchronized with conjunctures of right-wing electoral support (cf. Zimmermann and Saalfeld 1993, 58–63).

In the late 1970s and 1980s, at the radical conservative periphery of the Christian Democrats a new "intellectual" Right emerged around organizations such as the "Deutschland Stiftung" (Germany Foundation), the "Konservative Aktion" (Conservative Action), a number of journals and independent intellectuals, such as Klaus-Gerd Kaltenbrunner, Günther Rohrmoser, Hermann Lübbe, Robert Spaemann, and Odo Marquard. These intellectual conservatives represent the German equivalent of the new French right-wing intelligentsia, organized around the organization GRECE.[9] The German intellectual Right was mostly concerned with themes such as social order, natural inequality, and the resurrection of stable moral beliefs, but not with the free market liberalism of the paradigmatic "New" Radical Right that manifested itself in French or Scandinavian extreme rightist politics. Moreover, the German intellectual conservatives have not been close to political protoparties on the right of the Christian Democrats and thus cannot be considered the intellectual inspirators of such organizations as the German Republicans (cf. Betz 1990, 50).

Changing Opportunity Structure for the New Right

While the configuration of German political party competition was generally unfavorable to rightist mobilization throughout the 1970s and early 1980s because the major moderate conservative party was confined to the opposition benches, this situation began to change in the mid-1980s. The coming to office of the Christian Democratic–Free Democratic coalition government in 1982 in due course of time improved the opportunities for a new extremist Right. At the same time, changes in West Germany's economic and social structures made more voters potentially receptive to an extreme-rightist message.

Just as in other advanced capitalist market societies, in the 1980s Germany underwent a rapid process of structural economic transformation and modernization. In this process, the number of highly skilled jobs, particularly white-collar jobs in service sectors, expanded at the expense of more traditional unskilled and skilled industrial jobs. This gradual deindustrialization was more profound than the size of economic sectors, by itself, suggests. Even within the industrial sector, many skilled and unskilled manual jobs were displaced by automation and highly trained technicians capable of mastering computerized machine tools and work processes (Kern and Schumann 1984). While negotiations between business and labor both at the sectoral level as well as through works councils at the factory and corporate level buffered the economic hardship resulting from these changes, especially for already employed middle-aged and older workers, including skilled *Facharbeiter*, whose jobs now often were threatened, the major burden of the adjustment was experienced by young, unskilled workers and entrants into the labor force faced with rapidly shrinking employment opportunities. These "losers of the modernization process" began to represent a reservoir of political dissatisfaction that could be harnessed by new rightist parties. Accelerated economic adjustment, by itself, however, does not explain the *timing* of right-wing success in Germany (Jaschke 1990, 51). Two further conditions must be taken into account.

The first of these conditions was political and resulted from the policies of the Christian Democratic-Liberal government that came into office under Chancellor Kohl in 1982. In the campaign preceding the March 1983 elections, the Christian Democrats had promised not only a revival of the economy and a return to full employment but also a more profound political and cultural "reversal" (*Wende*) that was to mark the end of the social-liberal era of 1969–82. The nebulous concept of the *Wende* was designed to reinforce the loyalty of fundamentalist conservative and German-nationalist forces in the electorate and among the Christian Democrats' party activists who wanted to undo whatever libertarian political and cultural opening had taken place under the previous government. Within less than two years after winning the 1983 elections, however, it became clear that the Christian Democratic government would neither be able nor willing to engineer such a basic reversal. In part, Christian Democrats were hampered by their liberal coalition partner; in part, their own vocal moderate and social wing, as well as increasingly outspoken women's groups inside the party, imposed severe constraints on the scope of the politically feasible changes.

As a consequence, in most respects the government led by the Christian Democrats continued much of the "politics of centripetalism" that had been the hallmark of the preceding moderate and technocratic SPD government headed by Chancellor Helmut Schmidt. The persistence of policies of the previous government was first of all visible in the area of foreign policy where the new government continued detente and reconciliation with the East, including close contacts with the GDR leadership. In the sphere of economic and social policies, the changes were much less dramatic than promised. The Schmidt government had already enacted serious social budget cuts that eventually led to its collapse. The Kohl government continued this policy for some time, but was then faced with so much dissatisfaction in its own ranks that it returned to a course of gradual social policy expansion.

Many other policy areas—concerning industrial modernization and technology, environment and agriculture, health care and maternity leave—could be cited to show the rather substantial continuity in German government policies from the pre-1982 Schmidt government to the post-1982 Kohl government. This "politics of centripetalism" was reinforced by the growing strength of the social democrats at the level of state government. Germany's cooperative federalism constrained the federal government's capacity for policy innovation (cf. Katzenstein 1987). An area that deserves special mentioning is that of women's affairs. Conservative hopes to restore the paternalist family structure through policies to discourage female labor market participation and to tighten the German abortion law were disappointed; moreover, in competition with Greens and SPD, even the Christian Democrats had to show more openness toward an equalization of women's roles in all spheres of life, including that of politics.

The policy convergence in the German party system created an opening for voter defections to new left-libertarian (Green) and rightist party alternatives (cf. Leggewie 1987; Pappi 1990, 38). The Christian Democrats' failure to engineer the cultural and political *Wende* contributed to a growing disaffection of its conservative-national militants and fringe voters. The CDU became increasingly incapable of combining its three major "pillars," namely, a social Christian, a market-liberal, and a national-conservative pillar (Leggewie 1990, 11). In Berlin, for example, the CDU suffered a mass exodus of middle-level functionaries in 1987. In their letters of resignation, the dissenters declared they were disappointed by the party's continuation of detente policy toward communist regimes, the unwillingness of the party to cut back on women's abortion rights, the toleration of a statue for the Marxist Rosa Luxemburg in Berlin, and the failure to decrease the flow of political asylum-seekers to Berlin (Malzahn 1989, 45). These grievances quite accurately reflect the themes that conservative-nationalists in the CDU had associated with the implementation of a cultural and political *Wende,* which then never came: more nationalism, less libertarianism, fewer women's rights, more confrontation with Eastern European socialist countries, and a reversal of the ethnic and cultural pluralization of German society brought about by the influx of foreigners. The practice of centripetalism in German politics, even without the Grand Coalition, made elements of the Christian Democratic Right willing to defect to a new, more extremist party organization.

The second condition favoring the growth of right-wing extremism in Germany in the late 1980s was a political-demographic one, already touched upon in the declarations of those who left the Berlin CDU in 1987. In the 1980s, the number of asylum seekers in Germany began to skyrocket, as (1) it became more widely known that the German constitution in light of the experience with national socialism had one of the most liberal provisions for granting the right to political asylum and as (2) professional services began to organize the flow of asylum-seekers to West Germany. Moreover, as a result of detente policy, West Germany experienced a considerable inflow of ethnic Germans from Eastern Europe throughout the 1980s. While in the long run these developments might be welcomed economically because they counterbalance Germany's low birth rate and guarantee that future generations of retirees can count on their social security benefits, in the short run the influx of foreigners imposed considerable strains on the German legal system and social services, particularly at the municipal level in those large cities where the new arrivals typically settled first. A national survey in early 1989 showed that no less than 75 percent of all respondents indicated that there were too many foreigners in Germany, and 37 percent of all respondents, but only 16 percent of those younger than 24 years of age, even saw some justification for the slogan "foreigners out" (Jaschke 1990, 51). Respondents who expected to be negatively affected by the process of industrial modernization were most disaffected with the influx of asylum-seekers and ethnic Germans because they anticipated that they would compete directly with such new arrivals for the remaining low-skill jobs in the German economy.[10]

Beyond economic modernization, strategic convergence of the dominant parties and demographic changes, the German unification of October 1990 was a key event for understanding the trajectory of extreme-rightist forces in the early 1990s. Initially, the unification had rather ambivalent consequences for the electoral opportunities of the far Right. Most Germans were not overcome by a wave of nationalist sentimentality that might have helped the extreme Right to benefit from unification. Moreover, it was the main moderate conservative party that engineered the unification process and was electorally rewarded for that by East and West Germans in the December 1990 federal election.

Ironically, supporters of the nationalist Right around the Republican Party and smaller extremist groups showed the least sympathy for the plight of East German refugees in fall 1989. Because immigration had increased the anxiety about labor market opportunities and the viability of German social security institutions and provided a catalyst for right-wing mobilization before unification, the same West German rightists now could not welcome the rush of GDR immigrants into West Germany and the very sizable financial transfers from West Germany into the collapsing East German economy. The "welfare chauvinism" behind ethnocentrist feelings expressed by considerable contingents of West German voters who insisted on preserving the status quo of material affluence against any redistribution to "outsiders" contradicted a right-wing nationalist enthusiasm that might have displayed charity and altruism toward the new citizen and might have gladly accepted economic redistribution toward the East for the sake of unification with the territories of the former GDR.

In many ways, the ensuing socioeconomic difficulties and conflicts over the unification process, including the wave of asylum-seekers from Eastern Europe—but not the fact of unification itself—helped the German extreme Right to mobilize in the early 1990s. At the same time, however, these difficulties also promoted a differentiation within the German Right. There are indications that the West and East German extreme Right might develop a rather different momentum. As the integration process created strains in Germany's economy, rightist protests in each region of the country appear to be driven by somewhat different grievances. The single common denominator of the extreme Right in East and West, however, is racism, ethnocentrism, and xenophobia. But the West German far Right continues to thrive on "welfare chauvinist" sentiments, which at least indirectly depict East Germans as "free riders" on the welfare state. It is easy to see that the East German extreme Right cannot embrace welfare chauvinism because it would undercut subsidies precisely to those East Germans who are now most inclined to support right-wing extremism because of their often desperate economic difficulties.

Future research will have to determine the extent and the severity of conflicts of interest between the West and East German extreme Right. In addition to the legacy of national socialism on contemporary rightist appeals in Germany, the unique strategic situation of the contemporary German extreme Right might explain why it cannot combine authoritarian and racist appeals with economic market liberalism in the same fashion as French or Scandinavian NRR parties. If there is a common denominator, in addition to racism, between rightist currents in East and West Germany, it is a defense *against* free markets and *for* social protection. In the West, the extreme Right is able to appeal to certain working-class constituencies with such slogans but may sacrifice non–working-class support with this strategy, a choice yielding a lower electoral payoff than the "winning formula" of right-authoritarian politics. At the same time, abstention from free market rhetoric is important in attracting East German rightist voters to the Republicans. The latter are definitely motivated by misgivings about the consequences of market economic reforms in the former GDR and would not support a market-liberal extreme Right. At the same time, however, the perception of the Republicans as a West German party may explain the lower level of right-wing party support in East Germany and the higher level of physical and psychological violence there against foreigners than in West Germany.

Reorganization and Success of a New Extreme Right in Germany

The realignment of the German extreme Right that eventually was to take advantage of the emerging favorable opportunity structure in the party system began in 1983. At that time, the Prime Minister of Bavaria and chairman of the Christian Social Union (CSU), Franz-Josef Strauß, a man with the reputation of being a national-conservative hardliner but a clever tactician, visited East Germany and extended a credit of 10 billion Deutschmarks to the GDR. This action underlined the continuity between the social democratic detente policy in the 1970s and that of the newly installed Christian Democratic federal government, but it sorely disappointed national-conservatives who initially backed the new government. The huge credit for East Germany prompted a breakaway from the Bavarian CSU that established itself under the name "The Republicans." The name of the party was to symbolize its affinity to a Reagan-style nationalist conservatism, paired with cultural conservatism and anticommunist rhetoric.

The party developed roots primarily in Bavaria but also created subsidiaries in Berlin, Hamburg, and Bremen, although these state organizations remained rather weak. Its hard core was primarily drawn from the organizations of expellees and Christian Democratic party activists, as the example of the wave of resignations in the Berlin CDU in Berlin in 1987 has already illustrated. The Republicans achieved their first modest success in the 1986 Bavarian state elections with 3 percent of the vote. Party slogans were centered on the rejection of asylum-seekers in Germany, the arrogance of the dominant parties, as well as the need for a new sense of family and patriotism (cf. Jaschke 1990, 65). The party targeted the votes of expellees, small businesspeople, farmers, policemen, and generally those who were disappointed that the Christian Democratic *Wende* had not inaugurated a new era of moral conservatism and nationalism.

The intention of the Republicans' founders to institute a new rightist, but nonextremist party were soon subverted by the entry of militants from the spectrum of unsuccessful sectarian neo-Nazi organizations. In 1985, these forces quickly managed to displace the founder of the party, Franz Handlos, and instead elected as new chairman Franz Schönhuber, a former television journalist who had to resign from his position when he published the recollections of his life as an SS officer during the Nazi regime (Lepszy 1989, 3). Since the mid-1980s, at the time of Schönhuber's takeover, the party was embroiled in constant infighting between different cabals and tendencies. Some of these conflicts concerned matters of ideological extremism, others just personal ambition and the control of the party's organizational and financial apparatus that grew with its electoral success and eligibility for public party finance. Internal conflict among the Republicans has been associated with a high turnover of members, which may explain why the party did not manage to exceed 14,000 members in 1989 (Stöss 1989, 202). In May 1990, Schönhuber was even forced to resign as party chairman but was soon reelected to his previous position of leadership. Jaschke characterizes the Republicans at the turn to the 1990s in the following way:

> The party is internally divided, supported by an extremely fragile balance of power, lacks professional mechanisms to regulate conflicts, and is perpetually threatened by split-offs to the right or in a Christian-conservative direction. It lacks qualified, professional elected representatives and intra-party democracy. Schönhuber's role as integrator which far exceeds the intra-party position of other party chairmen, makes it appropriate to call the Republicans a "leader party" [*Führerpartei*], also with respect to its authoritarian and right extremist definition of politics. (1990, 80)

The conservative pro-Western basic program of the Republicans chosen at the first party conference was soon replaced by a succession of increasingly right-wing extremist programs at conferences in 1985, 1986, and 1988 (Stöss 1989, 205–6). The party continued to lack a conception for economic and social policy that would go beyond general support for small business at the expense of large corporations (Kieserling 1991, 47). Instead, the Republicans' propaganda has been entirely geared to social, political, and cultural questions situated on the libertarian versus authoritarian issue dimension. The party espouses racism, nationalism, and a quest for law and order. It employs a vocabulary that is close to national socialist rhetoric, especially through the usage of terms such as *Volk* (folk), *deutsches Volk* and *Lebensraum* ("living space").[11] The Republicans endorse a traditional view of women's roles in home and society and militantly reject women's right to choose an abortion. They intend to restrict civil rights protecting the articulation of political disagreements through strikes, demonstrations, and free speech and call for a strong authoritarian state. Moreover, the party wishes to "decriminalize" German history and belittles or denies the crimes of the Nazi regime. Directly and indirectly, it employs anti-semitic hate messages and racial stereotypes.

It is important to emphasize that, unlike the Scandinavian or French NRR, the German Republicans do not highlight support for a capitalist market economy and do not criticize the bureaucratic welfare state (Pappi 1990, 39). The Republicans share a rejection of immigrants and the call for a strong state and traditional morality with the NRR in these other countries. Even on these issues, however, Republicans often employ a vocabulary reminiscent of the national socialist legacy that is specific to Germany. At the same time, their economic predilections for a corporatist, antiliberal organization of the economy are more consistent with those of German national socialism than with market liberalism featured by parties of the NRR in other countries. The Republicans here follow the footsteps of their precursors from DRP to NPD with whom they have in common an authoritarian and nationalist view of social order that also is wary of free market capitalism:[12]

> Neutralism between the two blocs, reunification as confederation, a "third way" between Soviet communism and American cultural imperialism, and national identity and patriotism as surrogates of the old imperial idea of the Reich. (Zimmermann and Saalfeld 1993, 58)

The Republicans project themselves primarily as the party of the "little people," a party of those worried about their economic existence and seeking social protection from the vagaries of the marketplace (Lepszy 1989, 8). Based on this appeal by the political elites, we would expect the German Republicans to attract a different electoral support coalition than true parties of the NRR in France or Scandinavia.

Parallel to the Republicans, in northern Germany in the 1980s another party more directly linked to neofascist organizations began to thrive, the *Deutsche Volksunion* (DVU, German People's Union). This party was initially founded by a right-wing editor of a daily newspaper and of numerous extremist periodicals, Gerhard Frey. The party grew from less than 4,000 members in 1971 to 6,000 in 1979 and then from 12,000 in 1984 to more than 24,000 members in the late 1980s.[13] Many of its members directly transferred from the NPD of the 1960s and 1970s and on several occasions NPD and DVU formed joint electoral lists. The DVU's political appeal is similar to that of the Republicans, once the latter had defeated their moderate Christian-national wing in the mid-1980s. The DVU won its first modest success in the 1987 state elections in Bremen where it received 3.1 percent and one seat in the state parliament. The NPD/DVU scored further modest successes at the local level in the March 1989 Frankfurt elections and in the Bremen and Schleswig-Holstein state elections of 1991 and 1992. Overall, however, the DVU is less significant for German politics than the Republicans and is unlikely to establish itself nationwide.[14]

The major electoral breakthrough of the German extreme Right came in the January 1989 state election in West Berlin where the Republicans received 7.5 percent of the vote. Since the early 1980s, Berlin had been governed by moderate CDU lord mayors, although it had a vocal and increasingly restless right-wing led by the Christian Democrats' Senator of the Interior, Heinrich Lummer. At the same time, Berlin was a focus of immigration because the authorities did not impose border controls on individuals entering the city from East Berlin. Most importantly, however, conservative-nationalist forces considered the noisy West Berlin left-libertarian scene of social movements and countercultural projects to be a provocation that stirred right-wing resentments. In general, the rise of the extreme Right is not a "countermovement" that directly responds to the wave of left-libertarian mobilization in the 1970s and 1980s (cf. Koopmans and Duyvendak 1991). But in the particular circumstances of Berlin, the interference of left-libertarian forces with public manifestations of the extreme Right in the late 1980s may have contributed to a polarization of the public and to growing sympathies with the extreme Right. Confronted with the vocal protests of the Left, extreme-rightist militants appeared as "underdogs" attracting sympathies also from generally moderate conservatives and unpolitical citizens (Blattert and Ohlemacher 1991).

The party's electoral breakthrough in Berlin became self-sustaining because it triggered a flood of media attention and introduced the Republican leader Franz Schönhuber to millions of readers and television viewers. At the same time, the indecisive reactions of the established parties and their inability to take a clear stance on immigration policy, the issue featured most in Republican election campaigns, increased the new challenger's appeal. This momentum was manifested in the 1989 European elections when the party won 7.1 percent of the vote. The regional distribution of party support is particularly interesting. It ranged from 14.6 percent in the party's home state of Bavaria and 8.7 percent in the neighboring state of Baden-Württemberg to less than 5 percent in most of the northern German states, including Northrhine-Westfalia. While the differential organizational entrenchment of the Republicans played a role in the regional stratification of the party's electoral support base, it is also plausible that the relatively weak organization of the social democrats in the quite affluent southern German working-class neighborhoods made available a voter constituency to the extreme Right whose equivalent in the northern German states is still more firmly linked to the parties and unions of the labor movement.[15]

For reasons already elaborated, the fall of the Berlin Wall in November 1989 and the ensuing process of German unification were an electoral disaster for the Republicans, because the established parties stole the national limelight and the unification temporarily reduced the salience of immigration on the political agenda. Beginning in November 1989, opinion polls signaled a collapse in the Republicans' electoral base (Roth 1990, 28), and the party managed to win barely 2 percent of the national vote in the first federal election after unification, in December 1990.

The Republicans' comeback in 1992 when it received 11 percent of the vote in the Baden-Württemberg state elections and support of between 5 and 10 percent in several other state elections was intimately linked to the changing issue agenda of German politics. First of all, the problems of unification magnified the stress imposed on the German social and economic system by an accelerating stream of immigrants from Eastern Europe and other regions of the world. Moreover, those social groups that felt endangered by the industrial modernization process in the 1980s now had even more reason to be anxious about their social well-being, as increasingly scarce resources for social welfare had to be shared with the new East German states to rebuild that region. As a consequence, a strong "welfare chauvinist" sentiment, upset about the declining standard of living and social protection in West Germany resulting from the new financial burdens and taxes imposed after the unification, fed into the revival of the Republican party.

Moreover, the Christian Democratic government contributed to the intensifying debate about immigration and asylum-seekers both by its insistence on a change of the federal constitution that was initially rejected by the opposition social democrats as well as its lax handling of a rising wave of extremist hate crimes against foreigners, asylum-seekers, and even disabled citizens in East and West Germany.[16] These developments provided respectability to the demands of the Republicans and reinvigorated their electoral support. Only in 1993, after Social Democrats and Christian Democrats had agreed on a compromise law to restrict immigration and political asylum and after international outrage about racist hate crimes in Germany compelled state and federal governments to contain right-wing terrorism in more resolute ways, the favorable popular reception of one of the Republicans' main themes began to wane, and the party's public support retreated again (Falter 1994, 160–62).

By 1993–94, the political opportunity structure of the German extreme Right was more complicated than that of other countries because of the division between eastern and western extremist constituencies and their unique socioeconomic problems and cultural experiences over the preceding decades. Moreover, it was constrained by the long-term historical legacy of Germany's Nazi past. Because the national socialist ideological heritage was transmitted by actors and ideas over a span of more than 50 years, none of the contemporary rightist organizations, including the Republicans, has been seeking to overcome traditional collectivist, social protectionist, and corporatist economic appeals. For that reason, the German parties of the extreme Right have not been able to bring together an encompassing coalition of (1) small business and farmer antitax protestors with (2) a racist and authoritarian lower-class constituency revolting against the process of economic structural adjustment—that is, the elements that constitute the winning formula of the NRR in other countries. At the same time, in East Germany, extreme-rightist appeals are constrained by the absence of both a middle-class antitax constituency and a "welfare chauvinist" lower-class electorate protecting its social entitlements from redistribution to those who have not contributed to the West German social insurance systems. For these historical and structural politico-economic reasons, the appeal of the German extreme Right has been confined to racism, ethnocentrism, and a general populist call for protection from the marketplace, yielding a rather narrower and more volatile electoral coalition than that attracted by NRR parties in other countries.

Structure and Regional Distribution of the German Right-Wing Electorate

Based on the ideological legacy of the German extreme Right and what is known about the electoral appeal of the Republicans' leaders, we cannot characterize the (West) German Republicans as a pure NRR right-authoritarian party, but rather as a "welfare chauvinist" party that attracts a lower social clientele but not the independent businesspeople and farmers that the NRR parties in France or Scandinavia do. Like these parties, however, the Republicans are likely to be underrepresented among educated white-collar employees and professionals in the German occupational structure. Let us explore these hypotheses now with 1990 *World Values Survey* data bearing in mind that this survey is less than ideal for exploring the structure of the German right-wing electorate because it was taken in the months before unification when Republican electoral support had virtually collapsed. As a consequence, only about 2 percent in a sample of 2,100 respondents expresses a preference for the Republicans. Because it is difficult to test our hypotheses with such a small number of cases, we must supplement it with data from other surveys and empirical studies. The other handicap is that the data include only West

TABLE 6.1.   Ideological Divisions in West Germany: An Exploratory Factor Analysis (Principal Components)

	Factor I	Factor II	Factor III
	(Left-)Libertarian versus (Right-)Authoritarian	Capitalist Right versus Socialist Left	Deep Ecology versus Modern Industry
Economic Issues			
1. Business management	−.35	+.42	+.20
2. Income inequality	−.25	+.58	−.03
3. Competition	−.22	+.61	+.16
Ecology and Industry			
4. Environmental taxes	+.28	+.35	+.36
5. Urgency of ecology	+.53	+.29	+.18
6. No nuclear plants	+.57	−.23	+.54
Race and Nation			
7. Objections to neighbors of different race	−.30	−.34	−.12
8. Priority for own nationals in labor markets	−.39	−.20	−.02
9. National pride	−.64	+.08	+.13
Authority and Participation			
10. More respect for authority	−.60	−.09	+.26
11. Confidence in the army	−.58	+.21	+.07
12. Would participate in lawful demonstration	+.61	+.12	−.08
13. Would participate in disarmament protest	+.55	−.20	+.58
Women and Family			
14. Choice over abortion	+.51	+.05	−.42
15. Women as homemakers	−.47	−.23	+.35
16. Women's right to a job	+.53	+.27	+.12
Eigenvalues	3.70	1.55	1.27
Party Factor Scores			
Greens (N = 60)	+1.35	−.28	−.12
Social Democrats (N = 312)	+.28	−.19	+.01
Free Democrats (N = 70)	−.07	+.48	−.27
Christian Democrats (N = 313)	−.51	+.19	+.02
Republicans (N = 20)	−.57	−.01	−.70

Source: World Values Survey. Own Calculations.

German respondents. The East German 1990 *World Values Survey* has no respondents who would endorse an explicitly extremist right-wing party.

Table 6.1 presents the results of an exploratory principal components factor analysis on the political issue items familiar from previous chapters. It shows that the major division in the German electorate with a strong eigenvalue of 3.7 is between left-libertarian and right-authoritarian politics. It is

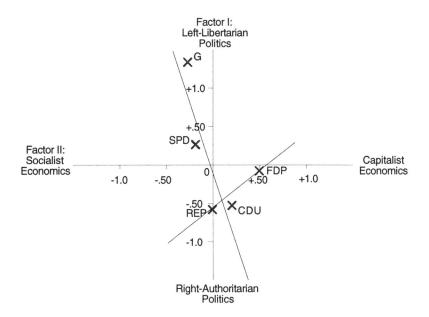

Fig. 6.1. The political space of European democracies: Germany

supplemented by a much weaker capitalism versus socialism second factor (eigenvalue 1.55) and an even weaker deep ecology versus modern industry factor (eigenvalue 1.27). Overall, the German profile of voter preferences does not look much different than what we found in most other countries, except that the first factor discriminates more than anywhere else. Examining the party supporters' mean factor scores and their geometric representation in figure 6.1 shows that mean scores on factor I are correlated with those on factor II. The competitive space between the parties is thus by and large unidimensional in Germany, with one important qualification. Liberals and Republicans may form the opposite poles on a subordinate competitive dimension that divides pro- and anticapitalist feelings on the second factor but only moderately divides the parties on the first factor.[17]

A regression of the three factors on general ideological dispositions also suggests that the first dimension organizes the German political space (table 6.2). The left-libertarian versus right-authoritarian factor is a powerful predic-

TABLE 6.2. General Ideological Dispositions Predicted by Voters' Issue Positions (Factor Scores of the Exploratory Factor Analysis) in West Germany

	Constant		Factor I (Left-)Libertarian versus (Right-)Authoritarian		Factor II Capitalist Right versus Socialist Left		Factor III Deep Ecology versus Modern Industry		adj. R^2
	PE	t	PE	t	PE	t	PE	t	
Left/right Self-Placement	5.25	102.76	−.90	18.46	+.34	6.54	+.03	.52	.32*** (N = 823)
Postmaterialism	2.18	122.51	+.32	18.71	+.03	1.74	−.02	−1.05	.28*** (N = 888)
Church attendance⁺	5.15	73.80	+.63	9.43	+.03	.48	−.52	7.77	.14*** (N = 887)

Source: World Values Survey. Own calculations.
Note: PE = parameter estimate; t = t ratio.
***significant at the .001 level.
**significant at the .01 level.
*significant at the .05 level.
⁺Scale inversed: High values indicate infrequent or no church attendance.

tor of left/right self-placements, postmaterialism, and secular orientation. The second capitalism versus socialism factor is a much weaker predictor of ideological self-placements and is unrelated to the religion/secularism divide on which the third factor has a rather powerful influence. Deep ecologists tend to be more religious.

As expected, in table 6.1 and figure 6.1 the position of the Republicans is near the right-authoritarian pole of factor I, but not that much differentiated from that of the Christian Democrats. Also as expected, Republican supporters do not take a clearly procapitalist position on factor II, in contrast to their counterparts in France, Norway, Austria, or Italy. These results signal the limited support Republican voters lend to the right-authoritarian agenda: authoritarianism—yes; liberal market capitalism—with hesitation. Republicans are clear outliers on factor III in that they oppose the deep ecology agenda and are ardent supporters of modern industrialism. This finding may signal the "welfare chauvinist" concerns of the Republican clientele with industrial employment that is challenged by environmentalist movements. Interestingly, there is no separate factor for race and nation on which the Republicans would stand out. Here as in the other countries, the racist-nationalist party appeal is embedded in a broader authoritarian message that organizes the ideological map of Republican voters.

Our findings about the general orientation of Republican voters are by and large confirmed by other studies. Such voters are especially disinclined to endorse postmaterialist (or antiauthoritarian, participatory) political orientations (cf. Minkenberg 1992a).[18] They are also more nationalist and racist than any other party's electorate.[19] Further, Republican voters militantly oppose women's right to abortions (Leggewie 1990, 20) and generally have the most sexist and traditional views of women's role in a German society that is generally more inclined to endorse traditional sex stereotypes than most other European countries (Morgan and Wilcox 1991; Wilcox 1991).[20]

We have not found studies that would explicitly analyze the Republican following's support of capitalism, but our *World Values Study* results reported in chapter 2 (table 2.10) are highly suggestive. Whereas voters of the NRR in France or Scandinavia endorse liberal capitalism more than the supporters of any other party family, this does not apply to the German extreme Right. Christian Democratic and liberal voters typically approve capitalism more than Republicans. For example, 64.9 percent of West German liberal voters and 60.5 percent of Christian Democratic voters believe that more state property should pass into private hands (survey average: 51.9%), but only 42.3 percent of Republican voters hold the same opinion. Republican voters are close to social democrats (43.6%) and Greens (38.6%) on this account. The views of the Republican electoral constituency thus directly correspond to the programmatic statements and public pronouncements of the German Republican party

TABLE 6.3. Ideological Divisions in West Germany: Confirmatory Factor Analysis (missing values set equal to zero)

	Capitalism versus Socialism	Authoritarianism versus Libertarianism	Parochialism versus Cosmopolitanism
A. Economic Distribution			
1. For more income inequality	+.45	—	—
2. For private business ownership	+.67	—	—
3. For more competition	+.60	+.12	—
4. For owner-managed business	+.36	+.25	—
B. Libertarian versus Authoritarian Issues			
5. Postmaterialism	—	−.58	—
6. Respect for authority	—	+.59	—
7. Participation in lawful demonstration	—	−.60	—
8. Women's right to abortion	—	−.53	—
9. Role of housewife fulfilling	—	+.44	—
C. Cosmopolitan/Particularist Dimension			
10. Acceptance of neighbor of different race	—	—	+.51
11. Acceptance of foreigners as neighbors	—	−	+.85
12. Members of one's nationality have priority in the labor market	—	+.30	+.28
Average Factor Scores of Party Followers			
Greens (N = 144)	−.44	−.88	−.27
Social Democrats (N = 700)	−.15	−.19	−.07
Free Democrats (N = 146)	+.29	−.17	−.10
Christian Democrats (N = 697)	+.20	+.37	+.06
Republicans (N = 41)	−.05	+.18	+.88

Source: World Values Survey. Own calculations.
Note: The confirmatory factors were estimated with unweighted least squares (ULS).

that has always abstained from a market-liberal rhetoric and has emphasized social protection and populist slogans supporting the "little people."

Our analysis so far provides little insight into the role of racism for Republican electoral support or into the occupational structure of party support. Unfortunately, a more refined analysis is heavily constrained by the small number of Republicans in the response pool. Nevertheless, we want to present calculations equivalent to those already discussed for the other countries, even though our German results rest on much weaker empirical foundations. In table 6.3, we have run a confirmatory factor analysis to force the appearance of a separate racist-ethnocentric dimension. The mean positions of each party's supporters on the three factors at the bottom of the table (10, 11, and 12) show that the Republicans are more racist, nationalist, and ethnocentric than the followers of other parties. At the same time, they take an intermediate position on the capitalism versus socialism dimension and are no more authoritarian than the Christian Democrats on the politico-cultural dimension. What is the net effect of each issue dimension on voting behavior? How do voters' opinions relate to their sociodemographic attributes?

Table 6.4 shows a generally more authoritarian, more parochial, and somewhat more anticapitalist tendency among working-class constituencies, an orientation that should predestine a significant share of blue-collar workers to support the extreme Right. In contrast, professionals and white-collar sectors tend to be somewhat more procapitalist, rather strongly libertarian, and more cosmopolitan. Therefore, libertarian and left-libertarian parties are likely to overrepresent these occupational groups. While this second prediction is borne out by the occupational support of the German Greens and the Free Democrats reported at the bottom of the table, results for the Republicans are uninformative. For all occupational categories, the Republicans amount to no more than 2.0 to 2.5 percent of the vote. The number of Republicans in the sample is too low to generate sharper findings, a reason why we will return to other studies of Republican electoral support below.

Given the small number of Republicans in the sample, the logit regressions of occupational background, sociodemographic attributes, and issue opinions on voter preference have to be interpreted with some caution. The data do suggest, however, a rather clear-cut pattern. Republican voters are primarily more racist-ethnocentric parochials. Moreover, they are more likely to be male, young, and less educated. Probably because of these rather strong effects, occupational variables wash out. What does *not* distinguish Republicans from the other parties are procapitalism and authoritarianism. In fact, if we pit Republican voters against Christian Democratic voters (equation 2, table 6.5), Republican voters are significantly less capitalist and almost significantly less authoritarian traditionalists than their conservative counterparts. As discussed in chapter 2, authoritarian compliance with traditional norms may be observed by radical rightists only up to a certain threshold beyond which their efforts to challenge the status quo conflict with existing norms and institutions.

The logit results for the Republicans are significantly different than those for the mainline NRR parties, which tended to be more promarket, more ethnocentrist, and typically also more authoritarian than the voters of all other parties. Compared to conventional rightist parties, none of the NRR parties was significantly less procapitalist, but this is exactly what we find in the case of the Republicans. Moreover, the populist antistatist parties in Italy and France stood out from the conventional Right primarily by being either significantly more promarket or significantly more libertarian, but they were only marginally

TABLE 6.4. Occupation, Ideological Dispositions, and Party Preferences in West Germany

	Professions (percent)	White Collar (percent)	Nonactive in the Labor Force (percent)	Workers (percent)	Independent Business and Farmers (percent)
A. Issue Positions					
1. For business-managed enterprises	48.3 (118)	44.4 (951)	50.0 (136)	43.7 (575)	75.5 (139)
2. Endorse stronger authority	17.6 (125)	25.6 (1023)	44.8 (154)	30.1 (639)	49.0 (147)
3. Against women's choice of abortion	22.8 (110)	38.1 (930)	51.1 (141)	44.7 (582)	59.4 (138)
4. Against neighbors of different race	3.2 (125)	8.0 (1029)	12.9 (134)	13.4 (643)	12.0 (150)
5. Proud to belong to one's nation	10.8 (102)	17.1 (870)	21.1 (142)	24.6 (553)	22.5 (129)
B. Percentage of Occupational Group Supporting a Party					
Green Party	15.8	8.6	8.1	4.1	0.8
Social Democratic Party	34.7	38.6	32.4	52.5	18.9
Free Democratic Party	14.9	10.2	8.1	4.1	10.7
Christian Democrats	30.7	39.4	53.7	34.9	64.8
Republicans	2.0	2.5	2.2	2.3	2.5

Source: World Values Survey. Own calculations.

more ethnocentrist. In contrast, what differentiates the Republicans from the moderate German Right more than anything else is its degree of ethnocentrism and racism. Moreover, in the German case, but not in that of most other countries, being male, younger, and less educated all have a significant influence on the probability of extreme-rightist voting.

We conclude that the Republicans tend to be a male, racist, and xenophobic lower-class party attracting younger voters that is unable or unwilling to appeal to market liberalism. Because so much rides on the mobilization of electoral support on ethnocentrism, electoral support of the party has remained volatile and the party has remained unsuccessful in the most important German national elections.

Because our findings on the electoral coalition of the German extreme Right are weak, given the small case number in our sample, it is useful to survey a few other studies of the sociodemographic basis of rightist party support in Germany. Similar to the electorates of the French National Front or the Scandinavian Progress parties, German extreme-rightist voters are predominantly male (cf. Hofmann-Göttig 1989; Falter 1994, 29–32). Surveys show that about two thirds of all Republican voters are men. If our theory is correct, the gender composition of the extreme Right is not a transitory phenomenon of a new party but pertains to the antifeminist thrust of authoritarian parties and the socialization and occupational experiences of, in particular, younger women.[21]

The German extreme Right also shares with NRR parties in other countries an underrepresentation of white-collar voters, particularly those with more advanced educational degrees (cf. Roth 1989; Falter 1994: 38–39, 75). All right-extremist parties cater to voters with lower educational accomplishments, but this is not because such parties are oriented to older and therefore generally less educated constituencies. In Germany, as elsewhere, the NRR electorate is evenly distributed across age groups or even skewed in favor of young voters. The overrepresentation of voters with low education signals the appeal of the extreme Right to the "losers of the economic modernization process" in the transition to knowledge-intensive postindustrial economies.

Beyond these general characteristics, the electorate of the Republicans differs from that of the prototypical NRR parties in other European countries. Whereas these other parties engineer a rather balanced coalition between blue-collar supporters, small businesspeople, and farmers, in the German Republicans the only group clearly overrepresented relative to its proportion in the population is the blue-collar segment. Young unskilled, semiskilled, and skilled laborers, in particular, were strongly attracted by the Republicans. This is shown both by general population surveys (cf. Roth 1989, 13; Falter 1994, 75) as well as regional election studies.[22] In the Bavarian state election of October 1990, for example, where the Republicans managed to receive 4.9

TABLE 6.5. Determinants of Political Orientations and of Party Preferences in Western Germany

A. Determinants of the Republican Party Vote, Entire Sample (Maximum likelihood estimates)

	Parameter estimate	Standard error	Probability	Percentage of voters supporting the rightist party if all other variables are held constant but value on the focal variable is at its—	
				Minimum	Maximum
Intercept	-1.30	3.13	.68		
Market Liberalism (Factor I)	-.14	.20	.49	0.8	0.5
Authoritarianism (Factor II)	+.17	.25	.50	0.4	0.7
Parochialism/Racism (Factor III)	+.76	.14	.0001	0.5	4.1
Gender (Female = 2)	-1.09	.36	.002	1.7	0.6
Age	-.02	.01	.06	0.9	0.3
Education	-.22	.10	.03	0.9	0.2
Business or Farmer	+.07	.83	.93	0.6	0.6
Professional	+.54	.95	.57	0.6	1.0
White Collar	+.40	.62	.52	0.6	0.8
Worker	-.45	.65	.49	0.6	0.4

Note: concordant cases: 75.1; cases *N:* 2068 (missing values on independent variables were substituted by mean values); missing cases *M:* 33.

B. Determinants of Vote: Republicans versus Christian Democratic Voters (Maximum likelihood estimates)

	Parameter estimate	Standard error	Probability	Percentage of voters supporting the rightist party if all other variables are held constant but value on the focal variable is at its—	
				Minimum	Maximum
Intercept	−1.31	3.36	.70	4.7	0.9
Market Liberalism (Factor I)	−.46	.23	.04	3.6	0.9
Authoritarianism (Factor II)	−.43	.27	.10	1.4	11.1
Parochialism/Racism (Factor III)	+.74	.15	.0001	4.1	1.7
Gender (Female = 2)	−.90	.37	.02	3.1	0.7
Age	−.02	.01	.04	2.6	0.6
Education	−.22	.10	.03	1.7	2.0
Business or Farmer	+.14	.87	.87	1.7	4.2
Professional	+.92	1.04	.37	1.7	3.0
White Collar	+.58	.66	.38	1.7	1.5
Worker	−.12	.70	.86		

Source: World Values Survey. Own calculations.
Note: concordant cases: 77.8; cases *N:* 730.

percent of the vote, in spite of the party's nationally weak support in this phase of the German unification process, 6.5 percent of workers, 6 percent of farmers (but only 4.4 percent of white-collar employees), 3 percent of the self-employed, and a mere 1 percent of voters still in education supported the Republicans (Schultze 1991, 54).[23] The Republicans' electorate in Bavaria—as everywhere else—was a mirror image of the Green constituency. Whereas the Greens won 6.4 percent statewide, 27.2 percent of voters still in education, 9.5 percent of state officials, 7.7 percent of white-collar employees, and 9.1 percent of the self-employed supported this party, but only 2.7 percent of workers and 1.3 percent of farmers.

The social pattern of Republican support is demonstrated even more convincingly by exit polls taken at the 1992 Baden-Württemberg state elections when the Republicans staged their comeback from the unification slump with more than 11 percent of the vote. In the entire electorate, the question of restricting asylum had salience for 43 percent of voters and thus ran ahead of all other issues. The Republicans received no less than 19.4 percent of the workers' vote and even 16.6 percent among labor unionists but managed to attract only 6.7 percent of civil servants and 7.9 percent of voters still in education (although 16.1 percent of all voters in the 18-to-24 year age bracket supported the party).[24] Among young, male, uneducated workers, the Republicans were the strongest of all parties in Baden-Württemberg. Republican support, therefore, is recruited not just from the Christian Democrats whom 42 percent of 1992 Republican voters had supported in the previous election, but also from the Social Democrats who contributed 26 percent of the Republican voters in 1992.

In contrast to NRR parties in other countries, which engineer an "inter-class" coalition of various occupational groups, the German extreme Right is a distinctly working-class and lower social status party. It is elected by those who are or fear becoming losers of the industrial modernization process (Minkenberg 1992a).[25] The occupational profile of far Right support in Germany distinguishes the party not only from the NRR elsewhere but also from pre-1933 national socialism (cf. Hamilton 1972). The Republicans and other German rightist groups at times appear to be closer to the "Strasserite" labor union and socialist wing of the Nazi party than the overall composition of the national socialist vote in 1930 to 1933. Today's far rightist groups lack the broad cross-class support the Nazi party enjoyed at that time, especially among white-collar employees, professionals, and businesspeople. German extreme-rightist electoral constituencies are thus *neither* identical with the NRR elsewhere in Europe *nor* with the "old" profile of national socialist support in Germany. Whereas national socialism could draw on significant elements of the German elite, these groups and strata have become unavailable to the extreme Right in the Federal Republic so that extremist political currents are now confined to the least advantaged and to workers in marginalized labor market positions. The structural transformation of the economy and of political institutions (bureaucracy, judiciary, etc.) since the 1940s removed more educated strata from the far rightist reservoir. But what may be more important, the *political organizations of the working class have changed since the mid-twentieth century.* Lipset (1981, 87–126) observed a distinctly authoritarian, intolerant streak in working-class political attitudes that he related to the lack of education and to the unique circumstances of workers' political socialization, which nurture anti-intellectualism and myopic economic orientations. At the same time, however, the elites of working-class parties typically expressed politically libertarian orientations. Lipset reasoned that as long as the working class was "encapsuled" by hierarchical socialist organizations governed by libertarian politicians and intellectuals, it would be willing to follow more libertarian politicians in spite of authoritarian subcultural inclinations (124). As the German social democrats gradually became a white-collar party and as tightly knit organized working-class subcultures disappeared in the 1970s and 1980s, young workers in particular no longer developed organizational ties to the social democratic political milieu. As a consequence, they were set free to follow their authoritarian inclinations and to drift toward extreme-rightist parties.

The interaction between class and organizational affiliation explains why workers unaffiliated with the social democratic Left have the highest propensity to join the extreme Right. Because lower-class voters won over to the extreme Right usually had little contact with the organizations of working-class politics and supported conservative parties, the Christian Democrats appear to lose voters to the Republicans at about two times the rate social democrats lose voters to the extreme Right (Klär et al., 1989a, 10). Only in the 1990 Northrhine-Westfalian state election, where the Republicans received a weak 1.8 percent of the electorate, a voter flow analysis showed that 38 percent of the party's support came from the SPD, compared to 24 percent from the CDU and 21 percent from nonvoters (Feist and Hoffmann 1990, 445). In instances where the Republicans were electorally more successful, however, most voters appear to come from the electorally unaffiliated segment of the working-class population. The case of Baden-Württemberg is instructive in this regard. Republicans are able to thrive on working-class support because class organization has always been weak in that region and many workers supported the Christian Democrats before they were won over by the Republicans.

The general socioeconomic profile of right-wing support is also consistent with ecological patterns of voting for the German extreme Right. First of all, in line with the interpretation that the contemporary German extreme Right does not show a profile similar to the national socialist electorate and its early successor parties in the 1950s and 1960s, the strongholds of the Nazi party in the 1930s and later of the NPD in the 1960s are usually *not* identical with those of the Republicans and other contemporary right-wing extremist parties. Whereas the old Right often excelled in rural areas, small towns, or urban middle-class districts, the contemporary Right is strong in urban and semi-urban working-class districts. These neighborhoods are typically not areas with a high percentage of immigrants and many marginal social residents (Leggewie 1990, 30), but locations with residents whose occupational background increases their anxiety about immigration.[26]

A closer ecological analysis of elections in which the Republicans performed particularly well, such as the 1989 Berlin state elections and the 1992 Baden-Württemberg elections, yields a rather clear-cut pattern.[27] The Republicans are weak in "bourgeois" areas where the Christian Democrats and social democrats receive about even support and where the Greens perform above average. Republican support also tends to be weak in the countryside and in marginal urban areas with a high percentage of immigrants and students. Whereas in the former the Christian Democrats are hegemonic, in the latter the Greens are particularly strong. On the other hand, the Republicans excel in metropolitan working-class districts and in suburban regions or medium-sized towns with mixed industrial employment where a mostly indigenous German population works in manufacturing jobs.[28]

At the risk of committing an ecological fallacy, the fact that most of the Republican blue-collar voters are not former social democrats, but generally unaffiliated workers, is suggested, though not proven, by a comparison of regions at a level of higher aggregation. The German extreme Right is particularly strong in states where social democrats have traditionally been weak. In the June 1989 European elections, the extreme Right, combining Republicans and the DVU-NPD alliance "Liste D," received 15.6 percent in Bavaria and 11.1 percent in Baden-Württemberg, both states where the social democrats won less than a third of the vote. In contrast, in northern and central German states where the social democrats typically exceed 40, if not 50, percent of the vote, the far Right remained below its national average of well over 8 percent: Northrhine-Westfalia (5.4%), Schleswig-Holstein (5.9%), Rhineland-Palatinate (6.1%), Lower Saxony (6.4%), Saarland (7.1%), Hamburg (7.5%) and Bremen (7.7%). Only in Hesse, the various extremist lists added together received 8.8 percent. This ecological inference is buttressed by individual-level data that in northern Germany the extremist electorate predominantly consists of young unaffiliated workers in industrial areas (Leggewie 1990, 17), whereas their parents are still strongly affiliated with the social democratic party. In other areas, where blue-collar constituencies have much weaker ties to social democracy, older workers may also be more inclined to support the Republicans.[29]

Although the socioeconomic and ideological pattern of Republican voters is thus quite clear-cut, one should be careful not to overemphasize the homogeneity of the German rightist electorate. The supporters of the German Republicans may not constitute as broad a social coalition as that of the NRR parties in France and Scandinavia, let alone the even broader coalitions of populist-rightist parties in Austria and northern Italy. Nevertheless, it contains considerable internal diversity. A series of in-depth narrative interviews with German right-wingers finds at least six different types (cf. Klär et al. 1989b). There are (1) neo-Nazis who always supported the extreme Right as well as (2) voters disappointed by the fizzling out of the conservative *Wende* promised by the Christian Democrats in 1982. Moreover, the Republicans are supported by (3) some economically threatened farmers and small businesspeople. In the past, these three traditional rightist groups primarily voted for the Christian Democrats. The remaining three groups of Republican followers, however, may have voted for either Christian or Social Democrats before moving over to the extreme Right. They consist of (4) alienated petit bourgeois in the broader cultural sense, including skilled workers, forepersons, lower-white collar employees, and civil servants, such as policemen, (5) authoritarian young workers without any ties to working-class organizations, and (6) victims of the economic modernization process. The in-depth interviews among 35 former SPD voters found that xenophobia and "welfare chauvinism"—the refusal to share one's social security with immigrants and refugees who have not contributed to the German social insurance systems—provided the strongest motivation to support the extreme Right, not a broader nationalist and authoritarian orientation. Within the spectrum of Republican voters, former SPD supporters may thus develop the weakest ties to the far Right.

Strategic Dilemmas of Established Parties and Republicans

The new challenge of the extreme Right, particularly that of the Republicans, poses strategic dilemmas for the established German political parties. By not giving in to xenophobic, welfare chauvinist, and authoritarian slogans, the social democrats lose predominantly young male blue-collar workers, a rather limited constituency. By catering to racist authoritarian sentiments, social democrats would suffer infinitely greater losses among educated white-collar employees, particularly in the public-sector personal services (health care, education, etc.), who then might support the left-libertarian Greens or the culturally centrist and economically conservative Liberals. Overall, the social democrats are "locked into" a strategic situation in which they must sacrifice young working-class constituencies if they wish to remain electorally success-ful with more significant socioeconomic groups. For this reason, the social democrats resisted concessions on a tightening of the German asylum and immigration laws until right-wing violence and terrorist activities appeared to get out of control in fall 1992. Like the social democrats, the Greens and the Free Democrats have no electoral incentives to cater to racist and authoritarian attitudes and may lose only a few general protest votes by remaining insensi-tive to far rightist clienteles.

As the general configurative analysis in figure 6.1 shows, the situation is much more complex for the Christian Democrats whose voters are generally closer to the Republicans than those of any other established party and who compete with the latter for just about all the voter segments that may be drawn to the new extreme Right: manual workers unaffiliated with working-class organizations, petit bourgeois, and farmers. As a consequence, the Christian democrats have been embroiled in internal divisions over a new policy toward immigration and the extreme Right in general. With the rise of the new extrem-ist challenge, the CDU eventually adopted a restrictive approach to immigra-tion and asylum policy, but in the competition with the other parties, the CDU faces ambiguous, if not contradictory, incentives to highlight and politicize or to tone down issues of national identity, ethnocentrism, and immigration. On the one hand, a clear anti-immigration stance and appeal to patriotism would contain the electoral attractiveness of the Republicans and maximize the pro-pensity of authoritarian workers to abandon their support of the social democrats in favor of the moderate conservatives. This strategy also maintains the integrity of the core Christian Democratic electorate. On the other hand, this approach may alienate white collar-constituencies with economically centrist but culturally more libertarian stances. They will be tempted to aban-don the party in favor of the liberals or even the social democrats, provided the latter choose a centrist rather than a left-libertarian strategic appeal.

Moreover, given the obvious historical sensitivities about German right-wing politics in Europe and the world, a nationalist, ethnocentric, and racist politics that is even remotely supported by the main German governing party is bound to damage Germany's international reputation and may even bring about negative economic consequences for Germany as an "investment loca-tion," as the German Federation of Industry has signaled in various public declarations. International anxieties about Germany's democratic and peaceful commitment surfaced for the first time when the Kohl government hesitated to accept the irreversibility of Poland's western Oder-Neiße border in 1990 for fear of losing the conservative-nationalist electorate in the first all-German elections. These anxieties increased dramatically in 1992 in view of the pas-sivity the German government exhibited when the first wave of racist and xenophobic violence against immigrants swept over Germany. The government party's response was equally half-hearted on the occasion of the second wave of attacks on foreigners in spring 1993 when the chancellor refused to attend a funeral for Turkish victims of xenophobic hate crimes.

The strategic dilemmas of the German moderate conservatives in dealing with the Republicans do not automatically guarantee the electoral success of the extreme Right. At least five factors are likely to undercut the extreme Right's ability to attract sufficient support to entrench itself in German state and national legislatures. First, the social populism of the Republicans attracts segments of the working class but depresses the support of other constituencies that were decisive for the success of NRR parties elsewhere in Europe with antitaxation and antipartocracy market-liberal appeals. The Republicans are electorally constrained because they combine economically more leftist and politically more authoritarian perspectives.[30] Second, the national socialist ideological legacy, West German welfare chauvinism, and East German backlash tendencies against liberal market society, particularly among the losers of the unification process, remove much strategic flexibility that right-wing parties enjoy elsewhere. Third, West German welfare chauvinist right-wingers and East German losers of the economic process of adaptation are difficult to unite under the same ideological umbrella, once the party is compelled to go beyond ethnocentric and social populist slogans. Because of the massive transfers of funds from western to eastern Germany in the postunification decade, in February 1990 Republican sympathizers were less enthusiastic about the prospects of a unified Germany than Christian Democrats (cf. Betz 1990, 53). Hence, beyond xenophobic and nationalist slogans, the Republicans may have little to offer that would unite their East and West German electorates.[31] Fourth, even if the Republicans had the appropriate mix of appeals to attract East German electorates, they would have to overcome their stigma of being a West German party. Their potential East German voters are precisely those voters who have the greatest inclination to hold up their East German identity against the onslaught of West German market reforms and the imposition of deprivations (unemployment, early retirement). The East/West cleavage, however, is increasingly served by the postcommunist Party of Democratic Socialism (PDS), which has been able to regroup in 1993–94 and attract a rather substantial following in the East German states. Because of its impeccably East German credentials, it is much more likely to capture economically marginalized East Germans than the Republicans.

Fifth, the difficulties the Republicans have encountered in coming to terms with these intricacies of the East/West division in the German electorate have surfaced in severe internal conflicts within the party's East German state organizations. Moreover, the Republicans could not prevent the growth of a number of independent East German right-wing protoparties, many of which are more radical than the Republicans. At the time of this writing, it is unclear whether the Republicans can establish their hegemony over the extreme Right in East Germany. If a cleavage between East and West Germans articulates itself anywhere in German electoral politics, it may do so first in an East-West split of the extreme Right. This division makes it harder for the Republicans to gain sufficient national support to become a serious player in the arena of party competition.

Internal party conflicts inside the Republicans, however, are not confined to East Germany, and their frequency and intensity may repel voters who may otherwise be attracted to the party. From the time the Republicans entered state parliaments there has been a constant flow of scandals about the abuse of party funds and the subversion of party statutes by cabals of party members. Moreover, the party has been marred by conflicts over where to draw the line in the right-wing terrorist scene in Germany, many of whose activists are too unruly to be ever organized by a party. Intraparty conflicts thus reflect the constant pressure to mediate between more moderate voter groups that must be attracted in order to enable the Republicans to overcome the 5 percent threshold of electoral representation in Germany, on the one hand, and the core groups of radical right-extremists who infiltrate the party and attempt to convert it into an unrestrained neofascist organization, on the other.

Conclusion

The German extreme Right does not rally around a right-authoritarian or a populist antistatist appeal, but a social authoritarianism and ethnocentrism. Therefore it is electorally less successful than the rightist parties who found the winning formula in the countries we have discussed in previous chapters. The Republican strategy is shaped by the legacy of German national socialism, but this does not make the party identical with a national socialist organization.

Alternative hypotheses about the rise of the extreme Right introduced in chapter 2 do not account for the German Republicans' performance. The Republicans or the DVU are clearly not single-issue phenomena, as their location in the ideological space demonstrates.[32] Moreover, its supporters are definitely not "right-libertarians," and our analysis of the party leaders' appeal has confirmed this judgment. Among all of the rival hypotheses, the idea that the German extreme Right is neofascist is most plausible, but that proposal may also not be fully on the mark, given the electoral support coalition behind the Republicans.

Minkenberg (1992a) has contrasted two interpretations of the German extreme Right. One interpretation sees the Republicans as the organizational equivalent of the restyled extreme Right elsewhere in Europe that rallies the losers of the modernization process against the libertarian Left.[33] The other interpretation places the Republicans not within the context of the contemporary European NRR, but in the legacy of the German old Nazi Right and the national socialist successor organizations since World War II.[34] If our own analysis is correct, neither of these alternatives is entirely adequate, although both contain elements of truth. The new German extreme Right is different from NRR parties in other countries in terms of its ideological appeal and its electoral coalition. It has great difficulties thriving on a liberal market resentment of the welfare state that clearly drives NRR parties elsewhere. Historical legacies clearly matter in explaining the German Right's uniqueness. The German extreme Right has not been electorally "rational" and has not brought together an electoral coalition under the winning formula of market-liberal and authoritarian appeals because its activists, as well as its leaders, have inherited national and socialist patterns of thought that limit the parties' strategic flexibility. Moreover, the unprecedented event of the German unification, which is indirectly tied to the legacy of nondemocratic German political regimes, creates different strategic dilemmas for the extreme Right than for other European rightist parties.

Yet at the same time, the contemporary German extreme Right is removed from the Nazi past in important respects. The transformation of the social and political order over the past 50 years has made it impossible to build a party around the same forces that supported the Nazis of the early 1930s. In particular, white-collar employees, professionals and members of the administrative, political, and cultural elite who then backed the Nazi party are no longer available for right-wing appeals. Today, a rightist party with quasifascist appeals is confined to a primarily lower-class male electorate encompassing a hard core of actual or potential losers of economic and social postindustrialization. At this juncture, the German extreme Right represents a hybrid phenomenon that can no longer build on the broad base of the German national socialist movement of the Weimar years, but which also cannot entirely relinquish the symbols and appeals of the national socialist legacy. For this reason, the German extreme Right is likely to remain electorally less successful than its "pure" NRR counterparts in other European countries.

Racism, Right-Wing Populism, and the Failure of the Extreme Right in Britain

All right-wing extremist or populist parties discussed in the previous chapters have successfully established themselves in the national electoral arenas of their respective countries, with the partial exception of the German Republicans. In France, Denmark, and Norway, a political convergence of established socialist and bourgeois parties and the ability of rightist political entrepreneurs to find the winning formula for NRR parties in electoral contests accounts for the result. In Austria and Italy, objective conditions for the NRR were favorable, but the additional presence of an important institutional feature—partocracy—enabled right-wing populist and antistatist parties to capture an even broader electorate than pure NRR parties. In Germany, finally, by the late 1980s, general conditions for the mobilization of the NRR were favorable, but the Republicans failed to adopt the winning formula that would have moved them to the center stage of national politics.

We have not yet discussed a case in which the opportunity structure for the extreme Right has been unfavorable for the emergence of a successful NRR party and where one can reconstruct the failed efforts of the extreme Right to overcome these adverse conditions. The British extreme Right, which was organized around the National Front in the 1970s, may lend itself to this comparison. This case offers one special advantage, but also one disadvantage, when examined from the perspective of comparative logic. The advantage is that the British political opportunity structure changed from the early 1970s to the later 1970s and 1980s. Thus, our comparison includes not only a cross-national perspective, contrasting Britain with the countries discussed previously, but also a longitudinal perspective, tracing political conditions and right-wing activities within Britain over time.

The case of the British National Front, however, also has a serious disadvantage. Ideally, we would be looking for a configuration in which conditions for the rise of the NRR are unfavorable, but political entrepreneurs try hard to mobilize voters on precisely the right-authoritarian NRR appeal. In such instances, we could isolate the impact of the political opportunity structure on NRR party fortunes from the party's choice of political appeal. Unfortunately, the British National Front never engaged in what this study terms the "pure"

NRR appeal. In examining the electoral failure of the British National Front, it is thus difficult to disentangle the independent contribution of political opportunity structure and party leaders' strategic entrepreneurism on the electoral outcome. Our search for a better case in which the appropriate constellation of NRR appeals, but unfavorable opportunity structures, are present, however, has remained unsuccessful. For this reason, we have settled for the British National Front as a "second-best" test case.

The counterfactual reasoning, then, underlying the exploration of the British case is that if (1) there had been a favorable political opportunity structure in Britain and if (2) leaders of the extreme Right had chosen a NRR appeal, then an extremist party would have experienced electoral success. Britain does show some empirical variation in political opportunity structures within the party system from the 1960s to the 1970s and 1980s that allows for a partial empirical testing of the argument. With respect to the strategic choices by extremist leaders, however, the reasoning remains purely counterfactual. At no point in time did British extreme-rightist leaders subscribe to what turned out to be the electorally winning formula for NRR parties in other countries in the 1980s, namely, a combination of economic market liberalism with political and cultural authoritarianism, laced with xenophobia and racism. The reason why the National Front ultimately failed to win a significant electoral market share is that the British Conservatives adopted enough elements of the free market and authoritarian formula and blended them into their own unique right-wing populism ("Thatcherism") that they drained attention away from the National Front. Maybe because of the Conservatives' decisive moves in the late 1970s, the National Front never gained the time to experiment with new strategic stances. As we know from the Scandinavian Progress parties, it may take an iterative process of trial and error over the course of several elections before a party finds the winning formula. At the same time, however, in Britain there were also internal organizational reasons why the National Front never even pondered moving to a strategic posture close to the winning formula of the new extreme Right.

Historical Legacy of the British Far Right

In contrast to Germany and Italy, it is implausible to argue that the ideological legacy of the British extreme Right constrained the ideological appeal of political entrepreneurs in the 1970s and 1980s. Britain experienced only a tiny sectarian fascist movement and an array of other minuscule extreme-rightist organizations before and after World War II. Whatever constraint the extreme Right was facing had more to do with the position of the major parties in the dominant competitive arena than with the historical legacy of the extreme Right.

In the 1930s, Hitler's Germany had a certain demonstration effect for some politicians in Britain's liberal democracy, given the depth of the Great Depression and the desperate search for new economic and institutional recipes to rebuild modern capitalism. Nevertheless, in Britain fascist ideas never won wide circulation and remained confined to fringe elements that defected from the two major parties, the Conservatives and the Labour Party. Undoubtedly, the long-term stability of British political institutions limited the range of alternatives that was discussed within the political elites. At the same time, institutional continuity also constrained the options the electorate in general would have found acceptable and promising. Fascist and national socialist movements gained a large following only in countries characterized by extreme institutional instability in the decades preceding the Great Depression, thus generating a willingness of masses and elites alike to discount the risk of major institutional transformations in a general climate of political uncertainty.

There were several tiny fascist sects in Britain in the 1920s, but the extreme Right gained momentum on a modest scale only when a young aristocrat, former Tory and then Labour MP, Sir Oswald Mosley, founded the "Union of Fascists" in 1930. Mosley was initially impressed by Mussolini, but later modeled his movement on the German Nazi party, which prompted him to rename his British organization "British Union of Fascists and National Socialists." Mosley's organization never won more than a tiny fraction of the electorate outside a few burroughs of London's East End, where his anti-Semitic slogans apparently found a receptive audience, particularly among workers. At its high point around 1936, the party had about 3,000 active and 15,000 inactive members.[1] Turnover was extremely high so that an estimated 100,000 people at one point or another had been members. Mosley built a paramilitary guard and sought support with a corporatist and racist program. During the Depression, much of Mosley's following was recruited from declining elements of the petite bourgeoisie and young workers. Thus, the "Strasserite" tinge of the leader's political appeal is worth emphasizing. Mosley tried to link nationalist and socialist ideas, an orientation that also characterized many British neofascist sects of the post-World War II era.

Mosley abandoned his efforts to rebuild a fascist Right after World War II in 1951 and left others to run the newly founded Union Movement (Eatwell 1992b, 176). Instead, he waited in the wings hoping for a collapse of the postwar political order and reemerged on the political scene only when immigration from the British colonies and independent countries of the Commonwealth became an issue in the late 1950s. At that time, Mosley contested a by-election for a House of Commons seat on a right-wing ticket. With only 8.1 percent of the vote, this foray into electoral politics was perceived as unsuccessful, in part due to the splintering of the extremist vote among several lists. Even at the high point of immigration in the period 1960–62, rightist sects could nowhere win a substantial electorate in Britain (S. Taylor 1982, 13–14). The 1962 Immigration Act then reduced the number of immigrants and, in the short run, undercut the salience of the issue on the popular agenda and the chances of right-wing electoral politics. Nevertheless, in the longer run, the fact that a government took immigration seriously enough to pass new legislation prepared the way to make the issue acceptable in British political debates. The extreme Right began to benefit from this change in climate only when immigration numbers began to rise again in the second half of the 1960s and the rightist sects united under the umbrella of the National Front.

Explicit fascist and anti-Semitic sects in Britain stood in the legacy of a "Strasserite" socialist fascism. Yet it is important to recognize there were other extreme-rightist groups in Britain with a different ideological baggage. Building on Thurlow (1987), Stan Taylor (1993, 166) distinguishes die-hard conservatives who could not accept the loss of the colonial empire, conservative fascists who opposed the welfare state, anti-Semites and racial nationalists, and racial populists as currents that supplemented the radical socialist fascism in the Mosley tradition. An alliance of all these groups thus could pursue a rather wide range of possible ideological tacks had it not been constrained by the strategic movements of the established political parties.

The Political Opportunity Structure
of the Extreme Right

Discussions of the institutional and cultural constraints British politics is said to impose on the formation of new parties usually turn on two important arguments that are purported to show why Britain is different from continental Europe. First, the British population has been said to behave according to a "culture of deference" in politics and has thus been unlikely to challenge the political elites by opting for new and untried parties. Second, even if British voters would want to protest against the system by supporting a new party, they could not effectively do so because of the first-past-the-post plurality electoral system that compels all reasonable minds who want to make a difference in government formation and not waste their vote to stick to the two major parties. Neither of these arguments is entirely convincing as explanations for the absence of strong NRR mobilization.

The pervasive liberal-democratic tradition in Britain may prevent political forces that openly aim at replacing competitive democracy by a dictatorship from gaining strength. But the example of Progress parties in Scandinavian countries where democracy is entrenched to an extent similar to that in Britain shows that popular beliefs in the basic institutional justification of democracy is not necessarily a deterrent against the rise of NRR-type parties. Such parties may not directly assault the core institutions of liberal democracy but seek to complement them with a framework of legislation restricting political participation and cultural diversity. Moreover, the British electorate may not necessarily be impervious to such demands because it is deferential to political elites. Both public opinion surveys as well as the record of civil strife and noninstitutionalized political action in the 1970s and 1980s belie the claim that there is no protest potential and willingness to attack entrenched political institutions in Britain.

British political "deference" may have been vastly overstated and it would certainly be wrong to believe that Britain simply has no reservoir of voters with far rightist preferences who might be won over by an extremist competitor. Studies of British political opinion in the 1970s and 1980s reveal a rather large constituency of voters by European standards who endorse authoritarian and racist views *and* place themselves on the political right (Falter and Schumann 1988). As in other countries, authoritarianism is associated with low educational qualifications, lower income, more religious practice, and greater age (Heath, Evans, and Martin 1994, 126). The absence of a strong rightist party, therefore, is not so much one of "demand" for political alternatives but one of political "supply": such voters cannot identify a rightist political alternative outside the established spectrum of competitors for which it would be worth voting.

The second argument typically fielded to account for the weakness of the British extreme Right focuses on the institutional conditions for the supply of new party alternatives. According to this line of reasoning, the British plurality electoral system has erected prohibitive barriers against the entry of new parties and thus has thwarted the rise of a new extremist Right. While it is undeniable that electoral laws do matter in shaping the format of a party system, they nevertheless do not provide a convincingly complete explanation for the weakness of the British extreme Right.[2] To begin with, since 1945 the British electoral law has remained the same, but the fortunes of the extreme Right, as well as that of several other minor parties, especially that of the Liberals who received between 2 and 26 percent of the vote in national parliamentary elections, have varied dramatically over time. At least these variations cannot be accounted for by a stable electoral law. The electoral law also cannot be held accountable for the extreme fragmentation of the British Right throughout much of the post–World War II period. To the contrary, it should have made cooperation among the various right-wing currents and tendencies easier. In fact, whenever the external political opportunity structure for extreme-rightist activism improves, in Britain and other countries such sects appear to be capable of cooperation. Conversely, when electoral prospects recede, internecine warfare breaks out. The French National Front is a good example of the ability of currents to cooperate in light of electoral success. The German NPD after 1969 or the Italian MSI after 1976 illustrate the reverse process of factional disorganization after major electoral defeats. In a similar vein, the fractionalization of the British extreme Right varied inversely with its electoral prospects in the 1970s and 1980s.

Next, while plurality laws may make it difficult for new parties to become serious contenders for national government, such parties can focus on particular districts or on secondary local elections, which even in Britain at times are governed by rules of proportional representation and thus enable minor parties to enter the arena of municipal politics. Such opportunities have been successfully exploited by the British Liberals, but also at times by the extreme Right. The National Front in fact did manage to win local representation in areas with a high concentration of urban problems, yet nowhere could the party hold on to these gains in the 1980s.

Finally, in plurality electoral systems a significant proportion of voters may have incentives to defect from the major contenders *if these contenders offer political alternatives that are too similar.* At that point, a logic of "blackmail" begins to run its course in which extreme voters abandon the hegemonic parties to "teach them a lesson" and force them to return to ideologically more differentiated appeals. Such defections would be irrelevant for vote-seeking politicians in the two dominant parties provided they occurred symmetrically and reduced both major parties' electorate by exactly the same margin at the same time, thus canceling out the effect of right- and left-wing extremism on each moderate party. If issue conjunctures and defections, however, affect the major parties asymmetrically, it is well possible that one party's elites see the difference between winning and losing as intimately related to its capacity to attract the support of potential blackmail voters. Thus, the overall competitive opportunity structure of which the electoral law is only one aspect may make it possible for far rightist parties to thrive even if there are high institutional barriers to entry into the arena of parliamentary representation.

Such was the case in Britain where the electorate in the late 1960s and early 1970s was caught up in a general malaise about economic policy under the Wilson (Labour) and Heath (Conservative) governments. In the late 1950s and 1960s the major parties had difficulty responding to voters' increasing attentiveness to the problems of immigration to Britain from former British colonies. On the one hand, the British Labour Party was most vulnerable to losing voters inspired by racist and xenophobic feelings in marginal neighborhoods and working-class districts where residents felt economically and culturally threatened by the new migrants. On the other hand, the party was badly placed to seize on the immigration issue because it stood to lose libertarian followers by adopting a more ethnocentrist policy than it could retain among racist constituencies. In theory, Labour's predicament opened a unique opportunity for the Conservatives to attract traditional Labour voters by a more parochial and xenophobic stance. Conservative party elites could reckon that, as a rule, their own voters were generally less likely to defect to Labour if the Conservatives catered to ethnocentric sentiments than libertarian Labour voters were to stay home or vote for a leftist splinter party if Labour engaged in such political rhetoric. Nevertheless, for the Conservatives appeals to racism would have been a risky strategy, given the slim margins of victory and defeat that separated the two major contenders in elections in the 1950s and 1960s. As a consequence, in the 1960s both parties opted for a "conspiracy of silence" in which neither of them would try to exploit immigration and race questions for electoral gain. Thus, not the electoral law, as such, but the particular power relations and electoral alignments among the major parties shaped the opportunity structure for a new racist party to make electoral inroads.

In Britain, the question of immigration and race became a matter of popular concern long before the parties felt compelled to address it. The 1960s were characterized by political convergence between the Tories and the Labour Party, particularly in the areas of social and economic policy where governments of different political stripes accomplished equally unsatisfactory results. The Labour Prime Minister Harold Wilson invoked the "white heat of the industrial revolution" and economic growth as the formula for Britain's success, not the class struggle and economic redistribution. Conservative politicians conceded the necessity of the dense social safety net provided by the welfare state and advocated moderate Keynesian economic policies focused on growth and full employment at least as vigorously as the fight against inflation. Only a few dissident politicians sensed the new electoral opportunities offered by the voters' changing mood on the immigration issue, but they were punished for such escapades by their party leaders. The most famous case is that of the Conservative front-bencher and shadow minister Enoch Powell who began to stir anti-immigrant sentiments with a famous speech delivered on April 20, 1968, in which he predicted "rivers of blood" if immigration and the multiculturalization of British society continued. When he was removed from the party leadership, the incident triggered a "Powell for premier" movement. Opinion polls at the time showed that up to three quarters of the British population agreed with Powell's stance (S. Taylor 1993, 176–7). In the aftermath of this controversy, the regrouped British extreme Right for the first time attracted right-wing Conservatives and became more hopeful about a future electoral breakthrough.

Several more controversies within the Conservative government of Edward Heath boosted the chances of the extreme Right. As a prime minister in 1971, Heath did agree to a more restrictive immigration law, but then in 1972 he admitted to England a large number of Asian refugees persecuted by Idi Amin's brutal regime in Uganda (Layton-Henry 1986, 74). This led to a controversy between Heath and Powell at the October 1972 Conservative party conference and translated into electoral surges of the extreme Right later on. A rerun of a similar issue attention cycle took place in 1974 when Malawi President Hastings Banda expelled a small number of Asians who then opted for British passports and came to England (S. Taylor 1993, 179). In both cases, the ineptitude of the governing party to address or contain the issue within its own ranks benefited the extreme Right.

Thus, in general, up to the mid-1970s, the political opportunity structure for the extreme Right in Britain became increasingly favorable as long as the major parties converged on moderate strategic stances that ruled out any temptation to exploit the immigration issue for advantages in the arena of electoral competition. This situation began to change when Margaret Thatcher defeated Edward Heath in the competition for the office of the parliamentary leader of the Conservative opposition party in 1975. Unlike the political philosophy espoused by her predecessor, Thatcher brought to the fore a tradition of conservatism that is not mildly paternalistic and socially oriented, but that emphasizes free enterprise, moral discipline, and statecraft (Crewe and Searing 1988, 363). Her approach included elements of what some observers have called a "right-wing populism." This populism combines resolute support for the free market and opposition to the organized interests of labor and business with an authoritarian appeal to a small but strong state. It is evident that this approach is echoed by the themes exploited later on by the NRR in France and Scandinavia.

With the exception of Thatcher's staunch defense of law and order, an appeal that always goes well with electoral constituencies, only a minority within the Conservative electorate endorsed the party's new rightist populism (Crewe and Searing 1988, 373–74).[3] Nevertheless, right-populist platforms and policies could not break the Conservatives' uninterrupted string of electoral victories from 1979 through 1987. Leader and policies were changed only in 1990 when all signs indicated that the party would be voted out of office in the subsequent general election if it stuck to the right-wing populist program. The reason that for more than a decade Thatcher could defy the Downsian logic of centripetal competition in a two-party system, where in principle each party must try to capture the median voter in order to govern, involves the policies of the Labour Party. Throughout the 1970s and well into the 1980s, Labour adopted a gradually more radically leftist appeal. At the turning point of that development in 1981–83, leftist activists and labor unions managed to capture the party leadership and split the party in two.[4] In this situation, moderate British voters had a choice between two evils, a radicalized right-wing Conservative party and an even more radicalized left-wing Labour party. From 1979 on, a plurality of the electorate chose the Conservatives and a substantial share of disaffected moderates who had previously voted for Labour now sought refuge under the umbrella of an emerging third-party alternative, the Alliance of Liberals and Social Democrats, which was later transformed into the Liberal Democrats.

The strategic radicalism of the Conservatives changed the opportunity structure of the British extreme Right and removed whatever chances it had in the mid-1970s to make inroads into the electorate. This became clear when after municipal council elections in Greater London in which the extreme Right had performed surprisingly well the new conservative leader Thatcher declared in a television interview in January 1978 that she intended to win people back to the Conservatives who had been driven to the National Front by the inability of conventional politicians to address the immigration issue (Layton-Henry 1986, 75). Husbands (1988a, 76) comments on this interview that Thatcher "publicly flaunted [the Conservative opposition party's] 'hard' image on race and immigration in order to attract support that had hitherto gone to the National Front."

Starting in 1981, the new Conservative Thatcher government followed up on its pre-election rhetoric with legislative action. It took a high profile on immigration policy and engineered a fundamental revision of the citizenship and nationality laws in 1981. Moreover, administrative procedures for the review of immigration were tightened. The government also showed its determination to restrict the role of immigrants in British society in its handling of the antipolice violence, primarily committed by young blacks, that broke out in inner city areas in 1980–81 (cf. Layton-Henry 1986, 73). The second Thatcher government from 1983 to 1987 generally toned down the immigration question yet it introduced a requirement for holiday visitors from certain new Commonwealth countries to produce entry visas and attacked local governments that were led by black Labour politicians (cf. Husbands 1988a, 76–77).

Thus, the Conservative party kept its credentials on race issues in order, although such questions played a lesser role in the later years of the Thatcher government than in the early 1980s. The party's tough stance on immigration and immigrants removed a critical catalyst that might otherwise have permitted the crystallization of a right-wing protest party. Conservative party strategy thus at least partly explains the failure of the extreme Right in Britain (cf. Messina 1989). This explanation remains incomplete, however, without examining the strategic stances of the rightist groups themselves. As the experience of rightist parties in other countries may illustrate, race and immigration are important catalysts but are certainly not the entire story of NRR mobilization, which revolves around a much broader cluster of right-authoritarian beliefs and appeals. In Britain, the Conservative party was able to preempt race from becoming the mobilizing issue for a new party; but at the same time, the candidate for leading such a new rightist drive, the National Front, failed to identify the cluster of political appeals around which broad new right-authoritarian or populist and antistatist electoral coalitions have been brought together in other countries. While the tradition of Mosley's radical socialist "Strasserite" fascism certainly made it difficult for the extreme Right to find an authoritarian promarket position attractive, the persistence with which the Conservatives after the decade of convergence with Labour in the 1960s emphasized free market economics undercut the strategic mobility of the extreme Right. Internal dispositions as well as external opportunities prevented the extreme Right from experimenting with what became the winning formula of the extreme Right in other countries.

Rise and Decline of the National Front

The story of the National Front is a difficult one to summarize. The organization went through a long history of internal controversies, splits, fusions, and strategic reversals typical of marginal political forces in the throes of small bands of party activists divided by intense rivalries and personal animosities that affect their competition for organizational control. At the same time, stripped of such unessential historical details, the National Front's development can be sketched in very few words. Despite fierce intraparty fighting, the Front moved along a seesaw, upward trajectory yielding modest gains in membership and voter support until about 1977, as long as the external electoral opportunity structure improved. The Front then switched to a trajectory of steady electoral decline, internal fractionalization, and fission when the Conservatives expressed a stronger anti-immigration and authoritarian stance in the late 1970s. Throughout this time period, the National Front could never find the winning formula of market liberalism with authoritarianism that might have enabled it to build a more resilient electoral coalition.

The National Front was a product of the convergence of the major strands inside the British extreme Right engineered at a conference in late 1966, which agreed on the formation of the National Front as its umbrella organization. Its constituent members were imperialist colonialists and antiwelfare state conservative fascists, organized in the League of Empire Loyalists dating back to 1954, and racial populist groups such as the British National Party (BNP) and the Racial Preservation Society (RPS). The National Socialist Movement (NSM) and the anti-Semitic Greater Britain Movement (GBM) were not admitted as organizations, but their individual members joined the National Front and often assumed key positions (Taylor 1993, 169). The Front was initially led by John Tyndall, but he was soon challenged by a "Strasserite" wing advocating nationalist and socialist views. The Strasserites briefly managed to displace Tyndall from the party leadership in the early 1970s. But when Tyndall regained the leadership in 1975, the Strasserites left the Front and formed the National Party. The years after the Front's peak in 1976-77 were characterized by increasing divisions of the extreme Right, with some elements moving to open neo-Nazi propaganda. Eventually, Tyndall set up a New National Front and later in 1982 the British Nazi Party (BNP). But these organizations repre-

sented only a few segments of the British extreme Right and they were complemented by other extremists sects such as the National Action Party and the
National Socialist Action Group. In addition, there were fringe organizations
of the Conservatives that eventually associated with the extreme Right, such as
the Federation of Conservative Students, which became so extreme it was shut
down by the governing party.[5] Since 1977, the radical Right gradually had to
give up any pretense of a serious claim to electoral participation and electoral
politics (Husbands 1988a, 65). For the most part, after the National Front's
decisive defeat in the 1979 election and the triumph of the right-wing populist
Conservatives under Thatcher, rightist groups moved out of electoral politics.

The electoral history of the National Front can be told quickly. In its first
venture into national politics in the 1970 parliamentary election, the NF fielded
only 10 candidates who won an average of 3.6 percent of the vote. In the
February and October 1974 elections that number increased to 54 and 90, but
the average electoral support in these districts fell to 3.3 and 3.1 percent.
Taking into account, however, that the Front now contested a number of less
favorable seats and that the best results in 1974 were significantly above the
levels of 1970, the 1974 performance cannot be simply judged a failure.[6]
Between the 1970 and 1974 general elections, the NF reached its all-time high
in the West Bromwich by-election of 1973 with 16 percent of the vote. After
1974, the National Front did well in the municipal elections of May 1976 when
it reached 15 percent and more in a number of cities. In the 1977 local elections, the party was already in decline, but won 120,000 votes in the Greater
London Council elections. The average of 5.3 percent masks the fact that in the
poorer suburbs of East London the party often received more than 10 percent of
the vote.

Thatcher's intervention in the immigration debate and the growing right-
wing populism of the Conservative leadership then put an end to National
Front electoral progress. In 1979, the party fielded 303 candidates, but received
only an average of 1.4 percent in these constituencies. The party lost supporters
even in its strongholds. After that, with the fragmentation of the extreme Right,
fewer and fewer candidates were fielded in the ensuing elections. In 1987, a
single right-wing candidate ran and received 0.6 percent of the vote. In 1992,
14 candidates captured an average of 0.9 percent and a maximum of 1.2
percent.

Electoral upswings and intraparty divisions follow nicely the changing
opportunity structure for the extreme Right. The 1970 election yielded some
success after the Enoch Powell controversy in the British Conservatives. The
West Bromwich by-election of 1973 followed on the heels of the admission of
Asian refugees from Uganda and the controversy at the October 1972 Conservative party conference. What was perceived inside the party as stagnation in
the 1974 elections fueled intraparty controversies that momentarily subsided in

1976 after the admission of Malawian Asians and the local elections. Thereafter, with the change of the opportunity structure upon Thatcher's election as leader of the Conservatives and with the general electoral decline of the party, only interrupted by the Greater London Council vote of 1977, the internal divisions intensified as well.

While the increasingly unfavorable political opportunity structure of party competition undoubtedly contributed to the demise of the National Front in the late 1970s, the radical Right's internal roadblocks to finding the winning electoral formula of authoritarian capitalist appeals is the other cause. The National Front, in the main, advocated a combination of national authoritarianism and anticapitalism. This "national socialist" rhetoric could attract only that limited segment of the marginal working class and other economically deprived groups that, taken by themselves, have proved insufficient to launch an electorally successful extremist party in other countries. The electoral problems of the German Republicans in the early 1990s are a case in point, even though their situation was complicated by the German unification process.

Several detailed studies of the National Front, in part based on inside participant observation, document that the British extreme Right never supported liberal market capitalism in the 1970s when the external political opportunity structure was moderately favorable for rightist mobilization (cf. Fielding 1981, S. Taylor 1982). In addition, when the competitive opportunity structure later became unfavorable, the extreme Right's rejection of capitalism persisted, as was illustrated by the sympathies the National Front voiced with the 1984–85 miners' strike against the Thatcher government (Eatwell 1991, 21–22). Instead of a market-liberal and authoritarian appeal that might have attracted a broader electoral coalition, had there been more convergence between Labour and Conservatives, the National Front always crafted a "street-wise appeal to the white working class." (Husbands 1988a, 74) This appeal combined populist resentment against the rich and powerful, including the labor unions, with an authoritarian appeal that went beyond the racist and xenophobic stance to endorse antilibertarian positions on a wide range of issues, such as opposition to family planning and women's abortion rights (cf. Durham 1991).[7] The top-down authoritarian organizational structure of the Front served as a programmatic symbol and as an inducement for the core group of militants to contribute time and energy.[8]

Why did the National Front "miss the boat" on strategic matters, and why could it not identify the winning formula for the NRR in electoral politics? At least three complementary arguments can be advanced to account for this failure: the ideological patterns of British politics in the 1970s, the timing of the Front's favorable opportunity structure, and the internal historical legacy of the British extreme Right.

Although in no country did the NRR emerge as a direct backlash mobilization against the wave of left-libertarian social movements and political parties, the growth of left-libertarian activities set the stage for a realignment of political debates in which a space for right-authoritarian positions would be opened up. In this sense, France and Scandinavia, as well as Austria, Germany, and Italy provided the ideological infrastructure in which a New Right with authoritarian and promarket ideologies could find its place and its prime targets of attack. In Britain, in contrast, the libertarian Left remained weak throughout the 1960s and 1970s and by and large submerged in an ineffectual and strategically outmaneuvered Labour Party. Britain experienced a feeble student movement at a time when elsewhere in Europe student protests disrupted the normal political process. Britain also did not produce strong citizens' movements calling for greater political participation, such as environmental and antinuclear protests or women's movements in the 1970s. When the peace movement gained momentum in the early 1980s, the favorable opportunity structure for the far Right had already vanished.

In Britain, unlike most advanced capitalist democracies, the two major political parties managed to keep the competition in the party system focused on questions of economic distribution and social welfare that by and large excluded libertarian or authoritarian political and cultural concerns, with the exception since 1978 of race and immigration. Institutional conditions that shape British interparty competition, but also the parties' internal power structures and their ideological legacies, explain their resistance to a redefinition of the salient political issue space. The issue leadership of the conventional parties is a key to understanding the inability of new rightist parties to attract voters. Once the Conservatives and Labour party moved into opposite ideological directions on traditional economic questions of socialism and capitalism, they forced the electorate to focus its attention on economic issues of income distribution and property rights, even though voters might have welcomed a different political agenda. For example, there is evidence that British voters, like electorates in other advanced capitalist countries, divide most on a left-libertarian versus right-authoritarian issue dimension. Party positions in Britain, however, are clearly distinct only on a subordinate dimension of voter opinions that divide advocates and opponents of capitalism. Major political voter divisions thus have gone unrepresented in British politics.[9]

In addition to the general resistance of the key political forces and actors in British politics to represent the division between left-libertarians and right-authoritarians in the competitive arena of electoral politics, the *timing* of the favorable electoral opportunity structure for the extreme Right may explain its failure to find the winning formula of the NRR. Up to 1976–77, when the opportunity structure turned unfavorable for the British extreme Right, no single European rightist party had already found that very formula. In most European countries, only the first consequences of a reconfiguration of the political space from a simple economic left/right to a more complex left-libertarian versus right-authoritarian main dimension of party competition had become visible and had not yet reshaped the patterns of party alternatives.

In France, it may be recalled, only in the late 1970s did Le Pen begin to embrace market liberalism within the framework of a rightist-authoritarian appeal. In a similar vein, but from a different ideological starting point, the Scandinavian Progress parties at that time were amorphous market-liberal protest parties faced with an eroding electoral base that could be stabilized in the 1980s only when the parties began to inch toward the winning formula. As a consequence, at the high-water mark of the favorable opportunity structure for the British extreme Right in the mid-1970s, *there were no precedents elsewhere in Europe* on which the British Right could have relied to learn the NRR's winning formula. Yet by moving to a more populist-authoritarian stance under Thatcher, the Conservatives prevented the extreme Right from having the time to discover a successful appeal through trial-and-error iteration over a sequence of elections. In some ways, the *British conservatives became the model according to which emerging NRR parties elsewhere in Europe could learn to fashion their appeals.*

Because the opportunities to learn from other countries and to benefit from the dissemination of rightist ideas were so poor and the Conservatives clearly "owned" the issue of free market economics, even a weak social fascist tradition constrained the strategic flexibility of the British National Front. Mosley's social fascism provided a cadre of activists and a legacy of debates, materialized around an endless stream of pamphlets, journals, and books, that was inimical to the winning formula of authoritarian capitalism. Given the lack of favorable opportunities for experimenting with new appeals and strategies, the ideological pluralism of the small British extreme Right did not stimulate a search for the winning formula, but only sectarianism that generated social fascism as its comparatively strongest element. Thus, the British extreme Right has been caught up in a history and a path-dependent process of political learning that prevented it from articulating a new market-liberal plus authoritarian appeal.

Electoral Profile of the Far Right

Given the failure of the National Front ever to win a significant national following, it is inherently difficult to speculate about the characteristics of its electoral coalition because even in large random population samples, only a handful of respondents typically revealed their support of the National Front. As a consequence, what little evidence we have about the electorate of the Front for the most part relies on ecological analyses of the areas in which the National Front's voter support surged in the 1970s compared to those areas where the party failed to gain support or decided not even to field candidates. Ecological reasoning is vulnerable to the well-known "ecological fallacy" of drawing inferences about the behavior of individuals from traits measured at the level of populations. Given the absence of viable individual level data about National Front voters, however, research on the National Front is unfortunately caught between two bad alternatives—inferences fallaciously drawn from ecological comparisons or no analysis at all.

Ecological examinations find that the National Front performed best in areas with a high proportion of immigrants and working-class inhabitants. These districts were typically strongholds of the Labour Party. Thus, Fielding (1981, 31–32) emphasizes the correlation between National Front support and immigration in a precinct-by-precinct comparison of election results in the 1977 greater London Council elections and Taylor (1982, 111–19) infers from a review of the entire evidence based on the results of various elections between 1974 and 1977 that the rise of the National Front occurred at the electoral expense of the Labour Party. Thus, the National Front performed particularly well in London's poor East End, in Wolverhampton, West Bromwich, Leicester, and Bradford. In the 1979 parliamentary election, the National Front averaged only 1.3 percent in all the districts where it contested seats, but reached almost 5 percent in its best inner-city London districts (Husbands 1988a, 67).[10] The correlation between working-class base, proportion of immigrants, and NF vote is far from perfect. Sometimes NF support is also above average in working-class districts that feel potentially threatened by immigration and falling house prices rather than the actual experience of such developments (Taylor 1993, 181).

From the observation of such ecological patterns, it is only one further step to the conclusion that primarily economically marginal, culturally threatened white workers in heavily working-class districts felt attracted to the National Front. Thus, voters came from traditional Labour clienteles in the inner cities, whereas members and activists tended to come more from the Conservative Party (Gable 1991, 246). This pattern can be explained in terms of Lipset's (1981, 124) observation that working-class cadres in party politics have generally libertarian orientations and are thus impervious to the appeal of the authoritarian Right. The cadres of the National Front, therefore, had to come from the nonsocialist political Right. In contrast to party activists, voters of an extreme Right that engages in authoritarian, but also anticapitalist, rhetoric are more likely to be workers who have never established or who have subsequently lost their ties to working-class political organizations.

Although this interpretation of National Front support is consistent with its voter appeal and with the general theoretical framework developed in this study, it must be reiterated that ecological evidence is too thin to prove the individual-level argument about the nature of the British extreme Right's electoral coalition. The limits of ecological reasoning are demonstrated by the case of France, where ecological analyses do show some affinity between communist municipal strongholds in the 1970s and above average support for the National Front in the 1980s, but where closer individual-level analysis reveals that it is not former communist workers who support the extreme Right, but typically the uncommitted workers, marginal independents, and lower-level white-collar employees in working-class neighborhoods. In the case of the British National Front, ecological data may support the relatively weak hypothesis that Front voters tended to be workers but not the stronger hypothesis that Front voters were workers who previously supported the Labour Party.

Conclusion

In contrast to countries where the extreme Right has experienced electoral success and has undermined the capacity of moderate-conservative parties to govern without external support from the extreme Right or from the moderate Left, the British competitive situation does not yield important strategic dilemmas for the various players in the arena of electoral politics. Although the demonstration effect of successful NRR parties elsewhere in Europe may eventually facilitate a restructuring of the British extreme Right, in the early 1990s it is so insignificant and so deeply divided into a multiplicity of sects and groups that it is unlikely to constitute a serious challenge to the established political parties in the foreseeable future. At the same time, Labour's long stay in the opposition has lowered the probability that some workers support the extreme Right because they have been disappointed with Labour's government performance.

As a consequence, both Labour Party and Conservatives in Britain could safely ignore the extreme Right in their strategic calculations in the early 1990s. Given the internal state of the extremist camp, the Conservatives need not fear that a moderation of their strategic appeal in the post-Thatcher era will trigger a loss of critical constituencies. At the same time, Labour can continue to concentrate on the arduous process of shedding its leftist economic image and of establishing itself as a centrist alternative to the Tory government. The emerging convergence between moderate Left and Right in British politics may improve the opportunity structure for the extreme Right eventually, but this is unlikely to happen before a change in government office and a fairly long and disappointing performance for both Labour and Tory cabinets, a situation that from the vantage point of the early 1990s is some years off.

8

The New Radical Right, Cultural Pluralization, and the Welfare State

European societies have become increasingly "multicultural" as a result of immigration from the European periphery, from former colonies, and most recently from Eastern Europe following the fall of communism. Immigration and cultural frictions have contributed to the rise of the NRR, but the message of the analysis presented in the preceding chapters is that the dynamic of ethnic and national conflict must be placed within a broader context of social change, political (re)alignments, and strategic interaction among parties.

The rise of the NRR is not a "single-issue" phenomenon concerned only with immigration. To the contrary, the themes of racism and cultural intolerance are embedded in broader right-authoritarian political dispositions that are prominent among identifiable social groups. The postindustrialization of the occupational structure, precipitating a decline and restructuring of employment in the manufacturing sector and an expansion of personal service occupations, together with the growth of the welfare state that encompasses many personal service jobs have led to the rise of a dominant political division at the level of public opinions between left-libertarians and right-authoritarians. Whether or not this cleavage is articulated and represented by existing or by new parties depends on the strategic behavior of the established moderate leftist and rightist parties. The strategic convergence of such parties and their alternation or coalition in government facilitates the rise of new more extreme parties with left-libertarian or right-authoritarian constituencies.

Figure 8.1 sketches the logic of the argument laid out in this study. Postindustrialization and development of comprehensive welfare states are associated with each other and jointly contribute to a change of political preferences and interests such that a new configuration emerges pitting left-libertarians against right-authoritarians (arrows 1.1 and 1.2).[1] Postindustrialization and comprehensive welfare states, together with the restructuring of the arena in which political demands are formulated, whittle away existing class and other political cleavages and facilitate a convergence of the established left and right parties (arrows 2.1, 2.2, and 2.3). Immigration is a growing problem for postindustrial societies because their wealth attracts an increasing number

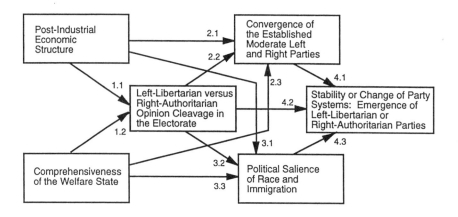

Fig. 8.1. The causal structure of party alignments

of enterprising or desperate individuals from less fortunate regions and because postindustrial societies develop segmented labor markets with employment sectors native citizens usually no longer want to enter (arrow 3.1). In this context, immigration can easily become a salient, controversial issue because political actors have no trouble interpreting it within the cognitive framework of left-libertarian versus right-authoritarian political views (arrow 3.2). Once immigration has been politicized, it feeds into the dynamic of party competition (arrow 4.3) that is fundamentally shaped by the political preference space (arrow 4.2) and the strategic positioning of the existing parties (arrow 4.1). The latter, of course, depends not just on the socioeconomic environment but also on the parties' objectives (vote seeking, office seeking, or policy seeking), constrained by mechanisms of intraorganizational interest articulation and aggregation (cf. Kitschelt 1994, chap. 4 and 5).

What the picture developed in this study ignores up to this point is the linkage between the welfare state and the salience of immigration (arrow 3.3). The welfare state politicizes immigration not only indirectly (arrows 1.2 and 3.2), but also directly, as can be seen from the phenomenon of "welfare chauvinism." If the welfare state in fact is a strong force in promoting racism, ethnic particularism, and xenophobia, this would raise theoretically interesting questions that at the same time would lead to troubling policy conclusions. Is the rise of comprehensive welfare states predicated on ethnic homogeneity or at least plural ethnic stability of a country, whereas immigration and ethnic mobility explain the weakness of welfare states in settler societies (such as the United States)? Conversely, will the multiculturalization of still by and large homogeneous or ethnically stable Western Europe lead to a decline of the welfare state?

In light of the analysis in the preceding seven chapters, the linkage between welfare state and immigration is perceived in different ways by the elements of the New Right electoral coalition. It is unlikely that the petit bourgeois element of that coalition, emphasizing ethnocentrism *and* free markets, will be much disturbed by a trade-off between welfare state and ethnic pluralization. These groups do not like either. In contrast, modernization losers of the postindustrial economy, particularly young less educated blue-collar workers, may be driven by a welfare chauvinism that stimulates their rejection of foreigners in order to preserve the social safety net for all native citizens in their country. These people prefer an ethnically closed, but egalitarian society, and can be convinced to support market liberalization in the New Right mode only if this is the only way to deprive immigrants and asylum-seekers from welfare benefits.[2] The dynamic of this "welfare chauvinism" will be the topic of this chapter.

In policy terms, the linkage between welfare state and racism would produce difficult strategic dilemmas for parties of the Left and the Right. Those on the Left who wish to preserve a comprehensive welfare state *and* create a multicultural society would be faced with the following trade-off: either they endorse economic redistribution within the confines of an ethnically stable and in most cases homogeneous bounded national community, or they are willing to give up the welfare state in favor of ethnic pluralization. A mirror image of this strategic dilemma may affect the New Right: if it succeeds in stopping the process of multiculturalization, it may have less capacity to fight for market liberalism because in a homogeneous country pressures to remove the welfare state will subside and it might lose its blue-collar constituency of modernization losers. Conversely, if the New Right succeeds with its market-liberal program, even losers of the modernization process may be more willing to accept multiculturalization because the influx of immigrants will have few financial consequences for the well-being of those who have previously lived in the country.

Before we explore these policy dilemmas, the linkage between the political salience of multiculturalization and comprehensive welfare states must be reconstructed in a more fundamental way. Behind the correlation between ethnic stability and size of the welfare state, we must identify the "mechanisms" in actors' thought processes and strategies that explain why critical subsegments of the population believe that a universalist welfare state and ethnic pluralization are incompatible. We begin with a reconstruction of the relationship between the growth of the welfare state and ethnic pluralization. We then discuss the creation of boundaries between "insiders" and "outsiders" as a critical problem of democratic theory underlying the trade-off between welfare state and multiculturalization. The final section discusses discursive strategies that could help the Left overcome the strategic dilemma cast upon it by "welfare chauvinism." In this section, we clearly go beyond the analytical themes of this study and trespass into the realm of normative political theory.

The Welfare State and Ethnic Pluralization

Let us begin with the facts already established from previous chapters. Those for whom the welfare state is most important as a buffer against the vagaries of capitalist labor markets, the less educated wage earners, and among them especially blue-collar workers, display an above average disposition to support right-authoritarian and racist claims. Except where rightist parties engage in a populist antistatist appeal, such as in Austria and Italy, blue-collar respondents are heavily overrepresented not only among the supporters of racist and ethnically particularist claims, but also among the sympathizers of extreme-rightist parties, particularly those with an NRR appeal. We made this observation with respect to the French, Danish, and Norwegian NRR parties. In the countries with less successful extreme rightist parties, such as Britain and Germany, our survey evidence generated too few voters of such parties to test the hypothesis. Ecological analyses and previously conducted surveys, however, suggest that the blue-collar sector is even more overrepresented among the supporters of these parties than the NRR parties in general.

The call for ethnic, racial, and religious closure among Western European blue-collar laborers may, however, have a different character than the sense of cultural superiority that is often associated with particularist group claims. In-depth qualitative interviews with former supporters of the German social democrats who were won over by the extremist Republicans, for example, yielded no sense of cultural superiority, but a strong anxiety about the future of the welfare state (cf. Klär, Ristau, Schoppe, and Stadelmaier 1989). Vote switchers to the extreme Right expect to lose some of their social insurance and other benefits, such as subsidized housing, to which they feel entitled as income and payroll taxpayers, due to the channeling of funds to immigrants who have not contributed to the system. In this sense, the rejection of immigration is a form of "welfare chauvinism," or the unwillingness to accept social redistribution to the worse-off if they are immigrants. This "welfare chauvinism" is not culturally bounded. In the German case, targets of resentment also include ethnic Germans from Eastern Europe and even East Germans who fled from the collapsing GDR in fall 1989.

At the aggregate level, empirical studies suggest, but do not prove, that in countries where comprehensive welfare states were introduced in ethnically homogeneous societies and immigrants followed later, ethnic racism is likely to be complemented by vigorous "welfare chauvinism." In bivariate statistical analysis of advanced industrial democracies, Betz and Swank (1991) did find a correlation between electoral support for the racist and anti-immigrant New Right in the period 1985–90 and the percentage of residents who are immigrants seeking asylum. This percentage, in turn, is highly correlated with the per capita income of countries. In multivariate analysis, however, the independent effect of asylum-seekers on New Right electoral support disappears, but per capita income, levels of taxation, and increases in youth unemployment are positively related to New Right strength, while the size of the service sector is negatively linked to it.[3] Betz and Swank do not mention whether they tested for the size of the welfare state as a determinant of New Right growth, but the variables included in their model suggest a corresponding pattern. Countries with high income and high levels of taxation happen to be comprehensive welfare states. They often have large industrial sectors trapped in structural adjustment problems and thus are likely to generate youth unemployment.

The underlying logic of the relationship between comprehensive welfare states, rejection of immigrants, and support for the extreme Right in an era of immigration is quite simple. As long as "minimalist" welfare states represent nothing but the equivalent of a private market insurance system in which people receive benefits strictly in proportion to their contributions based on calculations of their actuarial risk to the insurer, the influx of new residents from a hitherto nonexistent or very small ethnic grouping does not undermine the pubic acceptance of social programs. Where a comprehensive welfare state goes beyond the insurance principle, however, and redistributes funds from contributors to beneficiaries, a changing ethnic balance does matter. Individuals may welcome redistribution, even if they become net contributors to the welfare state because a comprehensive welfare state produces certain "club goods" such as lower crime and less poverty,[4] but also cultural goods such as a greater sense of moral worth and autonomy among the recipients of help than in a charity-based private and voluntary system.[5] If individuals were free to contract for private social insurances, many might fail to enroll and would be exposed to particularly severe risks of exploitation by those who take advantage of their predicament in labor markets and in other social power relations (Goodin 1988a).

Net contributors to the welfare state, however, are most willing to accept redistribution to the less fortunate where they can envision that they themselves could, in theory, be in the same predicament that calls for social benefits. By definition, immigrants are excluded from that comparison when residents see them not as members of the "club" that redistributes internal funds. In a similar vein, while members may accept welfare state policies for the sake of producing the "club goods" of social solidarity, this principle would not cover individuals who want to become members of the club in the first place. In other words, the welfare state appears acceptable to a large proportion of net contributors if those who are net beneficiaries are very much "like" those who contribute because they belong to the same "club" of citizens. Carens summarizes this logic of justifying the welfare state through particularist boundary-drawing:

> The will to support the welfare state comes, it can be argued, from a sense of common bonds, from a mutual identification by the members of the community. These feelings are more likely to emerge when people share a common language and a common culture and when they belong to groups that have developed habits of cooperation with other groups. (1988, 209)

What is most important in practical terms, however, is that if immigrants in a precarious economic position are seen as a threat to such "club goods" as low levels of civic anxiety, low costs of crime control, and high social stability, members of the club may call for a different way of handling the problem than in the case of the less fortunate among the original members of the club. Whereas the problems of the latter can be addressed only by repression or redistribution, the problems of the former can be handled by exclusion or expulsion. Particularly where the costs of including immigrants are high due to comprehensive and redistributive social policies that address most needs of health care, housing, and education, a substantial number of citizens will be inclined to support expulsion of immigrants as a last resort in order to preserve national club goods and to limit redistributive expenses.

In countries with changing ethnic boundaries, the derivative of the comprehensive welfare state is thus a "welfare chauvinism" that is not necessarily rooted in cultural patterns of xenophobia and racism but in a "rational" consideration of alternative options to preserve social club goods in efficient ways. "Welfare chauvinism" is likely to appeal particularly to less well-off members of the community who expect to gain from the redistributive welfare state but fear an antiwelfare state backlash if the number of net beneficiaries swells due to the special needs of immigrants. Thus racism and intolerance to cultural diversity, a traditional attribute of the authoritarian Right (Lipset and Raab 1978, 5–6), may be generated not only by low educational sophistication and high cognitive rigidity, but also by the redistributive schemes of the welfare state. There is a politically important difference, however, between cultural racism and welfare chauvinism.

Whereas racists and cultural-ethnic particularists turn only against immigrants from a different culture than citizens of the national club, sober calculating welfare chauvinists oppose any kind of immigration, *no matter* whether they belong to a different or the same ethnicity as actual citizens. As Klär et al.'s (1989) study of German vote switchers from the social democrats to the Republican party suggests, workers who oppose immigration tend to be "welfare chauvinists" because they fear their material well-being may deteriorate if a welfare state backlash occurs. In contrast, cultural racists and ethnic particularists may be more prominent among petit bourgeois and bourgeois strata whose members do not typically expect to be net beneficiaries of the welfare state and many of whom would welcome an antiwelfare state backlash.

The role of welfare chauvinism without racial and ethnic particularism is also evident in two recent cases of ethno-regional mobilization, Belgium and Italy. In both countries, the trigger was not immigration from the outside but increasing domestic regional economic disparities highlighted by institutional changes in the territorial organization of the state. In Belgium, the construction of the welfare state antedates the intensification of ethno-regional conflicts. With the economic decline of Wallonia relative to thriving Flanders, citizens in the latter have become increasingly less willing to redistribute social funds to the poorer South. As a consequence, but also as a cause of further ethnolinguistic division, the regions have been given more areas of self-governance, deepening the unwillingness to accept redistribution across the divide.

In Italy, the administrative regionalization of government after 1970 made redistributive fiscal flows more obvious and publicly highlighted the general discrepancy in the effectiveness of public policy making in northern Italy compared to much of southern Italy.[6] These changes have contributed to politicizing regional divisions and giving rise to a populist antistatist movement in the North.

The linkage between welfare state, perceptions of economic redistribution, and exclusionary definitions of citizenship can be explored not only with respect to the *consequences* of a large welfare state in previously homogeneous societies with now substantial immigration but also with regard to the *causes* of comprehensive welfare states. If cultural homogeneity and the stability of ethnic relations count in support of the welfare state, the initial construction of the welfare state may be shaped by these factors as well. In the founding periods of the welfare state from about the turn of the century until the 1950s, one can distinguish at least four configurations: (1) stable cultural homogeneity (Scandinavia); (2) cultural plurality, but no immigration (Lijphart's [1977] "plural" societies); (3) immigration but cultural homogeneity (Australia, Canada, New Zealand); and (4) immigration and cultural heterogeneity (United States). The potential for the rise of comprehensive welfare states is likely to decline from the first to the fourth configuration.

First, in stable homogeneous societies, it was not class politics but the common sense of national fate that served as the catalyst of the comprehensive welfare state. Baldwin (1990, 134–46) has shown that the Swedish working-class organizations, by themselves, were initially not interested in an encompassing welfare state that also benefited non–working-class clienteles, but just in means-tested programs for the working poor. It took the initiative of political representatives of the middle class during and right after World War II in a period that highlighted the significance of national solidarity to bring about a strategic shift in working-class politics in favor of a comprehensive welfare state. In this process, reform advocates redefined workers' interest in economic redistribution from a short-term to a long-term perspective. The atrocities of fascism and communism and the precarious position of the Scandinavian countries may have served as a catalyst to transform class interests from the perception of short-term zero-sum games to long-term positive-sum games and to realize that the well-being of the working class also depends on a thriving middle class.

Second, in stable plural societies, political divisions eventually lead to a compromise that is based on the segmentation of constituencies and benefits, particularly in small European democracies traditionally threatened by a volatile international environment of competing powers (cf. Lijphart 1977; Katzenstein 1985). Such countries typically did not build comprehensive and universalistic welfare states, but welfare states with fewer redistributive effects and a division of clients into subgroups (cf. Esping-Andersen 1990).

Third, in settler societies with substantial immigration but an ethnically homogeneous background, such as in Australia, Canada, and New Zealand, the construction of a comprehensive welfare state may be slower and less comprehensive than in stable societies without much immigration. Nevertheless, here also a substantial welfare state eventually did emerge that organizes a modicum of redistribution from the affluent to the poor. Fourth, the United States, in contrast, as a country with high immigration and ethnic plurality, has been unable to organize even a modestly comprehensive welfare state.[7] In the United States, the sense of citizenship was not strong and universal enough to make it acceptable to democratic majorities that public funds to hedge social risks should be transferred from one cultural group to others, primarily recent arrivals. The latter always had the greatest need for public resources, yet at the same time had the least justification to claim such resources. A similar logic applies to the treatment of African-Americans. Because European Americans did not see them as members of their community and because African-Americans were perceived as likely net beneficiaries of comprehensive social policy schemes, the majority of white citizens has opposed many comprehensive social programs.

The different trajectories of welfare state growth also throw some light on patterns of working-class formation in the nineteenth and early twentieth centuries. The political appeal to ethno-cultural identities is a mixed blessing for working-class movements. On the one hand, the success of class politics of economic redistribution is closely intertwined with a strong national identity. In this context, Miller (1988, 661) reminds us that liberal economic opponents of working-class movements such as Hayek rejected both nationalism and socialism. On the other hand, national and ethnic appeals may also be an elite strategy to undermine class identities, particularly in ethnically divided societies.[8] Depending on the configuration of ethno-cultural groups and the juncture in the development of capitalism and welfare states, appeals to ethnocultural identities may thus have rather different effects on class formation and the rise of the welfare state.

Explaining Boundaries between Ethnocultural Collectivities

Liberal theory of democracy and theories of collective political action presuppose an explanatory account of the "boundaries" of democracy and collective action, but they typically do not deliver this explanation within their own frameworks. Democracy, for example, presupposes a delineation between citizens and noncitizens, but this delineation cannot be accomplished by democratic mechanisms itself (Dahl 1989). A similar problem is encountered by theories of collective action (Hardin 1982; Olson 1965; M. Taylor 1987). We can analytically define collective goods by the attributes of nonexcludability and nonrival consumption, but practically most goods are "club" or "positional" goods that are enjoyed by a bounded collective and from which outsiders can be excluded.[9] The nation-state is one possibility for framing the boundaries within which democracy can be enjoyed and collective goods will be provided. But the boundaries of that state are introduced as a crude fact that, in itself, remains unexplained. In stark contrast to liberal democratic and public choice theorists, antidemocratic political theorists such as Carl Schmitt (1932) have virtually *defined* the primary activity of politics as boundary-drawing rather than as the production and distribution of scarce goods within an already constituted collectivity.

In order to understand why questions of citizenship, migration, and the welfare state are so closely intertwined in the politics of the advanced capitalist democracies, it may be worthwhile to review theories of boundary-drawing among collectivities—the manufacturing of "we-groups" (Elwert 1989)—that may shed light on the bases of contemporary ethno-culturally particularist mobilization. In light of these considerations, we can then consider normative arguments for and against boundary-drawing in the final section of this chapter.

Theories of ethnicity and boundary-drawing have advanced at least four arguments, none of which, taken by itself, appears to offer a satisfactory account of ethnicity. First, the older objectivist and naturalist approaches suggesting that ethnicity and nationality are primordial collective identifications have by and large been displaced by "constructivist" theories that interpret ethnicity and nationalism as the product of political (state) organization-building and discursive strategies in which a sense of collective identity is gradually "manufactured" by elites and external circumstances. All more recent approaches treat national and ethnic identities as a genuinely modern phenomenon, not a residual of traditional social organizations.

Second, economic distribution may explain the formation of ethnic and national "club" identities and political mobilization. Ethnic identities are created and become politicized when a group's relative resource endowment is shifting to its disadvantage ("reactive" ethnicity) or when a stable cultural division of labor is disrupted either by the prospect of disadvantages or advantages for one group ("competitive" ethnicity).[10] Groups seek autonomy through new boundaries if they have some rational expectation that they could be better off by introducing such boundaries (Meadwell 1992). Theories centering on rational economic considerations often work well to explain processes of bargaining among groups that have already constituted some kind of collective identity. Just like utilitarian theories of class formation, however, they fail to account for the cognitive and normative process that makes attributes, such as the physical location of one's residence, one's language, one's ethnicity, or one's religion, sufficiently *salient* to create common identities that override all the other economic differences and disparities that exist *within* such collectivities, particularly those of class. In other words, utilitarian theories cannot explain why individual actors frame distributive conflicts in terms of ethnicity and nationality rather than in terms of market position or class.

Third, boundary-drawing between ethnic groups may be a result of the *statecraft of political elites,* particularly their ability to structure differences among collectivities through administrative rules and the geographical distribution of the population that affects patterns of communication and interaction. Political actors are rational maximizers of self-interest, but this time the self-interest to be maximized is not that of the population but that of elite groups who try to protect and expand their power base. In order to mobilize resources for that end, they strive to weld together disparate economic groups into vertical singular collectivities, for example, through clientelistic organization, while they seek to divide others into separate identities (Elwert 1989, 452–53). In many ways, the statecraft approach suffers from the same problems as economic self-interest approaches. It cannot explain why populations would sometimes respond to administrative divisions and fusions by developing the desired identities, but sometimes would not. Why were peasants turned into Frenchmen, but not Flemings into Belgians? At the same time, the statecraft approach points toward a critical element that defines the fourth approach: the importance of social interaction and communication that facilitates the formation of collective identities. Elites structure the flow of information and thus shape the possible range of collective identities.

The fourth approach, then, may be termed a *communication theory of ethnicity and nationality* that, in some respects, was first charted by Deutsch

(1953), but has later been radicalized in various modernization theories. Whereas Deutsch perceived the modern mass media simply as the technological vehicle that disseminates a preexisting national sense of collective identification, later authors have argued that the technological vehicle shapes the message itself. The "reach" of means of communication and transportation that govern the spread of symbols and messages to a broad audience determines the territorial and ethno-cultural delineation of collectivities.[11] Together with the wide dissemination of ideas, economic and social change erodes primordial collective identifications and replaces them with ethnic and national collectives.

In this communication approach, ethnicity and nationalism are the product of a specific transition to modern social organization and its mode of communication. It is obvious that not only technological implements but also cultural elites and politics play an important role in shaping such identities. The structure of states and the administrative form of governance constitute bounded networks of dense communication, for example, through federalism and regional self-governance, that mold people's perception of groups and relative comparisons between groups with respect to their welfare and life chances.[12] But with the advent of multiple communications facilities, elites no longer have exclusive control over the formation of collective identities. Elite strategies to create new collective identities may thus have been particularly successful if they were well advanced *before* the advent of mass communication in the early nineteenth century. Conversely, they were less successful, once economic modernization had allowed for the emergence of a plurality of channels of communication that could disseminate other ethnocultural conceptions of collective identity.

Most likely, none of the four theories, singly, can explain ethno-cultural political mobilization. Preexisting cultural networks may or may not be a necessary (though certainly not a sufficient) determinant of ethnic mobilization. Economic modernization and the broadening of communication channels will promote ethnic mobilization *only* if it also interacts with economic imbalances that can be attributed to distinct culturally defined groups and if such ethnic and economic discrepancies are communicated by political entrepreneurs to the masses. For this to happen, politicians must have their own incentives to pursue strategies of ethnic mobilization. In other words, ethno-cultural mobilization is very much an interaction effect, a result of the conjuncture of primordial cultural collectivities, economic modernization and communications, imbalances of resource control, and strategies of elite politics.[13] Economic competition and elite strategies are complementary forces that account for the actual mobilization where there was only a dormant sense of ethnicity before. The trouble with a complex argument focusing on patterns of causal interaction among different mechanisms of collective boundary-drawing is that it lacks the elegance of parsimony and is empirically difficult to trace in a world in which the number of cases available for analysis is limited.[14]

Nevertheless, even this rudimentary conjunctural theory yields a simple analytical hypothesis that offers food for thought in any normative discussion about the political relationship between citizenship, migration, and the welfare state in contemporary democracies. As long as there are "imbalanced" processes of modernization that coincide with ethno-cultural divisions and economic stratification, there is a significant potential for the mobilization of exclusive, particularist conceptions of citizenship and threats to the comprehensive welfare state. This is the situation that prevails in the contemporary world system and affects the internal politics of advanced capitalist democracies. Let us conclude with a discussion of the normative arguments that may be marshaled by politicians on the Left and the Right in such democracies to cope with the strategic dilemmas that originate in the trade-off between immigration and welfare state.

Defending the Welfare State and Ethnic Pluralization against the New Right

Faced with the economic choice between a more spontaneous market-driven economy and a more politically regulated economy, and the cultural choice between a cosmopolitan multicultural community and a parochial and nationally homogeneous community, the strategic dilemmas of the New Right are mild compared to those of the New Left. The former faces no intrinsic conflict of goals between bringing about a market society without a comprehensive welfare state and preserving the ethnic homogeneity of the nation-state. The only strategic problem of the New Right is that the public salience of the cultural objective to preserve or restore national homogeneity may decline as the Right succeeds in realizing its economic objective to promote market relations, or vice versa. In contrast, the New Left faces a more difficult problem. Its quest to sustain a comprehensive welfare state *and* a multiculturalization of advanced European capitalist democracies may provoke a welfare chauvinist backlash among the indigenous population that skilled rightist politicians may incorporate into a broader right-authoritarian electoral coalition. The easy way out for the Left would be to choose between *either* the preservation of social solidarity through a comprehensive welfare state, while maintaining national cultural homogeneity, or the acceptance of ethnic multiculturalization, while renouncing a comprehensive system of social protection from market contingencies. This final section is intended to explore some arguments and political strategies that may enable the New libertarian Left to avoid such unpleasant choices and to advocate some measure of comprehensive social protection and multiculturalization simultaneously.

Let us begin by saying, however, that the choice between complete openness and closure of borders for migration is a false one and that even the advocates of multiculturalization may agree to certain constraints on free movement. These constraints can be justified in a universalist perspective by two different types of arguments—moral and pragmatic (Woodward 1992, 60–61). The moral arguments do not have to assume the superiority of one's ethnic community but can build on universalist ethical grounds that are also conceded by some of the most forceful proponents of free movement (e.g., Carens 1992, 37–39). The liberal conception of freedom of choice may include a right to the "context of choice," that is, the resources provided by a culture that enable individuals to realize their life plans. If immigration undermines this context of choice, citizens may reasonably claim that it must be reduced to a level at which this infringement on their life plans is eliminated.[15] Especially comprehensive universalistic welfare policies, which liberal egalitarians definitively value as a facility to increase freedom, may be undercut by high levels of immigration (Woodward 1992, 75–76). Of course, the precise circumstances and levels of permissible immigration within these parameters would be open to discussion.[16]

Beyond this universalist moral argument for limits to migration, there are at least four pragmatic arguments of expedience and efficiency that affect the desirability of open borders, even if we all agreed on the objective of maximizing individual rights and improving the lot of peoples from less developed countries (Woodward 1992). First, even through extensive migration to the West, only a small share of the people in less developed countries would be helped. Second, the wrong people would be helped because precisely those who have cognitive skills and psychic energies that would enable them to improve local institutions and welfare are also those who are most likely to leave. Hence, wealthy countries should not be compelled to accept members of the small middle class of educated and skilled individuals living in the less developed world (Carens 1988). Third, if continuous emigration was a safety valve, less developed countries might see fewer incentives to improve, for example, by relaxing their efforts at cutting population growth and at protecting the environment (Barry 1992, 282). Fourth, we must apply a pragmatic "lifeboat ethics" (Carens 1992, 30). Societies have a "carrying capacity" up to which their institutional viability can be maintained. Just as in the tragedy of the commons, if that threshold is exceeded everyone will be worse off rather than better off, and immigration becomes counterproductive.

Beyond these arguments, one might wonder whether global citizenship is realistic in a world in which communication is essentially concentrated around more limited national or regional communities, such as the European Union.[17] Miller's (1988; 1990) justification of national identity resorts to the argument that, in the present world, a universalist sense of community is not (yet) *feasible* so that collective goods—including distributive justice—can be provided only by smaller communities. Miller thus provides more a pragmatic *explanation* than a moral *justification* for boundaries delineating citizens from noncitizens:[18]

> We do not yet have global community in the sense that is relevant to justice as distribution to need. There is no consensus that the needs of other human beings considered merely as such make demands of justice on us, nor is there sufficient agreement about what is to count as a need. It is therefore unrealistic to suppose that the choice lies between distributive justice worldwide and distributive justice within national societies; the realistic choice is between distributive justice of the latter sort, and distributive justice within much smaller units—families, religious communities, and so forth. . . . The universalist case for nationality, therefore, is that it creates communities within the widest feasible membership, and therefore with the greatest scope for redistribution in favor of the needy. (Miller 1988, 661)

Against the backdrop of these moral and pragmatic arguments defending the limits of free movement across national or regional borders, let us now see how the political Left could defend multiculturalization. The range of arguments can be situated on a variety of levels that can be identified by Parsons's analysis of social action. In contrast to simple means/ends schemes of human action, Parsons (1951, 12–13) distinguished four "components of action": instruments (means), objectives (ends), norms, and values. Justifications for policies of multiculturalization combined with social protection relate a norm (citizenship regardless of cultural background) to either means, ends, or values of action. Norms can be advocated and enforced from "below," by considerations of expediency, such as the selection of efficient means in light of given ends and values, as well as pragmatic considerations, such as the choice of appropriate ends in light of fixed values. From "above," a norm can be defended by showing how it follows from basic values and principles that command respect in a community. We can thus analyze the options available to the New Left to justify the institutionalization of multicultural welfare states in the light of instruments, objectives, and principles.

At the level of instruments of policy, arguments for a multicultural welfare state postulate that objectives and principles of a good social order are agreed upon so that we search only for appropriate means to implement them. An instrumental argument for immigration and multiculturalization is the technical infeasibility of maintaining closed borders and the need to preserve comprehensive welfare states to cope with the negative side effects of immigration and multiculturalization. Given the growing ease and declining costs of moving goods, services, and people across borders, the struggle against immigration and multiculturalization is futile short of establishing a police state and withdrawing exactly those civil liberties that make it attractive to live in advanced capitalist democracies. The choice, then, is only between tacit unregulated or open and regulated immigration. Like settler nations hundreds of years ago, Western European countries now have to come to terms with the fact that they are nations of immigrants and must gear their institutions to the new conditions. If immigration is inevitable, it is better to endow immigrants with the skills and the competence that enable them to function in an advanced liberal capitalist society. Here the need for a comprehensive welfare state comes in. A sophisticated capitalist market society requires nonmarket safeguards that enable citizens to commodify their labor. The welfare state responds to an irreversible process in which institutions, such as family and friendship networks, can no longer provide such safeguards.

Instrumental arguments in defense of a multicultural welfare state limit the scope of political controversy by presuming that goals and principles of social organization cannot be changed by collective choice. Such arguments may be less convincing and motivating than more fundamental arguments for the desirability of multiculturalization as an objective and a moral principle. At the level of objectives, the libertarian Left could claim that the welfare state and multiculturalization through immigration serve two goals that mutually reinforce each other. Given the demographic development in advanced capitalist democracies, with a growing population of retirees, an increasing share of the adult population still in education, a fertility rate below the level of reproduction, and a shrinking proportion of the population in gainful employment, a steady flow of primarily young immigrants, often with a greater disposition to raise children than native citizens, is desirable to maintain the key institutions of the welfare state. Because social policies tend to transfer funds from working citizens to non-working citizens, immigration may increase the proportion of the gainfully employed in the population and thus preserve the fiscal viability of social security, health care, and education systems.[19]

If immigration is accepted for that purpose, a comprehensive welfare state is a necessity in an increasingly multicultural society in order to avoid the public bads of social disintegration and conflict that result when new arrivals do not receive the assistance that enables them to become fully functioning citizens inside the host society. In order to drive home this point, it suffices to take a brief look at the United States, where this lesson has not been learnt. The American residual welfare state has permitted the growth of a vast self-reinforcing poverty sector that is socially disruptive and economically inefficient. The residual welfare state, which does not offer comprehensive economic protection of minorities and less fortunate groups, creates public bads that affect all citizens, regardless of their ethnic identity. A small welfare state in an immigrant society appears attractive only to those well-to-do citizens who succumb to an extreme myopia and narrowness in their calculation of public welfare. It could be the task of the libertarian Left to counteract such views in defense of the welfare state. On balance, counting all costs and benefits, the welfare state is likely to be more efficient than the neoconservative visions of a new market liberal society (cf. Goodin 1988, chap. 8 and 9). The libertarian Left thus must fight the cognitive myopia that has befallen "welfare chauvinist" and market-liberal advocates of the NRR. The critical point is to demonstrate that ethno-cultural minorities and immigrants should benefit from comprehensive social policies because such measures help to stave off the collective bads of social conflict and individual deviance that otherwise might result.

Finally, there is no shortage of arguments to defend the welfare state and ethnic multiculturalization of advanced capitalist societies even on the most fundamental level of values and moral principles. Because human beings do not appear on this earth as fully functioning members of liberal society, but require an infrastructure of socialization and nurturing that enables them to exercise individual freedom and choice in the marketplace, in politics, and in cultural life, basic imperatives to create and preserve human autonomy and freedom call for the institutionalization of comprehensive welfare states (Goodin 1988a, chaps. 10 and 11). Without welfare states, many human beings would fall victim to dependency relations that directly contradict the liberal image of society. Economic and political liberals cannot want to preserve liberal freedoms in the marketplace and in democratic constitutions and at the same time intend to dismantle comprehensive welfare states.

In a similar vein, a political philosophy in the Western tradition that emphasizes individual autonomy and choice cannot deny the right to physical mobility and cannot endorse particularist arguments against redistribution across ethnic groups and regions of the globe. Following Rawls's principles of justice, inequality is permitted only as long as it makes the worst-off better off than in a society with overall greater equality. This principle can be applied to the global level (Carens 1988 and 1989). Advanced countries can help the world's worst-off in two ways: by transfers of capital to the less developed countries and by the acceptance of human transfers from such countries to the West. Very few might be prepared to argue that Western aid or acceptance of refugees violates Rawls's difference principle. In principle, capital transfers improve the conditions in the less developed countries if methods can be found to prevent their disappearance in the hands of small political elites. In principle, the acceptance of immigrants in advanced countries does not hurt the less developed countries, provided highly educated individuals from such countries are excluded from migration *or* are compelled to compensate less developed countries for the cost of higher education. For advanced countries, it is only morally justified to reject immigrants if they come from other almost equally wealthy countries (Carens 1988, 227–28). Within the boundaries of the moral and pragmatic arguments discussed above, however, migrants from less fortunate regions should be accepted.

Conclusion

Overall, the libertarian Left is faced with a range of arguments designed to defend a multicultural welfare state. Nevertheless, it is unlikely that "global" reasoning driven by principalist ethical concerns that invoke the moral obligations of rich countries to improve minimum standards of living on a global scale and to accept immigrants from poor regions of the world will persuade many of those who sympathize with "welfare chauvinist" and racist slogans. More instrumental and pragmatic arguments may have a slightly greater popular reach, but even here the power of the political argument should not be overestimated. Even though the battle against racism, xenophobia, and "welfare chauvinism" involves the entire arsenal of pragmatic and moral arguments that inform contemporary economic, political, and philosophical debates, the viability of a multicultural welfare state is ultimately decided by political competition and coalition-building and by socioeconomic changes in advanced capitalism. On the one hand, the advent of postindustrial society promotes a more skilled and sophisticated population and thus individual capacities that undermine the cultural acceptance of racism and xenophobia. On the other hand, however, the economic stress and polarization between winners and losers of the new socioeconomic order—but also the decline of existing modes of political mass organization through parties and interest groups—sets free new social potentials of unrest that can be harnessed by racist political entrepreneurs.

9

Conclusion

The main contention of this study is that the extreme Right in Western Europe can occupy a niche in the electoral market contingent upon three premises. First, societies have an advanced capitalist postindustrial structure that increases the salience of the political division between more left-libertarian and more right-authoritarian constituencies. Second, the major parties of the economic Left and Right, social democrats or socialists, on the one side, and Christian democrats or conservatives, on the other, go through a process of strategic convergence in which they alternate in government and/or join government coalitions. Third, the extreme Right can do well in this configuration *provided* it finds the winning formula to attract right-authoritarian support, namely a resolutely market-liberal stance on economic issues and an authoritarian and particularist stance on political questions of participatory democracy, of individual autonomy of lifestyles and cultural expressions, and of citizenship status. If rightist parties find the winning formula they will assemble an electoral coalition in which small independent businesspeople (shopkeepers, farmers, etc.) as well as blue-collar workers are overrepresented, but white-collar employees, particularly those with advanced training, and professionals are underrepresented. Right-authoritarian parties can appeal to primarily young and insecure workers based on the themes of authority, nation, and race, whereas they reach their petite bourgeois clientele with an extreme antistatist, promarket message against the "bureaucratic Moloch" of the advanced welfare state.

As we have seen, rightist parties have found the "winning formula" in Denmark, France, and Norway, but not in Britain, Germany, or in Italy (MSI). In Britain, a conservative party preempted the rise of a successful extreme Right in the 1970s by engaging in a populist-nationalist rhetoric. In Germany and Italy, strategic conditions for the rise of a right-authoritarian party were favorable, but the national socialist and fascist legacies of the direct or indirect successor rightist parties that were preserved by the memories and practices of the core party activists prevented these parties from choosing a new and electorally "profitable" appeal.

In countries with a patronage-based party system and political economy that is often labeled a "partocracy," such as Austria and Italy, rightist political entrepreneurs faced an even more favorable political opportunity structure than in other competitive democracies with a convergence between moderate Left and Right. Here, they could mobilize broad-based resentments against the hydra of a party state whose extremities extend into every corner of the economy and the society. As a consequence, they have been able to put together socially more amorphous electoral coalitions that span all strata and sectors of the social structure. In Italy, the Northern League was able to feed into a broad antipartocratic rebellion that eventually destroyed the foundations of the major Italian parties of the post-World War II era.

If our argument is correct, several rival theories of the extreme Right are implausible. First of all, it would be wrong to see the extreme Right as a *single-issue response* to the pressures of immigration in the 1980s. While it is true that popular anxiety about immigration varies with the percentage of non-European residents in a country (Fuchs, Gerhards, and Roller 1993), there is no clear-cut relationship between aggregate levels of anxiety and right-wing party performance, as we have shown in chapter 2. Moreover, the analysis of right-wing voters in six countries has demonstrated that racial attitudes are nowhere the one and decisive predictor of extreme-rightist party support. Instead, support for such parties is rooted in broader right-authoritarian dispositions. It is true that the support of the extreme Right in Western Europe draws on anti-immigrant resentments against cultural pluralization. Such feelings have become increasingly salient in the course of the transition to a postindustrial economic structure in which European countries have encountered many social and political difficulties. Racist and "welfare chauvinist" resentments, however, are only one catalyst for the emergence of extreme-rightist parties. Such attitudes lead to the choice of extreme-rightist parties only when they are embedded into a broader ideological syndrome that combines authoritarian and market-liberal orientations.

The second hypothesis our study has disproved is that the extreme Right expresses *a diffuse politics of protest* against a political system in which the existing alternatives have become too similar. If the protest hypothesis is correct, then voters of the extreme Right should not be characterized by identifiable patterns of belief and social circumstances. But we have shown that the clientele of such parties is not a random sample of the overall population in European countries. Moreover, the protest hypothesis would lead us to expect that rightist protest parties also emerge in countries where established major parties have converged, but postindustrialization and the welfare state are less far developed, such as Ireland, Portugal, or Spain. These countries, however, do not have strong rightist parties.

A third hypothesis claims that the new rightist mobilization in Western Europe is *not* primarily economically rightist and politically authoritarian, as we argue, but combines rightist *promarket liberalism with political and cul-*

tural libertarianism. Nothing in the data we have analyzed would substantiate this rival claim. Nowhere are successful rightist parties less nationalist, less concerned about authority, more willing to grant women's equality and cultural autonomy, and more environmentally protectionist than most of their competitors. The only partial exception to this rule are the populist and antistatist parties in Austria and Italy, which for the very specific reasons we have explained are able to assemble a broader electoral coalition than the pure NRR parties.

A fourth hypothesis is so implausible that it hardly deserves restatement were it not for its importance in political rhetoric, especially among certain strands of the European Left. This is the claim that the contemporary Right is *a neofascist continuation of the totalitarian movements* in earlier decades of this century, particularly in Germany and Italy. There is no question that neofascist elements have entered the new extreme Right, but it is an entirely different matter whether this qualifies these parties and movements as neofascist. Our book has argued precisely the opposite: the success of extreme-rightist parties is inversely proportional to their proximity to neofascist patterns. The successful New Right does not combine authoritarianism, nationalism, and corporatist economic visions, but authoritarianism, ethnic particularism, and market liberalism. Moreover, unlike the situation in the 1920s and 1930s, the white-collar and professional middle-class has by and large become unavailable to the extreme Right. Both in intellectual appeal as well as in electoral coalition, the successful contemporary extreme Right is different from the historical extreme Right, as represented by German national socialism or Italian fascism.

If our analysis survives the first test against rival theories how can it be exposed to tougher tests in the future? For one thing, further studies may examine the cases on which we have not presented data. For example, are the Swiss Automobilists' Party and the Swiss Democrats, the former National Action party, driven by similar right-authoritarian appeals and voter coalitions as the extreme Right in other European parties? It is known that the two parties place special emphasis on the struggle against environmental protection.[1] Moreover, they subscribe to an authoritarian and xenophobic agenda. Another test case is Belgium, particularly the "Vlaams Blok" in Flanders. In the Belgian national election of November 1991, it drew about one fifth of its voters from the socialist party and about two fifths from the main bourgeois parties, the Christian Democrats, the Flemish People's Union, and the Liberals (cf. Billiet, Swyngedouw, and Carton 1993).[2] The "Vlaams Blok" appears to mobilize primarily on racist sentiments within the framework of authoritarian orientations, but also on bourgeois market-liberal protests against the corporatist Belgian welfare state.

Other possibilities to test our argument will arise in the future, as electoral competition continues. For example, while in the Netherlands opportunities for the extreme Right were bad throughout the 1980s, when the Labor Party and the bourgeois Christian-liberal government were quite polarized, such conditions have gradually improved since the installation of the Labour-Christian government coalition in 1989. Indeed, in the June 1994 parliamentary election, the Dutch extreme Right, misleadingly labeled Center Democrats, could more than double its electoral take to about 2.5 percent of the vote and five seats in parliament. In a similar vein, it is important to monitor the extent to which the strategic movements and the electoral payoffs of the Swedish parties—social democrats, bourgeois parties, and the potentially right-wing New Democracy—are consistent with the predictions of our model.

It is important to realize, however, that the future of the present generation of extreme-rightist parties in Western Europe depends not only on socioeconomic developments and political opportunity structures determined by the moves of their competitors, but also in part on their own strategic actions. There is little question that a lingering on of the structural difficulties of the European economy in the transition to a postindustrial economy, such as the persistence of high unemployment particularly among less educated young males, maintains a receptive rightist constituency. Moreover, the centripetal competitive dynamic among the conventional parties of the moderate Left and Right continues to encourage disappointed voters to experiment with new alternatives.

At the same time, however, new rightist parties encounter a considerable challenge to developing viable party organizations and routines of internal decision making. In many instances, these parties initially were one-man affairs and remained under the spell of a charismatic leader for some time, thus sticking to a system of governance that becomes increasingly unwieldy and inflexible as parties grow. At the grassroots level, new rightist parties are often characterized by unrestrained hand-to-hand combat among different cabals and sects vying for control of party locals and party funds. Only the smaller portion of these conflicts is fueled by policy disagreements, whereas pure personal ambition and rivalry is the driving force behind divisions in most instances. Given the lack of respect for democratic collective decision-making procedures that is characteristic of activists in such parties, it may be difficult for them to overcome such impediments to organizational consolidation. Opponents of the extreme Right may therefore hope that even if they cannot decisively defeat the new extreme Right from the outside forces within these parties will bring about their demise. Such parties may be unable to institutionalize party organization, to develop effective mechanisms of internal conflict resolution, and therefore ultimately to consolidate loyal electoral constituencies.

The volatility of the extreme Right brings us finally to the question of what can be learnt from our study for party theory in general and the dynamics of party systems in postindustrial democracies more specifically. The main message, of course, is that the trajectory of parties can be accounted for only if we carefully analyze conditions of social demand, political opportunity structure, and the elite supply of new alternatives that is affected by the intricacies of organizing a new party. In that regard, hypotheses about left-libertarian as well as right-authoritarian parties are too simplistic if they expect these parties to disappear because their major issues will be absorbed by their conventional competitors. These competitors, however, face their own electoral dilemmas and experience their own difficulties in holding on to voter coalitions, so that for one reason or another they may not be able to absorb the electorate of new challengers.

It would also be premature to interpret the rise of the New Right as yet another indicator of party dealignment (Dalton, Flanagan, and Beck 1984) or, to stick with more fashionable postmodern concepts, party "disarticulation" in the 1990s. There are definitive social coalitions behind parties, but social background has very little impact on the decision to vote once we control for political attitudes (on economic liberalism, politico-cultural libertarianism/ authoritarianism, ethnic parochialism). What this shows is not the disappearing significance of social structure for politics, but the mediation of *political deliberation* between social structure and electoral choice. Moreover, the changes of advanced capitalism call for greater sophistication in characterizing social market locations and lifestyles than is possible on the basis of most survey data. In other words, the new rightist parties provide evidence for new electoral alignments in advanced democracies, but the nature of these alignments varies across countries for reasons of political opportunity structure and elite appeal.

Appendix: Wording of Questions in the *World Values Survey*

In a number of instances the values on the variables have been recoded for the analysis performed in this book. This is reflected in the values provided below for each variable.

I. Economic Management

V 126 (business management)

There is a lot of discussion about how business and industry should be managed. Which of these four statements comes closest to your opinion? (One response)
  1 = The government should be the owner and appoint the managers.
  2 = The employees should own the business and should elect the managers.
  3 = The owners and the employees should participate in the selection of managers.
  4 = The owners should run their business or appoint the managers.

V 250 (income inequality)

How would you place your views on this scale?
  1 = incomes should be made more equal.
  . . .
  10 = There should be greater incentives for individual effort.

V 254 (competition)

How would you place your views on this scale?
  1 = Competition is good. It stimulates people to work hard and develop new ideas.
  . . .
  10 = Competition is harmful. It brings out the worst in people.

II. Ecology and Industry

V 13 (environmental taxes)

For each statement I read out, can you tell me whether you agree strongly, agree, disagree, or strongly disagree?
"I would agree to an increase in taxes if the extra money is used to prevent environmental pollution."
1 = strongly disagree; 4 = strongly agree

V 17 (urgency of ecology)

For each statement I read out, can you tell me whether you agree strongly, agree, disagree, or strongly disagree?
"Protecting the environment and fighting pollution is less urgent than often suggested.
4 = strongly disagree; 1 = strongly agree

V 291 (no nuclear plants)

There are a number of groups and movements looking for public support. For each of the following movements, which I read can you tell me whether you approve or disapprove of this movement?
antinuclear energy movement:
1 = strongly disapprove; 4 = strongly approve

III. Race and Nation

V 70 (objections to neighbors of different race)

On this list are various groups of people. Could you please sort out any that you would not like to have as neighbors?
people of a different race:
1 = not mentioned; 2 = mentioned

V 77 (immigrants/foreign workers)

On this list are various groups of people. Could you please sort out any that you would not like to have as neighbors?
immigrants/foreign workers:
1 = not mentioned; 2 = mentioned

V 130 (priority for own nationals in labor markets)

Do you agree or disagree with the following statements?
"When jobs are scarce, employers should give priority to [own nationality] over immigrants."
1 = disagree; 3 = agree;

V 322 (national pride)

How proud are you to be [own nationality]?
1 = not at all proud; 4 = very proud;

IV. Authority and Participation

V 268 (more respect for authority)

Here is a list of various changes in our way of life that might take place in the near future. Please tell me for each one, if it were to happen whether you think it would be a good thing, a bad thing, or don't you mind?
Greater respect for authority.
1 = bad; 3 = good;

V 273 (confidence in the army)

Please look at this card and tell me, for each item listed, how much confidence you have in them, is it a great deal, quite a lot, not very much or none at all?
b. the armed forces
1 = none at all; 4 = a great deal;

V 244 (lawful demonstrations)

Now I'd like you to look at this card. I'm going to read out some different forms of political action that people can take, and I'd like you to tell me, for each one, whether you have actually *done* any of these things, whether you might do any of them, or whether you would never, under any circumstances, do them.
c. attending lawful demonstrations
1 = would never do; 3 = have done

V 292 (disarmament movement)

There are a number of groups and movements looking for public support. For each of the following movements, which I read can you tell me whether you approve or disapprove of this movement?
c. disarmament movement:
1 = strongly disapprove; 4 = strongly approve

V. Women and Family

V 309 (abortion)

Please tell me for each of the following statements whether you think it can always be justified, never be justified, or something in between.
    n. abortion
    1 = never justified; 10 = always justified

V 221 (women as homemakers)

People talk about the changing roles of men and women today. For each of the following statements I read, can you tell me how much you agree with each. Please use the responses on this card.
    d. Being a housewife is just as fulfilling as working for pay.
    1 = strongly agree; 4 = strongly disagree.

V 128 (women's right to a job)

Do you agree or disagree with the following statements?
    "When jobs are scarce, men have more right to a job than women.
    3 = disagree; 1 = agree;

VI. General Ideological Dispositions

V 405 (materialism - post-materialism)

    3 = post-materialism (priority for free speech, citizens' participation)
    2 = mixed
    1 = materialism (priority for fighting rising prices, law and order)

V 248 (left-right self-placement)

    1 = left
    10 = right

V 368 (urban-rural residence)

    1 = community under 2,000
    8 = community over 500,000

V 147 (attendance in religious services)

    1 = more than once a week
    8 = never, practically never

Notes

Chapter 1

1. A similar explanation accounts for the rise of left-libertarian parties and the strategic interaction between them and their main competitors, moderate-leftist socialist and social democratic parties. See Kitschelt (1988) and (1994).

2. In a similar vein, it proved to be naive to expect the disappearance of left-libertarian parties as a result of better labor market conditions and political access for young academics. For this argument, see Alber (1985) and Bürklin (1987).

3. For example, in postcommunist Eastern Europe, proponents of market liberalism tend to be libertarians, whereas in Western Europe market liberalism goes together with more authoritarian inclinations. Cf. Kitschelt (1995).

4. This protection is not primarily due to tariffs and export subsidies but to the high transaction costs of international trade in certain industries that buffer the domestic market from foreign competition. For example, this applies to most personal services as well as to highly fragmented industries that engage in on-site customized production and services.

5. Actually, there is evidence that the share of classical industrial workers in internationally exposed sectors has been falling, as Gösta Esping-Andersen reminded the authors in a private communication. At the same time, however, many business services that used to be domestically sheltered are now in the internationally competitive sector.

6. See, for example, studies of the "new service class" by Brint (1984) on the United States and by Kriesi (1989) on the Netherlands. An interesting analysis is also provided by Bob Altemeyer (1988, 93), who shows that liberal arts college majors over the course of their undergraduate studies show a much greater drop in their right-wing authoritarianism index than other majors. Miller et al. (1985) demonstrate that among Polish and American workers job flexibility and complexity of work, which we can presume to be particularly high in personal services, decreases authoritarianism and increases what they call "ideational flexibility."

7. Such two-dimensional schemes are not new to social psychology, where they have been developed for a considerable time. For a critical review of the literature and a particularly sophisticated confirmation of the two-dimensional attitude structure that is consistent with the dimensions postulated here, see Fleishman (1988). An instructive analysis of economic left/right and politico-cultural authoritarianism/libertarianism scales can be found in Heath et al. (1994).

8. We are not referring to "consumption" in the sense of Dunleavy and Husbands

(1985), who distinguish between consumption based on private income or public services and benefits (pensioners, students, users of public transportation, welfare recipients, etc.). As critics have pointed out, Dunleavy and Husbands's distinction is derivative of class divisions and has relatively little independent power to discriminate among political opinions.

9. For this argument, see Bjorklund (1992) and more generally Betz (1994, 179).

10. Altemeyer's (1988, 92–95) experiments with University of Manitoba students show that over time students become more libertarian.

11. A recent investigation within the framework of the British Election Studies group also found that among social characteristics of respondents, authoritarianism, measured by a six-item scale, is rather strongly and negatively related to income and educational qualifications. Other predictors of authoritarianism are age and religious devotion. See Heath et al. (1994, 126).

12. It is misleading to treat Lipset and Rokkan (1967) as representatives of a purely sociological analysis of political parties because they emphasize the role of political elites and institutions in translating societal divisions into political cleavages. In similar veins, later treatments of party formation and success that emphasize political leadership include Dalton and Flanagan (1984), Przeworski and Sprague (1986), and Carmines and Stimson (1989).

13. For a sophisticated analysis of the relationship between sociological determinants of party positions and political issue leadership, seen Iversen (1994).

14. A refinement of this simple model, with hypotheses predicting variance across countries, can be found in Kitschelt (1994, chap. 4).

15. One may think of farmers or other rent-seeking economic status groups. Riker's (1986) voluntarist theory of "heresthetics" according to which parties that consistently lose on a given dominant issue dimension will "create" a new dimension, just as the Republicans in the middle of the nineteenth century "created" the political issue of slavery to combat Democratic hegemony, ignores the fact that there must be a *structural propensity of the electorate to treat an issue as salient.* Politicians cannot create political dimensions out of thin air. Studies estimating the dimensionality of European party appeals thus have failed to come up with complex ideological spaces and instead usually fall back on an economic left/right and a new politics dimension closely linked to my conception of libertarian versus authoritarian politics. See Budge et al. (1987).

16. It is, of course, true that conservative parties as well always appealed to more authoritarian issue positions. But for the sake of simplicity and analytical contrast between the periods I have ignored this fact in figure 1.1.

17. All these conjectures depend on certain further assumptions we cannot detail here. For example, voters are held to act sincerely rather than strategically.

18. For an analysis of the interaction between electoral competition and government formation, see Laver (1989).

19. Similar views of the "master case" of the New Right can be found in other investigations. Ignazi (1992, 18–19) writes on the "new liberalism":

> This new attitude to socio-economic policy comes together with major value changes, as a result of which authority, patriotism, the role of the family and traditional moral values have been partly reemphasized and partly redefined in

response to postmaterialist issues. . . . However, in our opinion, the dominant emphasis is not on freedom and individualism against the danger of a bureaucratic and collectivist society but rather on traditional and neo-conservative values.

Betz (1993, 413–14) comments on the contemporary Right:

> In short, they tend to combine a classic liberal position on the individual and the economy with the socio-political agenda of the extreme and intellectual new right, and they deliver this amalgam to those disenchanted with their individual life chances and the political system.

20. Betz (1993, 419) explains the neoliberal agenda: "Primarily, it is a political weapon against the established political institutions and their alleged monopolization of political power which hampers economic progress and suppresses true democracy. The opponent is the bureaucratic, centralized state which is living off the work of the productive forces of society."

21. The existence of a clientelist political economy may even have effects on the parties of the libertarian Left. Libertarians faced with the alternatives of clientelist state-run enterprises and private-market capitalism may often prefer the latter to the former. As a consequence, even among extreme libertarians, in such circumstances their overall desire for leftist prowelfare state policies may be dampened. As a consequence, left-libertarian parties in such systems will be more libertarian than leftist, if they listen to their potential voters.

22. On the role of discursive traditions as a constraint on parties' strategic choices, see Kitschelt (1994, chap. 6).

23. In the theoretical literature, salience and directional theories of voting and party competition would provide the best reconstruction of the extreme Right's capacity to mobilize voters, if they were single-issue mobilizations (cf. Budge and Farlie 1983; Rabinowitz and MacDonald 1989; MacDonald and Rabinowitz 1993). If we find that no single issue is decisive for the rise of the extreme Right, then we have also some indirect evidence that spatial theories may be more powerful in accounting for party competition than directional theories. We will not, however, focus on a direct test of competing models of party competition, as this would require data we do not have at our disposal (cf. Iversen 1994).

24. This ideological thrust already surfaces in the Futurists' Manifesto of 1909:

> 9. We want to glorify war—the only cure for the world—and militarism, patriotism, the destructive gesture of the anarchists, the beautiful ideas which kill, and contempt for women.
> 10. We want to demolish museums and libraries, fight morality, feminism and all opportunist and utilitarian cowardice. (Quoted in Sternhell 1976, 334)

25. In that sense, the European NRR is more in the tradition of American nativist and xenophobic movements in the nineteenth and twentieth centuries that have been described so well by Lipset and Raab (1978) than of the European fascist movements of the interwar period.

26. For studies of fascist party membership and electoral support, see especially Larsen, Hagtvet, and Myklebust (1980) and Mühlberger (1987).

27. This "layered" explanatory approach is explicitly or implicitly advocated by de Felice (1977, 11–12), Griffin (1991, 210–11), Hagtvet and Rokkan (1980, 146–47), Moore (1966, chap. 8), and Payne (1980, 204–5).

28. Arjomand (1988) and Brooker (1991) have recently brought this Durkheimian argument to bear on the comparative analysis of fascist movements.

29. The fascists' love of technology has been stressed by Sternhell (1976, 341). Because of its activist, creative character, Payne (1980, 11) sees fascism as a late product of the Enlightenment.

30. A similar approach has recently been proposed by Rogowski (1989), who argues that the exposure of factors of production to international competition in societies with more or less economic development determines cleavages. Scarce factors of production call for protectionism because they are expensive; abundant factors call for free trade. In times of expansion of the world economy, free traders are assertive, in times of a contraction, protectionists are assertive. Western European fascism is that particular configuration of forces in which abundant labor and capital struggle against scarce land in a time of contracting world markets (Rogowski 1989, 12, 69–70). This account however, is quite unconvincing. Rogowski needs not only to introduce the auxiliary hypothesis that fascism matters only where agriculture still captures a significant proportion of the employed population, but the hypothesis also ignores the fact that fascist movements started in the cities, organized large constituencies there, and cannot be reduced to an agrarian protest movement, as Rogowski suggests (78–80). Further, it is unclear in which sense capital in interwar Europe was ever abundant. Finally, as with other modernization theories, this approach completely ignores the role of political actors and institutions in the rise of fascist movements. As a consequence, Rogowski's study cannot account for the empirical variance in the strength of European fascist movements.

31. This is not to imply, however, that peasants were the driving force of fascism, but only that an intermediate level of modernization made a variety of socioeconomic groups available to fascist appeals.

32. This operationalization is not too far off Organiski's rule of thumb that fascism's window of opportunity exists where 40 to 55 percent of the population is in the nonmodern sector (Organski 1968, 25). If we add to the peasantry other nonmodern employment, particularly in crafts and services, the 25 to 50 percent range for agriculture in table 1.2 translates into a nonmodern sector roughly the same size as the one Organski suggests.

33. On Japan, see Beasley (1990, chap. 10), Griffin (1991, 154), Linz (1976, 103–4), and Payne (1980, 161–71). On Spain, compare Luebbert (1991, 276–77, 302), Payne (1980, chap. 6), and Solé-Tura (1968).

34. Arjomand (1988) interprets the Shiite movement in Iran in this context. In a similar vein, fundamentalist mass parties in Egypt or Algeria have striking resemblances to Western European fascist movements of the interwar era.

35. Our summary of similarities and differences to a large extent overlaps with Prowe's (1991) observations. It disagrees, however, with Griffin's (1991, 161–74) more traditional analysis of the European post-World War II extreme Right, which tends to equate it with fascism.

36. Klingemann's (1979) empirical analysis of left/right conceptualizations in

five democracies shows that Europeans have in general a much more articulate understanding of left and right than do American citizens.

37. In part, this may be due to the fact that Eatwell violates a simple rule of typological-classificatory work: create exhaustive, mutually complementary, but nonoverlapping categories based on clear dimensions along which alternatives can vary (Kaplan 1964).

38. Eatwell's (1992a) most recent effort to define fascism does not go beyond essentialist analysis toward pragmatic, constructivist, and explanatory concept formation. Eatwell distinguishes between *conceptual* approaches that define fascism in terms of ideology and practice, but provide no explanation, and *theoretical* approaches that employ diffuse definitions of fascism, but attempt to explain the occurrence of fascism. Rather than trying to marry a rigorous explanatory approach with a precise definition of the phenomenon to be explained, Eatwell opts for yet another purely conceptual elaboration of the notion of fascism.

Chapter 2

1. For a review of this literature, see Kitschelt (1989b), and for a systematic model of issue leadership, see Iversen (1994).

2. Taggart (1993, 14–16) extends this argument beyond these four countries to Australia, Canada, New Zealand, and the United States, arguing that social services in these countries are not sufficiently decommodified for right-extremists to emerge as a powerful political force.

3. A similar argument has been made by Hainsworth (1992a) and Taggart (1993). Hainsworth writes

More favorable terrain for the extreme right has often been situations where the ideological distance between the major parties was reduced, thereby creating a vacuum on the right conducive to extreme right success, e.g. "the opening to the Left" in Italy in the 1960s . . . , the West German Grand Coalition of 1966–69 and the French "power sharing" (*cohabitation*) phase of the 1980s. (11)

Taggart (1993, 21) calls the conditions conducive to the extreme Right, "party system cartellization," but he gives no precise measure for it:

We can define the "cartelization" of the party system as the securing of power for a small number of parties through overt or covert cooperation and premised upon a foreshortening of the "policy distance" between the affected parties.

4. This incorporation can be done by simply adding the parties' values on the libertarian/authoritarian issues to the economic scores or by calculating the Euclidean distance of parties in a two-dimensional space created by an economic left/right and a political libertarian/authoritarian dimension. For the latter procedure, see Kitschelt (1994, chap. 4).

5. This did not prevent the extreme Right from performing better in local elections, particularly in large cities with many immigrants, although the ecological associa-

tion between percentage of foreigners living in a precinct and support of the extreme Right is far from straightforward (cf. Husbands 1992a). A further impediment for the new extreme Right in the Netherlands may be the existence of fundamentalist-Protestant parties that appeal to authoritarian and capitalist values.

6. New Democracy's devastating defeat in the September 1994 election, when the party declined from 6.7 to 1.2 percent, follows after a polarized campaign in which the Conservatives, advocating a free market liberal policy in the most pronounced fashion, won votes at the expense of the other bourgeois parties. The latter also lost to the social democrats who did not take a particularly radical socialist or libertarian stance, but clearly distinguished themselves from the conservative camp. Furthermore, New Democracy may have been hurt by its indecisiveness and inability to project a clear image during its three-year stint in the Swedish parliament. It appears to be a party that has not yet found the winning formula of right-wing electoral success, akin to the Danish and Norwegian Progress parties in the late 1970s and early 1980s.

7. For a detailed analysis of Belgian voter flows from 1987 to 1991, see Billiet, Swyngedouw, and Carton (1993).

8. On the situation in Flanders and Wallonia in the late 1980s, at the time when the "Vlaams Blok" took off and the National Front in Wallonia was founded after the model of the French party with the same name, see Fitzmaurice (1993) and Husbands (1992a).

9. In addition, however, it must be appreciated that Belgium has significant attributes of a patronage-driven political economy, an arrangement that fuels a market-liberal backlash.

10. Ignazi (1992, 20) claims that new rightist parties rise when the established moderate conservatives engage in a strategy of polarization against the Left, but then fall short of satisfying the expectations they have created among certain voter groups. Even Ignazi's own comparison, however, shows that this argument commands little plausibility. Some countries with strong right-extremist parties never experienced a polarization strategy (Austria, Switzerland); in others, the presumed polarization has not induced strong rightist parties (Germany, the Netherlands); in still others, the extent of presumed polarization, at least in the time periods when the extreme Right grew the most, is questionable (Denmark, Norway).

11. Even in the Swiss case, the National Action declined after an initial spurt in the early 1970s and the field of rightist parties, now supplemented by the Automobilists' Party, grew again only after the libertarian Left and Center Left (Greens) had made significant electoral inroads in the 1980s.

12. For an analysis of this logic for four countries with or without new leftist parties, see Rohrschneider (1993).

13. See also Grofman and Lijphart (1986) and Taagepera and Shugart (1989).

14. For a similar result with different data, see Fuchs, Gerhards, and Roller (1993).

15. The weakness of the correlation between patterns of immigration and rightist politics can also be reconstructed from time series data on foreign residents collected by Fassmann and Münz (1993, 460). Neither cross-national nor intertemporal differences in the proportion of the immigrant population appear to be directly linked to right-wing mobilization.

16. A multivariate cross-national analysis of right-wing electoral support by Betz and Swank (1991) also found that, once holding constant for affluence, service sector employment, change in youth unemployment and taxation (size of the welfare state?), a measure of political asylum-seeking had no independent effect on the strength of the extreme Right. Betz and Swank operationalize the effects of postindustrial social organization on the extreme Right, but they have no indicators of political convergence between conventional left and right parties as a predictor of extremist performance.

17. Nevertheless, in the late 1970s, one survey of party activists managed to include a fair number of extreme rightist-parties. Results will be reported below.

18. For a critique of the party manifestos data set in light of odd results it yields for the strategic interaction between socialist and nonsocialist parties, see Kitschelt (1994, chap. 4, footnote 35, and addendum).

19. Moreover, the German NPD is marginally more nationalist on Third World aid than the other parties of the extreme Right.

20. This explains the weakness of the extreme Right in postauthoritarian Spain (see Ellwood 1991, 1992, and 1993 and Gilmour 1992). Also, in Portugal (1992, 242) and in Greece (Dimitras 1992), extreme-rightist groups are still chasing the mirages of the past, without developing a nontraditional appeal to new voter groups. Of course, in all three countries, the comparatively less advanced industrial structures and welfare states are probably most important in accounting for the absence of a powerful new extreme Right.

21. One exception is that German Republicans are more inclined to participate in unconventional action than the average voter (row 8).

22. This comparability, of course, remains handicapped by the general problems of cross-national survey research. Identical absolute values of voters in two countries on the same measure may mean different things, and different values may mean identical things.

23. It is irrelevant for our purposes whether this "Keynesian" perception of government macroeconomic intervention is borne out by the facts or whether anti-inflationary policies in fact generate jobs. All that counts is that the public *perception* of the consequences of macroeconomic policy is still consistent with the Keynesian framework.

24. Factor analysis is one of several ways to test the dimensionality of beliefs and traits. Other possible avenues include cluster analysis and multidimensional scaling techniques. Less appropriate, in our view, is discriminant analysis (cf. Knutsen 1989) because this technique seeks to find a latent variable that is the most efficient predictor of prespecified group memberships, for example, party preferences. The objective of discriminant analysis is thus not to represent the clustering of opinion variables as such but to find a clustering that serves a particular purpose, the prediction of party alignments. Even if voter opinions cluster along the left-libertarian versus right-authoritarian dimension and even if parties are aligned along that dimension, discriminant analyses may not reveal this fact because the most efficient predictor of voting for a particular party may be a single element of the dominant issue dimension. This element is most likely left/right self-placements. Conversely, discriminant analyses may find no left-libertarian versus right-authoritarian discriminant function because *no single item on that dimension* is a good predictor of group membership (i.e., adherence to a group of party sympathizers).

25. Factor loadings are nothing other than zero-order correlations between the observed variables and the unobserved factor construct.

26. Thus, arguments that ecology represents a separate competitive dimension of postindustrial politics, independent of other economic and political dimensions, are not borne out. Supporters of economic leftist and political libertarian parties tend to also be more environmentalist. The only exception to this rule in our data is Italy, where the parties' mean positions on the market/redistribution factor and the authority/liberty factor are in fact highly correlated. However, neither of these two factors has much linkage to the ecology dimension. In the Italian case, however, the ecology dimension is not only quite weak but also less clear than in other countries even in the varimax rotation because it includes significant factor scores on issue items relating to race and ethnicity and authority.

Chapter 3

1. Hainsworth (1992b, 33) characterizes these continuities in the following way: "Without doubt, the FN of Le Pen was to revive much of the substance and spirit of Poujadism: anti-intellectualism, anti-technocracy, demagogy, xenophobia, defence of 'the small man,' authoritarianism, opposition to 'the political class,' anti-statism, anti-bureaucracy, defence of the family, pro-French colonialism, strong law and order, *Jeanne d'Arc* reverence, rejection of perceived decadence, Vichyite nostalgia, populism, leadership cult, plebiscitarianism and so on."

2. A more comprehensive description of the changing ideological appeal of the National Front can be found in Calderon (1985), especially chapter 3; Dumont, Lorien, and Criton (1985), especially chapters 3 through 5; Plenel and Rollat (1984), especially chapter 1; and Roussel (1985). An overview of the ideological themes of Le Pen's rhetoric in the late 1980s can be found in Taguieff (1989a; 1989b).

3. The pro-Catholic view sets the Front National apart from the atheist, modernist extremism represented by G.R.E.C.E.. See Roussel (1985, 77–78).

4. All accounts of the rise of the French National Front focus on the disorganization and quarrels of the French conventional Right. See Hainsworth (1992b, 41–2) and Safran (1993, 35–9).

5. For a good analysis of this logic, see Blattert and Ohlemacher (1991).

6. For a description of the events in Dreux, see Bréchon and Mitra (1992, 71–79) and Perrineau (1989, 40–43).

7. The limited power of electoral laws is also evidenced by the failure of the French ecologists to benefit from the electoral system change in 1986. For a further discussion of why electoral systems are of limited use for explaining party system change, see chapter 7 on the extreme Right in Britain.

8. Perrineau (1989, 44) reports a correlation of 0.89.

9. Factors 4 and 5 are not depicted in table 3.1 because they barely exceed an eigenvalue of 1. All other factors are below that threshold. A varimax solution essentially confirms the picture reported by the principal components analysis. It only slightly sharpens the independence of the libertarian/authoritarian and the economic capitalism/socialism factors.

10. The uniqueness of the French ecologists, compared to most European Green parties, is discussed in Kitschelt (1990). In fact, the weakness of French ecologists in elections may be due to the fact that they have positioned themselves in mildly pro-capitalist positions and have not managed to wean a "leftist" electorate off socialists and communists and establish themselves as a "second Left" (Prendiville 1989).

11. For an in-depth analysis of openended interviews supporting this interpretation, see Blondel and Lacroix (1989).

12. The comparison between moderate and extreme Right in France shows once again that the ideological disparity between a party's activists and its voters is a contingent phenomenon. As I have argued elsewhere, radical parties that build on a highly mobilized issue cleavage are most likely to experience a disparity of political preferences between their voters and their activists. See Kitschelt (1989b).

Chapter 4

1. Arter (1992, 365–6) reports that the platform of New Democracy is a "fun-filled" and "weird" program, but that it has also a darker racist side that came across in some of the bills submitted by the party's parliamentary group to the Swedish parliament. Nevertheless, it is likely that the antiestablishment stance of the party in 1991 was more important than any particular policy positions.

2. The collapse of New Democracy in the 1994 Swedish parliamentary elections suggests that the party has not yet found a clear-cut ideological profile. Even so, in other countries parties also underwent extensive learning processes before they found a winning electoral formula.

3. We confine ourselves here to the "Western" Scandinavian countries and ignore Finland with its unique historical right-wing tradition, which originated in the war between "reds" and "whites" in the aftermath of the Russian October Revolution and World War II. It is quite possible that residues of the prominence of the "old" left/right conflict, pitting the former communists against the conservatives, have weakened the emergence of a "new" right-authoritarian versus left-libertarian division, despite the existence of a moderately successful Green Party. As discussed in chapter 2, the one possible candidate for the NRR party family, Vennamo's Rural Party, does not quite fully capture the spirit of the European New Right with its agrarian populism.

4. On the formation of social cleavages in the Scandinavian party systems, see especially Elder, Thomas, and Arter (1988), chapter 1.

5. In this respect, the Finnish Rural Party may be the exception that proves the rule.

6. See Sjölin's (1993) instructive analysis of coalition-building in Swedish parliament.

7. In this paragraph, we are drawing on the instructive article by Harmel and Svasand (1993), who link studies in the sociology of (business) organizations about the life cycle of entrepreneurial task structures to the challenges faced by new political parties in different stages of their development.

8. Most of the social democrats' decline, however, is accounted for by the rise of the left-libertarian Socialist People's Party from 5.5 to 10.1 percent.

294   Notes to Pages 136–72

9. Torben Iversen has drawn our attention to a study by Nielsen (1979) that illustrates this character of the Danish Progress Party's electorate with ample survey evidence.

10. This finding is also backed by Knutsen's (1989, 503) discriminant analysis of Norwegian voters and parties. Progress voters place themselves on the right of a materialist economic left/right dimension, whereas socialists are on the left. On the next two discriminant vectors, however, socialist and Progress voters are located quite closely to each other, indicating the affinity of working-class constituencies to the far Right. These dimensions are religion and postmaterialism, where both party formations are located at the secular and the materialist pole of the continuum.

11. A varimax rotated factor analysis links ethnocentrism/racism primarily to authoritarian positions. Varimax rotation yields three factors with just about equal eigenvalues in both Denmark and Norway: an economic distributive, a libertarian/authoritarian, and an ecology factor. However, when we examine the party supporters' mean positions on the three factors, they are highly correlated in all larger parties. Economically left parties are libertarian and proecologist. Economically right parties, including the Progress parties, are also more authoritarian and antiecologist. The only outliers to this pattern are the Radical Liberals (RV) in Denmark and the Liberals in Norway, both of which combine more procapitalist with libertarian and proecology positions. As in France, there is no separate factor for race/ethnocentrism.

12. Keep in mind that the standard deviations of the positions of each party's supporters on the three factors are between 0.7 and 1.0. The variance of means on factors two and three is therefore for all practical purposes too small to be interpretable.

13. One "anomaly," of course, is that the Danish SF also draws on a rather large working-class constituency. This result would be fully consistent with our theoretical framework, provided we found that the SF primarily attracts older workers who were affiliated with the party in the 1960s and 1970s before its left-libertarian turn. The Progress Party, in contrast, should attract younger workers. Due to the comparatively small sample size (N = 1000), our surveys do not allow us to test such specific hypotheses.

14. For this contention, refer back to table 2.10, line 15, where we compared the endorsement of the statement that being a housewife is a fulfilling role for the Progress Party as well as the next most conservative party in Denmark and Norway.

Chapter 5

1. If we follow Sidoti (1993, 155–56) and separate the early antisystem movement and the "Social Republic" of 1943, we have *three* strands of fascism in Italy.

2. For a discussion of these rightist strands, see Sidoti (1992, 159–67).

3. Knight (1992, 290) describes the change at the helm of the party: "Haider's coup against Steger in 1986 can be seen as the uprising of the 'national' provinces against a liberal leadership which, as in the early 1950s, had lost touch with the rank and file."

4. A good review of the MSI's strategic movements in the post-World War II period is provided by Ignazi (1993).

5. Ruzza and Schmidtke (1993, 4) single out two causes of the Northern League's success: "First, the media discourse has increasingly stressed themes which are objectively consonant with those espoused by the Lega. This is above all the indignation about the *partitocrazia,* namely, corrupt and inefficient domination by the cartel of political parties. Second, through an effective use of political symbolism and a channeling of anti-southern feelings, the Lega has successfully mobilized social groups previously alienated from the political sphere."

6. In both countries, varimax-rotated factor analyses yield almost identical substantive factors as the principal component analysis.

7. Compared to the population average of 31.6 percent, 35.6 percent of Northern League supporters would like to see some or even substantially more emphasis on individual responsibility, but 53.8 percent of MSI voters endorse that view. While 47.9 percent of the population support the statement that competition is fairly or very good, 52.5 percent of MSI adherents endorse the same position. In the Northern League, approval of this statement is only 46.8 percent.

8. In the overall population, 13.4 percent mention neighbors of another race as something they would not want to see. Among NL supporters, this position is 18.9 percent; among MSI supporters 18.1 percent. These figures should be compared to the French and Scandinavian New Right parties where the salience of race among rightist voters and the discrepancy between their views and the population average is much stronger: French National Front, 35.5 percent concerned about the neighbor's race (population: 9.4 percent); Danish Progress Party, 32.7 percent (population: 7.4 percent); and Norwegian Progress Party, 21.9 percent (population: 12.6 percent).

9. The difference between population and new right support for this statement is +17.5 percent for the Italian Northern League (MSI only +4.8 percent), +23.8 percent in Norway, +27.2 percent in Germany, + 33.8 percent in France, and +38.4 percent in Denmark.

10. Only the supporters of the most cosmopolitan party, the Greens, are more united on this issue (standard deviation: 0.55).

11. The greatest increases in voters from 1990 until 1994 accrued to the FPÖ among workers (+33 percent, 1990–94), the unemployed (+31 percent, 1990–94), pensioners (+30 percent, 1990–94), and the self-employed (+30 percent, 1990–94). At the same time, the share of FPÖ voters with an advanced secondary education degree permitting them to enter university stagnated from 1986 to 1994 at around 25 percent of that group (cf. Plasser and Ulram 1994, 35).

Chapter 6

1. However, the German Right Party/German Conservative Party (DReP/DKP), with five seats in the 1949 *Bundestag,* and the Bavarian Union for Reconstruction (WAV), with twelve seats in 1949, came close to being Nazi successor organizations.

2. From 1953 on, the election law required an average of 5 percent support on the entire territory of the Federal Republic for a party to be granted parliamentary representation. In 1949, the 5 percent threshold applied in individual states so that smaller groups at the national level still could get representation if they overcame the state-level 5 percent threshold.

3. For a while, areas with high levels of immigration of eastern refugees, such as Schleswig-Holstein and Lower Saxony, were candidates for a new right-wing entrenchment. But the new arrivals were rapidly integrated into the booming industrial economy of western Germany.

4. This can be illustrated by the performance of the Danish, French, and German extreme Right in the 1994 European elections. Although secondary elections such as the European elections should benefit minor parties, the German Republicans lost almost half of their voters compared to the 1989 election, whereas their counterparts in Denmark and France held about steady.

5. We have analyzed the 1990 *World Values Survey* for East Germany but do not report these data here because they do not evidence significant support for a far rightist party. What is clear, however, is that East German public opinion is shaped by somewhat different forces than West German public opinion. This result is confirmed by Falter's (1994) analysis of numerous surveys comparing East and West Germans. In eastern Germany, support for right-wing parties remains lower and relies on different sociodemographic bases than in western Germany.

6. Since there is a voluminous literature on the German post-World War II extreme Right, we will confine ourselves to basic information. As introductions to this literature, consult Childs (1991), Jaschke (1990, chap. 1 and 2) and Stöss (1989, chap. 2).

7. For a detailed description of the NPD's rise in English, see Nagle (1970).

8. For a schematic comparison of the NPD's electorate with that of other far rightist parties preceding the wave of the 1980s, see Husbands (1981, 16).

9. For a comparison of the German and French intellectual Right, see Greß, Jaschke, and Schönekäs (1990).

10. More generally, Falter (1994, 116–19) found that a sense of being economically vulnerable and disadvantaged is a rather good predictor of support for the extreme Right in the former West Germany.

11. For an analysis of national socialist language in the rhetoric of the Republicans, see Jaschke (1990, 100) and Lepszy (1989, 5). A further examination of the Republicans' program is in Leggewie (1990, chap. 4).

12. On the programs of DVP and NPD, see Dudek and Jaschke (1984, 210–11 and 300–301).

13. Membership data are reported in Jaschke (1990, 185) and Childs (1991, 80).

14. For that reason, in 1993 and 1994, the DVU sought electoral alliances with the Republicans.

15. Falter (1994, 87–90) shows that close links to labor unions reduce the propensity to vote for right-extremist parties such as the Republicans.

16. Karapin (1994) argues that the wave of extreme-rightist violence in Germany in 1992–94 can be explained in part by the initially indifferent behavior of the German law enforcement system. Violence began to decline when the public (and international) outcry led to more systematic prosecution of right-wing criminals and tougher prison sentences.

17. A varimax-rotated factor analysis (three factor solution) yields a similar space for the parties. The SPD and the Greens are consistently on the side of libertarian politics (factor I), ecology and multiculturalism (factor II), and social redistribution

(factor III). The CDU is consistently on the opposite side, that is, more authoritarian, antiecological, and procapitalist. The FDP and the Republicans defy this pattern. The Republicans are the most antiecological and racist party, but they are only slightly more procapitalist and authoritarian than the average voter. The FDP is more libertarian, but more antiecological and procapitalist.

18. In addition, in the 1990 *World Values Survey,* only 9.7 percent of Republican supporters scored as postmaterialists, compared to 28.2 percent in the sample overall and 68.3 percent among the supporters of the Green party.

19. Again, the issue items included in the *World Values Survey* and analyzed in chapter 2 demonstrate this item by item.

20. Again, selective findings of the *World Values Study* for the West German electorate are instructive: 50.4 percent of Republicans, but only 31.4 percent of the overall sample, believe than men have a greater right to jobs than women; 23.5 percent of Republicans, but 41.4 percent of the population approve of working mothers; 63.8 percent of Republicans, but only 54.4 percent of the population, believe that the role of being a housewife is fulfilling for women. In all but the last item, while Christian Democrats and Republicans have almost identical scores, the Republican voters are culturally most conservative.

21. In the past, other factors may have contributed to an underrepresentation of women that can be found also in national socialism and its successor parties in the 1950s and 1960s. The major factor may have been women's greater affiliation with churches and their proximity to religious parties.

22. In addition to the 1990 *World Values Study,* we are aware of one study that modifies this claim. Falter (1994, 65, 75) found in a variety of surveys that small business is also overrepresented in the Republicans.

23. A similar pattern can be gleaned from the January 1990 state elections in the Saarland (Sandschneider 1990) and the May 1990 state elections in Northrhine-Westphalia (Feist and Hoffmann 1990).

24. All data are from Roth (1993).

25. Falter (1994) demonstrates the same point with a wealth of data about social mobility, perceived risk to one's job, and perceived social decline.

26. See also chapter 3 where it was noted that the French National Front performs well not necessarily in areas with a high ratio of immigrants but in their immediate vicinity.

27. This analysis is based on the voter support of the political parties in all electoral precincts, as reported in the *Frankfurter Allgemeine Zeitung* of January 27, 1989, and April 7, 1992.

28. For a confirmation of this pattern, see Falter (1994, 44–60).

29. For a similar analysis and conclusion, see Klär et al. (1989, 24).

30. This is also the finding of Pappi's (1990, 42) more sophisticated analysis of spatial representations of German politics at the turn of the 1990s.

31. The presence of a rather large authoritarian constituency in the former East Germany has been empirically established by Minkenberg (1992b) and Stöss (1991).

32. Falter (1994, 127–35) shows that there is a rather coherent worldview that characterizes a substantial share of the hard-core Republican voters in early 1994 but

also the party's more numerous potential electorate in 1993. This right-wing ideological worldview includes anti-Semitism and xenophobia, nationalism and collectivism, and a defense of dictatorship and the national socialist regime.

33. Minkenberg identifies this position with the writings of Leggewie (1990) and Stöss (1990).

34. Minkenberg sees this position represented by Funke (1989) and Kühnl (1989).

Chapter 7

1. These estimates are reported in Carsten (1967, 222).

2. I have made a parallel argument against accounting for the weakness of British ecologists by the disincentives to party entry through the electoral law (see Kitschelt 1988).

3. In addition, Studlar and McAllister (1992) find that the Conservatives won the elections despite the government's right-wing populist positions.

4. A good reconstruction of this process can be found in Seyd (1987) and Seyd and Whiteley (1992). The British Labour Party's development is placed in a comparative framework in Kitschelt (1994, chap. 4 and 5).

5. An overview of the otherwise irrelevant splinter groups and splintering processes in the British extreme Right can be found in Gable (1991).

6. In 1970, 5.6 percent of the electorate supported the NF in its best constituency; in Feburary 1974, the top constituency was at 7.8 percent and in October 1974 at 9.4 percent.

7. The antilibertarian thrust of the National Front is also detailed in Fielding (1981, chap. 5).

8. On the organization, see Fielding (1981, chapter 4).

9. For data suggesting this interpretation, see Studlar and MacAllister (1992, especially 158–60) and Kitschelt (1994, chap. 4).

10. In an earlier study, Husbands (1983) found that only "strong" NF supporters are primarily working class, whereas the wider spectrum of "weak" or potential NF supporters does not overrepresent the working class. Of course, actual strong support, revealed through voting behavior, is much more significant for an analysis of the National Front's appeal than vaguer issue sympathies (cf. Eatwell 1992b, 183).

Chapter 8

1. Of course, this roundabout statement does not dwell on the reasons for the rise of the welfare state. As is well known, the welfare state is not entirely a product of industrial development. Its comprehensiveness and structure is determined rather profoundly by the relative strength and interaction among politically organized socioeconomic groups, although one can subscribe to slightly different accounts of how group interests and group interactions brought about different welfare state profiles (cf. Baldwin 1990; Esping-Andersen 1990).

2. Referring back to figure 1.1, "welfare chauvinist" positions are expressed by constituencies closer to position W than position R or P, the winning formulas for the NRR. While rightist parties with position W cannot win a significant share of the vote,

they incorporate constituencies close to that position, even if they announce positions *R* or *P*. In that sense, they must take "welfare chauvinist" demands into account.

3. In addition, Fuchs, Gerhards, and Roller (1993) found a positive bivariate relationship between the population share of immigrants from non-European Union countries and the percentage of respondents in each EU country who were willing to state that "too many" foreign nationals are residing in his or her country. This study, however, does not control other variables, such as income, economic performance, and occupational structure.

4. Empirical studies show that the welfare state is much more likely to re-distribute resources to the worse-off than systems of progressive income taxation. See Andrain (1980) and Heclo, Heidenheimer, and Teich-Adams (1990).

5. Moreover, in a charity-based system, the undesirable effects may extend to the donors because providing charity creates smugness, self-deception, and a false sense of nobility and generosity (cf. Munzer 1990, 111–12).

6. For a sophisticated analysis of this pattern, see Putnam (1993).

7. Kudrle and Marmor (1981) provides an instructive comparison between the United States and Canada. In addition to ethnicity, the structure of the American political system impeded the growth of the welfare state. See also, from different perspectives, Orloff and Skocpol (1984) and Piven and Cloward (1977).

8. See Haller (1993) and Przeworski and Sprague (1986) on ethnic cleavages as an obstacle to class formation.

9. For insightful typologies of goods between pure private and pure public goods, see Hirsch (1976), Green (1992, 133) and Warren (1992).

10. For a comparison of the explanatory power of these theories for ethnic mobili-zation in contemporary Western Europe, see Ragin (1987, 134–49). Ragin's analysis, however, suffers from the counterintuitive coding of the cases. In Ragin's scores, the North Friesians in Germany have about the same level of intermediate ethnic mobiliza-tion as the Flemings in Belgium! See Ragin (1987, 141).

11. Ernest Gellner (1983, 126) writes in this regard: "[I]t is the media themselves, the pervasiveness and importance of abstract, centralized, standardized, one to many communication, which itself automatically engenders the core idea of nationalism, quite irrespective of what in particular is being put into the specific messages transmitted. The most important and persistent message is generated by the medium itself, by the role which such media have acquired in modern life. That core message is that the language and style of the transmissions is important, that only he who can understand them, or can acquire such comprehension, is included in a moral and economic community, and that he who does not and cannot, is excluded."

12. This is a somewhat modified rendering of what I take to be the core hypoth-esis of Horowitz's (1985) important book.

13. One may interpret Smith's (1991) account of nationalism and ethnic identities as an effort to synthesize different strands of theoretical propositions on this phenomenon.

14. Ragin's (1987, 144–49) work represents a more rigorous effort to combine at least a particular version of modernization/communications theory of ethnicity with a theory of competitive mobilization.

15. This argument could be restated also in terms of "embeddedness" in the

communitarian tradition of political theory. Following Aristotle, Van Gunsteren (1988) sees the conception of citizenship inherently related to a historical community that is embodied in institutionalized practices that articulate a culture, a set of socioeconomic relations, and political and legal rules. The limits of communication within and through this set of institutions also delineates citizenship.

16. Carens (1992), for example, recommends considering the alternatives that potential immigrants face in realizing their life plans.

17. Fuchs, Gerhards, and Roller (1993) show that mass publics in the European Union draw boundaries not so much among nation-states who are members of the union but between members of the Occidental civilization at large and those who come from cultural backgrounds beyond that realm.

18. Goodin (1988a, 282 n. 50) rightly points out that Miller does not so much provide a justification for nationality than a statement of fact of why nationality at this time is still politically significant.

19. A study of the Institute of German Business in Cologne reckons that until 2020 Germany needs 12.5 million immigrants and the European Union 28 million immigrants in order to make up for the decline in the workforce as the result of demographic developments such as the declining birth rate and rising life expectancy (*This Week in Germany,* December 17, 1993, 5).

Chapter 9

1. Analysts of Swiss politics have observed a recentering of party competition in the direction of a left-libertarian versus right-authoritarian configuration. See, for example, Church (1989), Finger and Hug (1992), and Finger and Sciarini (1991). The Swiss extreme Right actually goes back to the early 1970s when the National Action/ Mouvement républicaine pursued an authoritarian agenda without a clear economic left/ right profile (cf. Inglehart and Sidjanski 1975). In Switzerland, as well as in the Scandinavian countries, the rightist party experienced decline in the late 1970s but began to rise again in the 1980s (Klöti and Risi 1988, 785–86) when the questions of race and immigration gained renewed salience (cf. Schmitter-Heisler 1988). Since that time, a new rightist party that more vigorously combines authoritarianism with free market liberalism, the Swiss Automobilists' Party, has surpassed the National Action in political support and influence (cf. Longchamp 1988).

2. The remaining two fifths were previous "Vlaams Blok" voters and new voters or previous nonvoters.

Bibliography

Adorno, Theodor W., Else Fraenkel-Brunswick, David J. Levinson, and R. N. Sanford. 1950. *The Authoritarian Personality.* New York: Harper and Row.

Aimer, Peter. 1988. "The Rise of Neo-Liberalism and Right Wing Protest Parties in Scandinavia and New Zealand. The Progress Party and the New Zealand Party," *Political Science* 40 (2): 1–15.

Alber, Jens. 1985. "Modernisierung neuer Spannungslinien und die politischen Chancen der Grünen," *Politische Vierteljahresschrift,* 26(2): 211–26.

Altemeyer, Bob. 1988. *Enemies of Freedom. Understanding Right-Wing Authoritarianism.* San Francisco: Jossey-Bass.

Andersen, Jorgen Goul. 1990. "'Environmentalism,' 'New Politics' and Industrialism: Some Theoretical Perspectives," *Scandinavian Political Studies,* 13(2): 101–18.

———. 1992. "Denmark: The Progress Party. Populist Neo-Liberalism and Welfare State Chauvinism," in *The Extreme Right in Europe and the United States,* ed. Paul Hainsworth, 193–205. New York: St. Martin's Press.

Andersen, Jorgen Goul, and Tor Björklund. 1990. "Structural Change and New Cleavages: The Progress Parties in Denmark and Norway," *Acta Sociologica* 33(3): 195–218.

Anderson, Benedict. 1991. *Imagined Communities.* Revised and extended ed. London: Verso.

Andrain, Charles. 1980. *Politics and Economic Policy in Western Democracies.* North Scituate, Mass.: Duxbury Press.

Andreski, Stanislav L. 1968. "Some Sociological Considerations on Fascism and Class," in *The Nature of Fascism,* ed. S. J. Woolf, 97–102. London: Weidenfeld and Nicolson.

Arjomand, Said. 1988. *The Turban for the Crown.* New York: Oxford University Press.

Arter, David. 1992. "Black Faces in the Blond Crowd: Populist Racism in Scandinavia," *Parliamentary Affairs* 45(3): 357–72.

Backes, Uwe. 1990. "Extremismus und Populismus von Rechts. Ein Vergleich auf europäischer Ebene," *Aus Politik und Zeitgeschichte* 40 (November 9–16) B46-47: 3–14.

Bailer-Galanda, Brigitte. 1990. *Die Neue Rechte.* Zeitdokumente 52. Wien: Verlag Zukunft.

Baldwin, Peter. 1990. *The Politics of Social Solidarity. Class Bases of the European Welfare State.* New York: Cambridge University Press.

Barry, Brian. 1992. "The Quest for Consistency: A Sceptical View," in *Free Movement. Ethnical Issues in the Transnational Migration of People and of Money,* ed. Brian

Barry and Robert E. Goodin, 279–87. University Park, Penn.: Pennsylvania State University.

Bartolini, Stefano, and Peter Mair. 1990. *Identity, Competition, and Electoral Availability: The Stability of European Electorates 1885–1985*. Cambridge: Cambridge University Press.

Bauer, Petra and Oskar Niedermayer. 1990. "Extrem rechtes Potential in den Ländern der Europäischen Gemeinschaft," *Aus Politik und Zeitgeschichte* 40 (November 9–16) B46-47: 15–26.

Beasley, W. G. 1990. *The Rise of Modern Japan*. New York: St. Martin's Press.

Bell, David, and Byron Criddle. 1989. "Review Article: The Decline of the French Communist Party," *British Journal of Political Science* 19 (4): 515–36.

Berger, Suzanne. 1981. "Regime and Interest Representation. The French Traditional Middle Classes," in *Organizing Interests in Western Europe*, ed. Suzanne Berger, 83–101. Cambridge: Cambridge University Press.

Betz, Hans-Georg. 1990a. "Political Conflict in the Postmodern Age: Radical Right-Wing Parties in Europe," *Current Politics and Economics of Europe* 1(1): 67–83.

———. 1990b. "Politics of Resentment. Right-Wing Radicalism in West Germany," *Comparative Politics,* 23 (1): 45–60.

———. 1991. "Radikal rechtspopulistische Parteien in Westeuropa," *Aus Politik und Zeitgeschichte,* 41 (October 25) 44: 3–14.

———. 1993. "The New Politics of Resentment. Radical Right-Wing Populist Parties in Western Europe," *Comparative Politics,* 25 (4): 413–27.

———. 1994. *Radical Right-Wing Populism in Western Europe*. New York: St. Martin's Press.

Betz, Hans-Georg, and Duane Swank. 1991. "Electoral Support for Right-Wing Populist Parties. A Comparative Analysis of 16 Western European Democracies in the 1980s." Paper prepared for the annual meeting of the Midwest Political Science Association, Chicago, April 18–20.

Beyme, Klaus v. 1988. "Right-Wing Extremism in Post-War Europe," *West European Politics,* 11 (1): 1–18.

Bille, Lars. 1989. "Denmark: The Oscillating Party System," *West European Politics,* 12, (4): 41–58.

Billiet, Jaak, Marc Swyngedouw, and Ann Carton. 1993. "Protest, ongenoegen en onverschilligheid op 24 november . . . en nadien," *Res Publica* 35(2): 221–35.

Birnbaum, Guy, and Bastien François. 1989. "Unité et diversité des dirigeants frontistes," in *Le Front National à Decouvert,* ed. Nonna Mayer and Pascal Perrineau, 83–106. Paris: Presses de la Fondation Nationale des Sciences Politiques.

Björklund, Tor. 1988. "The 1987 Norwegian Local Elections: A Protest Election with a Swing to the Right," *Scandinavian Political Studies* 11(3): 211–34.

———. 1992. "Unemployment and Party Choice in Norway," *Scandinavian Political Studies* 15(4): 329–52.

Blattert, Barbara, and Thomas Ohlemacher. 1991. "Zum Verhältnis von Republikanern und anti-faschistischen Gruppen in West-Berlin: Dynamik, wechselseitige Wahrnehmungen und Medienresonanz," *Forschungsjournal NSB* 4(2): 63–74.

Blondel, Jacqueline, and Bernard Lacroix. 1989. "Pourquoi votent-ils Front National?"

in *Le Front National à Decouvert,* ed. Nonna Mayer and Pascal Perrineau, 150–70. Paris: Presses de la Fondation Nationale des Sciences Politiques.

Borre, Ole. 1974. "Denmark's Protest Election of December 1973," *Scandinavian Political Studies* 9: 197–203.

———. 1988. "The Danish General Election of 1987," *Electoral Studies* 7 (1): 75–78.

———. 1991. "The Danish General Election of 1990," *Electoral Studies* 10 (2): 133–38.

Boy, Daniel, and Nonna Mayer. 1990. "L'électeur français en question," in *L'électeur français en question,* ed. Daniel Boy and Nonna Mayer, 197–217. Paris: Presses de la Fondation Nationale des Sciences Politiques.

Boy, Daniel, and Elisabeth Dupoirier. 1990. "L'électeur est-il stratège?" in *L'électeur français en question,* ed. Daniel Boy and Nonna Mayer, 175–96. Paris: Presses de la Fondation Nationale des Sciences Politiques.

Bréchon, Pierre, and Subrata Kumar Mitra. 1992. "The National Front in France. The Emergence of an Extreme Right Protest Movement," *Comparative Politics* 25 (1): 63–82.

Brint, Steven. 1984. "'New Class' and Cumulative Trend Explanations of the Liberal Political Attitudes of Professionals," *American Journal of Sociology* 90(1): 30–71.

Brooker, Paul. 1991. *The Faces of Fraternalism. Nazi Germany, Fascist Italy, and Imperial Japan.* Oxford: Clarendon Press.

Budge, Ian, and Dennis Farlie. 1983. *Explaining and Predicting Elections. Issue Effects and Party Strategies in Twenty-Three Democracies.* London: Allen and Unwin.

Budge, Ian, David Robertson, and Derek Hearl, eds. 1987. *Ideology, Strategy, and Party Change.* Cambridge: Cambridge University Press.

Bürklin, Wilhelm P. 1987. "Governing left parties frustrating the radical non-established Left: The rise and inevitable decline of the Greens," *European Sociological Review* 3(2): 109–26.

Caciagli, Mario. 1988. "The Movimento Sociale Italiano—Destra Nazionale and Neo-Fascism in Italy," *West European Politics* 11 (2): 19–33.

Calderon, Desiré. 1985. *La Droite Française. Formation et Projet.* Paris: Messidor/ Editions Sociales.

Calhoun, Craig. 1992. "Why Nationalism? Sovereignty, Self-Determination and Identity in a World System of States." Manuscript, Department of Sociology, University of North Carolina, Chapel Hill.

Camus, Jean-Yves. 1989. "Origine et Formation du Front Nationale," in *Le Front National à Decouvert,* ed. Nonna Mayer and Pascal Perrineau, 17–36. Paris: Presses de la Fondation Nationale des Sciences Politiques.

Carens, Joseph H. 1988. "Immigration and the Welfare State," in *Democracy and the Welfare State,* ed. Amy Gutman, 207–30. Princeton: Princeton University Press.

———. 1989. "'Membership' and Morality. Admission to Citizenship in Liberal Democratic States," in *Immigration and the Politics of Citizenship in Europe and North America,* ed. William Rogers Brubaker, 31–49. Lanham, Md.: University Press of America.

———. 1992. "Migration and Morality: A Liberal Egalitarian Perspective," in *Free*

Movement. Ethnical Issues in the Transnational Migration of People and of Money, ed. Brian Barry and Robert E. Goodin, 25–47. University Park, Penn.: Pennsylvania State University.

Carmines, Edward G., and James A. Stimson. 1989. *Issue Evolution. Race and the Transformation of American Politics.* Princeton: Princeton University Press.

Carsten, Francis. 1967. *The Rise of Fascism.* Berkeley: University of California Press.

Castles, Francis G. 1978. *The Social Democratic Image of Society. A Study of the Achievements and Origins of Scandinavian Social Democracy in Comparative Perspective.* London: Routledge and Kegan Paul.

Charlot, Monica. 1986. "L'Emergence du Front National," *Revue Française de Science Politique* 36 (1): 30–45.

Chiarini, Roberto. 1991a. "The 'Movemento Sociale Italiano:' A Historical Profile," in *Neo-Fascism in Europe,* ed. Luciano Cheles, Ronnie Ferguson, and Michalina Vaughan, 19–42. New York: Longman.

———. 1991b. "The Italian Right: The Paradox of an Illegitimate Identity." Paper presented at the Conference on the Radical Right in Western Europe, Center for Western European Studies, University of Minnesota, Minneapolis, November 7–9.

Chiche, Jean. 1990. "L'univers ideologique et politique des français. Une exploration par l'analyse factorielle," in *L'électeur français en question,* ed. Daniel Boy and Nonna Mayer, 219–28. Paris: Presses de la Fondation Nationale des Sciences Politiques.

Childs, David. 1991. "The Far Right in Germany Since 1945," in *Neo-Fascism in Europe,* ed. Luciano Cheles, Ronnie Ferguson, and Michelina Vaughan, 66–85. New York: Longman.

Church, Clive H. 1989. "Behind the Consociational Screen. Politics in Contemporary Switzerland," *West European Politics* 12(2): 35–54.

Cole, Alistair. 1988. "La France unié? Francois Mitterrand," in *The French Presidential Elections of 1988. Ideology and Leadership in Contemporary France,* ed. John Gaffney, 81–100. Aldershot, U.K.: Gower.

Conovan, Margret. 1981. *Populism.* New York: Harcourt, Brace, Jovanovich.

Conover, Pamela, and Stanley Feldman. 1981. "The Origins and Meaning of Liberal/ Conservative Self-Identifications," *American Journal of Political Science* 25 (4): 617–46.

Cotarelo, Ramon Garcia, and Lourdes Lopez Nieto. 1988. "Spanish Conservatism, 1976–1987," *West European Politics* 11 (2): 80–95.

Cox, Gary W. "Centripetal and Centrifugal Incentives in Electoral Systems," *American Journal of Political Science* 34 (4): 903–35.

Crewe, Ivor, and Donald D. Searing. 1988. "Ideological Change in the British Conservative Party," *American Political Science Review* 82 (2): 361–84.

Dahl, Robert. *Democracy and Its Critics.* New Haven: Yale University Press.

Dalton, Russell, J. et al., eds. 1984. *Electoral Change in Advanced Industrial Democracies.* Princeton.: Princeton University Press.

Dalton, Russell J., Scott Flanagan, and Paul Allen Beck. 1984. "Political Forces and Partisan Change," in *Electoral Change in Advanced Industrial Democracies,* ed. Dalton et al., 451–76. Princeton: Princeton University Press.

Damgaard, Erik. 1974. "Stability and Change in the Danish Party System over Half a Century," *Scandinavian Political Studies* 9: 103–25.

De Felice, Renzo. 1977. *Interpretations of Fascism.* Cambridge, Mass.: Cambridge University Press.

Della Porta, Donatella. 1993. "Bewegungen und Protest in Italien. Mögliche Szenarien für die neunziger Jahre," *Forschungsjournal NSB* No. 1: 59–68.

Deutsch, Karl W. 1953. *Nationalism and Social Communication.* Cambridge, Mass.: MIT Press.

Dimitras, Panayote Elias. 1992. "Greece: The Virtual Absence of an Extreme Right," in *The Extreme Right in Europe and the United States,* ed. Paul Hainsworth, 246–68. New York: St. Martin's Press.

Dudek, Peter, and Hans-Gerd Jaschke. 1984. *Entstehung und Entwicklung des Rechtsextremismus in der Bundesrepublik. Zur Tradition einer besonderen politischen Kultur.* Vol. 1. Opladen, Germany: Westdeutscher Verlag.

Dumont, Serge, Joseph Lorien, and Karl Criton. 1985. *Le Système Le Pen.* Anvers, France: Les Editions EPO.

Durham, Martin. 1991. "Women and the National Front," in *Neo-Facism in Europe,* ed. Luciano Cheles, Ronnie Ferguson, and Mihalina Vaughan, 264–83. New York: Longman.

Duverger, Maurice. 1954. *Political Parties.* London: Methuen.

———. 1986. "Duverger's Law: Forty Years Later," in *Electoral Laws and Their Political Consequences,* ed. Bernard Grofman and Arend Lijphart, 69–84. New York: Agathon Press.

Dyson, Kenneth. 1977. *Party, State, and Bureaucracy in Western Germany.* Beverly Hills, Calif.: Sage.

Eatwell, Roger. 1982. "Poujadism and Neo-Poujadism: From Revolt to Reconciliation," in *Social Movements and Protest in France,* ed. Philip G. Cerny, 70–93. New York: St. Martin's Press.

———. 1989. "Approaches to the Right," in *The Nature of the Right. European and American Politics and Political Thought Since 1789,* ed. Roger Eatwell and Noël O'Sullivan, 3–77. London: Pinter.

———. 1991. "Neo-Fascism and the Right: Conceptual Conundrums?" Paper presented at the Conference on the Radical Right in Western Europe, Center for Western European Studies, University of Minnesota, Minneapolis, November 7–9.

———. 1992a. "Toward a New Model of Generic Fascism," *Journal of Theoretical Politics* 4(2): 161–94.

———. 1992b. "Why Has the Extreme Right Failed in Britain?" in *The Extreme Right in Europe and the United States,* ed. Paul Hainsworth, 175–92. New York: St. Martin's Press.

Eatwell, Roger and Noël O'Sullivan, eds. 1989. *The Nature of the Right. European and American Politics and Political Thought Since 1789.* London: Pinter.

Elder, Neil, Alastair H. Thomas, and David Arter. 1988. *The Consensual Democracies?* 2d ed. Oxford: Blackwell.

Ellwood, Sheelagh M. 1991. "The Extreme Right in Spain. A Dying Species?" in *Neo-Fascism in Europe,* ed. Luciano Cheles, Ronnie Ferguson, and Michalina Vaughan, 147–66. New York: Longman.

————. 1992. "The Extreme Right in Spain. Past, Present and Future." Paper presented at the Conference on the Radical Right in Western Europe, Center for Western European Studies Center, University of Minnesota, Minneapolis, November 7–9.

————. 1993. "The Extreme Right in Post-Francoist Spain," *Parliamentary Affairs* 45(3): 373–85.

Elwert, Georg. 1989. "Nationalismus und Ethnizität. Über die Bildung von Wir-Gruppen," *Kölner Zeitschrift für Soziologie und Sozialpsychologie* 41(3): 440–64.

Esping-Andersen, Gösta. 1990. *The Three Worlds of Welfare Capitalism.* Princeton: Princeton University Press.

Esser, Hartmut. 1988. "Ethnische Differenzierung und moderne Gesellschaft," *Zeitschrift für Soziologie* 17(4): 235–48.

Evans, Geoffrey. 1993. "Is Gender on the 'New Agenda'? A Comparative Analysis of the Politicization of Inequality Between Men and Women," *European Journal of Political Research* 24(2): 135–58.

Falter, Jürgen W., in cooperation with Markus Klein. 1994. *Wer wählt rechts? Die Wähler und Anhänger rechtsextremistischer Parteien im vereinigten Deutschland.* München: Beck.

Falter, Jürgen, and Siegfried Schumann. 1988. "Affinity Towards Right-Wing Extremism in Western Europe," *West European Politics* 11 (2): 96–110.

Farneti, Paolo. 1985. *The Italian Party System (1945–1980).* New York: St. Martin's Press.

Fassmann, Heinz, and Rainer Münz. 1992. "International Migration in Western Europe," *Population and Development Review* 18 (3): 457–80.

Feist, Ulrike, and Hans-Jörg Hoffmann. 1990. "Die Landtagswahl in Nordrhein Westfalen vom 13. Mai 1990," *Zeitschrift für Parlamentsfragen* 21 (3): 449–61.

Ferraresi, Franco. 1988. "The Radical Right in Postwar Italy," *Politics and Society* 16(1): 71–119.

Fielding, Nigel. 1981. *The National Front.* London: Routledge and Kegan Paul.

Finger, Matthias, and Simon Hug. 1992. "Green Politics in Switzerland," *European Journal of Political Research* 21 (3): 289–306.

Finger, Matthias, and Pascal Sciarini. 1991. "Integrating 'New Politics' into 'Old Politics.' The Swiss Party Elite." *West European Politics* 14 (1): 98–112.

Fitzmaurice, John. 1993. "The Extreme Right in Belgium: Recent Developments," *Parliamentary Affairs* 45(3): 300–308.

Flanagan, Scott. 1987. "Value Change in Industrial Society," *American Political Science Review* 81(4): 1303–19.

Fleishman, John A. 1988. "Attitude Organization in the General Public. Evidence for a Bidimensional Structure," *Social Forces* 67(1): 159–84.

Ford, Glyn, ed. 1992. *Fascist Europe. The Rise of Racism and Xenophobia.* London: Pluto Press.

Forgacs, David. 1986. "Introduction. Why Rethink Italian Fascism?" in *Rethinking Italian Fascism. Capitalism, Populism, and Culture,* ed. David Forgacs, 1–10. London: Lawrence and Wishart.

Fuchs, Dieter, Jürgen Gerhards, and Edeltraut Roller. 1993. "Wir und die Anderen. Ethnozentrismus in den zwölf Ländern der europäischen Gemeinschaft," *Kölner Zeitschrift für Soziologie und Sozialpsychologie* 45(2): 238–53.

Funke, Hajo. 1989. *Republikaner. Rassismus, Judenfeindschaft, nationaler Größen-wahn*. Berlin: Aktion Sühnezeichen.

Fysh, Peter, and Jim Wolfreys. 1992. "Le Pen, the National Front and the Extreme Right in France," *Parliamentary Affairs* 45(3): 309–25.

Gable, Gerry. 1991. "The Far Right in Contemporary Britain," in *Neo-Fascism in Europe*, ed. Luciano Cheles, Ronnie Ferguson, and Michalina Vaughan, 245–63. New York: Longman.

Gallagher, Tom. 1992. "Portugal: The Marginalization of the Extreme Right," in *The Extreme Right in Europe and the United States*, ed. Paul Hainsworth, 232–45. New York: St. Martin's Press.

———. 1993. "Regional Nationalism and Party System Change: Italy's Northern League," *West European Politics* 16(4): 616–21.

Gellner, Ernest. 1983. *Nations and Nationalism*. Oxford: Blackwell.

Gilmour, John. 1992. "The Extreme Right in Spain: Blas Pinar and the Spirit of the Nationalist Uprising," in *The Extreme Right in Europe and the United States*, ed. Paul Hainsworth, 206–31. New York: St. Martin's Press.

Gluchowski, Peter. 1987. "Lebensstile und Wandel der Wählerschaft in der Bundes-republik Deutschland," *Aus Politik und Zeitgeschichte* 37 (March 21) 12: 18–32.

Goodin, Robert E. 1988a. *Reasons for Welfare. The Political Theory of the Welfare State*. Princeton: Princeton University Press.

———. 1988b. "What Is So Special About Our Fellow Countrymen?" *Ethics* 98 (4): 663–86.

Gordon, Bertram M. 1991. "Theory and Practice of the French Extreme Right, 1945–1991." Paper presented at the Conference on the Radical Right in Western Europe, Center for Western European Studies, University of Minnesota, Minneapolis, November 7–9.

Green, Donald Philip. 1992. "The Price Elasticity of Mass Preferences," *American Political Science Review* 86 (1): 30–51.

Greß, Franz, Hans-Gerd Jaschke, and Klaus Schönekäs. 1990. *Neue Rechte und Rechtsextremismus in Europa*. Opladen, Germany: Westdeutscher Verlag.

Grieco, Joseph. 1989. "Realist Theory and the Problem of International Cooperation. Analysis with an Amended Prisoner's Dilemma Model," *Journal of Politics* 50 (3): 600–624.

Griffin, Roger. 1991. *The Nature of Fascism*. New York: St. Martin's Press.

Grofman, Bernard, and Arend Lijphart, eds, 1986. *Electoral Laws and Their Political Consequences*. New York: Agathon Press.

Grüner, Erich, and Kenneth J. Pitterle. 1982. "Switzerland's Political Parties," in *Switzerland at the Polls. The National Elections of 1979*, ed. Howard R. Penniman, 30–59. Washington, D.C.: American Enterprise Institute.

Grunberg, Gérard, and Etienne Schweisguth. 1990. "Liberalisme culturel et liberalisme économique," in *L'électeur français en question*, ed. Daniel Boy and Nonna Mayer, 45–70. Paris: Presses de la Fondation Nationale des Sciences Politiques.

Gyomarch, Alain, and Howard Machin. 1989. "François Mitterrand and the French Presidential and Parliamentary Elections of 1988. Mr. Norris Changes Trains?" *West European Politics* 12 (3): 196–210.

Habermas, Jürgen. 1982. *Theorie des kommunikativen Handelns*. Frankfurt am Main: Suhrkamp.

————. 1992. *Faktizität und Geltung*. Frankfurt am Main: Suhrkamp.

Haerpfner, Christian. 1987. "Lineare Modellierung von Wähler-Partei-Beziehungen in Österreich," *Österreichische Zeitschrift für Politikwissenschaft* 16(3): 259–75.

Hagtvet, Bernt, and Stein Rokkan. 1980. "The Conditions of Fascist Victory: Toward a Geoeconomic-Geopolitical Model for the Explanation of Violent Breakdowns of Competitive Mass Politics," in *Who were the Fascists?*, ed. Stein Ugelvik Larsen, Bernt Hagvet, and Jan Petter Myklebust, 131–52. Bergen: Universitetsforlaget.

Hainsworth, Paul. 1982. "Anti-Semitism and Neo-Fascism on the Contemporary Right," in *Social Movements and Social Protest in France*, ed. Philip G. Cerny, 146–71. New York: St. Martin's Press.

————. 1992a. "Introduction. The Cutting Edge: The Extreme Right in Post-War Western Europe and the United States," in *The Extreme Right in Europe and the United States*, ed. Paul Hainsworth, 1–28. New York: St. Martin's Press.

————. 1992b. "The Extreme Right in Post-War France: The Emergence and Success of the National Front," in *The Extreme Right in Europe and the United States*, ed. Paul Hainsworth, 29–60. New York: St. Martin's Press.

Haller, Max. 1993. "Klasse und Nation. Konkurrierende und komplementäre Grundlagen kollektiver Identität und kollektiven handelns," *Soziale Welt* 44(1): 30–51.

Hamilton, Richard F. 1972. *Who Voted for Hitler?* Princeton: Princeton University Press.

Hammar, Tomas. 1991. "'Cradle of Freedom on Earth.' Refugee Immigration and Ethnic Pluralism," *West European Politics* 14 (3): 183–96.

Hardin, Russell. 1982. *Collective Action*. Baltimore: Johns Hopkins University Press.

Harmel, Robert, and Rachel Gibson. 1991. "Right-Libertarian Parties and the 'New Values.'" Prepared for delivery at the annual meeting of the American Political Science Association. Washington, D.C. August 28–September 1.

Harmel, Robert, and Lars Svasand. 1989. From Protest to Party. Progress on the Right. Prepared for delivery at the annual meeting of the American Political Science Association. Atlanta August 31–September 3.

————. 1993. "Party Leadership and Party Institutionalization: Three Phases of Development," *West European Politics* 16(1): 67–88.

Harris, Geoffrey. 1990. *The Dark Side of Europe. The Extreme Right Today.* Savage, Md.: Barnes and Noble.

Hauss, Charles, and David Rayside. 1978. "The Development of New Parties in Western Democracies Since 1945," in *Political Parties: Development and Decay*, ed. Louis Maisel and James Cooper, 31–57. Beverly Hills, Calif.: Sage.

Hayek, Friedrich A. 1979. *The Political Order of a Free People. Law, Legislation, and Liberty.* Vol. 3. Chicago: University of Chicago Press.

Heath, Anthony, Geoffrey Evans, and Jean Martin. 1994. "The Measurement of Core Beliefs and Values: The Development of Balanced Socialist/Laissez Faire and Libertarian/Authoritarian Scales," *British Journal of Political Science* 24(1): 115–32.

Heclo, Arnold Heidenheimer, and Carolyn Teich Adams. 1990. *Comparative Public Policy.* 3d ed. New York: St. Martin's Press.

Heinelt, Hubert. 1983. "Immigration and the Welfare State in Germany," *Germany Politics* 2, (1): 78–96.

Hellemans, Staf. 1990. *Strijd om de moderniteit. Sociale bewegingen en verzuiling in Europa sinds 1800.* Leuven: Universitaire Pers Leuven.

Hennig, Eike, with Manfred Kieserling and Rudolf Kirchner. 1991. *Die Republikaner im Schatten Deutschlands. Zur Organisation der mentalen Provinz.* Frankfurt am Main: Suhrkamp.

Herz, Thomas A. 1990. "Die Dienstklasse. Eine empirische Analyse ihrer demographischen, kulturellen und politischen Identität," *Soziale Welt* 41 (special issue): 231–52.

Hibbs, Douglas J., and Henrik J. Madsen. 1980. "Public Reactions to the Growth of Taxation and Government Expenditure," *World Politics* 33 (3): 413–35.

Hirsch, Fred. 1976. *The Limits of Growth.* Cambridge: Harvard University Press.

Hoel, Marit, and Oddbjörn Knutsen. 1989. "Social Class, Gender, and Sector Employment as Political Cleavages in Scandinavia," *Acta Sociologica* 32(2): 181–201.

Hofmann-Göttig, Joachim. 1990. "Die Neue Rechte: Die Männerparteien," *Aus Politik und Zeitgeschichte* 39 (November 6): 21–31.

Holmstedt, Margareta, and Tove-Lise Schou. 1987. "Sweden and Denmark 1945–1982: Election Programmes in the Scandinavian Setting," in *Ideology, Strategy, and Party Change,* ed. Ian Budge, David Robertson, and Derek Hearl, 177–206. Cambridge, U.K.: Cambridge University Press.

Horowitz, Donald. 1985. *Ethnic Groups in Conflict.* Berkeley: University of California Press.

Huber, John D. 1989. "Values and Partisanship in Left-Right Orientations: Measuring Ideology," *European Journal of Political Research* 17(5): 599–621.

Husbands, Christopher T. 1981. "Contemporary Right Wing Extremism in Western European Democracies. A Review Article," *European Journal of Political Research* 9 (1): 75–99.

———. 1983. *Racial Exclusion and the City. The Urban Support of the National Front.* London: George Allen and Unwin.

———. 1988a. "Extreme Right-Wing Politics in Great Britain. The Recent Marginalization of the National Front," *West European Politics* 11 (2): 65–79.

———. 1988b. "The Dynamics of Racial Exclusion and Expulsion: Racist Politics in Western Europe," *European Journal of Political Research* 16 (6): 701–20.

———. 1991. "Militant Neo-Nazism in the Federal Republic of Germany in the 1980s," in *Neo-Fascism in Europe,* ed. Luciano Cheles, Ronnie Ferguson, and Michalina Vaughan, 86–119. New York: Longman.

———. 1992a. "The Netherlands: Irritants on the Body Politic," in *The Extreme Right in Europe and the United States,* ed. Paul Hainsworth, 95–126. New York: St. Martin's Press.

———. 1992b. "Belgium: Flemish Legions on the March," in *The Extreme Right in Europe and the United States,* ed. Paul Hainsworth, 126–50. New York: St. Martin's Press.

———. 1992c. "The Other Face of 1992: The Extreme-Right Explosion in Western Europe," *Parliamentary Affairs* 45(3): 267–84.

Ieraci, Guiseppe. 1992. "Centre Parties and Anti-System Oppositions in Polarized Systems," *West European Politics* 15 (2): 17–34.

Ignazi, Piero. 1989. "Un Nouvel Acteur Politique," in *Le Front National à Decouvert*, ed. Nonna Mayer and Pascal Perrineau, 63–80. Paris: Presses de la Fondation Nationale des Sciences Politiques.

———. 1992. "The Silent Counter-Revolution. Hypotheses on the Emergence of Extreme Right-Wing Parties in Europe," *European Journal of Political Research* 22 (1): 3–34.

———. 1993. "The Changing Profile of the Italian Social Movement," in *Encounters with the Contemporary Radical Right*, ed. Peter H. Merkl and Leonard Weisberg, 75–92. Boulder, Colo.: Westview.

Ignazi, Piero, and Colette Ysmal. 1992. "New and Old Extreme Right Parties. The French Front National and the Italian Movimento Sociale," *European Journal of Political Research* 22 (1): 101–21.

Inglehart, Ronald. 1977. *The Silent Revolution. Changing Values and Political Styles among Western Publics*. Princeton: Princeton University Press.

———. 1990. *Culture Shift*. Princeton: Princeton University Press.

Inglehart, Ronald, and Dusan Sidjanski. 1975. "Electeurs et Dimension Gauche-Droite," in *Les Suisses et la Politque. Enquete sur les attitudes d'electeurs suisse*, ed. Dusan Sidjanski, Charles Roig, Henry Kerr, and Ronald Inglehart, 83–124. Berne: Lang.

Iversen, Torben. 1994. "Political Leadership and Representation in West European Democracies. A Test of Three Models of Voting," *American Journal of Political Science* 38(1): 45–74.

Janda, Kenneth, and Desmond S. King. 1985. "Formalizing and Testing Duverger's Theories on Political Parties," *Comparative Political Studies* 18 (2): 139–69.

Jaschke, Hans-Gerd. 1990. "Frankreich," in *Neue Rechte und Rechtsextremismus in Europa*, ed. Franz Greß, Hans-Gerd Jaschke, and Klaus Schönekäs, 17–103. Opladen, Germany: Westdeutscher Verlag.

———. 1990. *Die 'Republikaner.' Profil einer Rechtsaußen Partei*. Bonn: Dietz Verlag.

Jelinek, Yeshayahu. 1980. "Clergy and Fascism: The Hlinka Party in Slovakia and the Croatian Ustasha Movement," in *Who were the Fascists?*, ed. Stein Ugelvik Larsen, Bernt Hagvet, and Jan Petter Myklebust, 367–78. Bergen: Universitetsforlaget.

Kaplan, Abraham. 1964. *The Conduct of Inquiry. Methodology for Behavioral Science*. Scranton, Penn.: Chandler.

Karapin, Roger. 1994. "Political Opportunities for Right-Wing Violence in Reunified Germany." Center for International Affairs, Harvard University, March.

Katzenstein, Peter. 1985. *Small States in World Markets*. Ithaca: Cornell University Press.

———. 1987. *Policy and Politics in West Germany: Politics in a Semi-Sovereign State*. Philadelphia: Temple University Press.

Katznelson, Ira, and Aristide Zolberg, eds. 1986. *Working Class Formation*. Princeton: Princeton University Press.

Kern, Horst, and Michael Schumann. 1984. *Das Ende der Arbeitsteilung*. München: Beck.

Kieserling, Manfred. 1991. "Zur Psychologie der Republikaner," in *Die Republikaner im Schatten Deutschlands. Zur Organisation der mentalen Provinz,* Eike Hennig, with Manfred Kieserling and Rudolf Kirchner, 24–56. Frankfurt am Main: Suhrkamp.

Kirfel, Martina, and Walter Oswalt, eds. 1989. *Die Rückkehr der Führer. Modernisierter Rechtsradikalismus in Westeuropa.* Wien: Europa Verlag.

Kirkpatrick, Jeanne. 1976. *The New Presidential Elite. Men and Women in National Politics.* New York: Russell Sage Foundation.

Kitschelt, Herbert. 1988. "Left-Libertarian Parties. Explaining Innovation in Competitive Party Systems," *World Politics* 40 (2): 194–234.

———. 1989a. *The Logics of Party Formation: Structure and Strategy of Belgian and West German Ecology Parties.* Ithaca, N.Y.: Cornell University Press.

———. 1989b. "The Internal Politics of Parties. The Law of Curvilinear Disparity Revisited," *Political Studies* 37(3): 400–421.

———. 1990. "La gauche libertaire et les écologistes français," *Revue Française de Science Politique* 40 (3): 339–65.

———. 1991. "The 1990 German Federal Election and National Unification: A Watershed in German Electoral History?" *West European Politics* 14 (4): 121–48.

———. 1992. "The Formation of Party Systems in East Central Europe," *Politics and Society* 20(1): 7–50.

———. 1993. "Class Structure and Social Democratic Party Strategy," *British Journal of Political Science* 23 (2): 299–337.

———. 1994. *The Transformation of European Social Democracy.* New York: Cambridge University Press.

———. 1995. "A Silent Revolution in Europe? Political Preference Formation and Social Movements in Eastern and Western Europe," in *Governing the New Europe,* ed. Jack Hayward, 123–65. Cambridge, UK.: Polity Press.

Kivinen, Markku. 1989. "The New Middle Classes and the Labour Process," *Acta Sociologica* 32(1): 53–73.

Klär, Karl-Heinz, Malte Ristau, Bernd Schoppe, and Martin Stadelmaier. 1989. *Die Wähler der extremen Rechten.* 3 Vols. Bonn: Vorwärts Verlag.

Klingemann, Hans-Dieter. 1979. "Ideological Conceptualization and Political Action," in *Political Action,* ed. Samuel Barnes and Max Kaase, 279–305. Beverly Hills, Calif.: Sage.

Klöti, Ulrich, and Franz-Xavier Risi. 1988. "Neueste Entwicklungen im Parteiensystem der Schweiz," in *Das österreichische Parteiensystem,* ed. Anton Pelinka and Fritz Plasser, 717–37. Wien: Boehlau.

Knight, Robert. 1992. "Haider, the Freedom Party and the Extreme Right in Austria," *Parliamentary Affairs* 45(3): 285–99.

Knutsen, Oddbjorn. 1989. "Cleavage Dimensions in Ten West European Countries. A Comparative Empirical Analysis," *Comparative Political Studies* 21 (4): 495–534.

Kogan, N. 1968. "Fascism as a Political System" in *The Nature of Fascism,* ed. S. J. Woolf, 11–18. London: Weidenfeld and Nicolson.

Koopmans, Ruud, and Jan Willem Duyvendak. 1991. "Gegen die Herausforderer. Neue Soziale Bewegungen in der Bundesrepublik, den Niederlanden und Frankreich," *Forschungsjournal NSBs* 4(2): 17–30.

Kriesi, Hanspeter. 1989. "New Social Movements and the New Class in the Nether-
  lands," *American Journal of Sociology* 94(5): 1078–116.
Kudrle, Robert T., and Theodore R. Marmor. 1981. "The Development of Welfare
  States in North America." *The Development of Welfare States in Europe and
  America,* ed. Peter Flora and Arnold Heidenheimer, pp. 81–121. New Brunswick:
  Transaction Books.
Kühnl, Reinhard. 1989. "Der (aufhaltsame) Aufstieg rechtsextremer Parteien," in *Dem
  Haß keine Chance,* ed. Matthias von Hellfeld, 24–44. Köln: Pahl-Rugenstein.
Lagrange, Hugues, and Pascal Perrineau. 1989. "Le syndrome lepéniste," in *Le Front
  National à Decouvert,* ed. Nonna Mayer and Pascal Perrineau, 228–46. Paris:
  Presses de la Fondation Nationale des Sciences Politiques.
Lane, Jan-Erik, Ruomo Martikainen, Palle Svensson, Gunnar Vogt, and Henry Valen.
  1993. "Scandinavian Exceptionalism Reconsidered," *Journal of Theoretical Poli-
  tics* 5(2): 195–229.
Larsen, Stein Ugelvik, Bernt Hagtvet, and Jan Petter Myklebust (eds.) *Who were the
  Fascists?* Oslo: Universitetsforlaget.
Laver, Michael. 1989. "Party Competition and Party System Change. The Interaction of
  Coalition Bargaining and Electoral Competition," *Journal of Theoretical Politics*
  1(3): 301–24.
Laver, Michael, and W. Ben Hunt. 1992. *Policy and Party Competition.* London: Rout-
  ledge and Kegan Paul.
Layton-Henry, Zig. 1986. "Race and the Thatcher Government," in *Race, Government
  and Politics in Britain,* Zig Layton-Henry and Paul B. Rich, 73–99. London:
  MacMillan.
Le Gall, Gérard. 1991. "L'effet immigration," in *L'état de l'opinion 1991,* ed. Olivier
  Duhamel and Jerome Jaffre, 119–36. Paris: Seuil.
Leggewie, Claus. 1987. "Die Zwerge am rechten Rand. Zu den Chancen kleiner neuer
  Rechtsparteien in der Bundesrepublik Deutschland," *Politische Viertel-
  jahresschriften,* 28 (4): 361–83.
———. 1990. *Die Republikaner. Ein Phantom nimmt Gestalt an.* Revised ed. Berlin:
  Rotbuch Verlag.
Lepszy, Norbert. 1989. "Die Republikaner. Ideologie—Programm—Organisation,"
  Aus Politik und Zeitgeschichte 39 (November 6), B41–42: 3–9.
Lewis-Beck, Michael S., and Glenn E. Mitchell II. 1993. "French Electoral Theory: The
  National Front Test," *Electoral Studies* 12(2): 112–27.
Lijphart, Arend. 1977. *Democracy in Plural Societies.* New Haven: Yale University
  Press.
Linz, Juan. 1976. "Some Notes Toward a Comparative Study of Fascism in Sociological
  Historical Perspective," in *Fascism. A Reader's Guide,* ed. Walter Laqueur, 3–121.
  Berkeley: University of California Press.
———. 1990. "The Perils of Presidentialism," *Journal of Democracy* 1(1): 51–70.
Lipset, Seymour Martin. 1961. *Political Man.* 2d ed., 1981. Baltimore: Johns Hopkins
  University Press.
Lipset, Seymour Martin, and Earl Raab. 1978. *The Politics of Unreason. Right-Wing
  Extremism in America, 1790–1977.* 2d ed. Chicago: University of Chicago Press.

Lipset, Seymour Martin, and Stein Rokkan. 1967. "Cleavage Structures, Party Systems, and Voter Alignments: An Introduction," in *Party Systems and Voter Alignments*, ed. Lipset and Rokkan, 1–64. New York: Free Press.

Lo, Clarence H. 1982. "Countermovements and Conservative Movements in the Contemporary United States," *Annual Review of Sociology* 8: 107–34.

Longchamp, Claude. 1988. "'Linke und Grüne and die Wand nageln und mit dem Flammenwerfer drüber.' Die Autopartei unter der sozialwissenschaftlichen Lupe." Paper presented at the meeting on "Rechtspopulismus in Europa." Wien, December 5.

Luebbert, Gregory. 1991. *Liberalism, Fascism, and Social Democracy*. New York: Oxford University Press.

MacDonald, Stuart Elaine, and George Rabinowitz. 1993. "Direction and Uncertainty in a Model of Issue Voting," *Journal of Theoretical Politics* 5(1): 61–87.

Malzahn, Claus Christian. 1989. "Der Aufstieg der Republikaner," in *Die Rückkehr der Führer. Modernisierter Rechtsradikalismus in Westeuropa*, ed. Martina Kirfel and Walter Oswalt, 43–52. Wien: Europa Verlag.

Mason, Tim W. 1968. "The Primacy of Politics. Politics and Economics in National Socialist Germany," in *The Nature of Fascism*, ed. S. J. Woolf, 165–95. London: Weidenfeld and Nicolson.

Mayer, Nonna. 1986. "Pas de chrysanthèmes pour les variables sociologiques," in *Mars 1986. la drôle de la défaite de la gauche*, ed. Elisabeth Dupoirier and Gérard Grunberg, 149–66. Paris: Presses Universitaires de France.

———. 1989. "Le vote Front National de Passy à Barbès," in *Le Front National à Decouvert*, ed. Nonna Mayer and Pascal Perrineau, 249–67. Paris: Presses de la Fondation Nationale des Sciences Politiques.

———. 1990. "Ethnocentrisme, racisme et intolerance," in *L'électeur français en question*, ed. Daniel Boy and Nonna Mayer, 17–43. Paris: Presses de la Fondation Nationale des Sciences Politiques.

Mayer, Nonna, and Pascal Perrineau. 1992. "Why Do They Vote for Le Pen?" *European Journal of Political Research* 22 (1): 123–41.

Mayer, Nonna, and Pascal Perrineau, eds. 1989. *Le Front National à Decouvert*. Paris: Presses de la Fondation Nationale des Sciences Politiques.

Meadwell, Hudson. 1992. Transitions to Independence and Ethnic Nationalist Mobilization. Revised Version of a Paper Presented at the Eighth International Conference of Europeanists, Palmer House, Chicago, Ill., March 27–29.

Merkl, Peter. 1980. "Comparing Fascist Movements," in *Who were the Fascists?*, ed. Stein Ugelvik Larsen, Bernt Hagvet, and Jan Petter Myklebust, 752–83. Bergen: Universitetsforlaget.

Messina, Anthony. 1989. *Race and Party Competition in Britain*. Oxford: Clarendon Press.

Meyer, John W., and Brian Rowan. 1977. "Institutionalized Organizations: Formal Structure as Myth and Ceremony," *American Journal of Sociology* 83(2): 230–63.

Michelat, Guy. 1990. "A la recherche de la gauche et de la droite," in *L'électeur français en question*, ed. Daniel Boy and Nonna Mayer, 71–103. Paris: Presses de la Fondation Nationale des Sciences Politiques.

Michels, Robert. 1911. *Political Parties*. English ed., 1962. London: Collier-Macmillan.

Middentorp, Cees P. 1993. "Authoritarianism: Personality and Ideology. Their Political Relevance and Relationship to Left-Right Ideology in the Netherlands (1970–1985)," *European Journal of Political Research* 24 (2): 211–28.

Middentorp, Cees P., and J. D. Meloen. 1990. "The Authoritarianism of the Working Class Revisited," *European Journal of Political Research* 18(2): 257–67.

———. 1991. "Social Class, Authoritarianism and Directiveness," *European Journal of Political Research* 20(2): 213–20.

Miller, David. 1988. "The Ethical Significance of Nationality," *Ethics* 98 (4): 647–62.

———. 1990. *Market, State, and Community. Theoretical Foundations of Market Socialism*. Oxford: Clarendon Press.

Miller, Joanne, Kazimierz M. Slomczynski, and Melvin L. Kohn. 1985. "Continuity of Learning-Generalization: The Effect of Job on Men's Intellective Process in the United States and Poland," *American Journal of Sociology* 91(3): 593–615.

Minkenberg, Michael. 1992a. "The New Right in West Germany. The Transformation of Conservatism and the Extreme Right," *European Journal of Political Research* 22 (1): 55–81.

———. 1992b. "The Wall after the Wall. On the Continuing Division of Germany and the Remaking of Political Culture." Paper presented at the Eighth International Conference of Europeanists, Council of European Studies, March 27–29.

———. 1993. *The New Right in Comparative Perspective: The USA and Germany*. Cornell Studies in International Affairs, Western Societies Papers, No. 32. Ithaca, N.Y.: Cornell University Press.

———. 1994. "The New Right in Western Democracies: France and Germany in Comparative Perspective." Paper prepared for the annual meeting of the American Political Science Association, New York September 1–4.

Mitra, Subtra. 1988. "The National Front in France. A Single Issue Movement?" *West European Politics* 11 (2): 47–64.

Moore, Barrington Jr. 1966. *The Origins of Democracy and Dictatorship*. Boston: Beacon Press.

Morgan, April, and Clyde Wilcox. 1991. "Anti-Feminism in Western Europe, 1975–87." Paper prepared for the annual meeting of the American Political Science Association, Washington, D.C. August 28–September 1.

Mühlberger, Detlef. 1987. *The Social Basis of European Fascist Movements*. London: Croom Helm.

Munzer, Stephen R. 1990. *A Theory of Property Rights*. New York: Cambridge University Press.

Nagle, John D. 1970. *The National Democratic Party. Right Radicalism in the Federal Republic of Germany*. Berkeley: University of California Press.

Niedermayer, Oskar. 1990. "Sozialstruktur, politische Orientierungen und die Unterstützung extrem rechter Parteien in Westeuropa," *Zeitschrift für Parlamentsfragen* 21 (4): 564–82.

Nielsen, Hans Jorgen. 1976. "The Uncivic Culture. Attitudes towards the Political System in Denmark and Vote for the Progress Party 1973–75," *Scandinavian Political Studies* 11: 147–66.

————. 1979. *Politiske Holdninger og Fremdskridsstemmen.* Kobnhavn: Politiske Studier.

Nolte, Ernst. 1966. *Three Faces of Fascism. Action Française—Italian Fascism—National Socialism.* New York: Holt, Rinehart and Winston.

Olson, Mancur. 1965. *The Logic of Collective Action.* Cambridge: Harvard University Press.

Orfali, Brigitta. 1989. "Le droit chemin ou les mécanismes de l'adhésion politique," in *Le Front National à Decouvert,* ed. Nonna Mayer and Pascal Perrineau, 119–34. Paris: Presses de la Fondation Nationale des Sciences Politiques.

Orloff, Sheila, and Theda Skocpol. 1984. "Why not Equal Protection? Explaining the Politics of Public Social Spending in Britain, 1900–1922, and the United States, 1880s–1920," *American Sociological Review* 49 (6): 726–50.

Organski, A. F. K. 1968. "Fascism and Modernization," in *The Nature of Fascism,* ed. S. J. Woolf, 19–41. London: Weidenfeld and Nicolson.

Panebianco, Angelo. 1988. *Political Parties: Organization and Power.* Cambridge, U.K.: Cambridge University Press.

Pappi, Franz Urban. 1984. "The West German Party System," *West European Politics* 7 (4): 7–26.

————. 1990. "Die Republikaner im Parteiensystem der Bundesrepublik. Protesterscheinung oder politische Alternative?" *Aus Politik und Zeitgeschichte* 40 (March 18) B 21: 37–44.

————. 1991. "Wahrgenommenes Parteiensystem und Wahlentscheidung in Ost- und Westdeutschland. Zur Interpretation der ersten gesamtdeutschen Bundestagswahl," *Aus Politik und Zeitgeschichte* 41 (October 25) 44: 15–26.

Parsons, Talcott. 1951. *The Social System.* Glencoe, Ill.: Free Press.

Payne, Stanley G. 1980. *Fascism. Comparison and Definition.* Madison, Wisc.: University of Wisconsin Press.

Perrineau, Pascal. 1989. "Les étapes d'une implantation électorale," in *Le Front National à Decouvert,* ed. Nonna Mayer and Pascal Perrineau, 37–62. Paris: Presses de la Fondation Nationale des Sciences Politiques.

Petersson, Olof, Anders Westholm, and Göran Blomberg. 1989. *Medborgarnas Makt.* Stockholm: Carlssons.

Pinto, Antonio Costa. 1991. "The Radical Right in Post-Authoritarian Portugal. From Crisis to What?" Paper presented at the Conference on the Radical Right in Western Europe, Center for Western European Studies, University of Minnesota, Minneapolis, November 7–9.

————. 1991. "The Radical Right in Contemporary Portugal," in *Neo-Fascism in Europe,* ed. Luciano Cheles, Ronnie Ferguson, and Michalina Vaughan, 167–90. New York: Longman.

Piven, Frances Fox, and Richard Cloward. 1977. *Poor People's Movements.* New York: Random House.

Plasser, Fritz, and Peter A. Ulram. 1989. "Major Parties on the Defensive," in *The Austrian Party System,* ed. Anton Pelinka and Fritz Plasser, 69–92. Boulder, Colo.: Westview Press.

————. 1992. "Überdehnung, Erosion und rechtspopulistische Reaktion. Wandlungsfaktoren des österreichischen Parteiensystems im Vergleich," *Österreichische Zeitschrift für Politikwissenschaft* 21(2): 147–64.

———. 1994. *Radikaler Rechtspopulismus in Österreich. Die FPÖ unter Jörg Haider.* Vienna: Fessel + GFK Institut für Marktforschung/Zentrum für angewandte Politikforschung.

Plasser, Fritz, Peter A. Ulram, and Alfred Grausgruber. 1987. "Vom Ende der Lagerparteien. Perspektivenwechsel in der österreichischen Parteien- und Wahlforschung," *Österreichische Zeitschrift für Politikwissenschaft* 16(3): 241–58.

Platone, François, and Henri Rey. 1989. "Le Front National en terre communiste," in *Le Front National à Decouvert,* ed. Nonna Mayer and Pascal Perrineau, 268–83. Paris: Presses de la Fondation Nationale des Sciences Politiques.

Plenel, Edwy, and Alain Rollat, eds. 1984. *L'Effet Le Pen.* Paris: Le Monde.

Plutzer, Eric, and Lee Ann Banaszak. 1991. "Support for Feminism in Nine Western Democracies. The Impact of National and Subnational Contexts." Paper presented at the annual meeting of the American Political Science Association, Washington, D.C., August 28–September 1.

Poguntke, Thomas. 1987. "New Politics and Party Systems: The Emergence of a New Type of Party?", *West European Politics* 10(1): 76–88.

Poulantzas, Nicos. 1974. *Fascism and Dictatorship. The Third International and the Problem of Fascism.* London: New Left Books.

Prendiville, Brendan. 1989. "France. 'Les Verts'." in *New Politics in Western Europe. The Rise and Success of Green Parties and Alternative Lists,* ed. Ferdinand Müller-Rommel, 87–100. Boulder, Colo.: Westview Press.

Prowe, Diethelm. 1991. Comparisons and Contrasts between 'Classic' Interwar Fascism and the New Radical Right in Europe. Paper presented at the Conference on the Radical Right in Western Europe. Minneapolis, November 7–9, 1991.

Przeworski, Adam. 1985. *Capitalism and Social Democracy.* Cambridge: Cambridge University Press.

Przeworski, Adam, and John Sprague. 1986. *Paper Stones. A History of Electoral Socialism.* Chicago: University of Chicago Press.

Putnam, Robert, with Robert Leonardi and Raffaella Y. Nanetti. 1993. *Making Democracy Work. Civic Traditions in Modern Italy.* Princeton: Princeton University Press.

Rabinowitz, George, and Stuart Elaine MacDonald. 1989. "A Directional Theory of Issue Voting," *American Political Science Review* 83 (1): 93–121.

Ragin, Charles. 1987. *The Comparative Method.* Berkeley: University of California Press.

Ranger, Jean. 1989. "Le cercle des sympathisants," in *Le Front National à Decouvert,* ed. Nonna Mayer and Pascal Perrineau, 135–49. Paris: Presses de la Fondation Nationale des Sciences Politiques.

Ray, J. J. 1991. "The Workers Are Not Authoritarian. Rejoinder to Middentorp and Meloen," *European Journal of Political Research* 20(2): 209–12.

Reif, Karlheinz, and Hermann Schmitt. 1980. "Nine Second Order National Elections. A Conceptual Framework for the Analysis of European Election Results," *European Journal of Political Research* 8(1): 2–44.

Reif, Karlheinz, and Oskar Niedermayer. 1990. "Supporters of Extremist Right Parties in Western Europe. Social Structure and Political Orientations." Paper prepared for the annual meeting of the American Political Science Association, San Francisco.

Rham, Gérard de. 1990. "Naturalization: The Politics of Citizenship Acquisition," in *The Political Rights of Migrant Workers in Western Europe,* ed. Zig Layton-Henry, 158–85. London: Sage.

Rogowski, Ronald. 1989. *Commerce and Coalitions.* Princeton: Princeton University Press.

Rohrschneider, Robert. 1993. "New Party versus Old Left Realignments: Environmental Attitudes, Party Policies, and Partisan Affiliation in Four West European Countries," *Journal of Politics* 55(3): 682–701.

Roth, Dieter. 1989. "Sind die Republikaner die fünfte Partei? Sozial- und Meinungsstruktur der Wähler der Republikaner," *Aus Politik und Zeitgeschichte* 39 (October 6) B41–42: 10–20.

———. 1990. "Die Republikaner. Schneller Aufstieg und tiefer Fall einer Protestpartei am rechten Rand," *Aus Politik und Zeitgeschichte* 40 (September 7) B37–38: 27–39.

———. 1992. *"Volksparteien* in Crisis? The Electoral Successes of the Extreme Right in Context. The Case of Baden-Württemberg," *German Politics* 2(1): 1–20.

Roussel, Eric. 1985. *Le Cas Le Pen. Les Nouvelles Droites en France.* Paris: J. D. Lattès.

Rucht, Dieter. 1991. "Das Kräftefeld sozialer Bewegungen, Gegenbewegungen und Staat. Einführende Bemerkungen," *Forschungsjournal NSBs* 4(2): 9–16.

Rüdig, Wolfgang. 1989. "Explaining Green Party Development. Reflections on a Theoretical Framework." Paper presented at the United Kingdom Political Studies Association Conference, University of Warwick, Coventry, 4–6 April.

Rusciano, Frank Louis. 1992. "Rethinking the Gender Gap. The Case of West German Elections, 1949–1987," *Comparative Politics* 24 (3): 335–57.

Ruzza, Carlo E., and Oliver Schmidtke. 1993. "Roots of Success of the Lega Lombarda: Mobilisation Dynamics and the Media," *West European Politics* 16(1): 1–23.

Safran, William. 1993. "The National Front in France: From Lunatic Fringe to Limited Respectability," in *Encounters with the Contemporary Radical Right,* ed. Peter H. Merkl and Leonard Weisberg, 19–49. Boulder, Colo.: Westview.

Sandschneider, Eberhard. 1990. "Die saarländische Landtagswahl vom 28. 1. 1990," *Zeitschrift für Parlamentsfragen* 21 (3): 418–29.

Sani, Giacomo, and Giovanni Sartori. 1983. "Polarization, Fragmentation and Competition in Western Democracies," in *Western European Party Systems,* ed. Hans Daalder and Peter Mair, 307–41. Beverly Hills, Calif.: Sage.

Sartori, Giovanni. 1966. "European Political Parties. The Case of Polarized Pluralism," in *Political Parties and Political Development,* ed. Joseph LaPalombara and Myron Weiner, 137–76. Princeton: Princeton University Press.

———. 1970. "Concept Misformation in Comparative Politics," *American Political Science Review* 64 (4).

Savage, James. 1985. "Postmaterialism of the Left and Right. Political Conflict in Postindustrial Society," *Comparative Political Studies* 17(4): 431–51.

Schain, Martin. 1987. "Racial Politics. The Rise of the National Front," in *The French Socialists in Power, 1981–1986,* ed. Patrick McCarthy, 129–58. Westport, Conn.: Greenwood.

———. 1988. "Immigration and Changes in the French Party System," *European Journal of Political Research* 16(6): 597–621.

———. 1990. "Immigration and Politics," in *Developments in French Politics,* ed. Peter A. Hall, Jack Hayward, and Howard Machin, 253–68. New York: St. Martin's Press.

Schepens, Luc. 1980. "Fascists and Nationalists in Belgium 1919–1940," in *Who were the Fascists?,* ed. Stein Ugelvik Larsen, Bernt Hagvet, and Jan Petter Myklebust, 501–16. Bergen: Universitetsforlaget.

Schmidtke, Oliver, and Carlo E. Ruzza. 1993. "Regionalistischer Protest als 'Life Politics.' Die Formierung einer sozialen Bewegung: die Lega Lombarda," *Soziale Welt* 44(1): 5–30.

Schmitt, Carl. 1932. *Der Begriff des Politischen.* New ed. München und Leipzig: Duncker und Humblodt.

Schmitt-Beck, Rüdiger. 1991. "Die hessische Landtagswahl vom 20. 1. 1991. Im Schatten der Weltpolitik kleine Verschiebungen mit großer Wirkung," *Zeitschrift für Parlamentsfragen* 22 (2): 226–44.

Schmitter, Philippe C. 1980. "The Social Origins, Economic Bases and Political Imperatives of Authoritarian Rule in Portugal," in *Who Were the Fascists?,* ed. Stein Ugelvik Larsen, Bernt Hagvet, and Jan Petter Myklebust, 435–66. Bergen: Universitetsforlaget.

Schmitter-Heisler, Barbara. 1988. "From Conflict to Accommodation. The 'Foreigners Question' in Switzerland," *European Journal of Political Research* 16 (6): 683–700.

Schoenbaum, David. 1966. *Hitler's Social Revolution.* Garden City, N.J.: Doubleday Anchor.

Schultze, Rainer-Olaf. 1991. "Die bayerische Landtagswahl vom 14. Oktober 1990: Bayerische Besonderheiten und bundesrepublikanische Normalität," *Zeitschrift für Parlamentsfragen* 22 (1): 40–58.

Schumpeter, Alois. 1950. *Capitalism, Socialism and Democracy.* New York: Harper.

Schweissguth, Etienne. 1988. "Les avatars de la dimension gauche-droite," in *Mars 1986. La drôle de défaite de la gauche,* ed. Elisabeth Dupoirier and Gérard Grunberg, 51–70. Paris: Presses Universitaires de France.

Seifert, Ruth. 1990. "Politik zwischen Interesse und Moral. Zum politischen Bewußtsein ausgewählter Berufsgruppen des sogenannten Kleinbürgertums," *Soziale Welt* 41 (special issue) 7: 455–79.

Seyd, Patrick. 1987. *The Rise and Fall of the Labour Left.* New York: St. Martin's Press.

Seyd, Patrick, and Paul Whiteley. 1992. *Labour's Grass Roots. The Politics of Party Membership.* Oxford: Clarendon Press.

Shepsle, Kenneth, and Ronald N. Cohen. 1990. "Multiparty Competition, Entry, and Entry Deterrence in Spatial Models of Elections," in *Advances in the Spatial Theory of Voting,* eds. Ames Enelow and Melvin J. Hinich, 12–45. Cambridge: Cambridge University Press.

Shields, James G. 1988. "Campaigning From the Fringe. Jean-Marie Le Pen," in *The French Presidential Elections of 1988,* ed. John Gaffney, 141–57. Aldershot, U.K.: Gower.

Sidoti, Francesco. 1992. "The Extreme Right in Italy: Ideological Orphans and Countermobilization," in *The Extreme Right in Europe and the United States,* ed. Paul Hainsworth, 151–74. New York: St. Martin's Press.

Sjölin, Mats. 1993. *Coalition Politics and Parliamentary Power.* Lund, Sweden: Lund University Press.

Smith, Anthony D. 1991. *National Identity.* Reno: University of Nevada Press.

Smith-Jespersen, Mary Paul. 1989. "A Danish Defense Dilemma: The Election of May 1988," *West European Politics* 12(3): 190–95.

Solé-Tura, J. 1968. "The Political 'Instrumentalism' of Fascism," in *The Nature of Fascism,* ed. S. J. Woolf, 42–50. London: Weidenfeld and Nicolson.

Sternhell, Zeer. 1976. "Fascist Ideology," in *Fascism. A Reader's Guide,* ed. Walter Laqueur, 315–76. Berkeley: University of California Press.

Stöss, Richard. 1988. "The Problem of Right-Wing Extremism in West Germany," *West European Politics* 11 (2): 34–46.

———. 1989. *Die Extreme Rechte in der Bundesrepublik. Entwicklung, Ursachen, Gegenmassnahmen.* Opladen: Westdeutscher Verlag.

———. 1991. "Right-Wing Extremism in East and West Germany, 1990. A Comparison." Paper presented at the Conference on the Radical Right in Western Europe, Center for Western European Studies. University of Minnesota, Minneapolis, November 7–9.

Strom, Kaare. 1994. "The Presthus Debacle: Intraparty Politics and Bargaining Failure in Norway," *American Political Science Review* 88(1): 112–27.

Studlar, Donley T., and Ian McAllister. 1992. "A Changing Political Agenda: The Structure of Political Attitudes in Britain, 1974–87," *International Journal of Public Opinion Research* 4(2): 148–76.

Suolinna, Kirsti. 1981. "The Popular Revival Movements," in *Nordic Democracy,* ed. Erik Allard, 589–608. Kobnhavn: Det Danske Selskab.

Svasand, Lars. 1991. "The Radical Right and the Conservatives in Scandinavia." Paper presented at the Conference on the Radical Right in Western Europe, Center for Western European Studies, University of Minnesota, Minneapolis, November 7–9.

Swenson, Peter. 1991. "Bringing Capital Back In, or Social Democracy Reconsidered: Employer Power, Cross-Class Alliances, and Centralization of Industrial Relations in Denmark and Sweden." *World Politics* 43 (4): 513–44.

Swyngedouw, Marc. 1994. "De opkomst en doorbraak van Agalev en Vlaams Blok in de jaren tachtig en negentig." *Acta Politica* 29 (4): 453–77.

Taagepera, Rein, and Matthew Shugart. 1989. *Votes and Seats.* New Haven: Yale University Press.

Taggart, Paul. 1993. "Muted Radicals: The Emerging 'New Populism' in West European Party Systems." Paper prepared for the annual meeting of the American Political Science Association Meeting, Washington, D.C.

Taguieff, Perre-André. 1989a. "La metaphysique de J.-M. Le Pen," in *Le Front National à Decouvert,* ed. Nonna Mayer and Pascal Perrineau, 173–94. Paris: Presses de la Fondation Nationale des Sciences Politiques.

————. 1989b. "Un programme 'revolutionaire'?" in *Le Front National à Decouvert,* ed. Nonna Mayer and Pascal Perrineau, 195–227. Paris: Presses de la Fondation Nationale des Sciences Politiques.

Tassani, Giovanni. 1990. "The Italian Social Movement: From Almirante to Fini," in *Italian Politics. A Review,* ed. Raffaela Y. Nanetti and Raimondo Cutanzaro, 124–45. Vol. 4: London: Pinter.

Taylor, Michael. 1987. *The Possibility of Cooperation.* New York: Cambridge University Press.

Taylor, Stan. 1982. *The National Front in English Politics.* London: MacMillan.

————. 1993. "The Radical Right in Britain," in *Encounters with the Contemporary Radical Right,* ed. Peter H. Merkl and Leonard Weinberg, 165–84. Boulder, Colo.: Westview.

Thurlow, Richard. 1991. The State and the Radical Right in Italy, France and Britain. A Historical Perspective. Paper presented at the Conference on the Radical Right in Western Europe. University of Minnesota, November 7–9, 1991.

Togeby, Lise. 1990. "Political Radicalism in the Working Class and in the Middle Class," *European Journal of Political Research* 18 (4): 423–36.

Valen, Henry. 1990. "The Storting Election of 1989: Polarization and Protest," *Scandinavian Political Studies* 13(3): 277–90.

Van Gunsteren, Herman R. 1988. "Admission to Citizenship," *Ethics* 98 (4): 731–41.

Vaughan, Michalina. 1991. "The Extreme Right in France. 'Lepenisme' or the Politics of Fear," in *Neo-Fascism in Europe,* ed. Luciano Cheles, Ravine Ferguson, and Michalina Vaughan, 211–33. New York: Longman.

Voerman, Gerrt, and Paul Lucardie. 1992. "The Extreme Right in the Netherlands. The Centrists and Their Radical Rivals," *European Journal of Political Research* 22 (1): 35–54.

Von Beyme, Klaus. 1988. "Right-Wing Extremism in Post-War Europe," *West European Politics* 11 (2): 1–18.

Warren, Mark. 1992. "Democratic Theory and Self-Transformation," *American Political Science Review* 86 (1): 8–23.

Weber, Eugene. 1964. *Varieties of Fascism. Doctrines of Revolution in the Twentieth Century.* Princeton: Van Nostrand.

Westle, Bettina, and Oskar Niedermayer. 1992. "Contemporary Right-Wing Extremism in West Germany. The Republicans and their Electorate," *European Journal of Political Research* 22 (1): 83–100.

Wilcox, Clyde. 1991. "Support for Gender Equality in Western Europe. A Longitudinal Analysis," *European Journal of Political Research* 20 (2): 127–47.

Wippermann, Wolfgang. 1983. *Europäischer Faschismus im Vergleich 1922–1982.* Frankfurt am Main: Suhrkamp.

Wolff, Reinhardt. 1989. "Fortschrittspartei gegen den Fortschritt," in *Die Rückkehr der Führer. Modernisierter Rechtsradikalismus in Westeuropa,* ed. Martina Kirfel and Walter Oswalt, 144–50. Wien: Europa Verlag.

Woods, Dwayne. 1992. "The Center No Longer Holds: Regional Leagues in Italian Politics," *West European Politics* 15 (2): 56–76.

Woodward, James. 1992. "Commentary: Liberalism and Migration," in *Free Movement. Ethnical Issues in the Transnational Migration of People and of Money,* ed. Brian

Barry and Robert E. Goodin, 59–84. University Park, Penn.: Pennsylvania State University.

Woolf, S. J. 1968. "Did a Fascist Economic System Exist?" in *The Nature of Fascism*, ed. S. J. Woolf, 119–51. London: Weidenfeld and Nicolson.

Ysmal, Colette. 1990. "La crise électorale de l'UDF et du RPR," *Revue Française de Science Politique* 40 (6): 810–29.

———. 1991. "Les cadres du Front National. Les habits neufs de l'extreme droite," in *L'état de l'opinion 1991,* ed. Olivier Duhamel and Jérôme Jaffré, 181–97. Paris: Seuil.

Zimmermann, Ekkart, and Thomas Saalfeld. 1993. "The Three Waves of West German Right-Wing Extremism," in *Encounters with the Contemporary Radical Right,* ed. Peter H. Merkl and Leonard Weisberg, 50–74. Boulder, Colo.: Westview.

Index

Experience, communicative, 7, 8
Experience, work, as determinant of attitudes, 7, 8, 9, 10, 12, 13, 18, 112
Expert studies, 53–56, 63–68, 71, table 2.9
Extra-Parliamentary Opposition (Germany), 209

Fabius, Laurent, 97
Factor analysis 53, 83–84
    confirmatory factor analysis, 87–88, 110, 188, tables 3.3, 4.6, 4.7, 5.4, 5.5, 6.3
    exploratory factor analysis, 86–87, 106, 222, figures 3.1, 4.1, 4.2, 5.1, 5.2, 6.1, tables 3.1, 3.2, 4.3, 4.4, 4.5, 5.1–5.3, 6.1, 6.2
Family, as determinant of attitudes, 12–13
Farmers. *See* Business people/farmers
Fascist movements, viii, 4, 42, 123, table 1.1
    appeals, 29–31, 36, 43
    causes, 35–42, table 1.2
    constituencies of, 33–35
    ideology of, 29–32, 43, 44
    new radical right as legacy of, viii–ix, 1, 3, 23–24, 27–28, 70, 75, 78, 90, 160, 162–66, 172–73, 203–6, 209, 221, 232, 237–38, 242–43, 252
    new radical right compared to, 22–23, 28–42, 43, 163–64
    organization, 32, 203
    Scandinavia, lack of in, 122–24
Federation of Conservative Students, 251
Federation of Expellees and People Deprived of their Rights (Germany), 208
Fini, Gianfranco, 173
Finland, 41
Flemish Block (Belgium), 50, 55, 58, 90, 277, table 2.1
Foreign-born population, 60–61, tables 2.5, 2.6
Forza Italia (Italy), 176, 200

Founding date. *See* New radical right parties, criteria for
France
    determinants, of vote of NRR, 113–15, table 3.5
    electoral coalition of NRR, 102–16
    emergence of NRR, 99–102
    historical background, 92–95
    political opportunity structure facing NRR, 95–99
    strategic dilemmas of NRR, 116–20
Free Democratic Party, 208, 227
Frey, Gerhard, 219
F-scale, 12

Gender issues, 20, 22, 67, 73, 82, 213, 218, 229, tables 2.10, 2.12
Gender, as determinant of attitudes, 7, 104, 229
German Confederation of Industry, 236
German Democratic Republic, relations with, 204, 210, 215, 216
German Empire Party, 207
German Party, 208
German Peoples' Union (Germany), 50–51, 64, 66, 67, 70, 72, 218–19, 234, 238, tables 2.1, 2.7, 2.8, 2.9
Germany
    determinants, of vote of the radical right, 227–29, table 6.5
    electoral coalition of the radical right, 221–35
    emergence of the radical right, 216–21
    historical background, 207–12
    political opportunity structure facing the radical right, 212–16
    strategic dilemmas of the radical right, 235–38
Germany Foundation, 211
Giscard D'Estaing, Valerie, 96, 98
Glistrup, Mogens, 122, 129, 130, 131, 132, 157
Greece, 52–53, 56, 72
Green Party (Italy), 180